NETNHϤⲨⲚⲚⲤⲀ
ⲚⲀ·ⲔⲀⲦⲠⲓⲤⲰ
ⲚⲦⲚ̄ⲦⲈⲠⲢⲞⲤ·Ⲟ
ⲢⲀⲈⲦⲞⲨⲀⲀⲂ·

ⲈⲦⲂⲈⲚⲈⲠⲢⲈⲤⲂⲨⲦⲈⲢⲞⲤ

ⲢⲈⲠⲈⲠⲒⲤⲔⲞⲠⲞⲤ·ⲆⲈ
ⲚⲀⲬⲒⲢⲞⲆⲞⲚⲈⲒϢⲠ
ⲠⲢⲈⲤⲂⲨⲦⲈⲢⲞⲤ·ⲈⲨⲚⲀ
ⲔⲀⲚⲒⲨⲆⲒⲬⲒⲬⲚ
ⲦⲒⲨⲀⲠⲒ·ⲈⲢⲈⲚⲈⲠ
ⲢⲈⲤⲂⲨⲦⲈⲢⲞⲤⲦⲎⲢⲞⲨ
ⲬⲰⲌⲈⲢⲞⲨ·ⲀⲨⲰ
ⲨⲀⲢⲈⲨⲨⲚⲀⲈⲢⲀⲒ
ⲈⲬⲰⲨ·ⲔⲀⲦⲀⲠ
ⲤⲨⲞⲦⲚ̄ⲦⲀⲚⲬⲆⲞⲨ
ⲈⲦⲂⲈⲠⲈⲠⲒⲤⲔⲞⲠⲞⲤ·

ⲈⲦⲂⲈⲚⲆⲒⲀⲔⲞⲚⲞⲤ·

ⲢⲈⲠⲈⲠⲒⲤⲔⲞⲠⲞⲤⲆⲈ
ⲚⲀⲔⲀⲨⲒⲤⲦⲀⲚⲞⲨ
ⲆⲒⲀⲔⲞⲚⲞⲤ·ⲀⲨⲰⲞⲦ
ⲠⲨⲔⲀⲦⲀⲠⲒⲈⲚⲦⲀⲚ
ϢⲢⲠⲒⲬⲆⲞⲨ·ⲈⲢⲈⲠ
ⲦⲒⲤⲔⲞⲠⲞⲤⲚⲀⲔⲀ
ⲚⲒⲨⲆⲒⲬⲒⲢⲀⲒⲈⲬⲰⲨ·
ⲦⲂⲒⲞⲨⲀⲀⲚⲬⲆⲞⲨ
ⲬⲠⲈⲠⲒⲤⲔⲞⲠⲞⲤ
ⲒⲨⲀϢⲠⲦⲚⲀ
ⲦⲠⲀⲚⲒⲨⲨⲖⲬⲈⲬⲒ
ⲠⲆⲒⲀⲔⲞⲚⲞⲤ
ⲨⲦⲠⲈⲦⲚⲦⲠⲒϢ

ⲠⲒⲨⲂ·ⲆⲈⲈⲨⲚⲀⲬⲒ
·ⲢⲞⲆⲞⲚⲈⲒϢⲨⲆϤⲈⲚ
ⲈⲨⲨⲠⲦⲞⲨⲎⲎⲂ·ⲆⲀ
ⲆⲀⲈⲨⲦⲠⲢⲈⲤⲒⲀϢ
ⲠⲈⲠⲒⲤⲔⲞⲠⲞⲤⲈⲦⲢⲈϤ
ⲒⲢⲈⲚⲚⲈⲦⲈⲨⲚⲆⲞⲨ
ⲈⲤⲆⲀⲈⲚⲈⲒϢϢⲞⲨⲚⲨ·
ⲞⲨⲆⲈⲈⲨⲚⲒⲔⲀⲨⲒⲤⲦⲀ
ϢϢⲞⲨⲀⲚⲈⲦⲢⲈϤ
ϢⲨⲦⲠⲚⲞⲨⲚⲂⲞⲨ
ⲚⲞⳝⲨⲠⲔⲀⲎⲢⲞⲤⲦⲎ
ⲢⲨ·ⲀⲖⲖⲀⲦ
ⲢⲈϤⲤⲎⲈⲒⲠⲢⲞⲞⲨϢ
ⲚⲈⲦϢⲨⲚⲈ·ⲀⲨⲰ
ⲚⲨⲦⲀⲨⲈⲠⲈⲠⲒⲤⲔⲞ
ⲠⲞⲤⲈⲢⲞⲞⲨ·ⲞⲨⲆⲈ
ⲈⲨⲚⲒⲔⲀⲨⲒⲤⲦⲀϢ
ϢⲞⲨⲀⲚⲈⲦⲢⲈϤⲬⲒ
ⲠⲒⲠⲒⲚⲀⲚⲦⲨⲈⲚⲦ
ⲚⲞⲚ·ⲠⲒⲈⲒ
ⲢⲈⲚⲈⲠⲢⲈⲤⲂⲨⲦⲈⲢⲞⲤ
ⲨⲦⲈⲬⲒⲈⲢⲞⲨ·
ⲀⲖⲀⲈⲦⲢⲈϤϢϢ
ⲚⲀⲌⲒⲞⲤ·ⲈⲢⲈⲠⲈⲠⲒⲤ
ⲔⲞⲠⲞⲤⲠⲒⳡⲨⲈ
ⲚⲒϢⲒⲚⲈⲦⲒϢϢⲒ·
ⲈⲦⲂⲈⲠⲀⲠⲈⲠⲒⲤⲔⲞ
ⲠⲞⲤⲨⲨⲖⲖⲀⲨⲨⲠⲈⲦ
ⲚⲀⲬⲒⲢⲞⲆⲞⲚⲈⲒϢ
ⲠⲆⲒⲀⲔⲞⲚⲞⲤ·
ⲠⲈⲠⲢⲈⲤⲂⲨⲦⲈⲢⲞⲤⲆⲈ
ⲈⲢⲈⲠⲈⲠⲒⲤⲔⲞⲠⲞⲤϢⲈ

hermeneia

Hermeneia —A Critical and Historical Commentary on the Bible

The Apostolic Tradition

A Commentary

by Paul F. Bradshaw, Maxwell E. Johnson,
and L. Edward Phillips

Edited by
Harold W. Attridge

**Fortress
Press**   Minneapolis

The Apostolic Tradition
A Commentary

Cover and interior design by Kenneth Hiebert
Typesetting and page composition by
The HK Scriptorium

Library of Congress Cataloging-in-Publication Data

Bradshaw, Paul F.
   The apostolic tradition : a commentary / by Paul Bradshaw,
Maxwell E. Johnson, and L. Edward Phillips ; edited by
Harold W. Attridge.
     p. cm.
   Includes bibliographical references and index.
   ISBN 0-8006-6046-3 (alk. paper)
   1. Hippolytus, Antipope, ca. 170–235 or 6. Traditio apostolica.
  2. Church polity. I. Johnson, Maxwell E., date– II. Attridge
Harold W. III. Phillips, L. Edward. IV. Title.

BRS65.H83 T7333 2002
270.1—dc21

                             2002016368

Manufactured in the U.S.A.   AF 1-6046

06   05   04   03   02   1   2   3   4   5   6   7   8   9   10

Paul F. Bradshaw was born in England in 1945. He received his Ph.D. in Liturgy from the University of London in 1971, and in 1994 was awarded the degree of Doctor of Divinity by the University of Oxford for his published works. In 1985 he came to teach at the University of Notre Dame, where he has been Professor of Liturgy since 1990. He has been president of the North American Academy of Liturgy (1993–94) and of Societas Liturgica (1993–95), and since 1987 he has been editor-in-chief of the journal *Studia Liturgica*. He has written widely on the subject of liturgy, and his major books include *Daily Prayer in the Early Church* (London: SPCK, 1981; New York: Oxford Univ. Press, 1982), *Ordination Rites of the Ancient Churches of East and West* (New York: Pueblo, 1990), and *The Search for the Origins of Christian Worship* (London: SPCK; New York: Oxford Univ. Press, 1992). He is coeditor with Lawrence Hoffman of a series of volumes of essays on Jewish and Christian worship (Two Liturgical Traditions, published by University of Notre Dame Press), as well as coeditor of the revised edition of *The Study of Liturgy* (London: SPCK; New York: Oxford Univ. Press, 1992). He has recently completed a revised and enlarged edition of his *Search for the Origins of Christian Worship* and a new version of the *Dictionary of Liturgy and Worship*, previously edited by J. G. Davies.

Maxwell E. Johnson was born in Benson, Minnesota, in 1952. He received his M.A. in Liturgy from Saint John's University, Collegeville, Minnesota, and completed his doctoral degree in Liturgy at the University of Notre Dame in 1992 with a dissertation on the prayers of Sarapion of Thmuis from the mid-fourth century. From 1993 to 1997 he was Assistant Professor of Liturgy at the School of Theology, Saint John's University, Collegeville. In 1997 he returned to the University of Notre Dame as Associate Professor and in 2002 became Professor of Liturgy. His major publications include: *The Rites of Christian Initiation: Their Evolution and Interpretation* (Collegeville, Minn.: Liturgical, 1999); *The Prayers of Sarapion of Thmuis: A Literary, Liturgical, and Theological Analysis*, Orientalia Christiana Analecta 249 (Rome: Pontifical Oriental Institute Press, 1995); *Liturgy in Early Christian Egypt* (JLS 33; Nottingham: Grove, 1995); and, as editor and contributor, *Living Water, Sealing Spirit: Readings on Christian Initiation* (Collegeville, Minn.: Liturgical, 1995).

L. Edward Phillips was born in Jackson, Tennessee, in 1954. He received his M.Div. in 1979 from Candler School of Theology, Emory University, and his Ph.D. in Liturgy in 1992 from the University of Notre Dame. From 1991 until 1997 he was head of the Department of Religion and Philosophy at Union College in Barbourville, Kentucky. From 1997 he has been Associate Professor of Historical Theology at Garrett-Evangelical Theological Seminary in Evanston, Illinois. He is the author or coauthor of several books and articles on liturgy and church history, including *The Ritual Kiss in Early Christian Worship* (JLS 36; Nottingham: Grove, 1996). His current research interests include the history of the relationship between Christian worship and money.

Contents
The Apostolic Tradition

■ **Commentary**

The name *Hermeneia,* Greek ἑρμηνεία, has been chosen as the title of the commentary series to which this volume belongs. The word *Hermeneia* has a rich background in the history of biblical interpretation as a term used in the ancient Greek-speaking world for the detailed, systematic exposition of a scriptural work. It is hoped that the series, like its name, will carry forward this old and venerable tradition. A second, entirely practical reason for selecting the name lies in the desire to avoid a long descriptive title and its inevitable acronym, or worse, an unpronounceable abbreviation.

The series is designed to be a critical and historical commentary to the Bible without arbitrary limits in size or scope. It will utilize the full range of philological and historical tools, including textual criticism (often slighted in modern commentaries), the methods of the history of tradition (including genre and prosodic analysis), and the history of religion.

Hermeneia is designed for the serious student of the Bible. It will make full use of ancient Semitic and classical languages; at the same time, English translations of all comparative materials—Greek, Latin, Canaanite, or Akkadian—will be supplied alongside the citation of the source in its original language. Insofar as possible, the aim is to provide the student or scholar with full critical discussion of each problem of interpretation and with the primary data upon which the discussion is based.

Hermeneia is designed to be international and interconfessional in the selection of authors; its editorial boards were formed with this end in view. Occasionally the series will offer translations of distinguished commentaries which originally appeared in languages other than English. Published volumes of the series will be revised continually, and eventually, new commentaries will replace older works in order to preserve the currency of the series. Commentaries are also being assigned for important literary works in the categories of apocryphal and pseudepigraphical works relating to the Old and New Testaments, including some of Essene or Gnostic authorship.

The editors of *Hermeneia* impose no systematic-theological perspective upon the series (directly, or indirectly by selection of authors). It is expected that authors will struggle to lay bare the ancient meaning of a biblical work or pericope. In this way the text's human relevance should become transparent, as is always the case in competent historical discourse. However, the series eschews for itself homiletical translation of the Bible.

The editors are heavily indebted to Fortress Press for its energy and courage in taking up an expensive, long-term project, the rewards of which will accrue chiefly to the field of biblical scholarship.

The editor responsible for this volume is Harold Attridge of Yale University.

Frank Moore Cross	*Helmut Koester*
For the Old Testament	For the New Testament
Editorial Board	Editorial Board

The anonymous early church order that became known as the *Apostolic Tradition* and conventionally attributed to Hippolytus of Rome has generated enormous scholarly discussion since its discovery in the nineteenth century. Surprisingly, however, there has never before been a comprehensive commentary on it such as there is for other patristic works. We have here attempted to remedy this defect, and at the same time we have offered the first full synoptic presentation in English of the various witnesses to its text. We have also taken the opportunity to develop our argument that it is neither the work of Hippolytus nor of any other individual. Instead, we believe that it is a composite document made up of a number of layers and strands of diverse provenance and compiled over a period of time, and therefore not representing the practice of any one Christian community. In spite of this conclusion, however, for the sake of convenience we have chosen to continue to refer to it by the familiar designation "Apostolic Tradition."

We are grateful to all who have given us assistance in various ways in this project, and above all to those who helped with the work of translation from languages in which we cannot claim competence: Carol Bebawi for the Arabic version and Professor James Vanderkam of the University of Notre Dame for the Ethiopic. Thanks are also due to the Appalachian College Association and the Andrew W. Mellon Foundation Trust for providing the funding for the preparation of the translation of the Coptic, to the University of Kentucky and the Divinity School at Duke University for providing library resources for that work, to Elizabeth Agnew for preparing the indices, and to George Kalantzis for assistance with proofreading.

We very much regret that access to the translation and commentary by Alistair Stewart-Sykes, *Hippolytus: On the Apostolic Tradition* (Crestwood, N.Y.: St. Vladimir's Seminary Press, 2001), with its interesting hypothesis on the origin of the work, came too late to permit its consideration within this volume.

Reference Codes

1. Abbreviations

aeth.	Ethiopic manuscript
AKG	Arbeiten zur Kirchengeschichte
ALW	*Archiv für Liturgiewissenschaft*
Ambrose	
De sacr.	*De sacramentis*
ANF	Alexander Roberts and James Donaldson, eds., *The Ante-Nicene Fathers* (10 vols.; New York: Scribner's, 1905–6)
ANRW	*Aufstieg und Niedergang der römischen Welt*
Ap. Trad.	*Apostolic Tradition*
Apoc. Mos.	*Apocalypse of Moses*
ar.	Arabic manuscript
ATR	*Anglican Theological Review*
Aug	*Augustinianum*
Barn.	*Letter of Barnabas*
BCE	*Bulletin du Comité des Études*
BLE	*Bulletin de littérature ecclésiastique*
BZNW	Beihefte zur Zeitschrift für die neutestamentliche Wissenschaft
c.	*circa*, approximately
CH	*Church History*
chap(s).	chapter(s)
1 Clem.	*The First Epistle of Clement*
Clement	Clement of Alexandria
Paed.	*Paedagogus*
Strom.	*Stromateis*
Comm.	*Commentary*
Const.	*Apostolic Constitutions*
CSCO	Corpus scriptorum christianorum orientalium
Cyprian	Cyprian of Carthage
De dom. or.	*De dominica oratione*
De laps.	*De lapsis*
Cyril of Jerusalem	
Myst. Cat.	*Mystagogical Catecheses*
d.	died
Did.	*Didache*
Didasc.	*Didascalia apostolorum*
diss.	dissertation
EHS	Europäische Hochschulschriften
EO	*Ecclesia Orans*
Ep.	*Epistola(e)*
EphLit	*Ephemerides Liturgicae*
ET	English translation
Eusebius	Eusebius of Caesarea
Hist. eccl.	*Historia ecclesiastica*
ExpT	*Expository Times*
f.	folio
FZThPh	*Freiburger Zeitschrift für Philosophie und Theologie*
GLS	Grove Liturgical Study
gr.	Greek manuscript
Greg	*Gregorianum*

Hippolytus	Hippolytus of Rome
Ref.	*Refutatio omnium haeresium*
Hom.	*Homily*
HTR	*Harvard Theological Review*
Ignatius	Ignatius of Antioch
Eph.	*Letter to the Ephesians*
Magn.	*Letter to the Magnesians*
Pol.	*Letter to Polycarp*
Smyrn.	*Letter to the Smyrnaeans*
Trall.	*Letter to the Trallians*
Irenaeus	Irenaeus of Lyons
Dem.	*The Demonstration of Apostolic Preaching*
Haer.	*Adversus haereses*
JAC	*Jahrbuch für Antike und Christentum*
JEH	*Journal of Ecclesiastical History*
JLS	Alcuin/GROW Joint Liturgical Study
JTS	*Journal of Theological Studies*
Justin	Justin Martyr
1 Apol.	*First Apology*
Dial.	*Dialogue with Trypho*
lit.	literally
LXX	Septuagint
m.	Mishnah
Ber.	*Berakot*
Bik.	*Bikkurim*
Menaḥ.	*Menaḥot*
Pesaḥ.	*Pesaḥim*
MS(s).	manuscript(s)
N.	name
Ochrid	Codex Ochrid
Mus. nat.	*Musée national*
or.	
OrChr	*Oriens Christianus*
OrChrA	Orientalia Christiana Analecta
OrChrP	*Orientalia Christiana Periodica*
Origen	
De or.	*De oratione*
par.	parallel(s)
PG	*Patrologia graeca* (ed. J.-P. Migne)
PO	Patrologia orientalis
QL	*Questions liturgiques*
QLP	*Questions liturgiques et paroissiales*
RBén	*Revue bénédictine*
RechSR	*Recherches de science religieuse*
RelSRev	*Religious Studies Review*
RevScRel	*Revue des sciences religieuses*
RHE	*Revue d'histoire ecclésiastique*
RHR	*Revue de l'histoire des religions*
RThAM	*Recherches de théologie ancienne et médiévale*
SC	Sources chrétiennes
StEphA	Studia ephemeridis Augustinianum

StLit	*Studia Liturgica*
StPatr	*Studia Patristica*
syr.	Syriac manuscript
Tertullian	Tertullian of Carthage
Ad. uxor.	*Ad uxorem*
Adv. Marc.	*Adversus Marcionem*
Adv. Prax.	*Adversus Praxeam*
Apol.	*Apologeticum*
De bapt.	*De baptismo*
De cor.	*De corona*
De ex. cast.	*De exhortatione castitatis*
De idol.	*De idololatria*
De ieiun.	*De ieiunio*
De monog.	*De monogamia*
De or.	*De oratione*
De praescr.	*De praescriptione haereticorum*
De pud.	*De pudicitia*
De res. carn.	*De resurrectione carnis*
De spect.	*De spectaculis*
De virg. vel.	*De virginibus velandis*
TextS	Texts and Studies
ThD	Theologische Dissertationen
ThH	Théologie historique
ThQ	*Theologische Quartalschrift*
TRev	*Theologische Revue*
TU	Texte und Untersuchungen
v(v).	verse(s)
VAL	*La vie et les arts liturgiques*
VC	*Vigiliae christianae*
VCSup	Vigiliae christianae supplements
ZKG	*Zeitschrift für Kirchengeschichte*
ZKTh	*Zeitschrift für katholische Theologie*
ZNW	*Zeitschrift für die neutestamentliche Wissenschaft*
ZPE	*Zeitschrift für Papyrologie und Epigraphik*

2. Short Titles of Frequently Cited Literature

Bartlet, "Ordination Prayers"
  J. Vernon Bartlet, "The Ordination Prayers in the Ancient Church Order," *JTS* 17 (1916) 248–56.
Botte, "Passage"
  Bernard Botte, "Un passage difficile de la 'Tradition apostolique' sur le signe de croix," *RThAM* 27 (1960) 5–19.
Botte, *Tradition*
  Bernard Botte, *La Tradition apostolique de saint Hippolyte: Essai de reconstitution* (1963; 5th ed. with addenda by Albert Gerhards; Liturgiewissenschaftliche Quellen und Forschungen 39; Münster: Aschendorff, 1989).
Bouyer, *Eucharist*
  Louis Bouyer, *Eucharist: Theology and Spirituality of the Eucharistic Prayer* (Notre Dame: Univ. of Notre Dame Press, 1968).
Bradshaw, "Baptismal Practice"
  Paul F. Bradshaw, "Baptismal Practice in the Alexandrian Tradition, Eastern or Western?" in

idem, ed., *Essays in Early Eastern Initiation* (JLS 8; Nottingham: Grove, 1988) 5–17.
Bradshaw, *Canons*
  Paul F. Bradshaw, *The Canons of Hippolytus* (JLS 2; Nottingham: Grove, 1987).
Bradshaw, *Daily Prayer*
  Paul F. Bradshaw, *Daily Prayer in the Early Church* (New York: Oxford Univ. Press, 1982).
Bradshaw, *Ordination*
  Paul F. Bradshaw, *Ordination Rites of the Ancient Churches of East and West* (New York: Pueblo, 1990).
Bradshaw, "Redating"
  Paul F. Bradshaw, "Redating the *Apostolic Tradition*: Some Preliminary Steps," in John Baldovin and Nathan Mitchell, eds., *Rule of Prayer, Rule of Faith: Essays in Honor of Aidan Kavanagh, OSB* (Collegeville, Minn.: Liturgical, 1996) 3–17.
Bradshaw, *Search*
  Paul F. Bradshaw, *The Search for the Origins of Christian Worship* (New York: Oxford Univ. Press, 1992).
Brent, *Hippolytus*
  Allen Brent, *Hippolytus and the Roman Church in the Third Century: Communities in Tension before the Emergence of a Monarch-Bishop* (VCSup 31; Leiden: Brill, 1995).
Brock and Vasey, *Didascalia*
  Sebastian Brock and Michael Vasey, eds., *The Liturgical Portions of the Didascalia* (GLS 29; Nottingham: Grove, 1982).
Brown, *Body*
  Peter Brown, *The Body and Society: Men, Women, and Sexual Renunciation in Early Christianity* (New York: Columbia Univ. Press, 1988).
Connolly, "Ancient Prayer"
  Richard H. Connolly, "An Ancient Prayer in the Mediaeval Euchologia," *JTS* 19 (1918) 132–44.
Connolly, *Egyptian Church Order*
  Richard H. Connolly, *The So-Called Egyptian Church Order and Derived Documents* (TextS 8/4; Cambridge: Cambridge Univ. Press, 1916; reprinted Nendeln, Liechtenstein: Kraus, 1967).
Connolly, "Eucharistic Prayer"
  Richard H. Connolly, "The Eucharistic Prayer of Hippolytus," *JTS* 39 (1938) 350–69.
Connolly, "Prologue"
  Richard H. Connolly, "The Prologue to the *Apostolic Tradition* of Hippolytus," *JTS* 22 (1921) 356–61.
Cuming, *Essays*
  Geoffrey J. Cuming, ed., *Essays on Hippolytus* (GLS 15; Nottingham: Grove, 1978).
Cuming, *Hippolytus*
  Geoffrey J. Cuming, *Hippolytus: A Text for Students* (2nd ed.; GLS 8; Nottingham: Grove, 1987).
Dix, *Apostolic Tradition*
  Gregory Dix, *Apostolike Paradosis: The Treatise on the Apostolic Tradition of St. Hippolytus of Rome* (New York: Macmillan, 1937; 2d ed. with preface and

corrections by Henry Chadwick, London: SPCK, 1968; reprinted Ridgefield, Conn.: Morehouse, 1992).

Dix, "Ministry"
Gregory Dix, "The Ministry in the Early Church," in Kenneth E. Kirk, ed., *The Apostolic Ministry* (London: Hodder & Stoughton, 1946) 183–303.

Dix, *Shape*
Gregory Dix, *The Shape of the Liturgy* (London: Dacre, 1945).

Duensing, *Aethiopische Text*
Hugo Duensing, *Der aethiopische Text der Kirchenordnung des Hippolyt* (Gesellschaft der Wissenschaften zu Göttingen, phil.-hist. Kl. 3/32; Göttingen: Vandenhoeck & Ruprecht, 1946).

Dugmore, *Influence*
Clifford William Dugmore, *The Influence of the Synagogue upon the Divine Office* (Oxford: Oxford Univ. Press, 1944; 2d ed. London: Faith, 1964).

Easton, *Apostolic Tradition*
Burton Scott Easton, *The Apostolic Tradition of Hippolytus* (New York: Macmillan, 1934; reprinted Hamden, Conn.: Archon, 1962).

Frere, "Early Forms"
Walter Howard Frere, "Early Forms of Ordination," in Henry Barclay Swete, ed., *Essays on the Early History of the Church and the Ministry* (London: Macmillan, 1918) 263–312.

Funk, *Constitutiones*
Franz Xaver Funk, *Didascalia et Constitutiones Apostolorum* (2 vols.; Paderborn: Schoeningh, 1905; reprinted Turin: Bottega d'Erasmo, 1979).

Hanssens, *Liturgie*
Jean Michel Hanssens, *La liturgie d'Hippolyte: Ses documents, son titulaire, ses origines et son charactère* (1959; 2d ed.; OrChrA 155; Rome: Pontificium Institutum Orientalium Studiorum, 1965).

Horner, *Statutes*
George W. Horner, *The Statutes of the Apostles or Canones Ecclesiastici* (London: Williams & Norgate, 1904).

Johnson, *Living Water*
Maxwell E. Johnson, ed., *Living Water, Sealing Spirit: Readings on Christian Initiation* (Collegeville, Minn.: Liturgical, 1995).

Johnson, *Sarapion*
Maxwell E. Johnson, *The Prayers of Sarapion of Thmuis: A Literary, Liturgical, and Theological Analysis* (OrChrA 249; Rome: Pontificio Istituto Orientale, 1995).

Kavanagh, *Confirmation*
Aidan Kavanagh, *Confirmation: Origins and Reform* (New York: Pueblo, 1988).

Kelly, *Creeds*
J. N. D. Kelly, *Early Christian Creeds* (New York: D. McKay, 1950).

Kilmartin, "Baptismal Cups"
Edward Kilmartin, "The Baptismal Cups Revisited," in E. Carr et al., eds., *Eulogema: Studies in Honor of Robert Taft, S.J.* (Studia Anselmiana 110, Analecta Liturgica 17; Rome: Pontificio Ateneo S. Anselmo, 1993) 249–67.

Lécuyer, "Episcopat"
Joseph Lécuyer, "Episcopat et presbytérat dans les écrits d'Hippolyte de Rome," *RechSR* 41 (1953) 30–50.

Markschies, "Wer schrieb"
Christoph Markschies, "Wer schrieb die sogenannte *Traditio Apostolica*? Neue Beobachtungen und Hypothesen zu einer kaum lösbaren Frage aus der altkirchen Literaturgeschichte," in Wolfram Kinzig, Christoph Markschies, and Markus Vinzent, *Tauffragen und Bekenntnis* (AKG 74; New York: de Gruyter, 1999) 1–74.

Mazza, *Origins*
Enrico Mazza, *The Origins of the Eucharistic Prayer,* trans. Ronald E. Lane (Collegeville, Minn.: Liturgical, 1995).

McGowan, *Ascetic Eucharists*
Andrew McGowan, *Ascetic Eucharists: Food and Drink in Early Christian Ritual Meals* (Oxford Early Christian Studies; Oxford: Clarendon, 1999).

Metzger, "Enquêtes"
Marcel Metzger, "Enquêtes autour de la prétendue *Tradition apostolique*," *EO* 9 (1992) 7–36.

Metzger, "Nouvelles perspectives"
Marcel Metzger, "Nouvelles perspectives pour le prétendue *Tradition apostolique*," *EO* 5 (1988) 241–59.

Mohlberg, *Liber Sacramentorum*
Leo Cunibert Mohlberg, *Liber Sacramentorum Romanae Aeclesiae ordinis anni circuli* (Rerum ecclesiasticarum documenta, Series major, Fontes 4; Rome: Herder, 1960).

Niederwimmer, *Didache*
Kurt Niederwimmer, *The Didache: A Commentary,* trans. L. M. Maloney (Hermeneia; Minneapolis: Fortress Press, 1998).

Phillips, "Daily Prayer"
L. Edward Phillips, "Daily Prayer in the *Apostolic Tradition* of Hippolytus," *JTS* 40 (1989) 389–400.

Phillips, *Ritual Kiss*
L. Edward Phillips, *The Ritual Kiss in Early Christian Worship* (JLS 36; Nottingham: Grove, 1996).

Rahmani, *Testamentum Domini*
Ignatius Rahmani, *Testamentum Domini nostri Jesu Christi* (Mainz: Kirchheim, 1899; reprinted Hildesheim: Olms, 1968).

Ratcliff, "Apostolic Tradition"
Edward C. Ratcliff, "Apostolic Tradition: Questions concerning the Appointment of the Bishop," *StPatr* 8 (1966) 266–70; reprinted in A. H. Couratin and David Tripp, eds., *E. C. Ratcliff: Liturgical Studies* (London: SPCK, 1976) 156–60.

Ratcliff, "Sanctus"
    Edward C. Ratcliff, "The Sanctus and the Pattern of the Early Anaphora," *JEH* 1 (1950) 29–36, 125–34; reprinted in A. H. Couratin and David Tripp, eds., *E. C. Ratcliff: Liturgical Studies* (London: SPCK, 1976) 18–40.

Richter, "Bischofsordination"
    Klemens Richter, "Zum Ritus der Bischofsordination in der 'Apostolischen Überlieferung' Hippolyts von Rom und davon abhängigen Schriften," *ALW* 17 (1975) 7–51.

Rordorf, "L'ordination"
    Willy Rordorf, "L'ordination de l'évêque selon la Tradition apostolique d'Hippolyte de Rome," *QL* 55 (1974) 137–50; reprinted in idem, *Liturgie, foi et vie des premiers chrétiens* (ThH 75; Paris: Beauchesne, 1986) 123–36.

Segelberg, "Benedictio Olei"
    Eric Segelberg, "The Benedictio Olei in the Apostolic Tradition of Hippolytus," *OrChr* 48 (1964) 268–81.

Segelberg, "Ordination Prayers"
    Eric Segelberg, "The Ordination Prayers in Hippolytus," *StPatr* 13 (1975) 397–408.

Stewart-Sykes, "Integrity"
    Alistair Stewart-Sykes, "The Integrity of the Hippolytean Ordination Rites," *Aug* 39 (1999) 97–127.

Taft, *Liturgy*
    Robert Taft, *The Liturgy of the Hours in East and West: The Origins of the Divine Office and Its Meaning for Today* (Collegeville, Minn.: Liturgical, 1986).

Vilela, *Condition*
    Albano Vilela, *La condition collégiale des prêtres au IIIe siècle* (ThH 14; Paris: Beauchesne, 1971).

Walls, "Latin Version"
    Andrew F. Walls, "The Latin Version of Hippolytus' Apostolic Tradition," *StPatr* 3 (1961) 155–62.

Werblowsky, "Baptismal Rite"
    R. J. Zwi Werblowsky, "On the Baptismal Rite According to St. Hippolytus," *StPatr* 2 (1957) 93–105.

Whitaker, *Documents*
    Edward C. Whitaker, *Documents of the Baptismal Liturgy* (2d ed.; Alcuin Club Collection 42; London: SPCK, 1970).

Yarnold, *Awe-Inspiring Rites*
    Edward Yarnold, *The Awe-Inspiring Rites of Initiation: Baptismal Homilies of the Fourth Century* (Slough: St. Paul, 1972).

This commentary offers the most comprehensive presentation of the evidence for the *Apostolic Tradition* available in English. The translations of the various witnesses and testimonies are the work of the authors of the commentary, with the exception of the translations of the Arabic version and the *Canons of Hippolytus,* which were done by Carol Bebawi, and the Ethiopic version, which was done by Professor James VanderKam. The translation of the *Testamentum Domini* is based on James Cooper and Arthur J. Maclean, *Testament of Our Lord Translated into English from the Syriac* (Edinburgh: T. & T. Clark, 1902).

The endpapers are produced from a microfilm of British Library Manuscript #OR1320 and are reprinted by permission of the British Library. This manuscript, which was made in 1006 C.E., preserves the oldest and most complete copy of the Sahidic Coptic version of *The Apostolic Tradition*. The pages printed for the endpapers are numbered 16 through 19 in Greek numbers and contain chapters concerning ordinations or consecrations of bishops, presbyters, deacons, confessors, readers, subdeacons, and widows.

1. Identification of the Document

During the course of the nineteenth century discoveries were made of a number of ancient Christian texts in a variety of linguistic versions that were similar in character to the *Apostolic Constitutions,* first published in 1563. These church orders, as they were termed by scholars, purported to offer authoritative "apostolic" prescriptions on matters of moral conduct, liturgical practice, and ecclesiastical organization and discipline.[1] Among them was a document that had earlier been known only through an incomplete Ethiopic version included by Job Leutholf in a 1691 study of Ethiopia.[2] The first complete text appeared in an 1848 edition by Henry Tattam of an ancient collection of church orders that had been translated into the Bohairic dialect of Coptic as recently as 1804.[3] Later in the century Paul de Lagarde published a much older translation of the same collection into the Sahidic dialect.[4] For want of a better title, this particular document within the collection was designated as the "Egyptian Church Order" by Hans Achelis when he produced a German translation of it in 1891,[5] and this name was generally adopted. In 1900 Edmund Hauler edited a fifth-century Latin version of the same collection,[6] and four years later George Horner completed the circle of extant witnesses by publishing Arabic and Ethiopic texts,[7] since—apart from a few fragments—the original Greek has never been found.

Although it was obvious that several of the church orders had a close literary relationship with one another, the "Egyptian Church Order" was at first unanimously judged to be a descendant of one of the other documents rather than their original source. Thus Achelis believed that it derived from the so-called *Canons of Hippolytus,* an attribution that he accepted as genuine, and that the *Epitome* of *Apostolic Constitutions* book 8 and then *Apostolic Constitutions* 8 itself were in turn descendants of it, via another work that had subsequently been lost. At the same time Franz Xaver Funk suggested almost exactly the opposite lineage: that *Apostolic Constitutions* 8 was the original source, with the *Epitome,* the "Egyptian Church Order," and the *Canons of Hippolytus* all being derived from it, in that order.[8] In 1899 Ignatius Rahmani published his edition of another obviously related church order, the *Testamentum Domini,* and he claimed that it was a second-century work from which *Apostolic Constitutions* 8 and the "Egyptian Church Order" derived directly, with the *Canons of Hippolytus* in turn being dependent on the latter.[9] Both John Wordsworth[10] and A. J. Maclean[11] came somewhat closer to the truth by conjecturing that there was a lost church order from which all the known ones had emanated.

1 See further Paul F. Bradshaw, *The Search for the Origins of Christian Worship* (New York: Oxford Univ. Press, 1992) 80–110.

2 Job Leutholf (Ludolfus), *Ad suam historiam Aethiopicam antehac editam commentarius* (Frankfurt: J. D. Zunneri, 1691) 323–29; reproduced in *Bullarium Patronatus Portugalliae Regum in Ecclesiis Africae, Asiae atque Oceaniae,* vol. 3: *Documenta Historiam Ecclesiae Habesinorum illustrantia inedita vel antea iam edita* (Olisipone: Ex Typographia Nationali, 1868) 2:145–98.

3 Henry Tattam, *The Apostolical Constitutions or the Canons of the Apostles in Coptic with an English Translation* (Oriental Translation Fund of Great Britain and Ireland Publications 63; London: Oriental Translation Fund of Great Britain and Ireland, 1848) 31–92.

4 Paul de Lagarde, *Aegyptiaca* (Göttingen: Hoyer, 1883; reprinted Osnabrück: Zeller, 1972) 248–66.

5 Hans Achelis, *Die ältesten Quellen des orientalischen Kirchenrechtes,* vol. 1: *Die Canones Hippolyti* (TU 6/4;

Leipzig: Hinrichs, 1891) 26. The German translation itself was the work of Georg Steindorff.

6 Edmund Hauler, *Didascaliae apostolorum fragmenta Veronensia latina. Accedunt canonum qui dicuntur apostolorum et aegyptiorum reliquies* (Leipzig: Teubner, 1900) 101–21.

7 George W. Horner, *The Statutes of the Apostles or Canones Ecclesiastici* (London: Williams & Norgate, 1904) 10–52, 95–108.

8 Franz Xaver Funk, *Die apostolischen Konstitutionen, eine litterar-historische Untersuchung* (Rottenburg: Bader, 1891; reprinted Frankfurt: Minerva, 1970); idem, "Die liturgie der Aethiopischen Kirchenordnung," *ThQ* 80 (1898) 513–47.

9 Ignatius Rahmani, *Testamentum Domini* (Mainz: Kirchheim, 1899; reprinted Hildesheim: Olms, 1968) VIII–XLVIII.

10 John Wordsworth, *The Ministry of Grace* (London: Longmans, Green, 1901) 18–21.

11 Arthur J. Maclean, *The Ancient Church Orders* (New York: Putnam, 1910) 141–73.

In 1906, however, Eduard von der Goltz came up with the suggestion that the "Egyptian Church Order" might in reality be a work by Hippolytus of Rome, the *Apostolic Tradition*, previously believed to have been lost,[12] and this theory was taken up and elaborated, first by Eduard Schwartz in 1910,[13] and then quite independently and much more fully by Richard H. Connolly in 1916.[14] Since that time it has been universally accepted that this document is the original source of the other church orders from which it was formerly presumed to derive. The questions of its identity, authorship, date, and provenance cannot, however, be considered definitively settled. While the majority of scholars have supported the position that it does originate from Rome and is the genuine work of Hippolytus, written in the early third century,[15] several scholars have raised doubts about this verdict. These have included Rudolf Lorentz in 1929,[16] Hieronymus Engberding in 1948,[17] and more recently Marcel Metzger in a series of articles from 1988 onward, which we shall consider in detail later.[18]

The traditional attribution rests on two principal arguments. The first is that, while no existing manuscript of the document itself bears a title or author's name, two of the derived church orders do refer to Hippolytus. One is actually titled *The Canons of Hippolytus*, and the other—the *Epitome* of *Apostolic Constitutions* 8—introduces a subheading, "Constitutions of the Holy Apostles concerning Ordinations through Hippolytus," at precisely the point where it begins to draw directly on a text of the document rather than on *Apostolic Constitutions* 8 itself (see below, p. 6). This appears to suggest that the two compilers knew of a tradition that linked their source with Hippolytus.[19]

The second argument is that the opening section of the document speaks of having "set down those things that were worthy of note about the gifts that God from the beginning according to his own will bestowed on human beings," and of having "arrived at the summit of the tradition that catechizes to the churches, so that those who have been well taught by our exposition may guard that tradition which has remained up to now." Moreover, the final section (chap. 43) also refers to "the apostolic tradition." This encouraged the identification of the document with an otherwise unknown treatise, the *Apostolic Tradition*, apparently included in a list of Hippolytus's works inscribed on the right-hand side of

---

12 Eduard von der Goltz, "Unbekannte Fragmente altchristlicher Gemeindeordnungen," *Sitzungsberichte der Preussischen Akademie der Wissenschaften* (1906) 141–57; see also idem, "Die Taufgebete Hippolyts und andere Taufgebete der alten Kirchen," *ZKG* 27 (1906) 1–51.

13 Eduard Schwartz, *Über die pseudoapostolischen Kirchenordnungen* (Strasbourg: Trubner, 1910); reprinted in idem, *Gesammelte Schriften* (5 vols.; Berlin: de Gruyter, 1938–63) 5:192–273.

14 Richard H. Connolly, *The So-Called Egyptian Church Order and Derived Documents* (TextS 8/4; Cambridge: Cambridge Univ. Press, 1916; reprinted Nendeln, Liechtenstein: Kraus, 1967).

15 Burton Scott Easton (*The Apostolic Tradition of Hippolytus* [New York: Macmillan, 1934; reprinted Hamden, Conn.: Archon, 1962] 25) dated it in 217, after Hippolytus's break with Callistus; Gregory Dix (*Apostolike Paradosis: The Treatise on the Apostolic Tradition of St. Hippolytus of Rome* [New York: Macmillan, 1937; 2d ed. with preface and corrections by Henry Chadwick; London: SPCK, 1968; reprinted Ridgefield, Conn.: Morehouse, 1992] xxxv–xxxvii) c. 215 just before the break; while Cyril C. Richardson ("The Date and Setting of the Apostolic Tradition of Hippolytus," *ATR* 30 [1948]

38–44) challenged both these dates and has been a lone voice arguing for 197.

16 Rudolf Lorentz, *De egyptische Kerkordening en Hippolytus van Rome* (Haarlem: Enschede, 1929). But see the response by Heinrich Elfers, *Die Kirchenordnung Hippolyts von Rom* (Paderborn: Bonifacius, 1938); and the unfavorable reviews by Odo Casel, *Jahrbuch für Liturgiewissenschaft* 9 (1929) 239–41; F. Rütten, *TRev* 30 (1931) 61–63; and Josef A. Jungmann, *ZKTh* 54 (1930) 281–85.

17 Hieronymus Engberding, "Das angebliche Dokument römischer Liturgie aus dem Beginn des dritten Jahrhunderts," in *Miscellanea liturgica in honorem L. Cuniberti Mohlberg* (2 vols.; Rome: Edizioni Liturgiche, 1948–49) 1:47–71. See the response by Bernard Botte, "L'authenticité de la Tradition apostolique de saint Hippolyte," *RThAM* 16 (1949) 177–85.

18 Marcel Metzger, "Nouvelles perspectives pour le prétendue *Tradition apostolique*," *EO* 5 (1988) 241–59; idem, "Enquêtes autour de la prétendue *Tradition apostolique*," *EO* (1992) 7–36; idem, "A propos des règlements écclesiastiques et de la prétendue *Tradition apostolique*," *RevScRel* 66 (1992) 249–61.

19 There is also a reference to Hippolytus in the heading of book 5 of the Arabic (but not the Syriac) ver-

the base of a statue discovered in Rome in 1551, especially since the list also seems to mention another unknown work, "Of the Gifts," apparently alluded to in the first quotation.

These two arguments can be challenged. The tendency to associate documents with apostolic figures or with those believed to have close connections to such persons so as to enhance their authority was common in the ancient Christian world. A good example is the claim of the *Apostolic Constitutions* to have been mediated from the apostles through Clement of Rome. While Hippolytus may not appear to be a particularly likely candidate for such pseudonymity, Palladius (c. 420) claims that he had been "the companion of the apostles," and later writers enhanced his reputation still further.[20] If he were believed to have belonged to the apostolic age, then the attribution of an anonymous text to him might be thought less surprising.[21] On the other hand, as Henry Chadwick has pointed out, this counterargument can be stood on its head: it could have been the very existence of a church order entitled *Apostolic Tradition* under the name of Hippolytus that was the source of the fifth-century idea that he had been known to the apostles.[22] Nevertheless, since other works are also known to have been falsely attributed to Hippolytus,[23] who can say with certainty whether this particular attribution is trustworthy?

Christoph Markschies has recently argued not only that the ascription of the *Canons of Hippolytus* to Hippolytus and the reference to him in the subheading of the *Epitome* were not made until the late fourth or early fifth century (and thus much too late to credit them with any historical reliability), but that the apparent references to "apostolic tradition" in the prologue and conclusion of the document, and to an earlier work that dealt with "gifts," have been misinterpreted by other scholars and so do not indicate the title of the work (see further the commentaries on those chapters). He believes that in the course of its transmission the document gradually went through a process first of "apostolicizing" and then of "Hippolyticizing."[24]

In any case, all church orders in one way or another profess an apostolic connection,[25] and it has been claimed that this one was actually known both to the compiler of the *Epitome* and to the editor of the collection of patristic quotations containing the text of chap. 36 (see below, p. 7) not as the "Apostolic Tradition," but as the "Constitutions of the Holy Apostles."[26] Bernard Botte, however, discounted this evidence by pointing out that Epiphanius cited under this same title six extracts from another church order, the *Didascalia Apostolorum*, and he suggested that this was the designation by which the collection of church orders that included both these texts was known.[27]

sion of the Clementine Octateuch, at the point where the section of *Apostolic Constitutions* 8 dealing with ordinations begins. Since it reads "The ordinance of the apostles concerning ordination through Hippolytus," however, it could well have been copied there from the *Epitome*: see Jean Michel Hanssens, *La liturgie d'Hippolyte: Ses documents, son titulaire, ses origines et son charactère* (2d ed.; OrChrA 155; Rome: Pontificium Institutum Orientalium Studiorum, 1965) 56.

20   Palladius *Lausiac History* 148. For other references see Allen Brent, *Hippolytus and the Roman Church in the Third Century: Communities in Tension before the Emergence of a Monarch-Bishop* (VCSup 31; Leiden: Brill, 1995) 183.

21   For the debate on the issue see n. 17 above.

22   In Dix, *Apostolic Tradition*, f.

23   See Hanssens, *Liturgie,* 84–85; Pierre Nautin, ed., *Homélies pascales* 1 (SC 27; Paris: Cerf, 1950) 34–36; Brent, *Hippolytus*, 192–93.

24   Christoph Markschies, "Wer schrieb die sogenannte *Traditio Apostolica*? Neue Beobachtungen und Hypothesen zu einer kaum lösbaren Frage aus der altkirchen Literaturgeschichte," in Wolfram Kinzig, Christoph Markschies, and Markus Vinzent, *Tauffragen und Bekenntnis* (AKG 74; Berlin: de Gruyter, 1999) 8–43.

25   See further Andrew F. Walls, "A Note on the Apostolic Claim in the Church Order Literature," *StPatr* 2 (1957) 83–92.

26   See Jean Magne, "La prétendue Tradition Apostolique d'Hippolyte de Rome s'appelait-elle, *AI ΔΙΑΤΑΞΕΙΣ ΤΩΝ ΑΓΙΩΝ ΑΠΟΣΤΟΛΩΝ Les statuts des saints apôtres?*" *Ostkirchliche Studien* 14 (1965) 35–67.

27   Bernard Botte, *La Tradition apostolique de saint Hippolyte: Essai de reconstitution* (1963; 5th ed. with addenda by Albert Gerhards; Liturgiewissenschaftliche Quellen und Forschungen 39; Münster: Aschendorff, 1989) iv. See also Aimé-Georges Martimort, "Nouvel examen de la 'Tradition apostolique' d'Hippolyte," *BLE* 88 (1987) 7–12. On the collections of church orders, see below, n. 55.

Moreover, the statue of Hippolytus has nearly as strange and complicated a history as the document itself: recent research has revealed that it was in origin a representation not of Hippolytus but of a female figure, which was restored in the sixteenth century as a male bishop because of the list of works inscribed on its base, using parts taken from other statues.[28] Even this list does not correlate exactly with the works of Hippolytus that are cataloged by both Eusebius and Jerome: most surprisingly, it omits those that are most strongly attested as genuinely his, including the commentary on Daniel.[29] These discrepancies led to several hypotheses: Pierre Nautin proposed the existence of two different authors, Hippolytus and Josephus;[30] Vincenzo Loi and Manlio Simonetti suggested that the works of two authors, both called Hippolytus, a Roman presbyter and a bishop from the East, had become confused;[31] and more recently Allen Brent has argued for a school of at least three authors as having been responsible for the works on the list.[32] Somewhat oddly, however, although acknowledging that there is no necessary association between the church order itself and the work on the list bearing the title "Apostolic Tradition," Brent still insists that it "must nevertheless be a document of the school of Hippolytus."[33]

In addition, it is not entirely clear how lines 9–11 of the inscription should be interpreted. They read:

[Π]ΕΡΙ ΧΑΡΙΣΜΑΤΩΝ   [C]ONCERNING CHARISMS
[ΑΠ]ΟΣΤΟΛΙΚΗ   [AP]OSTOLIC TRADITION
ΠΑΡΑΔΟΣΙΣ

Some believe this refers to two works, one called "Concerning Charisms" and the other "Apostolic Tradition,"[34] while others have espoused the view that "Apostolic Tradition concerning Charisms" was the title of a single work by Hippolytus.[35] Jean Magne adopted the latter position, but he argued that this document was not it: instead he thought that *Const.* 8.1–2 contained the genuine work by Hippolytus.[36] Botte responded with

---

28 See the essays by Margherita Guarducci, "La statua di 'Sant'Ippolito,'" in *Ricerche su Ippolito* (StEphA 13; Rome: Institutum Patristicum Augustinianum, 1977) 17–30; and "La 'Statua di Sant'Ippolito' e la sua provenienza," in *Nuove ricerche su Ippolito* (StEphA 30; Rome: Institutum Patristicum Augustinianum, 1989) 61–74. For further details concerning the statue, see Hanssens, *Liturgie*, 217–31; Brent, *Hippolytus*, 3–114. It has been suggested that the original figure was Themista of Lampsacus, but Markus Vinzent has recently made the intriguing proposal that it was an Amazon woman named Hippolyta: see Markus Vinzent, "'Philo biblie' in frühen Christentum," *Das Altertum* 45 (1999) 116–17.

29 Hanssens, *Liturgie*, 229–30, 247–49, 254–82; Brent, *Hippolytus*, 115–203.

30 Pierre Nautin, *Hippolyte et Josipe: Contribution à l'histoire de la littérature chrétienne du IIIe siècle* (Paris: Cerf, 1947); idem, "Notes sur le catalogue des oeuvres d'Hippolyte," *RechSR* 34 (1947) 99–107. But cf. the responses by Bernard Botte, "Note sur l'auteur du De universo attribué à saint Hippolyte," *RThAM* 18 (1951) 5–18; Bernard Capelle, "Hippolyte de Rome," *RThAM* 17 (1950) 145–74; idem, "A propos d'Hippolyte de Rome," *RThAM* 19 (1952) 193–202; the last two are reprinted in idem, *Travaux liturgiques de doctrine et d'histoire* (3 vols.; Louvain: Centre liturgique, Abbaye du Mont César, 1955–67) 2:31–70; Heinrich Elfers, "Neue Untersuchungen über die Kirchenordnung Hippolyts von Rom," in Marcel Reding, ed., *Abhandlungen über*

Theologie und Kirche: Festschrift für Karl Adam (Düsseldorf: Patmos, 1952) 169–211; and Marcel Richard, "Dernières remarques sur S. Hippolyte et le soi-disant Josipe," *RechSR* 43 (1955) 379–94.

31 Vincenzo Loi, "L'identità letteraria di Ippolito di Roma," in *Ricerche su Ippolito* (StEphA 13; Rome: Institutum Patristicum Augustinianum, 1977) 67–88; Manlio Simonetti, "A modo di conclusione: Una ipotesi di lavoro," in ibid., 151–56.

32 Brent, *Hippolytus*, 204–366. See also Paul Bouhot, "L'auteur romain des *Philosophumena* et l'écrivain Hippolyte," *EO* 13 (1996) 137–64; cf. the attack on Brent's position by M. Simonetti, "Una nuova proposta su Ippolito," *Aug* 36 (1996) 13–46.

33 Brent, *Hippolytus*, 301–2.

34 See, e.g., Connolly, *Egyptian Church Order*, 136–49; Botte, *Tradition*, xi; Markschies, "Wer schrieb," 21–24.

35 See, e.g., Edgar Hennecke, "Hippolyts Schrift 'Apostolische Überlieferung der Gnadengaben,'" in *Harnack-Ehrung: Beiträge zur Kirchengeschichte* (Leipzig: Hinrichs, 1921) 159–82; Hanssens, *Liturgie*, 109–10, 247–53.

36 Jean Magne, *Tradition apostolique sur les charismes et Diataxeis des saints Apôtres* (Origines chrétiennes 1; Paris: Magne, 1975) 7–104. See also idem, "Un extrait de la 'Tradition apostolique sur les charismes' d'Hippolyte sous les gloses du Constituteur, et les 'Diataxeis des saints Apôtres,'" in Franz Paschke, ed., *Überlieferungsgeschichtliche Untersuchungen* (TU 125; Berlin: Akademie, 1981) 399–402.

the assertion that this section of the *Apostolic Constitutions* was an adaptation by its compiler of a treatise about signs and miracles that was not the work of Hippolytus.[37]

Still further doubts may be raised concerning the identity of Hippolytus himself. In spite of the confident biographical account presented by Gregory Dix,[38] the historical data are very confused.[39] Eusebius and Jerome describe him as a bishop, but give no indication of his diocese.[40] Others associate him with either Rome itself or Porto (close to Rome) or even Arabia. Yet other sources speak of a Hippolytus who was a schismatic presbyter in the time of Novatian, and later hagiography complicates the story still further. It is certainly possible to try to reconcile some of this conflicting evidence, but such a reconciliation involves the assumption that Hippolytus was the author of the heresiological treatise *Refutatio* (or *Philosophoumena*),[41] which describes the opposition against Pope Callistus by a Roman presbyter elected bishop in 217. Some modern scholars, however, have challenged the attribution of that anonymous work to Hippolytus.[42] While we would wish to keep an open mind on that particular issue, without that sure attribution Hippolytus remains responsible for a series of exegetical works that provide no biographical informa-

tion at all about their author and offer no help to attempts to connect the *Apostolic Tradition* with this figure.

Some have judged the greatest weakness of the traditional attribution of the *Apostolic Tradition* to Hippolytus to be the paucity of close parallels between the liturgical practices prescribed in this document and the later Roman rites.[43] Even those that do exist might well have entered the Roman liturgy either as a result of the direct influence of the *Apostolic Tradition* itself or through some intermediate text, as earlier scholars have recognized, and so do not provide firm evidence for the Roman origin of the church order.[44] That certainly was the case with regard to the directions concerning the imposition of hands in ordination, which found their way into later Roman texts from the Gallican *Statuta Ecclesiae Antiqua*, which in turn derived them from the *Apostolic Tradition*.[45]

Moreover, the document apparently circulated more widely in the East than in the West, which has led some to suggest an Eastern provenance. For example, Jean Michel Hanssens championed the thesis that Hippolytus came to Rome from Alexandria, bringing with him the liturgy of his own country,[46] while Louis Bouyer pre-

---

37 Bernard Botte, "Le traité des charismes dans les Constitutions apostoliques," *StPatr* 12 (1975) 83–86.

38 Dix, *Apostolic Tradition*, xii–xxxv.

39 See Hanssens, *Liturgie*, 283–340; Brent, *Hippolytus*, 368–457; Victor Saxer, "La questione di Ippolito Romano. A proposito di un libro recente," in *Nuove ricerche su Ippolito* (StEphA 30; Rome: Institutum Patristicum Augustinianum, 1989) 43–60; Manlio Simonetti, "Aggiornamento su Ippolito," in ibid., 75–130.

40 Eusebius *Hist. eccl.* 6.20–22; Jerome *De viris illustribus* 61.

41 See the discussion in the most recent critical edition and introduction: Miroslav Marcovich, ed., *Hippolytus, Refutatio Omnium Haeresium* (PTU 25; Berlin: de Gruyter, 1986) 8–17.

42 The fundamental challenge was issued by Pierre Nautin, *Hippolyte et Josipe: contribution à l'histoire de la littérature chrétienne du troisième siècle* (Études et textes pour l'histoire du dogme de la Trinité 1; Paris: Cerf, 1947). For a concise statement of Nautin's position, see his article, "Hippolytus," in Angelo Di Berardino, ed., *Encyclopedia of the Early*

Church (2 vols.; New York: Oxford Univ. Press, 1992) 383–85.

43 The contrasts between the *Apostolic Tradition* and the later Roman baptismal liturgy are most fully discussed by A. Salles, "La 'Tradition apostolique' est-elle un témoin de la liturgie romaine?" *RHR* 148 (1955) 181–213; but see the response by Aimé-Georges Martimort, "La 'Tradition Apostolique' d'Hippolyte et le rituel baptismal antique," *BLE* 60 (1959) 57–62.

44 See Richard H. Connolly, "An Ancient Prayer in the Mediaeval Euchologia," *JTS* 19 (1918) 140–44; Josef A. Jungmann, "Beobachtungen zum Fortleben von Hippolyts 'Apostolische Überlieferung,'" *ZKTh* 53 (1929) 579–85; Damien van den Eynde, "Nouvelle trace de la 'Traditio apostolica' d'Hippolyte dans la liturgie romaine," in *Miscellanea liturgica in honorem L. Cuniberti Mohlberg* (2 vols.; Rome: Edizioni Liturgiche, 1948–49) 1:407–11. See also Metzger, "Nouvelles perspectives," 248.

45 See Bernard Botte, "Le rituel d'ordination des *Statuta Ecclesiae antiqua*," *RThAM* 11 (1939) 223–41.

46 Hanssens, *Liturgie*.

ferred a Syrian origin.[47] On the other hand, the absence of parallels with later Roman liturgy may not be quite as damaging to the traditional attribution as might appear. Since so little is known about Roman liturgical practice prior to the sixth century, it is impossible to say how great the changes might have been in the intervening period.

2. Textual Witnesses

Because the original Greek text is not extant (with the exception of several fragments), the document has to be reconstructed from various translations of it, together with the evidence provided by its use as a source for the other church orders.

a. Greek Fragments
1. The *Epitome* of *Apostolic Constitutions* 8
This work consists of a series of extracts from book 8 of the *Apostolic Constitutions*, some rendered word for word, others slightly altered. While Achelis and others thought that it represented a first draft of book 8, most modern scholars think that it is probably a subsequent abbreviation of that text. It is divided into five parts (*Const.* 8.1–2; 8.4–5, 16–28, 30–31; 8.32; 8.33–34, 42–45; and 8.46), each part being given its own subtitle. That for the second part is "Constitutions of the Holy Apostles concerning Ordinations through Hippolytus." Besides the apparent link with Hippolytus furnished by this title, what makes this section interesting for our purposes is that the author is thought to have had access to a Greek text of the *Apostolic Tradition* (or at least to the part of it dealing with appointment to ministries) as well as to his principal source, since at two points he seems to reproduce the form found there in preference to the version

from *Apostolic Constitutions* 8. These points are the ordination prayer for a bishop (*Apostolic Tradition* 3, in place of *Const.* 8.5) and the instructions for appointing a reader (*Apostolic Tradition* 11, in place of *Const.* 8.22). In addition, one manuscript alone has, for some reason, also preserved another Greek fragment of the *Apostolic Tradition:* Vienna *gr.* 7, and the passage concerned is chap. 23.[48] One should note, however, that Christoph Markschies has recently challenged the scholarly consensus and contended that what the *Epitome* had access to was not the original Greek text of the *Apostolic Tradition* as such but a version of it that had already undergone some modification.[49] We will consider this claim further at the relevant points in the commentary.

The *Epitome* was first published in full by Paul de Lagarde in 1856,[50] but Funk's text[51] (which was based on ten MSS.) is the one most commonly cited, and the one used for this edition. There is no published English translation, and only the passages that appear to be taken from a text of the *Apostolic Tradition* are included here, being substituted for the versions in the *Apostolic Constitutions*.

2. Chapter 5
An adaptation of the prayer for the blessing of oil in this chapter appears in the ritual for the anointing of the sick in an eleventh- or twelfth-century manuscript from the Monastery of St. Catherine on Mount Sinai.[52]
3. Chapters 31–32
The prayer for the offering of firstfruits in chap. 31 and the list of fruits that may be offered from chap. 32 are preserved in the oldest extant Byzantine *euchologion*, Barberini *gr.* 336 (8th century), although in a very defective state.[53]

---

47 Louis Bouyer, *Eucharist: Theology and Spirituality of the Eucharistic Prayer* (Notre Dame: Univ. of Notre Dame Press, 1968) 167. The same conclusion, for different reasons, was also reached by Michael A. Smith, "The Anaphora of *Apostolic Tradition* Reconsidered," *StPatr* 10 (1970) 426–30.

48 It was first found by Franz Xaver Funk and published both in his article, "Die apostolischen Konstitutionen III," *ThQ* 75 (1893) 664–66; and in Funk, *Didascalia et Constitutiones Apostolorum* (2 vols.; Paderborn: Schoeningh, 1905; reprinted Turin: Bottega d'Erasmo, 1979) 2:112. Connolly ("Ancient

Prayer," 138) also identified the existence of a fragment of *Ap. Trad.* 41.9 in this same manuscript.

49 Markschies, "Wer schrieb," 15–19.

50 Paul de Lagarde, *Reliquae iuris ecclesiastici antiquissimae* (Leipzig: Teubner, 1856; reprinted Osnabrück: Zeller, 1967) 1–23.

51 Funk, *Constitutiones*, 2:72–96.

52 See Eric Segelberg, "The Benedictio Olei in the Apostolic Tradition of Hippolytus," *OrChr* 48 (1964) 270, 274–75.

53 Critical editions in Giovanni Mercati, "Una

4. Chapter 36

A Greek text of this short chapter is preserved in an eighth-century collection of patristic quotations, which exists in two manuscripts, Ochrid *Mus. nat.* 86 (13th century), f. 192, and Paris BN *gr.* 900 (15th century), f. 112.[54]

b. Translations

It should be noted that the *Apostolic Tradition* is never found alone in any of the following manuscript traditions, but always as part of a collection of similar church orders, and is consistently placed after the *Apostolic Church Order* as though they constituted a single work, without any division to mark the two off from one another.[55]

1. Latin

This exists only as a single, incomplete manuscript, in the form of a palimpsest, that is, a parchment that was used once and then later scraped or washed clean so that it could be written on again. This manuscript, in the Verona Cathedral library, *Veronese* LV (53), now contains an eighth-century copy of the *Sentences* of Isidore of Seville (d. 636), but forty-one of its ninety-nine leaves once formed part of a late-fifth-century manuscript that included, among other things, a Latin translation of our document, which it is still possible to make out under the surface of the later text. The credit for this discovery belongs to the paleographer Wilhelm Studemund, but it was first read in full and published by Hauler in 1900.[56] While the titles or headings of the various chapters—which had been written in red ink—could not be retrieved at all, it was possible to decipher the rest quite successfully. More recently, however, a further edition by the Swedish philologist Erik Tidner has suggested alternative readings of the text at several points, and his edition is followed in our translation.[57] Tidner retains references to the page and line numbering of Hauler's edition, and this reference is given in parentheses at the beginning of each chapter in the translation.

The Latin text is incomplete because only certain leaves of the earlier manuscript were reused for the later work, and the rest have been lost. Three leaves, front and back, contain chaps. 1–8 of the document; another leaf contains part of the baptismal rite (chap. 21); two more cover chaps. 26–38, which are followed immediately by chaps. 42 and 43; and another preserves the last part of chap. 41, followed by a different version of chaps. 42 and 43 (the reasons for this repetition will be discussed more fully below, p. 16).

The date of the manuscript can be fixed fairly easily at about the end of the fifth century not only by its semi-uncial hand but also because it includes at the beginning a list of the *fasti consulares* down to 494. Scholars are agreed, however, that this manuscript does not constitute the original translation of the document itself, but is a later copy of the translator's work, because the text shows evidence of various interpolations by successive copyists. The translation itself appears to have been made sometime during the last quarter of the fourth century, and perhaps in an Arian community in North Italy, which because of its tendency toward liturgical conservatism would have been interested in preserving a pre-Nicene text.[58] But this is no more than a conjecture, whereas the date can be fixed fairly precisely, both on the basis of the Latin style and vocabulary and also because the form of the scriptural citations reflects a

Preghiera antichissima degli Eucologi medievali," in *Alcuni scritti e brevi saggi di studii sulla Volgata* (Rome: Tipografia della R. Accademia dei lincei, 1917); Stefano Parenti and Elena Velkovska, eds., *L'Eucologio Barberini gr. 336* (Rome: C.L.V.–Edizione Liturgiche, 1995) 258–59; ET in Connolly, "Ancient Prayer," 132–37, who attempts to reconstruct the original Greek of the *Apostolic Tradition*.

54 See Marcel Richard, "Quelques fragments des Pères anténicéens et nicéens," *Symbolae Osloenses* 38 (1963) 76–83; idem, "Le florilège eucharistique du Codex Ochrid. Musée national 86," in *Charistêrion eis Anastasion K. Orlandon* (4 vols.; Athens: Publications de la Société archéologique d'Athènes, 1966) 3:47–55.

Both are reprinted in his *Opera Minora* 1 (Turnhout: Brepols, 1976) nos. 5, 6.

55 See further Bradshaw, *Search*, 97–101; Bernard Botte, "Les plus anciennes collections canoniques," *L'Orient syrien* 5 (1960) 331–49; Hanssens, *Liturgie*, 171–216.

56 Edmund Hauler, *Didascaliae apostolorum fragmenta Veronensia latina: Accedunt canonum qui dicuntur apostolorum et aegyptiorum reliquiae* (Leipzig: Teubner, 1900).

57 Erik Tidner, *Didascaliae apostolorum Canonum ecclesiasticorum Traditionis apostolicae versiones Latinae* (TU 75; Berlin: Akademie, 1963) 117–50.

58 This suggestion is supported by Francis C. Burkitt,

Latin text of the Bible older than that known to Jerome. The translator seems for the most part to have followed the Greek text of the document before him very literally, even to the extent of retaining grammatical constructions from the Greek that are incorrect in Latin. A good example occurs in chap. 3, where the phrase "spirit of leadership," *principalis spiritus*, is followed first by a feminine relative pronoun, since the noun "spirit" is feminine in Latin, but then by a neuter relative pronoun in the next clause, which would have been there in the Greek text, since the Greek noun $\pi\nu\epsilon\hat{v}\mu\alpha$ is neuter.

2. Sahidic

Lagarde's edition was based on a single manuscript, BM *or.* 1320, dating from 1006 CE, although the original translation from Greek into Sahidic was probably made several centuries earlier. This manuscript has one folio torn out of the middle of the baptismal material, *Apostolic Tradition* 21, and the translator omits the texts of the eucharistic and ordination prayers as well as several other chapters (1, 5, 6, 22, 24 [= 29B], and 25 [= 29C]). Two other Sahidic manuscripts exist, but these are merely copies of the first and so have no independent value,[59] and a few fragments from another text are contained in BM *or.* 3580. A newer edition was published by Walter Till and Johannes Leipoldt in 1954.[60]

The Coptic language employs a large number of Greek loanwords, and both Dix and Botte reproduced a selection of these words from the Sahidic version in Greek in their editions of the *Apostolic Tradition*,[61] Dix even including some found only in the Bohairic version. We have instead included *all* the words found in the Sahidic, and none from the Bohairic, except where we have used that version in part of chap. 21. We have followed the convention of reproducing all verbs in the infinitive form, and nouns and adjectives in the nominative singular (a dash before or after a loan word indicates

its use in a compound Coptic word or phrase). Nevertheless, one must beware of assuming that these were always the exact words standing in the original Greek text used by the Coptic translator. They may often have been, but it is also possible that sometimes a translator might have chosen to render a Greek word before him by a quite different Greek loanword in the Coptic language.

The reader also needs to be aware that the Coptic language lacks the participle, so frequently used in Greek, and the translator would have to substitute for that a form of the verb that marked the subordination of the clause. It also lacks the passive voice, and thus a translator would need to render a phrase like "he was ordained by the bishop" either with an indeterminate subject in the third-person plural, "they ordained him by the bishop," or by inverting the construction, "the bishop ordained him." The first of these would signal that the Greek had used a passive, but not the second. Thus some differences between the Latin and the Sahidic may not be the result of deliberate alterations by the Coptic translator but variations made necessary by the structure of the language.

3. Arabic

Horner's 1904 text and translation of the Arabic was made on the basis of a single manuscript, *Vatic. ar.* 149, but a few years later a critical edition was published by Jean and Augustin Périer.[62] They used eight manuscripts, representing three different recensions:

1. Paris BN *ar.* 241 (13th-14th centuries)
   Rome *Vatic. Borgia ar.* 60 (1648 CE)
   Paris BN *ar.* 243 (1641 CE)
2. Paris BN *ar.* 251 (1353 CE)
   Rome *Vatic. ar.* 149 (14th century)
   Paris BN *ar.* 252 (1664 CE)
3. Rome *Barberini or.* 4 (1349 CE)
   London BM *Rich.* 7207 (1349 CE)

"The Didascalia," *JTS* 31 (1930) 261; Joseph H. Crehan in a review of Alois Stenzel, *Die Taufe,* in *JTS* 10 (1959) 421; and Andrew F. Walls, "The Latin Version of Hippolytus' Apostolic Tradition," *StPatr* 3 (1961) 161–62. See also Chadwick in Dix, *Apostolic Tradition,* f.

59 BM *or.* 440; and a manuscript of the Patriarchate of Alexandria, published by Urbain Bouriant, "Les canons apostoliques de Clement de Rome. Traduction en dialecte copte thebain d'apres un manuscrit

de la bibliothèque du Patriarche jacobite du Caire," *Recueil de travaux relatifs à la philologie et à l'archéologie égyptiennes* 5 (1884) 199–216; 6 (1885) 97–115.

60 Walter Till and Johannes Leipoldt, *Der koptische Text der Kirchenordnung Hippolyts* (TU 58; Berlin: Akademie, 1954).

61 See Botte, *Tradition,* xliii–lxiv.

62 Jean and Augustin Périer, *Les "127 Canons des Apôtres"* (PO 8/4; Paris: Firmin-Didot, 1912; reprinted Turnhout: Brepols, 1971) 590–622.

According to the colophon of one of the manuscripts, *Borgia ar.* 60, the translation from the Coptic was made in 1295, but since it was cited by the canonist Ibn-al-'Assâl, writing in the mid-thirteenth century, the true date may have been somewhat earlier.[63] It follows the Sahidic closely but has the advantage of having been made from a text that did not exhibit the lacuna in the baptismal material, nor does it have all the copyists' errors exhibited by the extant Sahidic manuscripts.

4. Ethiopic

Various errors found in this translation reveal clearly that it was made from an Arabic intermediary, but one that was more complete than the extant Arabic version, since it retained not only the full texts of prayers omitted in our Sahidic and Arabic manuscripts but also longer forms of certain chapters of which only traces remain in other witnesses. There are also indications in a few places that the translator may have had access to more than one version of the text. In addition, it includes a number of obvious interpolations, the most substantial of which is a set of baptismal prayers, located between *Apostolic Tradition* 30 and 31.

The full text of the Ethiopic published by Horner was based on a single manuscript, BM *or.* 793, dating from 1730–1735 CE.[64] In 1946, however, Hugo Duensing produced a critical edition from eight manuscripts.[65] He did not attempt to draw up a stemma for these, but in general showed a preference for the oldest manuscript, Vatican *Borgia aeth.* 2, dating from the fifteenth century.

5. Bohairic

This translation into the northern dialect of Coptic exists only in a single manuscript, Berlin *or.* quarto 519 (9488), the colophon of which states that it was made from Sahidic by a certain Georgios, son of Kosma, in 1804. It was thus done at a time when Coptic was a dead language, and consequently the translator's own native tongue would have been Arabic. The only published edition is that of Tattam in 1848, although Till and Leipoldt's edition of the Sahidic text contains notes on

the variants of the Bohairic version. Since none of these few variants is significant, and none suggests knowledge of a different text from that already known to us, we have not reproduced it in full in this edition. Use has been made of it only where the Sahidic is lacking in part of *Apostolic Tradition* 21.

c. Versions in Other Church Orders
1. *Apostolic Constitutions*

This composition reworks and weaves together several older sources, chief of which are the third-century church order known as the *Didascalia Apostolorum* (forming books 1–6 of the work), the *Didache* (in book 7), and the *Apostolic Tradition* (in book 8). It is generally agreed that it was written in Syria, and probably in Antioch, between 375 and 380. It is unlikely to be much earlier than that, because it includes a reference to the feast of Christmas, which was then only just beginning to make an appearance in Eastern churches, and it is unlikely to be much later, because its doctrine of the Holy Spirit is incompatible with the definition agreed at the Council of Constantinople in 381. The identity and theological position of the compiler, on the other hand, have been long debated. Indeed, the orthodoxy of the document became suspect at an early date, and it was thought by the Trullan Synod (691–692) that heretics must have falsified the original apostolic work. Photius, the patriarch of Constantinople (d. 891), criticized the whole compilation for its Arianism, although subsequent opinion was divided over this question.

Among modern scholars, Funk in his 1905 edition of the text (which has generally been treated as definitive) tended to play down the heterodoxy of the work by preferring orthodox variant readings wherever possible and by claiming that any suspect formulae came from the compiler's source and thus antedated the Arian controversy.[66] Cuthbert H. Turner criticized Funk's textual methods and argued strongly for an Arian compiler,[67] and Bernard Capelle later demonstrated that the text of

63 Ibid., 567.

64 Horner, *Statutes.*

65 Hugo Duensing, *Der aethiopische Text der Kirchenordnung des Hippolyt* (Gesellschaft der Wissenschaften zu Göttingen, phil.-hist. Kl. 3/32; Göttingen: Vandenhoeck & Ruprecht, 1946).

66 Funk, *Constitutiones*; ET based on this edition in

ANF 7:768–1008.

67 Cuthbert H. Turner, "A Primitive Edition of the Apostolic Constitutions and Canons," *JTS* 15 (1913) 53–65; idem, "Notes on the Apostolic Constitutions," *JTS* 16 (1914) 54–61, 523–38; 21 (1920) 160–68.

the *Gloria in Excelsis* found in the *Apostolic Constitutions* was not the original form of the hymn, as had been thought, but that the compiler had changed a hymn addressed to Christ into one addressed to the Father.[68] Because of similarities of language with the longer recension of the letters of Ignatius of Antioch, scholars have usually concluded that the compiler of the *Apostolic Constitutions*, whatever his theological stance, was also the interpolator of these letters. The most recent contributions to the authorship debate are by Georg Wagner (who drew linguistic parallels with the writings of Eunomius),[69] Dieter Hagedorn (who attributed the composition to an obscure bishop named Julian by a comparison of literary parallels),[70] and Marcel Metzger, who built on Hagedorn's suggestion and concluded that, although Julian's commentary on Job is much more explicitly Arian than the more moderate subordinationism of the *Apostolic Constitutions*, this difference could be explained by the fact that the latter was a liturgical work and so drew on traditional material. Metzger did not think, however, that its compiler could be considered a strict Arian.[71] He has also published a new edition of the text that makes use of a wider range of manuscripts and is free from the orthodox bias of Funk's edition;[72] our translation has been made from his Greek text.

2. Canons of Hippolytus

Although attention had been drawn as early as the seventeenth century to this collection of thirty-eight canons with a concluding sermon, it was first published in 1870.[73] It is extant only in Arabic, but there is general agreement that this text derived from a lost Coptic version, which was in turn a translation of an original Greek text. As indicated above, Achelis accepted the attribution to Hippolytus as genuine and concluded that this was the archetype from which all the other church orders containing similar material derived. As a consequence, interest was aroused in the document among liturgical scholars, but after Schwartz and Connolly had demonstrated that it was in reality merely a derivative of the *Apostolic Tradition*, it came to be considered as the latest of the group of related church orders, dating from the fifth or sixth century, and interest in it declined. In 1956, however, Botte suggested that it had been composed in Egypt around the mid-fourth century,[74] and in 1966 René-Georges Coquin, in the first and only proper critical edition of the text, followed up and amplified Botte's arguments, proposing on the basis of internal evidence a date between 336 and 340 for the work.[75] This would make it not the latest but the earliest known derivative of the *Apostolic Tradition*. On the other hand, Christoph Markschies has recently contested this conclusion and argued that, while the lost Greek original may date from that period, both the text in the form in which we now have it and the attribution to Hippolytus are no older than the late fourth or early fifth century.[76]

Nevertheless, it warrants more attention than it has hitherto received as it may well have something to contribute to the reconstruction of the underlying text of the *Apostolic Tradition*. Although the author seems to have freely paraphrased, supplemented, and adapted that source in the light of his own ecclesiastical situation and liturgical tradition, at least a few of these apparent

68 Bernard Capelle, "Le texte du 'gloria in excelsis,'" *RHE* 44 (1949) 439–57.

69 Georg Wagner, "Zur Herkunft der apostolischen Konstitutionen," in *Mélanges liturgiques offerts au R. P. Dom Bernard Botte OSB* (Louvain: Abbaye du Mont César, 1972) 525–37.

70 Dieter Hagedorn, *Der Hiobkommentar des Arianers Julian* (Patristische Texte und Studien 14; Berlin: de Gruyter, 1973) XXXVII–LVII.

71 Marcel Metzger, "La théologie des Constitutions apostoliques par Clement," *RevScRel* 57 (1983) 29–49, 112–22, 169–94, 273–94.

72 Marcel Metzger, *Les Constitutions apostoliques* (3 vols.; SC 320, 329, 336; Paris: Cerf, 1985–87); partial ET based on this edition in W. Jardine Grisbrooke, *The Liturgical Portions of the Apostolic Constitutions: A Text for Students* (JLS 13–14; Nottingham: Grove, 1990).

73 Daniel von Haneberg, *Canones S. Hippolyti arabice* (Munich: Academia Regia Boiea, 1870).

74 Bernard Botte, "L'origine des Canons d'Hippolyte," in *Mélanges en l'honneur de Mgr Michel Andrieu* (Revue de sciences religieuses; volume hors série; Strasbourg: Palais Universitaire, 1956) 53–63.

75 René-Georges Coquin, *Les Canons d'Hippolyte* (PO 31/2; Paris: Firmin-Didot, 1966); ET of the text in Paul F. Bradshaw, *The Canons of Hippolytus* (JLS 2; Nottingham: Grove, 1987).

76 Markschies, "Wer schrieb," 8–11, 63–69.

drastic recastings may not be that at all, but rather points at which he alone has retained primitive readings that have been revised by the other witnesses to the text. Coquin considered that it had been written by a priest rather than a bishop—though his arguments are not totally convincing[77]—and that its place of composition was Alexandria. This latter view has since been challenged by Heinzgerd Brakmann, who has argued instead that it originates from elsewhere in northern Egypt.[78]

3. *Testamentum Domini*

This church order incorporates the *Apostolic Tradition* within a much enlarged context of instructions given by Jesus himself to his disciples before his ascension, and beginning with an apocalyptic discourse. The author displays a somewhat perverse fidelity to his source: although he has retained much of its wording, he has interpolated so many words and phrases of his own that it frequently has an entirely different appearance and sense from the original. Thus all the various prayers are retained, but in a much expanded form, and others are added. The original Greek text is lost, and reliance has usually been placed on the Syriac version published by Rahmani,[79] but here there are two problems. First, his edition was based on only one family of manuscripts, while a different manuscript tradition seems to underlie the text of the *Testamentum Domini* found in the West Syrian Synodicon,[80] which may offer indications of better readings at some points. Second, even if the earliest text of the Syriac can be established, it is not certain that it always accurately reproduced the original Greek, especially as there are also extant Arabic and Ethiopic versions of the document with significantly different readings. These are both probably dependent on a lost Coptic translation. Until recently any comparison with these versions was extremely problematic, as neither had

ever been published, but in 1984 Robert Beylot produced a critical edition of the Ethiopic,[81] which goes some way to meet the difficulty. Since both these versions are later than the Syriac, many differences can be dismissed as emendations (intentional and unintentional) of translators and copyists, but at least at some points they may retain older readings. For example, the doxologies in the Ethiopic have a much simpler—and hence seemingly more primitive—form than those in the Syriac. Most scholars believe that the work originates from Syria, though Asia Minor and Egypt have also been suggested, and it has usually been regarded as the last of the church orders to have been written, dating most probably from the fifth century. Grant Sperry-White, however, has proposed its origin as being in the second half of the fourth century.[82]

3. Reconstruction of the Text

For a considerable period of time after the discovery of the different linguistic versions of the *Apostolic Tradition* no serious attempt was made to compare variant readings and produce a full critical edition. Funk did note the readings of the Latin text in a reconstruction that he included in his edition of the *Apostolic Constitutions*, but he preferred to rely primarily on the Coptic.[83] While Connolly similarly included a full text in an appendix to his study of the *Apostolic Tradition*, he simply reproduced the Latin where it existed and an English translation of the Ethiopic where it did not, and made no pretense that it constituted a critical edition of the original.[84] The German translation by Ernst Jungklaus in 1928 adopted basically the same method.[85] The first real attempts to produce a complete reconstruction of the earliest text by a comparison of the different witnesses were made by

77 See Bradshaw, *Canons*, 8.

78 Heinzgerd Brakmann, "Alexandreia und die Kanones des Hippolyt," *JAC* 22 (1979) 139–49.

79 Rahmani, *Testamentum Domini*; ET by James Cooper and Arthur J. Maclean, *The Testament of Our Lord Translated into English from the Syriac* (Edinburgh: T. & T. Clark, 1902).

80 Arthur Vööbus, ed., *The Synodicon in the West Syrian Tradition* (CSCO 367, 368; Scriptores Syri 161, 162; Louvain: 1975). This is based on MS. 8/11 of the Syrian Orthodox Patriarchate of Damascus, dating from 1204 CE.

81 Robert Beylot, *Le Testamentum Domini éthiopien* (Louvain: Peeters, 1984).

82 Grant Sperry-White, *The Testamentum Domini: A Text for Students* (JLS 19; Nottingham: Grove, 1991) 6.

83 Funk, *Constitutiones* 2:97–119.

84 Connolly, *Egyptian Church Order*, 175–94.

85 Ernst Jungklaus, *Die Gemeinde Hippolyts dargestellt nach seiner Kirchenordnung* (TU 46/2; Leipzig: Hinrichs, 1928).

the German scholars Theodor Schermann in 1914[86] and Edgar Hennecke in 1924[87] and by the American scholar Burton Scott Easton in an English translation published in 1934.[88] However, Easton did not contain much of a critical apparatus or indicate all the variant readings. But in the meantime Gregory Dix had been working independently on an edition of the text that included, as well as a reconstruction in English, the Latin version in full and a critical apparatus indicating many variant readings from the other textual witnesses. This was first published in 1937, and was reissued with a preface and corrections by Henry Chadwick in 1968. Dix intended to produce a second volume containing a "detailed Introduction and all consideration of the book's contents and setting,"[89] but this never appeared. Against his better judgment,[90] he adopted the numbering of chapters that had been introduced by Jungklaus and continued by Easton.

Botte retained the same numbering in his French reconstruction that appeared in 1946.[91] He included in this publication only the Latin text and the Greek fragments then known, but in his major critical edition published in 1963 he added to this a Latin translation of the Sahidic text (or where this was lacking, of the Ethiopic or other witnesses), brief extracts from the *Apostolic Constitutions*, and a critical apparatus of variants.[92] He also devised a new system of chapter numbering, which has been followed by most later scholars in preference to that of Jungklaus/Easton/Dix.[93] Botte's reconstruction was not only superior to that of Dix (and has made his the standard edition down to the present day), but it was also easier to use, at least for those students able to read Latin, Greek, and French. For it set out two of the textual witnesses (mostly the Latin and the Sahidic) side by side in parallel columns, which made it much simpler to see the differences between them than when they were buried in the critical apparatus. Nevertheless, it can be criticized for failing to display all the versions in this way, which consequently obscured the full complexity of the task of reconstruction. Moreover, like all other editions, it gave the misleading impression that the reconstructed translation could be taken with confidence as reflecting what the author originally wrote, whereas any reconstruction involves a large number of subjective judgments, as well as the assumption that there was once a single "original" text from which all extant versions derive.[94]

For a full display of all the versions, students had to wait for the volume by Jean Michel Hanssens in 1970, which laid out in Latin translations nearly all the relevant witnesses to the text.[95] Hanssens was also unique in not attempting to present a reconstruction of what the original text might have been. Nevertheless, his work is unsatisfactory for several reasons. It does not always use the best editions of the texts now available, and does not include the various extant Greek fragments. It makes cross-reference difficult by adopting its own numbering system and idiosyncratic nomenclature. Moreover, the structure of the Latin language does not permit a reader to glimpse the very different form of the oriental-language versions, and it is in any case of no help to those who do not read Latin fluently.

Our own edition, therefore, seeks to overcome the limitations of earlier ones. We include all witnesses to the text, from the best editions available and in the most literal English translation possible.[96] While we make no attempt to present a reconstructed "original" text, we do provide what has been lacking from all earlier editions: a

86 Theodor Schermann, *Die allgemeine Kirchenordnung, frühchristliche Liturgien und kirchliche Überlieferung*, vol. 1: *Die allgemeine Kirchenordnung des zweiten Jahrhunderts* (Studien zur Geschichte und Kultur des Altertums 3; Paderborn: Schöningh, 1914; reprinted New York: Johnson, 1968) 35–100.

87 Edgar Hennecke, *Neutestamentliche Apokryphen* (2d ed.; Tübingen: Mohr, 1924) 569–83.

88 Easton, *Apostolic Tradition*.

89 Dix, *Apostolic Tradition*, x.

90 Ibid.: "They are not invariably quite those I would myself have chosen, but the disadvantages of diversity are obvious."

91 Bernard Botte, *Hippolyte de Rome: La Tradition apostolique* (SC 11; Paris: Cerf, 1946; 2d ed. SC 11bis, 1968).

92 Botte, *Tradition*.

93 Including the English edition by Geoffrey J. Cuming, *Hippolytus: A Text for Students* (GLS 8; Nottingham: Grove, 1976).

94 See the strictures of Metzger, "Enquêtes," 16–22.

95 Jean Michel Hanssens, *La liturgie d'Hippolyte: Documents et études* (Rome: Liberia Editrice dell'Universita Gregoriana, 1970).

96 Readers should note that, in the translation of the Sahidic text, "shall" is used in the second and third

comprehensive commentary on each chapter of the document, and within that commentary we discuss what the textual history of the various chapters might have been. In our approach to possible earlier forms of the text, however, we adopt a significantly different methodology from that of previously published reconstructions.

In attempting to discern the original text of the document, other editors have quite naturally preferred the evidence of the translations (Latin, Sahidic, Arabic, and Ethiopic) to that of the reworkings (*Apostolic Constitutions*, *Canons of Hippolytus*, *Testamentum Domini*), since the latter have clearly adapted the material to its new context. Among the translations, it is not surprising that the Latin has been given pride of place. Not only is it apparently much older than the others, but it seems to have been done in a very literal manner. Easton claimed that it was "generally reliable";[97] Dix affirmed that "its readings provide a standard by which we may judge those of other versions";[98] and Botte asserted that it had retained the order of the words from the original and, for the most part, the identical structure of the phrases: "One does not find any systematic modification that could be attributed to the translator."[99] While these scholars acknowledged that the Latin was not entirely infallible, they believed its errors to be few, easily discernible, and simple to correct.

Even these scholars, however, were willing to go against the clear evidence of the Latin on various occasions when its readings did not correspond with what they thought the document ought to have said, the most well-known example of this being the postbaptismal

prayer in chap. 21, where the Latin linked the gift of the Holy Spirit to the water rather than to the laying on of hands, as was the case in the other witnesses.[100] Moreover, in a short paper presented to the Oxford Patristic Conference in 1961, Andrew F. Walls questioned the reliance usually placed on the Latin version, and noted the duplication of the concluding chapters (see below, p. 16) and other apparent inconsistencies in the text, which suggested that it too may have been subjected to a greater measure of revision than was generally acknowledged.[101] Several other scholars have also challenged the assumption that the reconstructed text represents what the original author wrote, and suggested that at least in parts it was retouched by later hands in order to bring it into line with current doctrine and practice.[102]

4. A New Approach

In a series of articles,[103] Marcel Metzger has gone even farther and developed an idea earlier advanced by both Jean Magne and Alexandre Faivre, that not only is this document not the *Apostolic Tradition* of Hippolytus, it is not the work of any single author at all but rather a piece of "living literature."[104] Metzger has argued that its lack of unity or logical progression, its frequent incoherences, doublets, and contradictions, all point away from the existence of a single editorial hand. Instead, it has all the characteristics of a composite work, a collection of community rules from quite disparate traditions, a view also supported by Brent.[105]

person to designate a more emphatic sense (Coptic third future), with "will" indicating the simple future. The reverse applies in the first person.

97 Easton, *Apostolic Tradition*, 31.

98 Dix, *Apostolic Tradition*, lvii.

99 Botte, *Tradition*, xxxvi.

100 See below, pp. 127–28.

101 Walls, "Latin Version."

102 Edward C. Ratcliff, "The Sanctus and the Pattern of the Early Anaphora," *JEH* 1 (1950) 29–36, 125–34; idem, "Apostolic Tradition: Questions concerning the Appointment of the Bishop," *StPatr* 8 (1966) 266–70 (both reprinted in Arthur H. Couratin and David Tripp, eds., *E. C. Ratcliff: Liturgical Studies* [London: SPCK, 1976] 18–40, 156–60); Paul F. Bradshaw, "Ordination," in Geoffrey J. Cuming,

ed., *Essays on Hippolytus* (GLS 15; Nottingham: Grove, 1978) 33–38; idem, "The Participation of Other Bishops in the Ordination of a Bishop in the *Apostolic Tradition* of Hippolytus," *StPatr* 18/2 (1989) 335–38; Eric Segelberg, "The Ordination Prayers in Hippolytus," *StPatr* 13 (1975) 397–408.

103 See above, n. 18.

104 Jean Magne, *Tradition apostolique sur les charismes et Diataxeis des saints Apôtres* (Origines chrétiennes 1; Paris: Magne, 1975) 76–77; Alexandre Faivre, "La documentation canonico-liturgique de l'Eglise ancienne," *RevScRel* 54 (1980) 286.

105 Brent, *Hippolytus*, 195–96.

Metzger draws attention in particular to the way in which the text oscillates between an impersonal mode of address in the third-person singular or plural (e.g., chap. 36: "Let every faithful [person] take care to . . .") and an occasional personal mode, which may be either in the second-person singular or in the second-personal plural. Sometimes the subject appears in the first-person plural ("we . . ."), but only once in the first-person singular, and then only in the Latin version of the text (chap. 38A and its parallel in chap. 43).[106]

We believe that Metzger's general approach is correct, and would take it even farther. Because of the features to which he has drawn attention and others that we have observed, we judge the work to be an aggregation of material from different sources, quite possibly arising from different geographical regions and probably from different historical periods, from perhaps as early as the mid-second century to as late as the mid-fourth, since none of the textual witnesses to it can be dated with any certainty before the last quarter of that century. We thus think it unlikely that it represents the practice of any single Christian community, and that it is best understood by attempting to discern the various individual elements and layers that constitute it.

Such steps can be taken only very tentatively, however, because of the lack of many objective criteria to guide the way. In addition to looking for signs of dislocation in the document itself, one must employ a comparative method and ask at what period similar practices are attested in other sources. While this may provide a useful guide to the likely time when a particular part of the document originated, it is not infallible. It remains possible, for example, that the practice in question is in reality even older than the other extant witnesses to it, and so this part of the text should be assigned to an earlier date. Alternatively, the practice may have persisted much later than our other evidence suggests, and so this part

of the *Apostolic Tradition* is more recent than we might suppose.[107]

Furthermore, the process of comparative analysis must be undertaken carefully. Too many previous attempts at comparison of parts of the *Apostolic Tradition* with other ancient sources have been carried out with such superficiality as to render their results virtually worthless, and insufficient attention has generally been paid to differences as well as similarities between passages in the *Apostolic Tradition* and the alleged parallels. Above all, there has been a common failure to distinguish those that may also be found in a number of different authors, and often in different geographical regions and temporal periods, from those that are unique to one particular author, region, or time period. The test of exclusivity is vital to the value of the data adduced.[108] It is not enough, for instance, to show that phrases and vocabulary similar to those in parts of the *Apostolic Tradition* can also be found in the writings of Hippolytus or Irenaeus or whomever. It is essential to demonstrate that they can be found there *and nowhere else* for the data to have some value in determining either authorship or source or region or time period of composition of that section of the church order.[109]

Because of limitations such as these, it has rarely been possible for us to suggest a particular date or provenance for the various strata that we discern in the church order. Nevertheless, we offer a tentative proposal for what might have been the contents of the core document, perhaps from the mid-second century, to which the rest was later added. One must take care to note, however, that just because something is judged to be a later addition to the text does not mean that it is necessarily a later composition. Although in many cases this may be so, in others the material may be as old as the core itself, but only added to it at a later date. We believe that the core had three basic parts (or, alternatively, that

106 Metzger, "Enquêtes," 11–13.

107 See further Paul F. Bradshaw, "Redating the *Apostolic Tradition:* Some Preliminary Steps," in John Baldovin and Nathan Mitchell, eds., *Rule of Prayer, Rule of Faith: Essays in Honor of Aidan Kavanagh, OSB* (Collegeville, Minn.: Liturgical, 1996) 3–17.

108 See the essay by Robert F. Taft, "The Authenticity of the Chrysostom Anaphora Revisited. Determining the Authorship of Liturgical Texts by Computer," *OrChrP* 56 (1990) 5–51, esp. 27ff.

109 See further Paul F. Bradshaw, "The Problems of a New Edition of the *Apostolic Tradition*," in Robert F. Taft and Gabriele Winkler, eds., *Comparative Liturgy Fifty Years after Anton Baumstark (1872–1948)* (OrChrA 265; Rome: Edizioni Orientalia Christiana, 2001) 613–22.

three short collections of material were combined to form the document), although the various sections may not have been in precisely their present form:

  a) directives about appointment to ministry:
     2.1–4; 7.1; 8.1; 9.1–2(?); 10.1–3; 11; 12; 13; 14
  b) directives about the initiation of new converts:
     15; 16; 17; 18; 19; 20; 21.1–5, 12–18, 20, 25–26
     (perhaps also parts of 21.27–28, 31–32, 34, 37–38)
  c) directives about community meals and prayer:
     23; 24 (= 29B); 25 (29C); 26(?); 27; 28.4–6; 29A;
     30A; 31; 32; 33; 35

5. Order of the Document

At four points the various textual witnesses differ as to the position that different chapters of the text should occupy. The first concerns chap. 1. This appears at the beginning of the document in the Latin version, but is completely omitted by the Sahidic and Arabic manuscripts. It is included in the Ethiopic, on the other hand, but placed after chap. 30 and not at the beginning (designated as chap. 30B in our text). Since the *Apostolic Constitutions*, *Canons of Hippolytus*, and *Testamentum Domini* all include prologues before their equivalents of *Apostolic Tradition* 2, although only in that the *Apostolic Constitutions* exhibits any close verbal resemblance to the version in the *Apostolic Tradition*, this points to the position in the Latin as the original and the Ethiopic as a dislocation.

The second concerns chaps. 9–14. The Latin is missing here, and only the Arabic and Ethiopic agree on the sequence in which these chapters should be placed: the other four witnesses adopt a different order from one another. These variations can perhaps best be expressed in tabular form below:

It seems most likely that the Arabic and Ethiopic texts have preserved the original order. This sequence is largely supported by the *Testamentum Domini*, which differs only in moving the reference to the subdeacon to a position preceding the direction about the reader, thereby reflecting the higher standing granted to the subdiaconate over the office of reader by the late fourth century. The order found in the Sahidic looks like an attempt to reorganize the various categories of people so that references to women (widows and virgins) are placed after the ecclesiastical offices of reader and subdeacon, but without disturbing the original sequence within the two groups. The *Canons of Hippolytus* represents a similar tendency, but apparently understands the direction about virgins to refer to the celibacy expected of those who had been ordained to the subdiaconate while unmarried, and the direction about the gift of healing to refer to those seeking ordination on the grounds of their claim to possess that gift. Consequently, the *Canons of Hippolytus* places the reference to widows last of all, after inserting further instructions about the life of presbyters that do not derive from the *Apostolic Tradition*. The *Apostolic Constitutions* adopts an equally radical rearrangement of the material, placing the various categories of people in a more hierarchical format: subdeacon and reader (in that order) follow the chapter on the deacon, with the reference to the ordination of confessors relegated to the end of these directions about the clergy; virgin now precedes widow, since the author seems to have some reservations about the latter.

The third area of textual confusion concerns chaps. 24 and 25, which are preserved in full only in the Ethiopic, but placed between chaps. 29 and 30. For this, see the note on chaps. 24 and 25 below (p. 141).

Sahidic	Arabic	Ethiopic	*Const.*	*Can. Hipp.*	*Test. Dom.*
Confessor	Confessor	Confessor	Subdeacon	Confessor	Confessor
Reader	Widow	Widow	Reader	Reader	Widow
Subdeacon	Reader	Reader	Confessor	Subdeacon	Subdeacon
Widow	Virgin	Virgin	Virgin	Celibacy	Reader
Virgin	Subdeacon	Subdeacon	Widow	Healing	Virgin
Healing	Healing	Healing	Healing	Widow	Healing

Finally, there are also some significant differences in order toward the end of the document. In all the versions chap. 35, on the times for prayer, is duplicated as the beginning of chap. 41, a much longer chapter on the same subject, but in addition the Latin includes doublets of chaps. 42 and 43 immediately after chap. 38 (which are designated as chap. 38B in our text). Most scholars have accepted the view advanced by André Wilmart in 1919 that the Latin has conflated two versions of the *Apostolic Tradition* (a shorter one lacking chaps. 39–41 and a longer one that included them), both composed by Hippolytus himself.[110] However, the order of the material in the *Canons of Hippolytus* and the *Testamentum Domini* suggests that they were familiar with a version in which a form of chaps. 39–41 appeared in the place occupied by chaps. 34–35 in the texts known to us.[111]

All these variants can best be explained by the hypothesis of a gradual expansion of the material, with at least four stages: (1) a shorter version lacking chaps. 39–41 altogether; (2) an intermediate version, in which chap. 34 was *replaced* by an earlier form of what are now chaps. 39 and 40 (which are an adaptation of chap. 34), and chap. 35 was *replaced* by an earlier form that became the expanded chap. 41—the order apparently known to the compilers of the *Canons of Hippolytus* and of the *Testamentum Domini*; (3) a composite version, in which chaps. 34 and 35 were retained and chaps. 39–41 were instead *inserted* into the shorter version just before the conclusion (chaps. 42–43), thus creating the form underlying the oriental-language texts; and (4) the longer version, represented by the Latin alone, in which the final portion of the composite version (chap. 39 to the end)

was *appended* to the conclusion of the shorter version, resulting in a duplication of chaps. 42 and 43.

6. Principles Governing the Display of the Text in This Edition

The four principal linguistic versions (Latin, Sahidic, Arabic, and Ethiopic) are displayed in English translation in parallel columns on left-hand pages. The Bohairic (the northern dialect of Coptic) is only included in part of chap. 21, where the Sahidic (the southern dialect of Coptic) is lacking. In each case the text is given in full (apart from the obvious interpolations of the Ethiopic), and thus a series of periods (. . .) preceding or following a passage indicates a lacuna in the text, not an omission made by the editors. To give the reader as clear as possible an idea of the original documents, we normally reproduce the text in the exact order in which it occurs in the sources (which results in what Botte numbered as chaps. 24 and 25 being placed after chap. 29 and designated here as chaps. 29B and 29C).[112] The only real exception to this rule is in the case of chaps. 9–14, the order of which differs significantly from version to version. To facilitate comparison here these chapters have all been placed in what appears to have been the original sequence (see above, p. 15).

The three principal adaptations of the *Apostolic Tradition* (the *Apostolic Constitutions*, *Canons of Hippolytus*, and *Testamentum Domini*) appear in parallel columns on right-hand pages opposite the corresponding material in the translations. The *Epitome* is substituted for the *Apostolic Constitutions* at those points where it appears to pre-

---

110 André Wilmart, "Le texte latin de la *Paradosis* de saint Hippolyte," *RechSR* 9 (1919) 62–79.

111
Apostolic Tradition	Canons	Testamentum
33	22	2.18
34	24	2.21
35		
36	28a	2.25b
37	28b	
38A	29	
39	[?24a, 21]	[?2.21]
40	24b, 25a	2.23
41	25b–27	2.24–25a
42	29	
43		2.25c

112 For the reasons for this, see below, p. 141.

serve the Greek of the *Apostolic Tradition*, but any other witnesses are placed below the principal texts. No attempt has been made to reproduce the adaptations in full, and hence a series of periods here does indicate an omission made by the editors. Nor has the order of the original always been preserved, although the numbers attached to the various chapters by their ancient redactors have been included, so that readers may know where they differ in order and also more easily compare what is reproduced here with a complete text of the particular document so as to see its full context. The titles and other headings attached to the chapters by the redactors have also generally been omitted, as they usually seem to bear no linguistic relationship to the titles of the Sahidic, Arabic, and Ethiopic.

The translations of the Arabic and the *Canons of Hippolytus* were made by Carol Bebawi,[113] and that of the Ethiopic by James C. VanderKam, while our version of the *Testamentum Domini* is based on the English translation in Cooper and Maclean's edition,[114] with minor emendations. All other translations are the work of the editors themselves. They have been done in as literal a manner as possible so as to convey the character of the

original texts. Brackets indicate a word or phrase that needs to be supplied in order to make the text intelligible. The numbering of the individual chapters substantially follows that devised by Botte rather than the older system adopted by Dix (although to assist those unfamiliar with it, the correlation between the two is given in appendix A on p. 18), but with the restoration of the "verse" divisions introduced by Easton and modified by Dix, which Botte abandoned. We have retained these numbers in order to simplify the readers' task when attempting to locate a part of the document that is cited in another work, but they are not entirely satisfactory, since the chapter numbers introduce some divisions into the text where no break appears to have existed in the most ancient versions (see, e.g., chaps. 3 and 4). The headings also largely follow those used by Botte; most are based on the Sahidic version (where no title existed or can be discerned in one of the ancient versions, the heading is placed within brackets). Once again, they are given for convenience only, and readers should certainly not assume that the particular headings chosen are most likely to have existed in the oldest texts, nor even that the original included any divisions or titles at all.

---

113 Her translation of the *Canons of Hippolytus* originally appeared in Bradshaw, *Canons*.
114 See n. 79 above.

Appendix A:
Correlation between the Numbering of Dix and Botte

DIX	BOTTE	DIX	BOTTE	DIX	BOTTE
1	1	16.1–8	15	27	30
2	2	16.9–25	16	28.1–5	31
3	3	17	17	28.6–8	32
4	4	18	18	29	33
5	5	19	19	30	34
6	6	20	20	31	35
7	omitted	21–23	21	32.1	36
8	7	24	22	32.2	37
9	8	25–26.1	23	32.3–4	38
10	9	26.2–4	26	33	39
11	10	26.5–6	27	34	40
12	11	26.7–12	28	35–36	41
13	12	26.13	29	37	42
14	13	26.14–17	24	38	43
15	14	26.18–32	25		

The Apostolic Tradition

1

Latin (67.31—68.13)	Sahidic	Arabic	Ethiopic

[?Title]

1. We have worthily set down those things that were of the word[a] about the gifts that God from the first according to his own will bestowed on human beings, presenting to himself that image which had gone astray.

2. And now led on by the love that he had for all the saints, we have arrived at the summit of the tradition that catechizes to the churches,

3. so that those who have been well led by our exposition may guard that tradition which has remained up to now, and being aware [of it] may remain firmer,

4. on account of that fault or error which was recently invented through ignorance and those who are ignorant,

5. since the Holy Spirit bestows perfect grace on those who rightly believe, that they may know how those who preside over the church ought to hand on and preserve all things.

[See chap. 30B]

Syriac Epitome:

We have indeed then set down equally and rightly the first points of the word regarding the gift, all those that God, from the beginning by his will, conferred on human beings, offering to him the image that went astray; also how we confuted the way of those who dare to speak false things or are moved by a foreign spirit, as we explain through the word to those who either unwittingly or purposely are cast into error; also that many times God indeed used wicked ones for prophecy and for the doing of miracles. Now, however, out of love for all the saints we have been diligent for that which is the foremost and highest of the faith that is proper and fitting in the churches, we have done eagerly. And concerning the ordinance and the constitution the word urges us on, how that when you bishops learn this order from us, those things that you have learned well from us by the will of Christ, how those commandments that were handed to us—all of them—you should do, knowing that the one who listens to us listens to God his Father, to whom belongs glory for ages of ages. Amen.

---

[a] Reading *verbi*, "of the word," for *verba*, "words."

Apostolic Constitutions 8.3.1–2

So, then, in the first [part] of the discourse we have given an explanation concerning the charisms, which God, according to his own will, gave to human beings, and how he refuted the way of those who attempted to speak falsely or who were moved by an alien spirit, and how God frequently used evil people for both prophecy and the doing of wonders. But now our discourse comes to the major part of the ecclesiastical arrangement, so that learning this appointment from us, bishops who are ordained through us by the command of Christ may do all things according to the commands that have been delivered to us, knowing that the one who hears us hears Christ, and the one who hears Christ hears his God and Father, to whom be glory forever. Amen.

Canons of Hippolytus 1

Before all else we speak of the holy and true faith in our Lord Jesus Christ, Son of the living God. And we have set it down faithfully, and we are firmly in agreement [with it], and we say, we, that the Trinity, equal and perfect in honor, is equal in glory. He has no beginning or end, the Word, the Son of God, and he is also the creator of every creature, visible and invisible. This we have set down and we truly agree with it. And those who have dared to say what they ought not about the Word of God, according to what our Lord Jesus Christ said concerning them, we have assembled ourselves, being the great majority, in the power of God, and we have cut them off because they are not in accord with the Holy Scriptures, the Word of God, or with us, the disciples of the Scriptures. . . .

Testamentum Domini 1.14

. . . Turning therefore to the church, setting right, duly ordering, and arranging, and doing all things in uprightness and holiness, speak to everyone as is helpful to him, so that your Father who is in heaven may be glorified. Be wise, that you may persuade those who are in captivity to error, and those who are sunk in ignorance, that coming to the knowledge of God, and living piously and purely, they may praise my Father and your God. . . .

[17] But to us also Jesus said: Because you also have asked me concerning the ecclesiastical rule, I deliver and make known to you how you ought to order and command him who stands at the head of the church. . . .

[18] . . . But it shall be spoken and given to those who are firm and fixed, and do not fall away, who keep my commandments and this tradition, so that they, keeping these [things], may abide holy and upright and strong in me, fleeing from the downfall of iniquity and the death of sin; the Holy Spirit bestowing on them his grace, that they may believe rightly. . . .

1

Text

Although this chapter is found only in the Latin and Ethiopic versions, and in the latter case at a quite different point in the text, after chap. 30 (= 30B in this edition), yet its authenticity seems to be guaranteed by the *Apostolic Constitutions*, *Canons of Hippolytus*, and *Testamentum Domini*, all of which include prologues to their work, even if only *Apostolic Constitutions* shows any close verbal similarity to that in the Latin. It is also attested by a Syriac epitome contained in book 5 of the ancient collection of church orders known as the Clementine Octateuch and preserved in the Vatican ms. *Borgia syr.* 148 of 1575/1576 CE (f. 91verso–92recto). This witness combines the text of the prologue of the *Apostolic Constitutions* with that of the *Apostolic Tradition*.[1] The absence of the prologue from the Sahidic and Arabic versions may simply be an accident, the result of damage to a manuscript, or it may be a deliberate omission, since these translations also regularly omit the text of prayers in the *Apostolic Tradition*. Why it should have been displaced in the Ethiopic remains a mystery, but it may be noted that it now occurs just before a lengthy block of interpolated baptismal ritual and so in a strange sense could be seen as supplying some sort of transition to that material.

Both the Latin and Ethiopic texts appear somewhat confused throughout this section, and translation is more difficult than in many other chapters.

■ **1** Botte judged that the plural *verba* in the Latin was an error for the genitive singular, *verbi*, since the Ethiopic, Syriac, and *Apostolic Constitutions* all had the singular here, and he rendered the phrase "those things that were of the word" as "the [part] of the discourse."[2] Cuming, on the other hand, took up a suggestion by Dix and thought that the Latin *verba . . . digne* should actually read *verbi . . . digna*, translating the whole phrase as "those things which were worthy of note," the equivalent of a possible original Greek ἀξιόλογα.[3] The last part of the sentence is unclear in both the Latin and Ethiopic,

as well as the Syriac, but the general sense appears to be that humankind, made in God's image (Gen 1:26), had gone astray but God had drawn it back to himself.

■ **2** The Syriac supports the view that "by the love that he had for all the saints" in the Latin is the result of a misunderstanding of the original Greek, which was probably "by love toward all the saints" (a possible allusion to Eph 1:15) and so referred to the author's love and not God's.[4] Similarly, both the Syriac and Ethiopic suggest that the Latin translator also mistook the Greek καθήκει, "is fitting" for κατηχεῖ, "catechizes."[5]

■ **3** The Ethiopic suggests that *ducti*, "led," in the Latin is a copyist's error for *docti*, "taught." More significantly, where the Latin and Ethiopic have "the tradition," the Syriac instead has "the faith" and the *Apostolic Constitutions* has "the . . . arrangement." This has led Markschies to argue that the original Greek word was not παράδοσις, "tradition," as is usually assumed, but διατύπωσις, "configuration, arrangement, custom, rule," as in the *Apostolic Constitutions*, which could have been translated in the other ways by the various witnesses.[6]

Comment

■ **1** As noted in the introduction (above, pp. 2–3), the apparent references here to an earlier work on the subject of "gifts" and to "tradition" have been among the factors that have encouraged the identification of this document with the *Apostolic Tradition* of Hippolytus. If Markschies is correct in his assertion that the word "tradition" was not part of the Greek text, however, then the case is weakened; and if he is correct in a further claim about the opening words of the passage, then the case is weaker still. For he disputes the interpretation adopted by other scholars (influenced by the word "first," πρῶτα, in the *Apostolic Constitutions*), that the first sentence refers to an earlier work, or to an earlier part of this work, arguing that the reference is instead intended to

---

1   Text in Richard H. Connolly, "The Prologue to the *Apostolic Tradition* of Hippolytus," *JTS* 22 (1921) 356–61; see also Edgar Hennecke, "Der Prolog zur 'Apostolischen Überlieferung' Hippolyts," *ZNW* 22 (1923) 144–46.

2   Botte, *Tradition*, 3 n. 2.

3   Cuming, *Hippolytus*, 8.

4   Connolly, "Prologue," 360; Botte, *Tradition*, 3 n. 4.

5   Eduard von der Goltz, "Die Taufgebete Hippolyts und andere Taufgebete der alten Kirchen," *ZKG* 27 (1906) 8; Walter Howard Frere, "Early Ordination Services," *JTS* 16 (1915) 330–31; Connolly, "Prologue," 360.

6   Markschies, "Wer schrieb," 25–26.

be to this work itself and to the various charisms of ministry that it describes, and that "those things . . . of the word" should be understood as "those things of the Word [of God]," that is, of Christ.[7]

Whatever the truth of those particular claims, the author of this chapter clearly judged that the customs of the church with which he was familiar were under threat as a result of the ignorance of others and so needed recording/transmitting in this document for their preservation.

■ 4 It is not possible to establish precisely what the "fault or error that was recently invented" might have been. Writing before the church order was identified as the *Apostolic Tradition* of Hippolytus, Frere thought that it was referring to Montanism because of the earlier mention of spiritual gifts, and so dated it to the end of the second century.[8] Dix believed that it was a reference to the theological controversy between Hippolytus and Pope Zephyrinus (197–217), especially as Hippolytus

(*Ref.* 9.11.1) charges Zephyrinus with being "an ignorant man and unlettered and unversed in the ecclesiastical ordinances."[9] But if the author was not Hippolytus, then the phrase is sufficiently vague that it might refer to almost any dispute in the first few centuries of Christianity, whether known to us or not. This chapter shows some similarities to the epilogue of the work (chaps. 42 and 43) and so may have been added to it at about the same time, whenever that was.

■ 5 These lines seem to suggest that the work is addressed not to bishops or clergy but to faithful laity ("those who rightly believe"), who through the charism of discernment that they have received from the Holy Spirit have the right and duty to correct "those who preside over the church."[10] This last phrase, moreover, could be seen as implying the existence of a plurality of ministerial leaders rather than a monarchical episcopate in the community to which this prologue refers.

7   Ibid., 26–29.
8   Walter H. Frere, "Early Ordination Services," *JTS* 16 (1915) 331.
9   Dix, *Apostolic Tradition*, xxxv.
10   See Bernard Botte, *Hippolyte de Rome: La Tradition apostolique* (SC 11; Paris: Cerf, 1946; 2d ed.; SC

11bis; 1968) 26; John E. Stam, "Charismatic Theology in the *Apostolic Tradition* of Hippolytus," in Gerald F. Hawthorne, ed., *Current Issues in Biblical and Patristic Interpretation: Studies in Honor of Merrill C. Tenney* (Grand Rapids: Eerdmans, 1975) 269.

2

Latin (68.14-25)	Sahidic	Arabic	Ethiopic
[Title]	*31 Concerning the bishops* (ἐπίσκοπος)	*21 Concerning the ordination of bishops and the beginning of the liturgy*	*21 Concerning the ordination of bishops and the order of the oblation*
1 Let him be ordained bishop who has been chosen by all the people,	The bishop (ἐπίσκοπος) shall be ordained (χειρο-τονεῖν) according to (κατά) the word that we said before, having been chosen from the whole multitude and (δέ) being without sin.	The bishop is ordained as we said formerly. He is chosen from the whole community [as being] without sin.	A bishop is to be ordained, as we said before, one who has been chosen from all the people.
2 and when he has been named and accepted by all, let him assemble the people together with the presbytery and those bishops who are present, on the Lord's day.	When he has been named (ὀνομάζειν) and he pleases them, all the people (λαός) shall gather themselves together with the presbyters (πρεσβύτερος) and the deacons (διάκονος) on the Lord's day (κυριακή),	When he is named and they approve of him, all the people meet together, with the presbyters and deacons on a Sunday,	. . . together with the presbyters and deacons on the Sabbath.
3 When all give consent, let them lay hands on him, and let the presbytery stand by, being still.	all the bishops (ἐπίσκοπος) who have laid their hands on him giving consent (συνευδοκεῖν). The presbyters (πρεσβύτερος) also standing and waiting	and all the bishops proceed together gladly and they lay their hands on him, with the presbyters standing silently;	All the bishops are to go in with mutual accord and lay their hands on him. While the presbyters stand quietly,
4 And let all keep silence, praying in the heart for the descent of the Spirit;	with all of them shall keep silent together and shall pray in their heart that the Holy Spirit (πνεῦμα) come down on him; and as they request (ἀξιοῦν) one of the bishops (ἐπίσκοπος), every-	and they pray in their hearts that the Holy Spirit may come down upon him.	all will be silent together and pray in their heart that the Holy Spirit come down upon him.
5 from whom let one of the bishops present, being asked by all, laying [his] hand on him who is being ordained bishop, pray, saying thus:	one standing, he shall put his hand on the one who will be made bishop (ἐπίσκοπος) and pray over him.	And they ask one of the bishops, and with everyone standing, he lays his hand on the one being ordained bishop and prays over him thus.	Each one of the bishops is to pray, and every one of them, as they stand, is to place a hand on him who is to be ordained bishop. He is to pray over him thus:

Apostolic Constitutions 8.4.2–6	*Canons of Hippolytus* 2	*Testamentum Domini* 1.20
First, then, I Peter say, as we all together have appointed above: a bishop to be ordained [is to be] in all things blameless, the best, elected by all the people. After he has been nominated and approved, let the people come together on the Lord's day with the presbyterate and the bishops present. And let the leader of the others ask the presbyterate and the people if he is the one whom they want as ruler. . . . And when they have agreed for the third time that he is worthy, let them all be asked to give their assent, and giving it eagerly, let them be heard. And when silence comes, let one of the leading bishops, together with two others standing near the altar (the remaining bishops and presbyters praying in silence, and the deacons laying the holy Gospels open on the head of the one being ordained), say to God:	Let the bishop be chosen by all the people, and let him be without reproach, as it is written concerning him in the apostle. The week when he is ordained, all the clergy and the people say, "We choose him." There shall be silence in all the flock after the approbation, and they are to pray for him and say, "O God, behold him whom you have prepared for us." They are to choose one of the bishops and presbyters; he lays his hand on the head and prays, saying:	. . . Let the bishop be appointed, being chosen by all the people according to the will of the Holy Spirit, being without fault . . . . [21] Being such as this, let him receive laying on of the hand on the first day of the week, all consenting to his appointment and bearing witness to him, with all the neighboring presbyters and bishops. Let those bishops lay hands on him, having first washed their hands, but let the presbyters stand beside them, not speaking, in fear, lifting up their hearts in silence. Next, [let] the bishops lay hands on him, saying: . . . After this, let one bishop, commanded by the other bishops, lay hands on him, saying the invocation of the ordination thus:

Text

The versions vary considerably from one another in this chapter.

■ **1** The equivalent of the phrase "according to the word that we said before" in the Sahidic is included in the Arabic and Ethiopic, but not in the other witnesses.[1] It may well have been added to the textual tradition behind these oriental versions after this document was appended to the *Apostolic Church Order* (see above, p. 7), since that too contains brief directives for the appointment of bishops and other ministers.

In the same sentence "by all the people" is attested by the Latin, *Apostolic Constitutions*, and *Testamentum Domini*, while the oriental versions all have the equivalent of "from all the multitude." Botte believed that "by" was the original reading, because the Coptic phrase ⲈⲂⲞⲗ ⲊⲘ̄ (ⲊⲚ̄), here translated as "from," could also be used in an instrumental sense,[2] but Ratcliff argued that the reading of the oriental versions was preferable. He believed that the direction would thus have meant that candidates for the episcopate must be chosen from the laity and not from among the deacons and presbyters, who were ineligible because their offices were originally bestowed for life and so there could be no movement from one order to another.[3] Whether he was correct in this supposition is open to question, however, since we do have evidence as early as the second century of some episcopal figures who had previously served as deacons or presbyters.[4] Botte also regarded the second mention of "by all" (*omnibus*) in the Latin as an addition to the text, since its absence from the Sahidic and Arabic texts was supported by the *Apostolic Constitutions*.[5]

Although the word translated as "without sin" (Coptic ⲀⲦⲚⲞⲂⲈ, perhaps influenced by ἀνέκλητον in 1 Tim

3:2 or ἀνεπίλημπτον in Titus 1:7) is missing from the Latin, it was clearly present in the textual tradition known to nearly all the other witnesses: the Sahidic and Arabic, the *Canons of Hippolytus* and *Testamentum Domini*, and the *Apostolic Constitutions* (although in this last case the Greek word used was ἄμεμπτον). It is impossible to determine, however, whether it was in the oldest stratum but had accidently fallen out of the version used by the Latin translator, or whether it represents an early addition to the core.

■ **2** In the light of the other versions, most scholars have treated the Latin text "let him assemble the people" (*conveniet populum*) as merely an accidental corruption, the word "people" having been written by mistake in the accusative form (*populum*) instead of the nominative (*populus*). But James O'Regan has tried to argue that the reading was intentional and reflects the initiative taken by the bishop in ancient ordination practice.[6] This seems improbable.

The versions differ most with regard to their mention of the participation of other bishops in the whole procedure. While both the Latin text and the *Apostolic Constitutions* include "those bishops who are present" in the list of those who are to assemble for the ordination, the Sahidic, Arabic, and Ethiopic versions have "deacons" instead, and insert a somewhat clumsy reference to bishops in the next sentence: "all the bishops who have laid their hands on him giving consent." On the other hand, the *Canons of Hippolytus* does not refer to the presence of bishops at all until the final sentence of this section, when it suddenly and rather oddly says: "They are to choose one of the bishops and presbyters; he lays his hand. . . ." Dix thought that this was a sign of what he called "theoretical presbyterianism" on the part of the redactor of the *Canons of Hippolytus*.[7] But in the light of

---

1   Although the *Apostolic Constitutions* appears to support this reading, Botte (*Tradition*, 5 n. 4) noted that the phrase found there was a common expression used by the redactor.

2   Botte, *Tradition*, 5 n. 5.

3   Edward C. Ratcliff, "Apostolic Tradition: Questions concerning the Appointment of the Bishop," *StPatr* 8 (1966) 266–70.

4   See, e.g., Michel Andrieu, "La carrière ecclésiastique des papes et les documents liturgiques du moyen âge," *RevScRel* 21 (1947) 90–120.

5   Botte, *Tradition*, 5 n. 7.

6   James O'Regan, "A Note on Keeping a Difficult Text in the Apostolic Tradition," *EphLit* 108 (1994) 73–76.

7   Dix, *Apostolic Tradition*, lxxviii–lxxix.

the variations in the other versions, it seems more likely that Ratcliff was correct when he claimed that "discernible between the lines of the several versions of *Apostolic Tradition* there are signs which can be taken as indicating that, in its original form, the direction instructed the presbyters to conduct the proceedings."[8] If this was so, then the various references to the involvement of other bishops in the procedure would have been supplied later by the individual editors of the versions in order to bring the text into line with what had by their day become the standard contemporary practice.[9]

■ **3** The above reconstruction also helps to resolve other oddities in this chapter. First, the Latin has no explicit subject for the action of the imposition of hands. Scholars generally presume bishops to be meant, because presbyters are apparently excluded in the next clause, although Allen Brent thinks a collective imposition of hands by the whole assembly was originally intended.[10] But, as Andrew F. Walls has pointed out, the instruction "let the presbytery stand by, being still" (*praesbyterium adstet quiescens*) in the Latin is also a curious feature: rubrics usually direct action, not enforce inactivity.[11] It becomes more intelligible, however, as an emphatic correction made by a redactor/translator to an earlier directive that instructed presbyters to perform the imposition of hands.[12] Furthermore, the otherwise puzzling absence of any reference to the involvement of bishops in the eucharistic celebration that follows the ordination is also explained if they were simply not there in the first place.

Comment

Although the divergences among the versions make generalizations difficult in this section, two principal features seem to emerge, which are also characteristic of other ancient ordination rites.[13] (a) The ordination process comprises *both* the election of the candidate *and* prayer for the Holy Spirit. The important place accorded to election should not be understood as pointing to some notion of the ideal of democracy in early Christianity, nor necessarily to the principle that a congregation had the right to choose its own ministers. Nor was it seen as in any way opposed to the divine calling of the bishop, but on the contrary it was understood as the means by which God's choice of a person for that office was discerned and made manifest. (b) Ordination is portrayed as primarily an act of the local ecclesial community: the candidate is elected by all the people and all pray for him. Even in the extant versions of the text, the bishops of the neighboring churches only attend the Sunday prayer service, give their assent, and lay their hands on the elect: they do not deprive the community of its central role.

If our conclusion is correct that mention of the presence of other bishops was absent from the oldest version, it would suggest that this section dates from a time after the office of bishop had emerged but prior to the time when it became the custom for other bishops to be involved in the ordination of the bishop of a neighboring church. The earliest reference to such involvement appears in North Africa in the mid-third century,[14] but this does not prove that the practice was universal by this date. Some evidence suggests that in Alexandria the older custom persisted at least until the mid-third century if not later,[15] and the same may well also have been the case elsewhere. Indeed, that the Council of Nicea (canons 4 and 6) found it necessary to legislate for the participation of other bishops suggests that it was not even accepted everywhere by the early fourth century.[16]

---

8   Ratcliff, "Apostolic Tradition," 269.

9   See Paul F. Bradshaw, "The Participation of Other Bishops in the Ordination of a Bishop in the *Apostolic Tradition* of Hippolytus," *StPatr* 18/2 (1989) 335–38.

10   Brent, *Hippolytus*, 467–68.

11   Walls, "Latin Version," 159.

12   See Albano Vilela, *La condition collégiale des prêtres au IIIe siècle* (ThH 14; Paris: Beauchesne, 1971) 345.

13   See Paul F. Bradshaw, *Ordination Rites of the Ancient Churches of East and West* (New York: Pueblo, 1990) 21–32.

14   Cyprian *Ep.* 55.8; 67.5. See Takeo Osawa, *Das Bischofseinsetzungsverfahren bei Cyprian* (EHS 25/178; Frankfurt: Lang, 1983).

15   See Vilela, *Condition*, 173–79, and the works cited in n. 5 there.

16   See C. Wilfred Griggs, *Early Egyptian Christianity: From Its Origins to 451 C.E.* (Coptic Studies 2; Leiden: Brill, 1990) 132–33.

■ **1–2** The selection of ordained ministers by the local community is reported in a number of sources from the end of the first century onward, though without any details of the process involved,[17] and the election of bishops in this way continued to be the standard practice throughout the Christian church for several centuries.[18] Ordination within the Sunday eucharistic celebration might be thought to be implied by *Did.* 15.1,[19] and once again later evidence shows it to be the custom in most places.[20]

■ **3–4** The form of the imposition of hands constitutes an unusual feature. The collective laying on of hands in silence here is followed in 2.5 by another imposition of the hand[21] by the minister who recites the ordination prayer. Although we have no other extant ordination rites of the third or fourth century for comparison, all known ancient ordination rites from later centuries have just a single imposition of the hand by one person—the bishop who is to say the prayer—as is also the case in the *Canons of Hippolytus.*[22] Some scholars have understood the supposed second laying on of the hand to be merely a continuation of the first, while others regard the double imposition of hands to be a primitive feature that did not survive in later practice, and have interpreted its significance in various ways.[23] For instance, some have seen the first imposition of hands as the moment when the Holy Spirit was bestowed;[24] and others have seen it instead as an expression of consent in preparation for the second, which constituted the ordination itself.[25] Willy Rordorf offered a variation of the latter theory, seeing the first imposition as making the candidate a member of the episcopal college, and the second as God bestowing the Spirit;[26] while Matthew Black linked the action with 1 Tim 4:14 and 2 Tim 1:6, where he believed that both a collective and an individual laying on of hands were mentioned in relation to the same ordination.[27] Alistair Stewart-Sykes has recently suggested that although the presbyters were not permitted to speak, it

---

17 The earliest examples are *Did.* 15.1: "elect for yourselves therefore bishops and deacons worthy of the Lord"; and *1 Clem.* 44.3: "we judge therefore that it is not right to remove from the ministry those appointed by them [the apostles] or afterward by other eminent men with the consent of the whole church." On the passage in the *Didache*, see Kurt Niederwimmer, *The Didache: A Commentary*, trans. L. M. Maloney (Hermeneia; Minneapolis: Fortress Press, 1998) 200–201.

18 See Roger Gryson, "Les élections ecclésiastiques au IIIe siècle," *RHE* 68 (1973) 353–404; idem, "Les élections episcopales en Orient au IVe siècle," *RHE* 74 (1979) 301–45; James F. Puglisi, *The Process of Admission to Ordained Ministry: A Comparative Study*, trans. M. S. Driscoll and M. Misrahi (Collegeville, Minn.: Liturgical, 1996) 29 n. 52; and the works cited therein.

19 See Willy Rordorf, "L'ordination de l'évêque selon la Tradition apostolique d'Hippolyte de Rome," *QL* 55 (1974) 142–43.

20 Bradshaw, *Ordination*, 21. The claim by Jean D. Zizioulas, *Being as Communion: Studies in Personhood and the Church* (Crestwood, N.Y.: St. Vladimir's Seminary Press, 1985) 192–93, that this implies an eschatological dimension to ordination may be reading too much into it.

21 The use of the right hand alone is usual in other evidence for ancient ordination practice. See Bradshaw, *Ordination*, 44.

22 The claim made by Bradshaw, "Ordination," in

Cuming, *Essays*, 34, that other ancient rites prescribe an imposition of hands by all the bishops present was mistaken. Except for the *Apostolic Tradition* and *Testamentum Domini*, the presiding bishop alone lays his hand on the candidate, and this continues to be the Eastern practice to the present day. It was only as a result of the reproduction of the directive from the *Apostolic Tradition* in the 5th-century Gallican *Statuta Ecclesiae Antiqua* that a collective imposition of hands was introduced into later Western practice. See further Bradshaw, *Ordination*, 44–45.

23 For a discussion of some of these theories, see John E. Stam, *Episcopacy in the Apostolic Tradition of Hippolytus* (ThD 3; Basel: Reinhardt, 1969) 19–22; Klemens Richter, "Zum Ritus der Bischofsordination in der 'Apostolischen Überlieferung' Hippolyts von Rom und davon abhängigen Schriften," *ALW* 17 (1975) 15–19.

24 See, e.g., Dix, *Apostolic Tradition*, 3 n. 4; Walter Howard Frere, "Early Forms of Ordination," in Henry Barclay Swete, ed., *Essays on the Early History of the Church and the Ministry* (London: Macmillan, 1918) 278–79.

25 See, e.g., Joseph Coppens, *L'imposition des mains et les rites connexes dans le Nouveau Testament et dans l'Église ancienne: Étude de théologie positive* (Paris: Gabalda, 1925) 145–56; Hanssens, *Liturgie*, 114.

26 Rordorf, "L'ordination," 145–50.

27 Matthew Black, "The Doctrine of the Ministry," *ExpT* 63 (1952) 114–15. But see the exegesis of

was nevertheless they who performed the first imposition of hands as a sign of their consent.[28]

A further possible explanation for the apparent double imposition of hands could be that what we have here is a fusion of two sets of directives, one that merely prescribed the collective imposition of hands in silence, and another that enjoined that one minister alone should impose his hand and recite an ordination prayer. (The statement in the Ethiopic that every bishop is to pray and lay his hands on the candidate is clearly based on the translator's misunderstanding of the text before him.) It would, however, be going too far to share the speculation of Octavian Bârlea that one tradition derived from the northern Mediterranean area and the other from the southern region.[29]

■ 5 The suspicion that this may be a composite text is encouraged by the nature of the phrase in the Latin that seems to provide the connecting link between the two parts, *ex quibus*, "from whom." Dix thought that it was translating the Greek ἐκ τούτων, "from these,"[30] while Botte judged that it probably represented ἀφ᾽ ὧν, "from whom."[31] But both agreed that the phrase was intended in a temporal sense here, "after which," which is certainly how the *Testamentum Domini* seems to have understood it, although the rest omit it entirely, probably because they could not make sense of it. Although this meaning would be unusual for either of the Greek expressions, if it predated the addition of the mention of bishops to the text, it could instead have been a clumsy attempt to link the two sets of directives: "let all keep silence, praying in the heart for the descent of the Spirit, of whom let one, being asked by all. . . ."

---

1 Tim 4:14 given by David Daube, *The New Testament and Rabbinic Judaism* (London: Athlone, 1956) 244–46.

28 Alistair Stewart-Sykes, "The Integrity of the Hippolytean Ordination Rites," *Aug* 39 (1999) 122.

29 Octavian Bârlea, *Die Weihe der Bischöfe, Presbyter und Diakone in vornicänischer Zeit* (Munich: Rumänische akademische Gesellschaft, 1969).

30 Dix, *Apostolic Tradition*, 3 n. 5.

31 Botte, *Tradition*, 7 n. 1.

3

Latin (68.26—69.24)	Sahidic	Arabic	Ethiopic

1 "God and Father of our Lord Jesus Christ, Father of mercies and God of all comfort,[a] who dwells on high and looks on that which is lowly,[b] who knows all things before they come to pass,[c]

2 you who gave limits in the church through the word of your grace,[d] foreordaining from the beginning a race of righteous ones [from] Abraham, appointing rulers and priests, and not leaving your holy place without a ministry, from the beginning of the age you were pleased to be given in those whom you chose:[e]

3 now pour forth that power which is from you, of the spirit of leadership[f] that you gave to your beloved Son Jesus Christ, which he gave to the holy apostles, who established the church in every place, your sanctification, for unceasing glory and praise to your name.

4 Bestow, knower of the heart,[g] Father, on this your servant, whom you have chosen for the episcopate, to feed your holy flock[h] and to exercise the high priesthood for you without blame, ministering night and day; unceasingly to propitiate your countenance, and to offer to you the holy gifts of your church;

5 and by the spirit of high priesthood to have power to forgive sins according to your command,[i] to assign lots according to your bidding, also to loose every bond according to the power that you gave to the apostles,[j] and to please you in gentleness and a pure heart, offering to you a sweet-smelling savor;[k]

6 through your Child, Jesus Christ, through whom [be] glory and power and honor to you, Father and Son with the Holy Spirit, both now and to the ages of ages. Amen."

Ethiopic:

"O God, the Father of our Lord Jesus Christ, our Savior, Father of mercies and Lord of all benefit,[a] who lives with the lofty but sees the lowly,[b] who knows everything before it happens,[c]

you have given the order to the church by the word of your grace,[d] which you ordained beforehand, from the beginning, as a race of righteous ones. From Abraham you have ordained rulers and priests, and you have not left your sanctuary without a minister. From before the creation of the world you have desired to be glorified through the one whom you have chosen.[e]

And now pour out the power that is from you, the spirit of a ruler[f] that you have given to your beloved Son Jesus Christ, whom you have given as a gift to your holy apostles of the church through the plough of your cross in every place, your holiness. To you be glory and unending praise for your name.

Father, you who know the heart,[g] grant to your servant whom you have chosen as bishop to pasture your flock[h] and serve as priest for you without reproach, ministering night and day, asking to see your face in a worthy way. May he offer your oblation of your holy church;

and in the Holy Spirit of the priesthood, having authority to forgive sins according to your command,[i] may he give the offices of your order and loosen all the bonds of wickedness in accord with the authority that you gave to your apostles.[j] And may he please you with gentleness and a pure heart as he offers to you a sweet fragrance;[k]

through your Son, Jesus Christ, through whom you have glory and power and honor, to the Father and the Son and the Holy Spirit in your holy church, now and always and forever and ever. Amen."

---

[a] 2 Cor 1:3.   [b] Ps 113:5-6.   [c] Sus 42.   [d] Acts 20:32.   [e] Eph 1:4-6.   [f] LXX Ps 50:14.
[g] Acts 1:24.   [h] Acts 20:28   [i] John 20:23.   [j] Matt 18:18.   [k] Eph 5:2.

Epitome 4.1–4	Canons of Hippolytus 3	Testamentum Domini
"God and Father of our Lord Jesus Christ, the Father of mercies and God of all comfort,[a] dwelling on high and looking on that which is lowly,[b] knowing all things before their creation,[c] you who gave [the] rules of [the] church through the word of your grace,[d] who foreordained from the beginning a righteous race from Abraham, appointing rulers and priests, and not leaving your sanctuary without a ministry, who from the beginning of the world was pleased to be glorified in those whom you chose;[e] and now pour forth the power that is from you, of the spirit of leadership[f] that you granted through your beloved Child Jesus Christ to your holy apostles, who established the church in the place of your sanctuary, to the unceasing glory and praise of your name.	"O God, Father of our Lord Jesus Christ, Father of mercies and God of all comfort, dwelling on high and looking upon the lowly, knowing everything before it comes to pass, you who have fixed the boundaries of the church, who have decreed from Adam that there should exist a righteous race by the intermediary of this bishop that is [the race] of great Abraham, who have established authorities and powers, look upon N. with your power and mighty spirit, which you have given to the holy apostles by our Lord Jesus Christ, your only Son, those who have founded the church in every place, for the honor and glory of your holy name.	". . . O God and Father of our Lord Jesus Christ, Father of mercies and God of all comfort, who everlastingly dwells in the pure heights, . . . who knows all things before they are, . . . you who gave illumination to the church by the grace of your only begotten Son; you who foreordained from the beginning those who delight in just things and do those things that are holy to dwell in your habitations; you who chose Abraham . . . ; who ordered princes and priests in your high sanctuary, Lord, who called [them] to praise and glorify your name and [the name] of your only begotten in the place of your glory. Lord God, who before the foundation of the world did not leave your high sanctuary without a ministry; . . . you, Lord, even now have been pleased to be praised, and have vouchsafed that there should be leaders for your people. Make shine and pour out understanding and the grace that is from your princely Spirit, which you delivered to your beloved Son Jesus Christ . . . .
Knower of the hearts of all,[g] bestow on this your servant, whom you have chosen for the episcopate, [to feed] your holy [flock] and to serve as high priest for you blamelessly, ministering night and day; unceasingly to propitiate your countenance, and to offer to you the gifts of your holy church; and by the high priestly spirit to have authority to forgive sins according to your command,[i] to assign lots according to your bidding, to loose every bond according to the authority that you gave to the apostles,[j] to please you in gentleness and a pure heart, offering to you a sweet-smelling savor;[k] through your Child Jesus Christ our Lord, with whom [be] glory, power, honor to you, with the Holy Spirit, now and always and to the ages of ages. Amen."	Since you know the heart of everyone, make him shepherd your people blamelessly, so that he may be worthy of tending your great and holy flock; make his life higher than [that] of all his people, without dispute; make him envied by reason of his virtue by everyone; accept his prayers and his offerings that he will offer you day and night; and let them be for you a sweet-smelling savor. Give him, Lord, the episcopate, a merciful spirit, and the authority to forgive sins; give him power to loosen every bond of the oppression of demons, to cure the sick and crush Satan under his feet swiftly; through our Lord Jesus Christ, through whom be glory to you, with him and the Holy Spirit, to the ages of ages. Amen." And all the people say "Amen."	O Father, who knows hearts, [grant] to this your servant whom you have chosen for the episcopate, to feed your holy flock, and to stand in the high priesthood without blame, ministering to you day and night. Grant that your face may be seen by him; make him worthy, O Lord, to offer to you the offerings of your holy church circumspectly, with all fear. Grant him to have your powerful Spirit to loose all bonds, just as you granted to your apostles. In order [that he might] please you in meekness, fill him full of love . . . and a pure heart . . . while he offers you praise and thanksgiving and prayers for a sweet savor. Through your beloved Son our Lord Jesus Christ, by whom to you be praise and honor and might, with the Holy Spirit, both before the worlds and now and always and to the generation of generations and to worlds without end of worlds. Amen." Let the people say, "Amen."

[Prayer for the Ordination of a Bishop]

Text

This is one of the rare chapters where what has been thought to be the Greek text behind the other versions has been preserved in the *Epitome*,[1] and we have included an English translation of it above in place of the expanded form in the *Apostolic Constitutions* itself. Scholars have expressed suspicions, however, that at some points in the prayer the Latin text may have retained better readings (which we shall consider below), and this has led Markschies to contend that what the compiler of the *Epitome* had access to was not the original Greek text of the *Apostolic Tradition* as such but a version of it that had already undergone some modification.[2]

Ratcliff had earlier gone further still, claiming that the text of the *Epitome* had "undergone considerable revision so as to be conformed to the standards and usage of the fourth century."[3] Segelberg has also attempted to discern an original text beneath what he regards as later strata, though admitting that one of these other layers might well be the redaction by the author himself of older liturgical material and not necessarily a subsequent interpolation.[4] In his judgment the original did not include anything in *Ap. Trad.* 3.1 after the initial "God," or anything in 3.3 after "the spirit of leadership," continuing in 3.4 only from "on this your servant" onward, and nothing again in 3.5 until after "apostles."

Segelberg's reconstruction is not entirely convincing. While there may be some merit to the main criteria used in his analysis—that the earliest liturgical texts tend to have biblical allusions rather than direct quotations, and that Old Testament allusions are likely to be more primitive than New Testament ones—these are not immutable laws, and it is difficult to share his conclusions without reservation.

■ 2 While the *Epitome*, *Apostolic Constitutions*, and *Canons of Hippolytus* all have the phrase "righteous race," the Latin and Ethiopic have "race of righteous ones." Botte regarded the latter as the original, and thought that the *Epitome* had been influenced here by the *Apostolic Constitutions*.[5] On the other hand, "you were pleased to be given" in the Latin appears to be the result of a mistranslation, the Greek participle εὐδοκήσας being read as the indicative εὐδόκησας (as also in 4.5) and the verb δοξασθῆναι ("to be glorified") as δοθῆναι ("to be given"), with the *Epitome* preserving the true reading.

■ 3 There has been more of a debate about the clause "that you granted through your beloved Child (παῖς) Jesus Christ to your holy apostles" in the *Epitome*, which is rendered in the Latin as "that you gave to your beloved Son (*filius*) Jesus Christ, which he gave to your holy apostles." Botte, Dix, and Frere all agreed that the Latin had preserved the original reading here, as confirmed by the Ethiopic, *Apostolic Constitutions*, and *Testamentum Domini*, and that the *Epitome* and *Canons of Hippolytus* had emended it in order to avoid any implication of subordinationism.[6] Segelberg and Walls dissented. Segelberg noted that the use of "Son" rather than "Child" in the Latin suggested that there had been later emendation. "There is no doubt that the text is at this point quite difficult."[7] Walls suggested that the Latin translator might have introduced the more subordinationist formulation ("which . . . which") to accord with his Arian sympathies.[8]

With regard to the phrase "in the place of your sanctuary" (*Epitome*) or "in every place, your sanctification/holiness" (in the Latin and Ethiopic, although a variant reading in the Ethiopic would support the *Epitome*), Botte again believed that the word "sanctification" (*sanctificationem*) in the Latin was an attempt to translate the accusative of the Greek word for "sanctuary" (ἁγίασμα), rendered a few lines earlier in the Latin as "holy place" (*sanctum*), and was to be preferred to the genitive in the *Epitome*, so that the phrase should read "in [every] place [as] your sanctuary."[9] Connolly suggested, on the basis

---

1   See above, p. 6.
2   Markschies, "Wer schrieb," 15–19.
3   Ratcliff, "Apostolic Tradition," 270 n. 13.
4   Segelberg, "Ordination Prayers," 397–402.
5   Botte, *Tradition*, 7 n. 4.
6   Ibid., 9 n. 9; Dix, *Apostolic Tradition*, lxxvi, 4–5; Frere, "Early Forms," 280 n. 2. See also Markschies,

"Wer schrieb," 17, who suggests that the *Epitome* here was trying to smooth out the roughness of the original.
7   Segelberg, "Ordination Prayers," 399.
8   Walls, "Latin Version," 161 n. 4.
9   Botte, *Tradition*, 9 nn. 1, 6.

of the appearance of the motif in other ancient texts, that "through the plough of your cross" in the Ethiopic was an authentic part of the original;[10] but he was opposed by Dix, who noted that this motif was especially common in Ethiopic literature and is thus more likely to have been an Ethiopic insertion, as there is no trace of it in the other versions.[11] Connolly's suggestion has not been followed by anyone else.

■ **4** There seems to be a consensus among scholars that the phrase "knower of the heart, Father" (in the Latin, supported by the Ethiopic and *Testamentum Domini*) is the original and that "knower of the hearts of all" (in the *Epitome* and *Canons of Hippolytus*) has been conformed more closely to the text of Acts 1:24.[12] The words "to feed the flock" ($\pi o\iota\mu\alpha\acute{\iota}\nu\epsilon\iota\nu$ $\tau\grave{\eta}\nu$ $\pi o\acute{\iota}\mu\nu\eta\nu$) also seem to have fallen out of the text of the *Epitome*.

■ **6** The *Epitome* has "with whom" in place of the "through whom" of the other witnesses. Dix again thought that the change had been deliberately made in order to avoid subordinationism, and there seems to be general agreement that the others have here preserved the older reading.[13] Botte regarded the phrase "in your holy church" in the Ethiopic as part of the earliest text, because the *Epitome*, like the *Apostolic Constitutions*, regularly omitted it whenever it occurred.[14] For the form of the rest of the doxology, see the commentary on 6.4 below.

Comment

Several scholars have drawn attention to apparent parallels between a number of phrases in the prayer and expressions that occur in *1 Clement*,[15] and this led Georg Kretschmar to go further and conclude that the prayer "clearly draws from the First Epistle of Clement in sev-

eral places."[16] However, this alleged literary dependency is scarcely certain. The passages in question are not numerous, and the close verbal similarities amount to little more than that both use such words as "high priest" and "blamelessly." At best, all that might be claimed is that the two documents derive from a similar world of ideas, which would not be too surprising if the prayer is indeed of Roman provenance.

Brent has alleged that the use of the term "high priesthood" to describe the office of a bishop here "represents the earliest usage of such sacred and hierarchical teminology in Christian literature and is absolutely unique" to this text and to Hippolytus's *Refutatio* I, proemium 6.[17] This claim, however, ignores (a) the usage in *1 Clement*, which certainly sees some sort of parallel—if not exact equivalence—between the Jewish high priesthood and the Christian ordained ministry; (b) the appearance of the word "high priest" in relation to Christian prophets in *Did.* 13.3; (c) Tertullian's use of the equivalent Latin term *summus sacerdos* to refer to the bishop, even if it is in a context that suggests that it may perhaps have been a metaphor occasioned by the particular argument rather than a regular term for the office (*De bapt.* 17.1);[18] and (d) the use of "Levitical high priest" for the bishop in *Didasc.* 2.26.4, which may well have been written at the same time or even earlier than this prayer.[19] Moreover, the passage in Hippolytus's *Refutatio* to which Brent refers speaks of "the charism of teaching and high priesthood," but he fails to note that this is in sharp contrast to the ordination prayer, which perhaps rather surprisingly lacks any direct reference to a prophetic or teaching ministry, suggesting that such a ministry was not seen as fundamental to the episcopal office in the tradition in which it arose.

Stewart-Sykes also fails to note this significant con-

10 Connolly, *Egyptian Church Order*, 24.
11 Dix, *Apostolic Tradition*, 86.
12 See, e.g., Easton, *Apostolic Tradition*, 34 n. 5, 67 n. 5.
13 Dix, *Apostolic Tradition*, 6. See also Botte, *Tradition*, 11; Markschies, "Wer schreib," 17.
14 Botte, *Tradition*, 9 n. 4.
15 See, e.g., Richter, "Bischofsordination," 21–23, 30–31; Rordorf, "L'ordination," 147.
16 Georg Kretschmar, "Early Christian Liturgy in the Light of Contemporary Historical Research," *StLit* 16.3/4 (1986–87) 33.
17 Brent, *Hippolytus*, 302.

18 Tertullian elsewhere implies that *sacerdos*, "priest," may have been a commonly used designation for the bishop in the North African church (see *De ex. cast.* 11.1–2; *De monog.* 12; *De pud.* 20.10; 21.17); and Cyprian regularly calls the bishop *sacerdos*, reserving *summus sacerdos* for Christ alone (e.g., *Ep.* 63.14).
19 See also Markschies, "Wer schreib," 51.

trast between the two sources, and furthermore advances the extremely improbable hypothesis that the prayer here in chap. 3 is older than the prayer for a presbyter in chap. 7, and was originally meant for a presbyter-bishop rather than a monepiscopus, in spite of its high priestly language.[20]

Since the only other text of an independent ordination prayer that we can date with any certainty before the end of the fourth century is that in the *Sacramentary of Sarapion*,[21] comparison with other prayers appears to be rather difficult. There are, however, reasons to suppose that the substance of at least some prayers in later Eastern ordination rites may well also go back to the late fourth century. Among all these texts, the prayer in the *Apostolic Tradition* stands out because of its authoritarian and sacerdotal language. While most later ordination prayers do have some reference to the priestly character of the episcopal office, in nearly every case this is peripheral to the main imagery of the prayer, and so appears to be a secondary addition. This is especially clear in a number of prayers from Eastern rites, which obviously share a common ancestor: the sacerdotal references are not part of their common nucleus but are added at different points and in different ways in the individual prayers.[22] Although in most other respects following closely its source in the *Apostolic Tradition*, even the *Canons of Hippolytus* lacks all reference to the high priestly ministry of the bishop. While it has generally been supposed that the redactor deleted these allusions because the early Eastern concept of the episcopate did not include this cultic dimension to the same extent as in the West, one cannot entirely rule out the possibility that he may have known an earlier form of the text to which this typology had not yet been added.[23] Only the classical Roman ordination prayer, the earliest manuscript of which dates from the seventh century, has as its central theme the priestly character of the episcopate, and draws on Old Testament cultic imagery to express this theme.[24]

Similarly, no other extant prayer from ancient times lists in its primary stratum the powers and functions of the episcopate in the way that the *Apostolic Tradition* does. In other prayers, the fundamental images are generally those of shepherd and teacher, with either the precise liturgical and pastoral functions associated with the office left largely unspecified (as in the case of the Byzantine rite) or with their being added in what are obviously secondary strata in the prayer originating in later centuries (as in the East and West Syrian rites).[25] Chief among these functions in Eastern prayers tends to be the ministry of healing, not mentioned at all in the prayer in the *Apostolic Tradition*. Even the Roman prayer with its strong sacerdotal emphasis does not enumerate the individual functions belonging to the order but concentrates instead on the inner qualities requisite in a true bishop.

The unique character of the prayer in the *Apostolic Tradition*, therefore, suggests that it took its present form in a particularly difficult situation in which the status of the bishop's office and his authority in the local Christian community were under attack from some quarters. Perhaps it was the whole idea of the existence of an episcopal figure distinct from the corporate presbyterate that was a novelty and needed support from Old Testament imagery, or perhaps it was the extent of the independent powers that such a person should possess that was being challenged, and led to their careful cataloging in the prayer in an attempt to bolster the leader's position. Whatever the precise circumstances, they produced a prayer that is unlike any other from Christian antiquity, except for those in the *Apostolic Constitutions* and *Testamentum Domini* that are consciously dependent on it, and for those in later Eastern rites that in turn copied these two prayers.

---

20 Stewart-Sykes, "Integrity."
21 See Maxwell E. Johnson, *The Prayers of Sarapion of Thmuis* (OrChrA 249; Rome: Pontificio Istituto Orientale, 1995) 60–61, 92–95, 148–62.
22 See Bradshaw, *Ordination*, 54.
23 J. Vernon Bartlet ("The Ordination Prayers in the Ancient Church Order," *JTS* 17 [1916] 248–56) sug-

gested that the prayer in the *Apostolic Tradition* had originally lacked the list of high priestly functions.
24 Bradshaw, *Ordination*, 215–16.
25 Ibid., 133–34, 164, 183–84.

But when might this situation have been? In the light of the parallels to the high priestly language adduced above, and on the basis that doctrinal developments generally appear in theological discourse well before they find a place in liturgical texts, which are by nature more conservative, it is unlikely that the prayer—at least in the form in which we have it—is older than the mid-third century, and may well be much later still. That is not to say, however, that it does not contain elements that are older than that, among them the two references in the *Epitome* to Jesus as the "Child" rather than "Son" of God, a usage not otherwise found in material later than the second century.[26]

■ **2** The meaning of the word "limits" or "rules" (Greek ὅρους; Latin *terminos*) is disputed. Botte thought that the reference was to the rules given in the Old Testament for the succession of "rulers and priests," and that the Latin had wrongly translated the Greek word in its other sense of "limits."[27] Georg Kretschmar, on the other hand, believed that what had been meant were the lines of demarcation between the different ordained ministries,[28] while Carlos-J. Pinto de Oliveira understood it more broadly in the sense of "you who fashioned your church."[29] Brent has drawn attention to parallel uses of the term to mean "canons" or "ordinances" rather than "limits" in Hippolytus *Ref.* 9.11.1; 9.12.21; 10.5.1, and claimed that its use in this sense is unique to these two documents;[30] but the examples cited by Lampe's *Lexicon* would seem to contradict Brent's assertion.[31]

The prayer then recalls God's activity among the people of the old covenant and especially his raising up of "rulers and priests." Such Old Testament imagery, both here and in other ordination prayers, is not merely incidental: it witnesses to a belief in the fundamental continuity of God's work throughout history, the promise of the new covenant in the old and the fulfillment of the old covenant in the new.[32] Thus the mention of both rulers and priests is an indication of the dual nature of the office to which the bishop was seen as succeeding.

■ **3** The relationship of the bishop's ministry to that of Christ and the apostles is given only a limited expression: they are merely said to have received the same spirit of leadership that is being sought for the ordinand—and even this meager reference is deleted in Segelberg's putative original version. Nor does the prayer seem to envisage any sort of transmission of the gift of the Holy Spirit from ordainer to ordinand in the manner commonly understood by later theologians. Indeed, it is not the gift of the person of the Holy Spirit as such that is asked for, in contrast to the directives in chap. 2, but rather "the power . . . of the spirit of leadership" (*virtutem . . . principalis spiritus*: δύναμιν τοῦ ἡγεμονικοῦ πνεύματος), and indirectly in 3.5 "the spirit of high priesthood" (*spiritum primates sacerdotii*: τῷ πνεύματι τῷ ἀρχιερατικῷ), expressions otherwise almost unknown in patristic literature.[33] Furthermore the gift is understood to be effected by a fresh outpouring of the Spirit directly from God upon the candidate.[34]

■ **4–5** The choice of the candidate is affirmed as the work of God ("whom you have chosen for the episcopate") and not just that of the congregation, and the dual nature of the episcopal office features again here.

26 See the commentary on chap. 4, below, n. 1.

27 Botte, *Tradition*, 7 n. 3. See also Roger Béraudy, "Le sacrement de l'Ordre d'après la *Tradition apostolique* d'Hippolyte," *BCE* 38–39 (1962) 340; Richter, "Bischofsordination," 22 n. 93.

28 Georg Kretschmar, "Die Ordination im frühen Christentum," *FZThPh* 22 (1975) 44.

29 Carlos-Josaphat Pinto de Oliveira, "Signification sacerdotale du ministère de l'évêque dans la Tradition Apostolique d'Hippolyte de Rome," *FZThPh* 25 (1978) 407.

30 Brent, *Hippolytus*, 303–4. The parallel was also noted by Joseph Lécuyer, "Épiscopat et presbytérat dans les écrits d'Hippolyte de Rome," *RechSR* 41 (1953) 32.

31 See also Markschies, "Wer schreib," 52.

32 See Lécuyer, "Épiscopat," 31–32.

33 Ibid., 35–36; but cf. Enrico Mazza, *The Origins of the Eucharistic Prayer* (Collegeville, Minn.: Liturgical, 1995) 108 n. 32, who draws attention to the occurrence of the expression "sovereign spirit" (= "spirit of leadership") in Pseudo-Hippolytus, *In Sanctum Pascha*.

34 See Gregory Dix, "The Ministry in the Early Church," in Kenneth E. Kirk, ed., *The Apostolic Ministry* (London: Hodder & Stoughton, 1946) 200; Ratcliff, "Apostolic Tradition," 269.

On the one hand, the power of the "spirit of *leadership*" that God is asked to pour forth is so that the bishop may be a *shepherd* to his people ("feed your holy flock"). On the other hand, it is also said to be in order that he may "serve as high priest," and various liturgical functions are then enumerated: "to offer . . . the gifts of your holy church" (i.e., to preside at the Eucharist; cf. *1 Clem.* 44.4, προσενεγκόντας τὰ δῶρα); "to have authority to forgive sins"; "to assign lots" (i.e., to assign ecclesiastical duties, derived from the allocation of priestly duties by lot in the OT);[35] and "to loose every bond" (as the authority to forgive sins has already been mentioned, this may be a reference to the power of exorcism).[36] The bishop is also described as "high priest" in *Ap. Trad.* 34 and in the Ethiopic text of 8.11.

---

35 For example, 1 Chr 24:5; 25:8; see also 1 Pet 5:3; and *Ap. Trad.* 8.3; 30A.2.

36 So John E. Stam, *Episcopacy in the Apostolic Tradition of Hippolytus* (ThD 3; Basel: Reinhardt, 1969) 88.

Text

The eucharistic prayer, together with chaps. 5 and 6, interrupts the sequence of directives pertaining to ordination and ministry, and may therefore be later additions to the primitive nucleus of the church order, although there is no textual evidence as such for this. This is not to say that these portions would necessarily have been later *compositions*, but only that they could have been added to this document at a later date, perhaps because a redactor thought it strange that nothing was said about a matter as important as the eucharistic prayer, not recognizing the directions about "the Lord's supper" (see below, chaps. 26–29B) as referring to a eucharist, since it was unlike the eucharistic practice known to him.

For the majority of this chapter the Latin and Ethiopic constitute the principal witnesses, the Sahidic and Arabic omitting the prayer itself in accordance with their usual practice. The *Apostolic Constitutions* and *Testamentum Domini* do offer some assistance, but the material has undergone such a major transformation in both cases that it is sometimes difficult to disentangle what might have originated in the *Apostolic Tradition* from the rest.

It has long been recognized that the eucharistic prayer has some elements that suggest a very early date, as, for example, references to Jesus as the "Child" of God[1] and the "angel" of God's will,[2] and other features that seem to point instead to a later time, for example, the appearance it gives of a seamless whole flowing continuously from initial dialogue to final doxology. Yet most scholars have been willing to accept without apparent difficulty virtually the entire prayer as the authentic work of Hippolytus. For instance, Bouyer dealt with the

tension by proposing that Hippolytus was a deliberate archaizer.[3]

Almost alone among scholars, Ratcliff claimed that the prayer as it stood did not date from the late second or early third century but had been reworked in the fourth century. At the same time he maintained that beneath the surface could be detected the remains of the original pattern of the prayer, which had consisted of more extensive thanksgiving for creation and redemption, the absence of any epiclesis, and the inclusion of a final thanksgiving for the admission of the gathered assembly to the worship of heaven, culminating in the singing of the Sanctus, later dropped from the text.[4] Although strongly supported by Arthur Couratin and Gilbert Mitchell,[5] this radical hypothesis failed to convince others. While his particular reconstruction may have been mistaken, that does not mean that Ratcliff was wrong in challenging the authenticity and integrity of the prayer as such.

■ **2** As Botte has noted, the plural "oblations" (*oblationes*) in the Latin seems to be a copyist's error, because it is followed by the singular pronoun "it" (*eam*), and all the oriental versions also have the singular.[6]

■ **3** The whole dialogue here appears in Greek rather than Coptic in the Sahidic version, as is also the case in the *Canons of Hippolytus*.

■ **5** As Botte notes, there seems to be the same confusion in the Latin here between the Greek participle εὐδοκήσας and the indicative εὐδόκησας as there was in *Ap. Trad.* 3.2,[7] resulting in the translation "and it was well pleasing to you" rather than the participle that the Ethiopic has retained (*faqidaka*), rendered here as "by your will."

■ **12** The only major textual debate about the prayer has concerned the invocation of the Holy Spirit here. Dix

1   Except for one occurrence in the *Apostolic Constitutions* (which may derive from the *Apostolic Tradition* itself), all other instances of this expression in early Christian literature belong to works dated no later than the mid-2d century: *Didache, 1 Clement, Barnabas, Martyrdom of Polycarp*.

2   An allusion to Isa 9:5 in LXX also found in *Ap. Trad.* 8.10 as well as in Justin *1 Apol.* 63; *Dial.* 56, 76, 126–28; and Irenaeus *Dem.* 55–56. Mazza (*Origins*, 107–10) adds a reference to Pseudo-Hippolytus, *In Sanctum Pascha*, but here it is simply part of a longer quotation from Isaiah and is not otherwise

applied directly as a christological title.

3   Bouyer, *Eucharist*, 180–81.

4   Edward C. Ratcliff, "The Sanctus and the Pattern of the Early Anaphora," *JEH* 1 (1950) 29–36, 125–34.

5   Arthur H. Couratin, "The Sacrifice of Praise," *Theology* 58 (1955) 285–91; Gilbert Arthur Mitchell, *Landmarks in Liturgy* (London: Darton, Longman & Todd, 1961) 84–89.

6   Botte, *Tradition*, 11 n. 7.

7   Ibid., 13 n. 6.

[Eucharistic Prayer]

	Latin (69.25—70.35)	Sahidic	Arabic	Ethiopic
1	When he has been made bishop, let all offer the mouth of peace, greeting him because he has been made worthy.	And (δέ) when he is made bishop (ἐπίσκοπος), let everyone give peace (εἰρήνη) with their mouth, greeting (ἀσπάζεσθαι) him.	And when he has become bishop, he greets each one and kisses him on the mouth.	After the bishop has been ordained, every one is to greet him with the mouth, paying respect to the one who has become bishop and to the one to whom this grace has been apportioned.
2	And let the deacons offer to him the oblations, and let him, laying [his] hands on it with all the presbytery, say, giving thanks:	And (δέ) let the deacons (διάκονος) bring the offering (προσφορά) to him. And (δέ) when he lays his hand on the offering (προσφορά) with the presbyters (πρεσβύτερος), let him say, giving thanks (εὐχαριστεῖν):	And the deacon brings the offerings in to him, and when he puts his hand on the offerings with all the presbyters, let him say and give thanks thus:	And a deacon is to bring the oblation to him, and when he has then with all the presbyters placed his hand on the oblation, he is to say as he offers thanks in this way:
3	"The Lord [be] with you." And let them all say: "And with your spirit." "Up [with your] hearts." "We have [them] to the Lord." "Let us give thanks to the Lord." "It is worthy and just." And so let him then continue:	"The Lord [be] with all of you. And let all the people (λαός) say: "With your spirit." And he says: "Up [with] your heart." And the people (λαός) say: "We have [them] to the Lord." And he says again: "Let us give thanks to the Lord." And the people (λαός) say: "Worthy and right." And let him pray again in this way and say the things which come after this, according to (κατά) the custom of the holy offering (προσφορά).	"The Lord be with you." And all the people say: "And with your spirit." And he says: "Where are your hearts?" And all the people say: "They are with the Lord." And he says: "Thank the Lord." And the people say: "[It is] right." And so he makes supplication and says what follows after that according to the rules of the liturgy.	"The Lord be with all of you." And the entire people are to say: "May he be with your spirit." And the bishop is to say: "Lift up your heart." And all the people are to say: "We have [them] with the Lord our God." And the bishop is to say: "Let us give thanks to the Lord." The people are to say: "It is right and a just thing." And then the bishop is to say what follows [of] the oblation:
4	"We render thanks to you, God, through your beloved Child Jesus Christ, whom in the last times you sent to us as savior and redeemer and angel of your will,			"We thank you, O God, through your beloved Son Jesus Christ, whom you sent to us at the end of time as our Savior and Redeemer, the messenger of your counsel,
5	who is your inseparable word, through whom you made all things[a] and it was well pleasing to you,			this Word who is from you, in whom you made everything by your will[a];
6	you sent from heaven into the virgin's womb, and who conceived in the womb was incarnate and manifested as your Son, born from the Holy Spirit and the virgin;			and you sent [him] from heaven into the womb of a virgin; who became flesh and was borne in a belly. And your Son was revealed by the Holy Spirit
7	who fulfilling your will and gaining for you a holy people[b] stretched out [his] hands when he was suffering, that he might release from suffering those who believed in you;			so that he might complete your will and make a people for you.[b] He spread out his hands in suffering so that he might release those who suffer, those who trust in you;
8	who when he was being			who was given up by his

Apostolic Constitutions 8.5.9–10	*Canons of Hippolytus*	*Testamentum Domini*
And after the prayer one of the bishops will present the sacrifice on the hands of the one that is ordained. And early in the morning let him be enthroned in the place offered him by the other bishops, all kissing him with a kiss in the Lord. . . . [8.12.4–5] "May the grace of almighty God and the love of our Lord Jesus Christ and the communion of the Holy Spirit be with you all." And let all say in unison: "And with your spirit." And the high priest: "Up with [your] mind." And all: "We have [them] to the Lord." And the high priest: "Let us give thanks to the Lord." And all: "[It is] right and just." And let the high priest say:	After that they are all to turn toward him and give him the kiss of peace, because he is worthy of it. Then the deacon brings the offerings, and he who has become bishop lays his hand on the offerings with the presbyters, saying: "The Lord be with all." The people reply: "And with your spirit." He says: "Lift up your hearts." They reply: "We have [them] to the Lord." He says: "Let us give thanks to the Lord." They reply: "It is fitting and right," that is to say, "It is fitting." After that he says the prayer and completes the liturgy.	Then let them cry out, "He is worthy, he is worthy, he is worthy." After he is [ordained], let the people keep the feast three days. . . . And let everyone give him the Peace. . . . [23] Let the bishop then place his hand on those loaves that have been set on the altar, and let the presbyters place [their hands] together with him. . . . Then let the bishop say, giving and rendering thanks, with an awed voice: "Our Lord [be] with you." And let the people say: "And with your spirit." Let the bishop say: "[Lift] up your hearts." Let the people say: "They are with the Lord." Let the bishop say: "Let us give thanks to the Lord." And let all the people say: "It is meet and right." . . .

8.12.7–50

". . . Only begotten Son, God the Word, living wisdom, firstborn of every creature, messenger of your great will. . . . For you, eternal God, made all things through him . . . coming to be from a virgin, God the Word coming to be in the flesh, the beloved Son. . . . And the one who forms all who are made came to be in the womb of a virgin, the one without flesh has been made flesh, the one timelessly begotten has been born in time . . . he fulfilled your will, he brought to perfection the work that you gave to him . . . in order that he might release those who suffer and rescue from death those for whom he came, and might break the chains of the devil and deliver men from his deceit. . . .		"We give you thanks, O God . . . and Father of the only begotten, our Savior, whom in the latter times you sent to us as a savior and proclaimer of your will. . . . You, Lord, sent your Word, son of [your] counsel and son of your promise, by whom you made all things, being well pleased with him, into a virgin womb; who, when he was conceived [and] made flesh, was shown to be your Son, being born of the Holy Spirit and the Virgin, who, fulfilling your will and preparing a holy people, stretched out his hands to suffering, that he might loose from sufferings and corruption and death those who have hoped in you; who when he was betrayed to voluntary suffering so that he might . . . loose [the pains of] death, and rend the bonds of the devil . . . and tread down Sheol . . . and guide the righteous to light, and fix the boundary . . . and reveal the resurrection;

	Latin	Sahidic	Arabic	Ethiopic

Latin

handed over to voluntary suffering, that he might destroy death and break the bonds of the devil, and tread down hell and illuminate the righteous, and fix a limit and manifest the resurrection,

9 taking bread [and] giving thanks to you, he said: 'Take, eat, this is my body that will be broken for you.' Likewise also the cup, saying: 'This is my blood that is shed for you.

10 When you do this, you do my remembrance.'

11 Remembering therefore his death and resurrection, we offer to you the bread and cup, giving thanks to you because you have held us worthy to stand before you and minister to you.

12 And we ask that you would send your Holy Spirit in the oblation of [your] holy church, [that] gathering [them] into one[c] you will give to all who partake of the holy things [to partake] in the fullness of the Holy Spirit, for the strengthening of faith in truth,

13 that we may praise and glorify you through your Child Jesus Christ, through whom [be] glory and honor to you, Father and Son with the Holy Spirit, in your holy church, both now and to the ages of ages. Amen."

Ethiopic

will to suffering so that he could condemn death and break the bonds of Satan and trample Sheol and lead forth the holy ones and fix the order and make the resurrection known.

Then, having taken bread, he gave thanks and said: 'Take, eat; this is my body that will be broken for you.' And in the same way [with] the cup he said: 'This is my blood that will be poured out for you. When you do this, you make a memorial of me.' As we therefore remember his death and his resurrection, we offer this bread and cup to you, giving thanks to you who have made us worthy to stand before you and to serve you as priests. We pray that you send your Holy Spirit on the oblation of the church. Having united [them], may you give to all who [par]take holiness, both for filling with the Holy Spirit and for strengthening the faith in truth

so that they may glorify and praise you through your Son Jesus Christ, through whom you have glory and power in the holy church both now and always and forever and ever. Amen."

[a] John 1:3   [b] 1 Pet 2:9   [c] John 11:52

Apostolic Constitutions	Canons of Hippolytus	Testamentum Domini

taking bread, gave [it] to his disciples, saying: 'Take, eat; this is my body that is broken for you for the forgiveness of sins. When you do this, you make my resurrection.' Also the cup of wine that he mixed he gave for a type of the blood that he shed for us." And also let him say: "Remembering therefore your death and resurrection, we offer you bread and the cup, thanking you who alone are God forever and our Savior, since you have promised to us to stand before you and serve you in priesthood . . . . O Lord the Holy Spirit, we have brought this drink and this food of your holiness; make it be to us not for condemnation, not for reproach, not for destruction, but for the medicine [and] support of our spirit. . . . Sanctify us all, O God; but grant that all those who partake [and] receive of your holy things may be made one with you, so that they may be filled with the Holy Spirit, for the confirmation of the faith in truth, that they may always offer a doxology to you, and to your beloved Son Jesus Christ, by whom praise and might be to you with your Holy Spirit, to the ages of ages." Let the people say: "Amen." . . .

Do this for my remembrance. . . . Remembering then his passion and death and his resurrection from the dead . . . we offer you . . . this bread and this cup, giving you thanks because you have made us worthy to stand before you and to offer you priestly service . . . And we ask you . . . send down your Holy Spirit upon this sacrifice . . . in order that those who receive . . . may be filled with Holy Spirit . . . For to you through him [be] all glory, worship, and thanksgiving; and through you and with you in him [be] honor and adoration in Holy Spirit, both now and always and to the unceasing and everlasting ages of ages. Amen."

41

argued that the incoherence of both the Latin and Ethiopic texts suggested that some interpolation had taken place and that the *Testamentum Domini*, which lacks a fully developed epiclesis, probably came closest to the original reading at this point.[8] Cyril Richardson, on the other hand, argued that the epiclesis was not an interpolation into the *Apostolic Tradition* but that the text had suffered corruption and could easily be restored.[9] Botte rejected both these solutions, and in a careful examination of the text of the *Testamentum Domini* concluded that by reworking the extant Syriac version back into Greek he could show that the original of the *Testamentum Domini* had included an epiclesis on the eucharistic elements (although mistranslated by the Syriac): "send the Holy Spirit upon this holy drink and holy food." This reconstruction, he believed, proved the existence of the epiclesis in the original of the *Apostolic Tradition*.[10] Richardson accepted Botte's criticism that his suggestions with regard to corruptions were an inadequate explanation for what had happened to the text but disagreed with Botte's particular reconstruction of the epiclesis.[11] Bouyer too challenged Botte's reasoning, accusing him of failing to read in the context of the whole sentence the particular words of the *Testamentum Domini* about which he had imputed a series of mistakes to the translator. Bouyer believed that no corrections were necessary, that there had never been an epiclesis on the eucharistic elements in the *Testamentum Domini*, and that therefore one was probably not there in the original of the *Apostolic Tradition* either, but instead was added later.[12] Botte nevertheless continued to maintain

his position.[13] More recently Mazza has suggested that only the second part of the epiclesis, which asks for the union of the communicants and their participation in the fullness of the Spirit for the strengthening of faith in truth, belongs to an older layer of the prayer, and that the first part, the invocation of the Spirit on the oblation, to which the second is not smoothly connected, is a later addition.[14] To Mazza's arguments on this point, we may add the studies on the evolution of epicleses in general undertaken by both Sebastian Brock and Gabriele Winkler,[15] which demonstrate that the earliest form was usually an imperative, "Come," addressed directly to the Son as Messiah or Logos and/or to his Spirit, and that imperatives which were addressed to the Father, as in "Send your Holy Spirit," or petitions to the Father to send the Spirit, as here, reflect successive stages of development.

Comment

■ 1 The ritual kiss appears to be a distinctively Christian practice that emerged in the New Testament period.[16] It is attested at the conclusion of congregational prayer within a baptismal eucharist in Justin Martyr and at the conclusion of common prayer in various settings by Athenagoras, Tertullian, Clement of Alexandria, and Origen.[17] This text, however, is the earliest explicit evidence for its use at the conclusion of an ordination, although it is a standard feature of all later rites.[18] The Latin expression "the mouth of peace" (*os pacis*) seems to be without parallel elsewhere, although the oriental

---

8 Dix, *Apostolic Tradition*, 75–79.

9 Cyril C. Richardson, "The So-Called Epiclesis in Hippolytus," *HTR* 40 (1947) 101–8.

10 Bernard Botte, "L'épiclèse de l'anaphore d'Hippolyte," *RThAM* 14 (1947) 241–51.

11 Cyril C. Richardson, "A Note on the Epicleses in Hippolytus and the Testamentum Domini," *RThAM* 15 (1948) 357–59.

12 Bouyer, *Eucharist*, 170–77.

13 See Botte, "À propos de la 'Tradition apostolique,'" *RThAM* 33 (1966) 183.

14 Mazza, *Origins*, 169–74.

15 Sebastian Brock, "The Epiklesis in the Antiochene Baptismal Ordines," in *Symposium Syriacum 1972* (OrChrA 197; Rome: Pontificium Institutum Orientalium Studiorum, 1974) 183–218; Gabriele

Winkler, "Nochmals zu den Anfängen der Epiklese und des Sanctus im Eucharistischen Hochgebet," *ThQ* 174 (1994) 214–31; idem, "Weitere Beobachtungen zur frühen Epiklese (den Doxologien und dem Sanctus). Über die Bedeutung der Apokryphen für die Erforschung der Entwicklung der Riten," *OrChr* 80 (1996) 1–18.

16 Cf. 1 Thess 5:26; 1 Cor 16:20; 2 Cor 13:12; Rom 16:16; 1 Pet 5:14.

17 See further L. Edward Phillips, *The Ritual Kiss in Early Christian Worship* (JLS 36; Nottingham: Grove, 1996) 5–25.

18 See Bradshaw, *Ordination*, 34–36.

versions also include an explicit reference to the mouth here, and in *Ap. Trad.* 21.26 all the versions—including the Latin—speak of giving "the peace with the mouth." Since this is not the usual way to say "kiss" in any of these languages (cf. *Ap. Trad.* 21.23: Latin *osculum*; Sahidic ⲡⲉⲓ), some expression must have included the word "mouth" in the underlying Greek in both places. The explanation for the kiss given in the Latin and echoed in the *Canons of Hippolytus*, "because he has been made worthy," suggests the acclamation "worthy" that occurs at the conclusion of episcopal ordination in the *Testamentum Domini* and in other Eastern rites. In the Armenian tradition and in Western rites, however, this acclamation is found at the beginning of the ordination rite rather than the end, which suggests that at least this clause, if not the whole directive, may be of Eastern rather than Western provenance.[19]

■ **2** The practice of deacons bringing up the eucharistic elements, which is also mentioned in chap. 21, is implied in the Syrian *Didascalia Apostolorum*, where the bishop is directed to let one deacon "stand always by the offerings of the eucharist; and let another stand outside the door and observe those who enter. But afterwards, when you offer the oblation, let them serve together in the church."[20] On the other hand, the practice of both bishop and presbyters laying their hands on the eucharistic offering before the prayer is otherwise unknown in Christian antiquity. Several scholars have interpreted it as expressing a sense of eucharistic concelebration between bishop and presbyters.[21]

■ **3** The dialogue preceding the eucharistic prayer is attested in other early sources but not in exactly the same form. The greeting, "The Lord be with you." . . .

"And with your spirit," does not occur in other texts before the fourth century and is characteristic of later Western rather than Eastern rites, which tend to have instead a variation of 2 Cor 13:13. The addition of "all" in the Sahidic and Ethiopic reflects the standard Egyptian version of the greeting. Robert Taft has argued that its earliest form in the East was "Peace to/with you/all," and that this form was later expanded.[22] Because chap. 21 has the same greeting at the postbaptismal kiss as it does here in the preanaphoral dialogue, and because a number of later Western sources omit any reference to this greeting when describing the dialogue before the eucharistic prayer, the suggestion has been made that it may originally have been connected with the exchange of the kiss of peace that preceded the eucharistic prayer rather than with the beginning of the eucharistic prayer as such.[23]

The earliest reference to the second member of the dialogue is found in Cyprian (*De dom. or.* 31). The final part of the dialogue, "Let us give thanks to the Lord/It is worthy and just," has often been ascribed to Jewish origins and cited as an example of the antiquity of the Christian pattern of eucharistic praying. While it may certainly have been used in first-century Jewish practice, it should be noted that (a) what became the standard invitation to say grace in later Judaism was "Let us bless, . . ." a quite different verb from "Let us give thanks";[24] and (b) the response is "no more than an acclamation of approval of the sort common in pagan antiquity as well as in Jewish culture"[25] and is found in a number of early Christian sources, including Hippolytus's *Comm. on Dan.* 2.29; 3.4; and *Didasc.* 6.14.11.

19 Ibid., 23–26.
20 *Didasc.* 2.57. ET from Sebastian Brock and Michael Vasey, eds., *The Liturgical Portions of the Didascalia* (GLS 29; Nottingham: Grove, 1982) 16.
21 See Bernard Botte, "Note historique sur la concélébration dans l'Église ancienne," *La Maison-Dieu* 35 (1953) 10–13; Gregory Dix, *The Shape of the Liturgy* (London: Dacre, 1945) 125–26; Emil J. Lengeling, "Der Bischof als Hauptzelebrant der Messe seiner Ordination," in Patrick Granfield and Josef A. Jungmann, eds., *Kyriakon: Festschrift Johannes Quasten* (Münster: Aschendorf, 1970) 889–91; Vilela, *Condition*, 345–49.
22 Robert Taft, "The Dialogue before the Anaphora in the Byzantine Eucharistic Liturgy (I)," *OrChrP* 52 (1986) 229–324.
23 L. Edward Phillips, "The Kiss of Peace and the Opening Greeting of the Pre-anaphoral Dialogue," *StLit* 23 (1993) 177–86.
24 See Paul F. Bradshaw, *Daily Prayer in the Early Church* (New York: Oxford Univ. Press, 1982) 12–16, 32–33.
25 Robert Taft, "The Dialogue before the Anaphora in the Byzantine Eucharistic Liturgy (III)," *OrChrP* 55 (1989) 63–74, quotation from 69–70.

■ **4–13** The paucity of ante-Nicene parallels for material in the *Apostolic Tradition* is perhaps at its greatest with regard to the eucharistic prayer itself. With the exception of the prayer texts in *Didache* 9 and 10 and some brief invocations over food in early apocryphal literature[26]—all of which are completely different in character from the prayer here—no extant eucharistic prayers can be dated with any certainty before the fourth century. Even texts that are often thought to have roots in this earlier period (the Strasbourg Papyrus and the anaphora of Addai and Mari)[27] manifest a number of significant differences from this text. For example, the Strasbourg Papyrus focuses its praise of God entirely on the theme of creation—which is passed over quickly in one clause here ("through whom you made all things")—and contains substantial intercession, which is completely lacking in this prayer. The anaphora of Addai and Mari consists of a series of discrete prayer units rather than a continuously flowing text. Both the papyrus and the anaphora lack a narrative of institution. Thus, if this prayer does belong to the third century in its present form, it is very advanced for its age, having some features that are otherwise first encountered only in the fourth century or later.

Many scholars have claimed that the prayer bears the marks of the Jewish grace after meals, the *Birkat hamazon*.[28] But even if we prescind from the question as to whether this Jewish prayer existed at this early period in the form in which we know it from later sources,[29] the connection between the two amounts to nothing more than that both offer thanksgiving to God and make petition for something, albeit in very different ways and with very different literary structures. These are simply not close enough similarities to posit a direct link between the two, however much those trying to trace the evolution of eucharistic prayers would like to find one in order to show continuity from the apostolic age to the fourth century.

For early parallels to the material in the eucharistic prayer, therefore, one is forced to resort instead to similarities of phrases and vocabulary in Christian theological writings of the second and third centuries. Resemblances to quite a number of words and phrases have been observed in the writings of Justin Martyr, Irenaeus, and Hippolytus himself.[30] Dix noted some affinity between the prayer and a passage in the Easter homily of Pseudo-Hippolytus (although believing it to be a genuine work of Hippolytus),[31] and later both Raniero Cantalamessa and Otto Perler pointed to an apparent connection between the prayer and the Easter homily of Melito of Sardis.[32] But it is only recently that Mazza has carried out a close comparison of these particular texts. He concludes:

> this anaphora depends *generally* on material contained in the Easter homilies, that is, on particular kinds of terms (for example, Christological titles), idioms, typological expressions, biblical quotations, and so on that are essential characteristics of the literary genre of the Easter homilies. Our anaphora in question depends not on the homilies of Melito or Pseudo-Hippolytus as such but . . . on material that is typical and constitutive of the literary genre of the

---

26 For the *Didache* see Niederwimmer, *Didache*, 139–61; for apocryphal texts, see G. Rouwhorst, "Bénédiction, action de grâces, supplication: Les oraisons de la table dans le Judaïsme et les célébrations eucharistiques des chrétiens syriaques," *QL* 61 (1980) 211–40; Cyrille Vogel, "Anaphores eucharistiques préconstantiniennes: Formes non traditionelles," *Aug* 20 (1980) 401–10.

27 For these prayers see Stephen B. Wilson, "The Anaphora of the Apostles Addai and Mari," and Walter D. Ray, "The Strasbourg Papyrus," in Paul F. Bradshaw, ed., *Essays on Early Eastern Eucharistic Prayers* (Collegeville, Minn.: Liturgical, 1997) 19–37 and 39–56, respectively.

28 See, e.g., Georg Kretschmar, "Early Christian Liturgy in the Light of Contemporary Historical

Research," *StLit* 16.3/4 (1986–87) 41; Mazza, *Origins*, 101.

29 See Bradshaw, *Search*, 24–26; Stefan Reif, *Judaism and Hebrew Prayer: New Perspectives on Jewish Liturgical History* (Cambridge: Cambridge Univ. Press, 1993) 22–87.

30 See, e.g., Richard H. Connolly, "The Eucharistic Prayer of Hippolytus," *JTS* 39 (1938) 350–69.

31 Dix, *Apostolic Tradition*, 74–75.

32 Raniero Cantalamessa, *L'omelia "In S. Pascha" dello Pseudo-Ippolito di Roma* (Milan: Vita e Pensiero, 1967) 61 n. 42; Otto Perler, ed., *Méliton de Sardes. Sur la Pâque* (SC 123; Paris: Cerf, 1966) 201 n. 780.

Easter homilies such as one finds in the homilies of Melito and Pseudo-Hippolytus and in many other texts as well.[33]

However, when the words and phrases in the anaphora of the *Apostolic Tradition,* which Mazza cites as characteristic of the genre of the Easter homilies, are examined more closely, most of them turn out also to have parallels in other types of early Christian literature of the same period.[34] Since it is necessary to show that a word or phrase is otherwise unique to a particular source in order to demonstrate a sure connection, Mazza appears to be claiming too much: the language certainly has close parallels with second-century sources, but not *exclusively* with the Easter homilies.

Mazza also believes that the author of the prayer inserted this "paschal" material into an older, simpler tripartite structure, one like that found in *Didache* 10. This assertion again may be going too far. In order to sustain the claim, he has to resort to the argument that in that transition the first thanksgiving of *Didache* 10 disappeared and was "replaced by the account of salvation in Christ such as it was presented in the literary genre of the Easter homilies."[35] Moreover, the parallel between the supposed second thanksgiving of the *Apostolic Tradition* ("giving thanks to you because you have held us worthy to stand before you and minister to you") and that of *Didache* 10 (praise for creation, the gift of food and drink, and "spiritual food and drink and eternal life through your Child Jesus") is hardly close. Mazza tries to resolve this problem by drawing into the argument the prayer in the *Martyrdom of Polycarp* and the grace from the intertestamental *Book of Jubilees* in an attempt to show that all four texts belong to one family in which the second thanksgiving is always in some way for the gift of the present moment.[36] Similarly, he seeks to establish a link between the final, petitionary sections of the anaphora of the *Apostolic Tradition* and of *Didache* 10 by setting them within what he believes to be an evolving process, beginning from the supplication in *Didache* 10

for God to perfect the church in his love and bring it into his kingdom. This request, he alleges, developed into different but related petitions in certain other liturgical texts. Thus *Const.* 7.26 asks God to "free [the church] from every evil and make it perfect in your love and your truth and unite us, all of us, into your kingdom"; the Egyptian version of the Liturgy of St. Basil asks God to "preserve us . . . in your faith and lead us into your kingdom"; and the *Sacramentary of Sarapion* prays "for the destruction of evil and for the confirmation of the church," and later asks God to give the departed "a place of rest in your kingdom." Mazza claims that the petitionary section of the anaphora of the *Apostolic Tradition* belongs to this family because it shares the phrase "for the confirmation" with *Sarapion,* "of faith" with Egyptian Basil, and "in truth" with *Const.* 7.26.[37]

Even if there are weaknesses in Mazza's line of reasoning, that does not necessarily invalidate his fundamental point that the material in the first part of the anaphora of the *Apostolic Tradition* appears to belong to a quite different world from some of the material in the second part. He would include within this "first part" the narrative of institution itself, even though he does not claim for it the same sort of parallel language to the Easter homilies as he does for the rest.[38] Against this, however, one may note that Ratcliff believed that the narrative in the *Apostolic Tradition* followed awkwardly upon the reference to the harrowing of the underworld and the resurrection and so thought it possible that "the want of smoothness and order at this point indicates that the older tradition has here been remodelled and stabilized in accordance with later fashion."[39] Furthermore, Mazza himself goes on to claim that the theology of the anamnesis section of the prayer, in linking death and resurrection together on the same plane, belongs to a different world of ideas and a later historical period than the so-called preface, in which it is Christ's death that is the salvific act par excellence.[40] Since other scholars generally accept that narrative and anamnesis have always

33 Mazza, *Origins,* 102–29; quotation from p. 103.
34 See further Paul F. Bradshaw, "A Paschal Root to the Anaphora of the *Apostolic Tradition*? A Response to Enrico Mazza," *StPatr* 35 (2001) 257–65, and the notes to specific words and phrases in this commentary.
35 Mazza, *Origins,* 176.
36 Ibid., 153–61.
37 Ibid., 161–66.
38 Ibid., 134–39.
39 Ratcliff, "Sanctus," 32.
40 Mazza, *Origins,* 167–69.

formed a single liturgical unit,[41] it would seem more reasonable to conclude that both the narrative and the anamnesis/oblation section were subsequent additions to the material in the first part of the prayer. These additions were perhaps not made until about the mid-fourth century, when the *Sacramentary of Sarapion* was also apparently experimenting with the novelty of inserting an institution narrative into the eucharistic prayer,[42] while in other regions the older tradition was still being maintained: both Cyril of Jerusalem and Theodore of Mopsuestia, for example, seem to have known eucharistic prayers that lacked such a development.[43]

We may perhaps conjecture, therefore, that the final clause before the institution narrative beginning, "who when he was being handed over to voluntary suffering, . . . ," was originally in the past tense like the relative clauses that precede it. But if the narrative and anamnesis were later additions, what then would originally have followed? We may note that although the anamnesis phrase itself, "remembering therefore his death and resurrection," may not have been part of the earlier text, this is not to say that the oblation clause, "we offer you the bread and the cup," may not already have been present, as Mazza assumes. Although the two elements are usually closely combined in later anaphoras, the Strasbourg Papyrus reveals a tripartite pattern of praise, offering, and petition, which is also remarkably similar to what has been suggested was the earliest form of the eucharistic prayer in the *Sacramentary of Sarapion*.[44] While in both these cases what is offered is more abstract than the bread and cup here, "the reasonable sacrifice and this bloodless service" in the Strasbourg text, "this living sacrifice, the unbloody offering" in *Sarapion*, yet they do offer parallels for a prayer that moves directly from praise through offering to petition.

Moreover, the explicit offering of bread and cup is mentioned as early as the writings of Justin (*Dial.* 41.3).

The original prayer, therefore, would appear to have been created by the combination of a substantial hymn of praise for redemption with perhaps a brief offering/thanksgiving formula and then with a short petition for the communicants and a concluding doxology (for the form of the doxology, see the commentary on chap. 6 below). Everything else was probably added in the course of the fourth century.

■ 6 Yet even some elements from the first half of the prayer may not belong to its earliest stratum. In particular, the textual witnesses imply that the original Greek spoke of Christ being "born from the Holy Spirit and the Virgin." While the use of the same preposition "from" (Latin: *ex*; Greek ἐκ) for both the Holy Spirit and the Virgin Mary is in line with several later creedal formulae, including the Niceno-Constantinopolitan Creed of 381, it does not agree with the versions of the baptismal creed preserved in both the Latin and Sahidic versions, and also in the *Testamentum Domini*, which use different prepositions for each of them (see *Ap. Trad.* 21.15 below), implying that it comes from a different source. But what is more significant is that any reference to the Holy Spirit in connection with Christ's birth rather than just the Virgin alone seems to be unknown in very early Christian writings, and this is still the case in many fourth-century Eastern creeds.[45] The oldest example of the inclusion of the Holy Spirit appears to be a single reference in Irenaeus (*Dem.* 40), and even this is not an exact parallel to the phrase here in the eucharistic prayer, for which we have to wait until the apparent citation of a creedal formula by Origen (*Comm. on the Gospel of John* 32.16; *De principiis* Preface, 4). Because some of the other vocabulary in this part of the prayer is

41 See, e.g., Louis Ligier, "The Origins of the Eucharistic Prayer: From the Last Supper to the Eucharist," *StLit* 9 (1973) 180; Thomas J. Talley, "The Eucharistic Prayer of the Ancient Church According to Recent Research: Results and Reflections," *StLit* 11 (1976) 151.

42 See Johnson, *Sarapion*, 219–26.

43 See E. J. Cutrone, "Cyril's Mystagogical Catecheses and the Evolution of the Jerusalem Anaphora," *OrChrP* 44 (1978) 52–64; Mazza, *Origins*, 302–9. But cf. Edward Yarnold, "Anaphoras without Institution Narrative?" *StPatr* 30 (1997) 395–410, who chal-

lenges the scholarly consensus.

44 Johnson, *Sarapion*, 255–59, 271–76.

45 See J. N. D. Kelly, *Early Christian Creeds* (New York: D. McKay, 1950) 146, 184–93.

characteristic of the early second century, it is possible that this whole phrase may have been added somewhat later.

■ **7** The phrase "stretched out [his] hands when he was suffering" is based on a common primitive Christian interpretation of Isa 65:2 ("I held out my hands all day long to a rebellious people") as a prophecy of the crucifixion.[46] The words that follow, "that he might release from suffering those who believed in you," refer not to immediate suffering in this life (which believers still have to endure) but to eternal torment, and are paralleled in several second-century sources.[47]

■ **8** The roots of the narrative summary of Christ's work of redemption, "that he might destroy death and break the bonds of the devil, and tread down hell and illuminate the righteous, and fix a limit and manifest the resurrection," seem to lie in passages like 2 Tim 1:10, which speaks of Christ having "abolished death and brought life and immortality to light," and *Barn.* 5.6, which apparently alludes to that verse, saying, "he endured, so that he might 'abolish death' and show forth the resurrection from the dead, because it was necessary for him to be 'manifested in the flesh' [1 Tim 3:16]." Irenaeus also records a somewhat similar narrative summary to that in the *Apostolic Tradition*: "Our Lord by his passion destroyed death, and dispersed error, and put an end to corruption, and destroyed ignorance, while he manifested life and revealed truth, and bestowed the gift of incorruption" (*Haer.* 2.20.3). Elsewhere he presents another such summary that has further parallels to that in the eucharistic prayer, speaking not only of Christ abolishing death, but also of his "releasing those bonds in which we had been chained," and adding that he "manifested the resurrection" (*Dem.* 38). The same expression is found in Hippolytus (*Ref.* 10.33), who states that Jesus "did not protest against his passion, but became obedient unto death and manifested his resurrection."

The idea of breaking the bonds of the devil is also similar to Heb 2:14-15, which affirms that Jesus partook of human nature "that through death he might destroy him who has the power of death, that is, the devil, and deliver all those who through fear of death were subject to lifelong bondage." As for treading down hell, Christ's descent into Hades is either stated or implied in several New Testament texts (Matt 12:40; Acts 2:24, 27, 31; Rom 10:7; Eph 4:9), and the idea is taken up by other early Christian writers, who saw his mission there as in order to liberate those, both Jew and Greek, who had lived righteously before his coming. An early allusion to this occurs in Ignatius (*Magn.* 9.2), but the concept is elaborated in Irenaeus (*Haer.* 4.22.1–2) and Clement of Alexandria (*Strom.* 6.6), although it is not until the *Gospel of Nicodemus* (4th century?) that we encounter the word "illuminate" in connection with this episode (5[21].3).

Finally, we should note that Justin Martyr presents a narrative summary that exhibits similarities more broadly with the first half of the prayer, stating that Christ "of old appeared in the shape of fire and in the likeness of an angel to Moses and to the other prophets; but now in the times of your reign, having, as we before said, become Man by a virgin, according to the will of the Father, for the salvation of those who believe in him, he endured both to be set at nought and to suffer, that by dying and rising again he might conquer death" (*1 Apol.* 63).

The meaning of the phrase "fix a limit" (*terminum figat*), however, continues to puzzle scholars. Connolly suggested that the limit was "for the resurrection";[48] Easton translated it as "boundary-post" and understood it to be the cross, "dividing the realms of life and death";[49] Dix thought that the limit was "probably of hell";[50] Botte translated the phrase as "fix the rule (of faith?)," though in a footnote wondered if "the limit of hell" might not be preferable;[51] Bouyer rendered it as

46 E.g., *Barn.* 12.4; Justin *1 Apol.* 35; *Dial.* 97.2. See Bernard Botte, "Extendit manus suas cum pateretur," *QLP* 49 (1968) 307–8; Emil J. Lengeling, "Hippolyt von Rom und die Wendung 'extendit manus suas cum pateretur,'" *QLP* 50 (1969) 141–44.

47 See, e.g., Justin *1 Apol.* 10, 57; *Dial.* 45; Irenaeus *Haer.* 4.24.

48 Connolly, "Eucharistic Prayer," 362.

49 Easton, *Apostolic Tradition*, 73.

50 Dix, *Apostolic Tradition*, 8 n. 8.

51 Botte, *Tradition*, 15 and n. 4. Ron Grove supported "rule of faith" ("Terminum figat: Clarifying the Meaning of a Phrase in the Apostolic Tradition," *OrChrP* 48 [1982] 431–34).

"set the guiding principle";[52] while Metzger preferred "established the rule (of the eucharistic celebration)."[53]

■ **9** The use of the future "will be broken" is unusual in early Christian citations of the words of Jesus. Botte thought that it was due to a misunderstanding of a present participle by the Latin and Ethiopic translators,[54] but it should be noted that the future tense (*confringetur*) also occurs in the narrative of institution in the eucharistic prayer in Ambrose *De sacr.* 4.21.

■ **10** The indicative "you do my remembrance" (Latin *meam commemorationem facitis*) rather than the imperative "do my remembrance" (cf. Luke 22:19 and 1 Cor 11:24-25) has been thought to be the result of a wrong translation of the Greek verb (which can be either indicative or imperative),[55] although again it should be noted that Ambrose *De sacr.* 4.26 has a similar phrase, though in the future tense, *commemorationem mei facietis*.

■ **11** There has been some discussion over the phrase "you have held us worthy to stand before you and minis-

ter to you." On the basis of the readings in the Ethiopic, *Apostolic Constitutions*, and *Testamentum Domini*, both Connolly and Botte judged that the original Greek verb translated in the Latin as "minister" had been $\iota\epsilon\rho\alpha\tau\epsilon\acute{v}\epsilon\iota\nu$, "to exercise the priesthood."[56] Ratcliff, however, believed that not only here but elsewhere in the *Apostolic Tradition* $\lambda\epsilon\iota\tau\sigma\upsilon\rho\gamma\epsilon\hat{\iota}\nu$ was the Greek verb underlying the Latin "ministrare," especially as this verb is found in several passages in the LXX of Deuteronomy combined with "stand before the Lord" in a liturgical context.[57] But Botte later went on to argue that the subject of the verb was the new bishop, who had just received the priesthood through his episcopal ordination.[58] A similar position had also been adopted by Bouyer.[59] Most scholars, however, have understood it to refer instead to the ministry of the whole priestly people of God.[60]

52 Bouyer, *Eucharist*, 169.
53 Marcel Metzger, "Les deux prières eucharistiques des Constitutions Apostoliques," *RevScRel* 45 (1971) 59.
54 Botte, *Tradition*, 15 n. 5. The Ethiopic also has the future in connection with the cup.
55 Ibid., 16 n. 1; Cuming, *Hippolytus*, 11; Easton, *Apostolic Tradition*, 73.
56 Connolly, "Eucharistic Prayer," 363; Botte, *Tradition*, 17 n. 3.
57 Ratcliff, "Sanctus," 126–30. Cf. Deut 10:8; 18:5; 18:7.
58 Bernard Botte, "Adstare coram te et tibi ministrare," *QL* 63 (1982) 223–26.
59 Bouyer, *Eucharist*, 178–79.
60 See, e.g., Mazza, *Origins*, 151 n. 222.

5

[Concerning the Offering of Oil]

Text

As in the case of chap. 4, the Latin and Ethiopic texts constitute the sole principal witnesses, with some slight support from the *Canons of Hippolytus* and *Testamentum Domini*, and also from the prayer for the anointing of the sick in the eleventh- or twelfth-century manuscript from the Monastery of St. Catherine on Mount Sinai.

■ 2 Antoine Chavasse thought that the first occurrence of the word "health" in the Latin text should be excised,[1] but both Dix and Botte suggested that a copyist might have misread *sanitatem* for *sanctitatem*, "holiness," Botte noting that the equivalent word (*qedsatika*) occurs as a variant reading for the verb "sanctify" (*qadisaka*) in some manuscripts of the Ethiopic.[2] Dix also raised the alternative possibility that the Latin translator might have misread the Greek ἁγίασμα as ὑγίασμα.[3] Segelberg, however, defended "health" as original.[4]

The discrepancy between "those using" in the Latin and "those who are anointed" in the Ethiopic is probably the result of confusion between the Greek χρωμένοις and χριομένοις. Botte preferred the Ethiopic reading as original, because it fitted the context better.[5] But while Chavasse judged the absence of "kings" from the Ethiopic as original because the twofold form "priests and prophets" also occurred in the baptismal prayers interpolated into the Ethiopic text, Botte instead favored the Latin here, since he thought it likely that an Ethiopic copyist could have accidentally omitted the word if he were familiar with the shorter form in his own tradition.[6]

at this point in the church order, as it was no doubt understood that these "offerings" would be made within the eucharistic rite. They were probably intended to be included within the eucharistic prayer itself, or at least within a similar thanksgiving format, because, although the bishop is said to give thanks, neither of the texts cited is a thanksgiving as such.[7] The equivalent prayer in the *Sacramentary of Sarapion* is also located among its postanaphoral prayers.

Neither the directive nor the prayer itself seems particularly well written, in contrast to the fluency of the eucharistic prayer, which suggests that the material may have come from a different source. In particular, the directive does not say explicitly who is to say the prayer: commentators assume that the bishop is intended, but the person offering the oil could conceivably have been meant.

The anointing of sick people with oil is attested in Mark 6:13 and Jas 5:14, but the earliest prayer for the blessing of oil other than this one occurs in the *Sacramentary of Sarapion*.[8] Several phrases from the prayer turn up in a number of later liturgical texts for the blessing of oil, both Eastern and Western. Segelberg listed them fully, and concluded that they did not directly derive from the *Apostolic Tradition*, but that they were all part of a common prayer tradition, intended originally for baptismal oil but later adapted for oil for the sick. He judged that this might be true also of the prayer from the Monastery of St. Catherine.[9]

Comment

It was presumably the location of the eucharistic prayer that led to both this chapter and chap. 6 being inserted

1   Antoine Chavasse, *Étude sur l'onction des infirmes dans l'Église latine du IIIe au XIe siècle* (Lyon: Librairie du sacré-coeur, 1942) 31–39.
2   Botte, *Tradition*, 18 n. 2.
3   Dix, *Apostolic Tradition*, 10.
4   Segelberg, "Benedictio Olei," 270.
5   Botte, *Tradition*, 18 n. 3.
6   Ibid., 19 n. 4.
7   See Emmanuel Lanne, "La bénédiction de l'huile," in Achille M. Triacca and Alessandro Pistoia, eds., *Les bénédictions et les Sacramentaux dans la liturgie* (Rome: C.L.V.-Edizioni Liturgiche, 1988) 165–68.
8   See Johnson, *Sarapion*, 52–53, 121–23.
9   Segelberg, "Benedictio Olei," 268–80.

5

Latin (71.1–9)	Sahidic	Arabic	Ethiopic

[Title]

Concerning the offering of oil

1 If anyone offers oil, let him render thanks according to the offering of bread and wine—and let him say [it] not word for word but to similar effect—saying:

He will offer oil like the offering of bread and wine just as he gives thanks in this order. If he does not speak with those words, he will give thanks in that power of his and then saying with another word:

2 "As, sanctifying this oil, you give, God, health to those using and receiving [it], whence you have anointed kings, priests, and prophets, so also may it afford strengthening to all tasting [it] and health to all using it."

"As you give this oil, having sanctified [it], to those who are anointed and [par]take—that with which you have anointed priests and prophets—so strengthen these and everyone who tastes and sanctify the ones who take it."

Apostolic Constitutions	*Canons of Hippolytus*	*Testamentum Domini* 1.24
	If there is any oil, he prays over it in this manner, though not the same expressions, but the same meaning.	If the priest consecrates oil for the healing of those who suffer, let him say thus, quietly, placing the vessel before the altar: "O Lord God. . . ."

Manuscript from the Monastery of St. Catherine on Mount Sinai:
"Send, Lord, the richness of your mercy upon this fruit of the oil, through which you anointed priests, prophets, kings, and also martyrs, and clothed in kindness with the garment of your righteousness, in order that for everyone coming for anointing it may be for advantage and benefit of soul and body [and] spirit, for averting of every evil, for health to the one anointed through our Lord Jesus."

6

Latin (71.10–19)	Sahidic	Arabic	Ethiopic

[Title]

1 Likewise, if anyone should offer cheese and olives, let him say thus:

2 "Sanctify this milk that has been coagulated, coagulating us also to our love.

3 Make also this fruit of the olive not depart from your sweetness, which is a symbol of your richness that you have poured from the tree for life for those who hope in you."

4 But in every blessing let there be said: "To you [be] glory, Father and Son with the Holy Spirit, in the holy church, both now and always and to the ages of ages."

Text

Although this chapter is found only in the Latin, the support given by both the *Canons of Hippolytus* and *Testamentum Domini* to different parts of it points to its authenticity. While its absence from the Sahidic and Arabic is in line with their normal practice of omitting prayer texts, the omission of such material from the Ethiopic is very unusual. In its place the Ethiopic text has five communion prayers that are clearly not an authentic part of the church order and have therefore not been reproduced in our translation.[1]

■ 4 It is noteworthy that the doxology, which is here said should end every "blessing" (a word that otherwise occurs in the *Apostolic Tradition* only in 23.4 and 28.6 = 29D.3, and the verb "bless" only in 32.1), is not found at the conclusion of every prayer in the church order. Apart from minor variations in the other cases (*Ap. Trad.* 3.6; 4.13; 7.5; 8.12; 21.21; 29C.9), at least some of

which could be attributed to translators or copyists, the Latin version of the offering of firstfruits in chap. 31 (largely supported by a surviving Greek fragment) ends simply: "through your Child Jesus Christ our Lord, through whom to you [be] glory to the ages of ages." Emmanuel Lanne tried to argue that because *Ap. Trad.* 23.4 distinguishes between a "blessing" and a "eucharist," the author intended the rule to apply only to formulae that were inserted into eucharistic prayers.[2] Josef Jungmann thought that "we would have here already the custom still in use today in the Roman liturgy whereby, depending on the solemnity of the rite, a longer or shorter conclusion is employed."[3] After a detailed comparison of all the doxological forms in the *Apostolic Tradition* (except, for some reason, that in 29C.9), Hanssens concluded that there had originally been just two forms, a longer and a shorter: the former, found in five instances, began with "through your Child Jesus Christ . . ."; the latter, found only in 21.21, did not;

---

1 Text in Duensing, *Aethiopische Text*, 25–31; ET in Dix, *Apostolic Tradition*, 11–12; see also ibid., 80.

2 Emmanuel Lanne, "La bénédiction de l'huile," in Achille M. Triacca and Alessandro Pistoia, eds., *Les bénédictions et les Sacramentaux dans la liturgie* (Ephemeredes Liturgicae, Subsidia 44; Rome: C.L.V.-Edizioni Liturgiche, 1988) 168–69.

3 Josef A. Jungmann, *The Place of Christ in Liturgical Prayer*, trans. A. Peeler (2d ed.; Staten Island: Alba, 1965) 8 n. 1.

Apostolic Constitutions	Canons of Hippolytus	Testamentum Domini
	If there are any firstfruits, anything edible, that someone has brought, he prays over it, and blesses the fruit that is brought to him, in his prayer. In each prayer that is said over each thing, there is said at the end of the prayer, "Glory to you, Father, Son, and Holy Spirit, to the ages of ages. Amen."	. . . Send on this oil, which is the type of your fatness, the delivering [power] of your good compassion, that it may deliver those who labor and heal those who are sick, and sanctify those who return, when they draw near to your faith; for you are mighty and [to be] praised forever and ever. The people: "Amen." . . .

but he believed both forms included "with the Holy Spirit," and thus treated it as having accidentally fallen out of the Latin and Greek of chap. 31.[4]

A more likely explanation than any of these, however, is that we are dealing with material deriving from different sources that has not been fully harmonized by an editorial hand. Attempts at such harmonization in other prayer endings in the church order have been clumsily done, probably by translators or copyists. Thus, as Botte has noted, the inclusion of "Father and Son" in several of them renders the doxology incoherent because in these cases it is preceded by a "through whom" referring to Christ.[5] But to this may be added the consideration that even the presence of the formula "Father *and* Son" here in chap. 6 would be quite unusual for a third-century text: the normal form was "to the Father *through* the Son," and it was only in the early fourth century, in reaction to Arianism, that formulae like this, which emphasized the divinity of Christ, began to be adopted.[6] This

suggests that this doxology too has been emended by a later hand.

Comment

■ **1** As in *Ap. Trad.* 5.1, the subject of the offering is imprecise.

■ **2–3** Segelberg has drawn attention to a number of later liturgical texts of both Eastern and Western provenance that include phrases reminiscent of the offering of olives here, usually in a prayer that is also related to the offering of oil in chap. 5.[7] Its combination with cheese is unparalleled, however, and as Cuming has pointed out, "the blessing consists of two unconnected sentences, either of which could stand on its own; and it may well be that they were really meant to be two separate blessings."[8] It is possible that one was added to the other by a later hand. Andrew McGowan has discussed the possible connection of the cheese prayer with a sect

4   Hanssens, *Liturgie*, 343–53.
5   *Ap. Trad.* 3.6: in the Latin and Ethiopic, but not in the *Epitome*; 4.13: in the Latin but not the Ethiopic; 7.5: in both the Latin and Ethiopic. See Botte, *Tradition*, 11 n. 3, 19 n. 7. But cf. Josef A. Jungmann, "Die Doxologien in der Kirchenordnung Hippolyts," *ZKTh* 86 (1964) 321–26.
6   See Jungmann, *Place of Christ*, chaps. 10 and 11.
7   Segelberg, "Benedictio Olei," 277–79.
8   Cuming, "The Eucharist," in Cuming, *Essays*, 51.

known as "Artotyritai" ("Bread-and-cheese-eaters"), and suggested that the understanding of cheese here as "coagulated milk" may point to a link more widely with ritual meals in some Christian groups that involved bread and milk.[9]

■ **3** Dix suggested that the "tree" here was intended to be the cross rather than the olive tree, but he also noted that in the apocryphal *Life of Adam and Eve* the "oil of mercy" is spoken of as flowing from the tree of life in paradise, with which Adam desires to anoint himself to give relief from his suffering.[10] The same narrative also appears in the *Gospel of Nicodemus* 3(19), where it is said that Christ will anoint with the oil of mercy all who believe in him.

■ **4** The strange phrase "with the Holy Spirit in the holy church" (perhaps related to Eph 3:21) occurs in doxologies five times in the *Apostolic Tradition*: 3.6 (Ethiopic only); 4.13 (Latin and Ethiopic); 6.4 (Latin only); 7.5 (Latin and Ethiopic); and 21.21 (Latin, Bohairic, Arabic,

and Ethiopic). Hanssens regarded it as a later interpolation,[11] but that does not answer the questions why anyone should want to add it, and who might have done so. The only close parallel to it in Greek patristic literature is in *Contra Noetum*, a work that has been attributed to Hippolytus, "To him be glory and power with the Father and the Holy Spirit in the holy church both now and always and to the ages of ages" (18.10). Some, however, would question the attribution of that work, and it should also be noted that doxologies in other works ascribed to Hippolytus are much simpler in form and show no sign of this phrase.[12] There is also a Latin phrase in a text attributed to Cyprian that connects "Holy Spirit" with "holy church" in a doxology, but the parallel is not nearly as close as in *Contra Noetum* 18.10; and some manuscripts of the Latin version of the *Acta Antiochena* of Ignatius of Antioch include the phrase in a doxology, although it does not occur in the Greek or Syriac versions.[13]

9 Andrew McGowan, *Ascetic Eucharists: Food and Drink in Early Christian Ritual Meals* (Oxford Early Christian Studies; Oxford: Clarendon, 1999) 95–107.

10 Dix, *Apostolic Tradition*, 11; *Adam and Eve* 36.2; 40.1–41.3, paralleled in *Apoc. Mos.* 9.3; 13.1–2. See Robert Henry Charles, *Apocrypha and Pseudepigrapha of the Old Testament* (2 vols.; Oxford: Clarendon, 1913) 2:143–44.

11 Hanssens, *Liturgie,* 368–70.

12 See Josef Frickel, "Hippolyts Schrift *Contra Noetum*: Ein Pseudo-Hippolyt," in Hanns Christof Brennecke, Ernst Ludwig Grasmück, and Christoph.

Markschies, eds., *Logos: Festschrift für Luise Abramowski* (BZNW 68; Berlin: de Gruyter, 1993) 87–123; Christoph Markschies, "Neue Forschungen zur sogenannten *Traditio Apostolica*," in Robert F. Taft and Gabriele Winkler, eds., *Comparative Liturgy Fifty Years after Anton Baumstark (1872–1948)* (OrChrA 265; Rome: Edizioni Orientalia Christiana, 2001) 583–98.

13 See Hanssens, *Liturgie,* 368–70.

Concerning Presbyters

Text

■ **1** The *Apostolic Tradition* here appears to require the same prayer to be used for a presbyter as for a bishop, but then quite contrarily goes on to provide the text of a different one. In 1915 Cuthbert H. Turner advanced the suggestion that what had really been intended was that the first part of the prayer for a bishop should also be used for a presbyter, but that when the petitions specific to the episcopate were reached, the prayer for a presbyter should be substituted.[1] This resolution of the problem was subsequently adopted by Frere, Dix, Hanssens, Segelberg, and Douglas Powell.[2] On the other hand, it was rejected by Botte,[3] Ratcliff,[4] and Walls, who pointed out that Turner's suggestion, "though apparently simple, involves no small subtlety of thought in the users of Hippolytus's manual";[5] but none of them offered an alternative solution to the apparent contradiction.[6]

Vernon Bartlet, however, responded to Turner by putting forward the suggestion that the original text had really intended the same prayer to be used for a presbyter as for a bishop, and that a different prayer had then been added by a later hand unable to accept that arrangement.[7] He was ignored once the whole text was judged to be the work of Hippolytus.[8]

More recently an alternative solution has been put forward by August Jilek, that it was confusion between the Greek verbs ἐκλέγειν, "to choose," and λέγειν, "to say," that led to the prayer rather than the election being described as "according to those things that have been said above."[9] It would, however, be odd for the directives to begin with the laying on of hands and then move to the election, rather than the other way around, and the alleged confusion would necessarily have occurred very early, since all the witnesses seem to have inherited the same misunderstanding.

Although Jilek's precise solution appears wide of the mark, the textual confusion here may well be an indication that some attempt has been made to correct an older reading. We have suggested earlier that the original form of the rite for the episcopate in chap. 2 may have directed that the presbyters rather than the bishops of neighboring churches should perform the imposition of hands on the candidate. If this were so, then it is possible that the words "and let him say" were originally absent from the directions here. Thus what was being enjoined was that the imposition of hands on a candidate for the presbyterate should follow the same pattern as for a candidate for the episcopate—all the presbyters touching him. When the practice of presbyters laying hands on a candidate for the episcopate ceased, the interpretation of this instruction would have become problematic. Hence it may then have been understood as referring in some way to the prayer, and this reference was eventually clarified by the insertion of "and let him say" into the Latin text and by recasting the entire end of the sentence in the oriental versions.

The author of the *Canons of Hippolytus* was apparently somewhat perplexed by the enigmatic nature of the direction, since he interpreted it to mean that everything in the rite for the episcopate was also to be done in the case of a presbyter, including the same prayer, except that the term "presbyter" be used instead of "bishop," and consequently he simply omitted the entire text of the presbyteral prayer.

■ **2** In accordance with their usual practice with regard to major prayer texts in the *Apostolic Tradition*, both the Sahidic and Arabic omit the text of the prayer itself, although it is interesting to note that the opening words, "God and Father of our Lord and our King Jesus Christ,

1   Cuthbert H. Turner, "The Ordination of a Presbyter in the Church Order of Hippolytus," *JTS* 16 (1915) 542–47.

2   Frere, "Early Forms," 283–84; Dix, *Apostolic Tradition*, 80–81; Hanssens, *Liturgie,* 121–22; Segelberg, "Ordination Prayers," 402; Douglas Powell, "Ordo Presbyterii," *JTS* 26 (1975) 310.

3   Botte, *Tradition*, 21 n. 1.

4   In a review of Botte's edition of the text in *JTS* 15 (1964) 406.

5   Walls, "Latin Version," 159.

6   For a discussion of their theories, see Bruno Klein-

heyer, *Die Priesterweihe im römischen Ritus: Eine liturgiehistorische Studie* (Trierer theologische Studien 12; Trier: Paulinus, 1962) 18–25.

7   Bartlet, "Ordination Prayers."

8   See Richard H. Connolly, "The Ordination Prayers of Hippolytus," *JTS* 18 (1917) 55–60.

9   August Jilek, *Initiationsfeier und Amt: Ein Beitrag zur Struktur und Theologie der Ämter und des Taufgottesdienstes in der frühen Kirche (Traditio Apostolica, Tertullian, Cyprian)* (EHS 23/30; Frankfurt: Lang, 1979) 40 n. 4.

7

Latin (71.20—72.5)	Sahidic	Arabic	Ethiopic
[Title]	*32 Concerning the presbyters* (πρεσβύτερος)	*22 Concerning the ordination of presbyters*	*22 Concerning the ordination of presbyters*

1 And when a presbyter is ordained, let the bishop lay [his] hand on his head, the presbyters also touching [him], and let him say according to those things that have been said above, as we have said above about the bishop, praying and saying:

And (δέ) when the bishop (ἐπίσκοπος) will ordain (χειροτονεῖν) the presbyter (πρεσβύτερος), he shall lay his hands on his head, all the presbyters (πρεσβύτερος) touching him. And let him pray according to (κατά) the pattern that we said concerning the bishop (ἐπίσκοπος).

If the bishop wishes to ordain a presbyter, he puts his hand on his head with all the presbyters touching him and prays over him in the same way as we have prescribed for the bishop.

If the bishop wishes to ordain a presbyter, he is to place his hands on his head. All the presbyters are to touch him, and he is to pray over him in the form that we have mentioned. He is to pray, saying:

2 "God and Father of our Lord Jesus Christ, look upon this your servant and impart the spirit of grace and of counsel of the presbyterate that he may help and govern your people with a pure heart,

3 just as you looked upon the people of your choice and commanded Moses that he should choose presbyters whom you filled with your Spirit that you gave to your servant.

4 And now, Lord, grant to be preserved unfailingly in us the spirit of your grace and make [us] worthy that believing in you we may minister in simplicity of heart, praising you

5 through your child, Christ Jesus, through whom to you [be] glory and power, Father and Son with the Holy Spirit, in the holy church, both now and to the ages of ages. Amen."

"My God, the Father of our Lord and our Savior Jesus Christ, look upon this your servant and apportion to him the spirit of grace and the wisdom of the presbyterate so that he may be able to guide your people with a pure heart, as you looked at the elect people and commanded Moses to choose presbyters whom you filled with the Spirit that you bestowed on your servant and minister Moses. And now, my Lord, give to this your servant that which does not perish, preserving for us the spirit of your grace; and give us a share as you have filled us in the heart with worship in gentleness, as we glorify you through your Son, Jesus Christ, in whom you have glory and power, to the Father and the Son and the Holy Spirit in your holy church both now and always and forever and ever. Amen." And all the people are to say, "Amen and amen, and it is proper for him."

Apostolic Constitutions 8.16.2–5

When ordaining a presbyter, O bishop, place the hand on his head, the presbyterate and deacons standing by you, and praying, say: ". . . And now look upon this your servant given into the presbyterate by the vote and judgment of the whole clergy, and fill him with spirit of grace and counsel to help and to assist in governing your people with a pure heart, just as you looked upon your chosen people and commanded Moses to appoint presbyters, whom you filled with Spirit. . . .

Canons of Hippolytus 4

When a presbyter is ordained, one is to do for him everything that one does for the bishop, except the sitting on the seat. One is to pray over him all the prayer of the bishop, except only the name of the bishop. The presbyter is equal to the bishop in everything except the seat and ordination, because to him is not given the power to ordain.

Testamentum Domini 1.30

Then let the appointment of the presbyter be thus: . . . the bishop laying his hand on his head, the presbyters touching him and holding him, let the bishop begin, and say thus: "O God, Father of our Lord Jesus Christ, . . . look upon this your servant, and make [him] a partaker and grant him the Spirit of grace and of reason and of strength, [the] Spirit of the presbyterate that does not grow old . . . that he may help and govern your people by labor, by fear, by a pure heart . . . in like manner as when you looked upon your chosen people, you commanded Moses to ask for the elders, and filling [them] with your Spirit you bestowed on your minister;

And now, Lord, preserve unceasingly the Spirit of your grace watching in us, so that, having been filled with works of healing and the word of teaching, he may teach your people in humility and serve you sincerely with a pure mind and a willing soul, and may fulfill without blemish the holy services of your people; through your Christ, through whom [be] to you glory, honor, and worship in Holy Spirit unto the ages. Amen."

so now, O Lord, bestow on [this man] abundantly your Spirit, which you gave to those who were made disciples by you, and to all those who through them truly believed in you. And make him worthy, being filled with your wisdom and your hidden mysteries, to shepherd your people in holiness of heart; pure and true; praising, blessing, lauding . . . bearing always the cross of your only begotten Son, our Lord Jesus Christ, through whom [be] praise and might to you with the Holy Spirit, to all ages of ages." Let the people say: "Amen.". . .

look upon your servant," do occur in some Arabic manuscripts,[10] suggesting that the translator or scribe had access to something other than just the Sahidic text with the prayers already excised.

■ **4** This petition is somewhat strange, in asking for "the spirit of your grace" to be preserved not in the ordinand but "in *us*, and make *us* worthy." While some have seen this as expressing the commonality of the Spirit shared by bishop and the whole presbyterate,[11] Segelberg argued that the change to the first-person plural here was an indication that this section of the prayer was not part of the original, although he allowed that it might already have been incorporated in the text by Hippolytus's time.[12] Both the *Apostolic Constitutions* and *Testamentum Domini* convert the prayer to differing extents into a petition for the ordinand. On this basis Dix was of the opinion that a similar clause referring to a preaching/teaching ministry had formerly stood in the *Apostolic Tradition* and had subsequently fallen out of the Latin text.[13] It seems more likely, however, that the later versions have tried to improve on what they found before them.

The disagreement between the Latin and the rest in the participle that follows the above clause ("believing," versus "filling" or "filled") is probably the result of the Latin translator misreading the Greek participle $\pi\lambda\eta\sigma\vartheta\acute{\epsilon}\nu\tau\epsilon\varsigma$ as $\pi\epsilon\iota\sigma\vartheta\acute{\epsilon}\nu\tau\epsilon\varsigma$, as Botte has suggested.[14] For the form of the concluding doxology, see the commentary on 6.4 above.

Comment

■ **1** The direction that the presbyters as well as the bishop are to lay their hands on the ordinand is almost unparalleled in ancient ordination rites. It is not part of the original Roman tradition as otherwise known to us, and with the exception of the *Testamentum Domini* and the Gallican *Statuta Ecclesiae Antiqua*, which are dependent on the *Apostolic Tradition* at this point, only the much later Armenian rite makes provision for something similar to this action.[15] Does the *Apostolic Tradition*, therefore, in this regard represent a very old tradition that antedates the emergence of a separate episcopal order, the development of which must inevitably have raised questions about the tradition, and led to the need to include in chap. 8 the explanation that the presbyters' touching did not mean that they were doing what the bishop did? And was it the possibility of misinterpretation that caused the practice subsequently to disappear from virtually all other ecclesiastical traditions? Or is it merely an invention of the compiler?

■ **2–5** Several scholars have claimed to see a strongly Jewish background to the prayer. Thus Easton considered it "conceivable that Hippolytus' formula reproduces the substance of a Jewish ordination prayer."[16] Dix was also of the opinion that its substance might go back to the earliest Jewish-Christian synagogues governed by a college of presbyters, or even to pre-Christian Jewish practice,[17] and a similar view was put forward by Albano Vilela.[18] Pierre-Marie Gy, however, was more cautious, admitting that "one could suspect some rabbinic background, especially in connection with the typology of the seventy elders and Moses." He added the warning that "for the ordination of rabbis, as for the berakah, one should not give excessive value to rather late texts."[19] This caution seems wise in the light of Lawrence Hoffman's conclusions that the term "rabbi" did not come into use until after the destruction of the Jerusalem temple in 70 CE. He also argues that although

10 Those of the Clementine Octateuch rather than the Alexandrine Sinodos; see Jean and Augustin Périer, *Les "127 Canons des Apôtres"* (PO 8/4; Paris: Firmin-Didot, 1912) 556.

11 See, e.g., Roger Béraudy, "Le sacrement de l'Ordre d'après la *Tradition apostolique* d'Hippolyte," *BCE* 38–39 (1962) 350; Lécuyer, "Episcopat," 44.

12 Segelberg, "Ordination Prayers," 403–4.

13 Dix, *Apostolic Tradition*, 14 n. 4: "The quasi-agreement of the versions suggests that something has been altered in L., but it seems hopeless to restore it." See also Dix, "Ministry," 218 n. 1.

14 Botte, *Tradition*, 23 n. 2.

15 See Bradshaw, *Ordination*, 59–60.

16 Easton, *Apostolic Tradition*, 77.

17 Dix, "Ministry," 218.

18 Vilela, *Condition*, 354.

19 Pierre-Marie Gy, "Ancient Ordination Prayers," *StLit* 13 (1979) 82. See also Georg Kretschmar, "Die Ordination im frühen Christentum," *FZPhTh* 22 (1975) 46–55.

individual rabbis subsequently did appoint disciples, if ever there was any liturgical ceremony associated with this act, we do not know anything about it.[20]

The prayer, however, certainly has a more ancient feel to it than the prayer for the bishop, especially as the text has only the briefest reference to Christ at the beginning and a total absence of any clear New Testament allusions. It shares some features in common with the prayer for a presbyter in the fourth-century *Sacramentary of Sarapion* (which also may be older than the prayers for a bishop and a deacon in that collection), specifically, the references to Moses appointing seventy elders (which also turns up in a Melkite ordination prayer) and the presbyter's role in governing. Otherwise, the prayer has no close parallels with other ancient ordination prayers.[21]

As was the case in the prayer for the episcopate, the office to which the candidate is being admitted is defined by use of Old Testament typology, this time that of the seventy elders appointed by Moses to govern the people (Num 11:16–17). Some scholars have seen this allusion as intended to express the subordinate nature of the presbyterate, deriving from and participating in the ministry of the episcopate, just as the elders received the Spirit that had originally been given to Moses.[22] As David Power has argued,[23] however, the parallel between Moses and the bishop is nowhere made explicit, and

there is no good reason to believe that it is implied. The parallel is between the elders and the Christian presbyterate, and the "counsel" and "help" that the presbyter is said to give appear to be directed toward the people and not the bishop, who is not mentioned at all in the prayer. What is certain is that the prayer viewed the presbyterate as a corporate body that existed primarily for the government of the Christian community and not as a priesthood or simply for the exercise of specific liturgical functions (for a somewhat different picture of the presbyterate, see chap. 8). Brent has argued that because this vision of the ordained ministry's role differs from the more sacerdotal picture of the episcopate in chap. 3, both prayers cannot have been "part of an original single rite of the Roman community."[24] Stewart-Sykes has taken Brent's line of argument further still and claimed, improbably, that chap. 3 is the older of the two and chap. 7 a third-century interpolation, but from within the same school as that in which chap. 3 arose.[25]

Whatever its origin, however, since there are signs that the earliest form of the instructions about the appointment of the bishop (chap. 1) and of the deacon (chap. 8) did not include any prayer texts, it is likely that this prayer too is a subsequent addition to the core document, even though the prayer itself may be very old.

20 Lawrence Hoffman, "Jewish Ordination on the Eve of Christianity," *StLit* 13 (1979) 11–41.
21 Bradshaw, *Ordination*, 63–64, 67; Johnson, *Sarapion*, 150–53.
22 See, e.g., Bernard Botte, "Holy Orders in the Ordination Prayers," in *The Sacrament of Holy Orders* (Collegeville, Minn.: Liturgical, 1962) 7; Lécuyer, "Episcopat," 42–43.
23 David N. Power, *Ministers of Christ and His Church* (London: Chapman, 1969) 33–36; see also Vilela, *Condition*, 355.
24 Brent, *Hippolytus*, 305; see also 465–91.
25 Stewart-Sykes, "Integrity."

Concerning Deacons

Latin (72.6-35)	Sahidic	Arabic	Ethiopic
[Title]	**33 Concerning the deacons** (διάκονος)	**23 Concerning the ordination of deacons**	**23 Concerning the ordination of deacons**

1 — **Latin:** And when a deacon is ordained, let him be chosen according to those things that have been said above, the bishop alone likewise laying on hands as we have prescribed. In the ordination of a deacon, let the bishop alone lay on hands,

Sahidic: And (δέ) when the bishop (ἐπίσκοπος) will appoint (καθίσταναι) a deacon (διάκονος), who has been chosen according to (κατά) what we said before, the bishop (ἐπίσκοπος) shall lay his hands on him. Why, then, have we said that the bishop (ἐπίσκοπος) alone is the one who will set his hands over the deacon (διάκονος)?

Arabic: If the bishop wishes to establish a deacon, he is chosen as we have said before, and the bishop puts his hand on him alone. Why have we said that the bishop alone is the one who puts his hand on him?

Ethiopic: And if the bishop wishes to ordain a deacon, he is to choose [a person] as we said before. The bishop alone is to place his hands on him. Why did we say that the bishop alone should place a hand on him?

2 — **Latin:** because he is not ordained to the priesthood but to the service of the bishop, that he may do those things that are ordered by him.

Sahidic: This is the reason (αἰτία): he is not ordained (χειροτονεῖν) to a priesthood, but (ἀλλά) to a service (ὑπηρεσία) of the bishop (ἐπίσκοπος), to do those things he will command him.

Arabic: The reason for this action is that he is not being raised to the priesthood, but is rather one of the bishop's helpers [called] to carry out the orders he gives him.

Ethiopic: [It is] because of the sign in this act that he was not ordained to the priesthood but to the service of the bishop so that he should perform the commands that he was given by him;

3 — **Latin:** For he is not a participant in the counsel of the clergy, but taking care of and indicating to the bishop what is necessary,

Sahidic: Neither (οὐδέ) is he appointed (καθίσταναι) to be adviser (σύμβουλος) of all the clergy (κλῆρος), but (ἀλλά) to take care of those who are sick and inform the bishop (ἐπίσκοπος) of them

Arabic: Nor is he established to teach the clergy, but rather to care for what is necessary as the bishop instructs him.

Ethiopic: and he was not ordained to be a teacher of all those ordained but to be one who thinks about what is proper and is to tell the bishop.

4 — **Latin:** not receiving the common spirit of the presbyterate, that in which the presbyters are participants, but that which is entrusted to him under the power of the bishop.

Sahidic: Nor (οὐδέ) is he appointed (καθίσταναι) to receive the spirit (πνεῦμα) of seniority, which the presbyters (πρεσβύτερος) share (μετέχειν), but (ἀλλά) to be worthy (ἄξιος) that the bishop (ἐπίσκοπος) entrust (πιστεύειν) to him those things that are proper.

Arabic: And he is not established to receive the spirit of power in which the presbyters have a share, but rather to take care to be worthy that the bishop should entrust to him and give him charge over what is necessary,

Ethiopic: And he was not ordained to acquire this great spirit that the presbyters share but to be eager for that which is proper so that the bishop may trust him and he may help him understand what is proper.

5 — **Latin:** Wherefore, let the bishop alone make a deacon,

Sahidic: Because of this, the bishop (ἐπίσκοπος) alone is the one who will ordain (χειροτονεῖν) the deacon (διάκονος).

Arabic: for it is only the bishop who puts his hand on him.

Ethiopic: For the bishop alone is the one who places a hand on him.

6 — **Latin:** but on a presbyter let the presbyters also lay on hands on account of the common and like spirit of the clergy.

Sahidic: But (δέ) as for the presbyter (πρεσβύτερος), the bishop (ἐπίσκοπος) shall share (μετέχειν) with him, and they will lay hand on him because the same spirit (πνεῦμα) comes down on him.

Arabic: As for the presbyters, the bishop and all the presbyters share in laying hands on them, for it is the one spirit who descends on them.

Ethiopic: And as for the presbyters, because the bishop and all the presbyters share with him, they are to place their hands on him, for it is one spirit that descends on him.

7 — **Latin:** For the presbyter has the power of this alone, that

Sahidic: For (γάρ) the presbyter (πρεσβύτερος) himself only

Arabic: The presbyter only receives, and so the clergy

Ethiopic: And the presbyter alone is the one who acquires [it].

Apostolic Constitutions 8.17

Concerning the ordination of a deacon, I, Philip, command: Ordain a deacon, O bishop, by laying hands on him, with the whole presbyterate and the deacons standing before you, and pray, saying. . . .

Canons of Hippolytus 5

When a deacon is ordained, one is to do for him according to the same rules, and one is to say this prayer over him. He is not appointed for the presbyterate but for the diaconate, as a servant of God. He serves the bishop and the presbyters in everything, not only at the time of the liturgy; but he serves also the sick of the people, those who have nobody; and he informs the bishop so that he may pray over them or give to them what they need, or also to people whose poverty is not apparent but who are in need. They are to serve also those who have the alms of the bishops, and they are able to give to widows, to orphans, and to the poor. He is to perform all the services. So this in truth is the deacon of whom Christ has said, "He who serves me, my Father will honor him."

Testamentum Domini 1.33

The deacon is appointed, chosen like the things that have before been spoken of. . . .
[34] But let him accomplish in the church those things that are right. Let [his] ministry be thus. First, let him do only those things that are commanded by the bishop as for proclamation; and let him be the counselor of the whole clergy, and the mystery of the church; who ministers to the sick, who ministers to the strangers, who helps the widows, who is the father of the orphans, who goes about all the houses of those that are in need. . . . For the help of those who are in need let him notify the church; let him not trouble the bishop. . . .

[38] Let the appointment of a deacon be thus. Let the bishop alone lay a hand on him, because he is not appointed to the priesthood, but for the service of attendance on the bishop and the church.

Latin	Sahidic	Arabic	Ethiopic
he may receive, but he does not have power to give.	receives. He has no authority (ἐξουσία) to bestow orders (κλῆρος). Because of this he will not appoint (καθίσταναι) the clergy (κληρικός), since he merely seals (σφραγίζειν) the presbyters (πρεσβύτερος) whom the bishop (ἐπίσκοπος) will ordain (χειροτονεῖν).	do not have power.	And those who are ordained do not have the authority. And for this reason the reader and the subdeacon are not ordained by an elder alone but the bishop alone is to ordain and he is not to place a hand on him.

8 For this reason he does not ordain the clergy, but at the ordination of a presbyter he seals while the bishop ordains.

And for this reason the clergy ordain only the presbyter and the bishop ordains him [with them].

9 And over a deacon let him say thus:

10 "God, who created all things and ordered [them] by [your] word, Father of our Lord Jesus Christ, whom you sent to serve your will and manifest to us your desire,

11 give the Holy Spirit of grace and caring and diligence to this your servant, whom you have chosen to serve for your church and to offer. . . ."

12

The prayer of the ordination of a deacon:
"O God, you who have created everything and have beautified [it] by your word, the Father of our Lord Jesus Christ whom you sent to serve by your will and to reveal to us your plan, give the spirit of your grace and diligence upon this your servant whom you have chosen to be a deacon in your church and to offer in your Holy of Holies that which is offered to you by your ordained high priest to the glory of your name so that he may acquire, having served without blame in a pure way of life, the great levels of ordination and your honor and may glorify you through your Son Jesus Christ our Lord, in whom you have glory and power and praise with the Holy Spirit, now and always and forever. Amen."

Apostolic Constitutions	Canons of Hippolytus	Testamentum Domini
	The bishop lays his hand on the deacon and prays over him, saying: "O God, Father of our Lord Jesus Christ, we beseech you, pour out your Holy Spirit on N.; count him among those who serve you according to your will like Stephen and his companions; fill him with power and wisdom like Stephen; make him triumph over all the powers of the devil by the sign of your cross with which you sign him; make his life without sin before all men and an example for many, so that he may save a multitude in the holy church without shame, and accept all his service; through our Lord Jesus Christ, through whom be glory to you, with him and the Holy Spirit, to the ages of ages. Amen."	Over the deacon then, let the bishop say thus: "O God, you who created all things, and who adorned [them] by the Word . . . Father of our Lord Jesus Christ, whom you sent to minister to your will, that all the human race might be saved, and you made known to us and revealed your Thought, your Wisdom . . . give the spirit of grace and earnestness to this your servant. . . . Enlighten, Lord, the one you have loved and chosen to minister to your church, offering in holiness to your sanctuary those things offered to you from the inheritance of your high priesthood, so that ministering without blame and purely and in a holy fashion and with a pure conscience, he may be counted worthy of this high and exalted office, by your good will, praising you continually through your only begotten Son Jesus Christ our Lord, by whom [be] praise and might to you forever and ever." The people: "Amen."

Text

Compared with the directions about ordination to the presbyterate, those for the diaconate are very lengthy and exhibit a somewhat confused air. They are rather defensive in tone, as though stemming from a situation of controversy over the role of the deacon and over the bishop alone laying his hand on the candidate. Most scholars have accepted without question the whole chapter as the authentic work of Hippolytus, but as these directions appear badly written and repetitious, they may well be the product of several different hands rather than a single author. Frere thought that the earliest form probably "contained no more than some brief directions analogous to those in the preceding sections," and consisted of just the first sentence of the Latin text, and possibly also the second.[1] His view was supported by Bartlet.[2]

The second sentence, however, is partly repetitive of the first; and its refusal to grant the deacon a share in the priesthood, like the denial of a place in the counsel of the clergy in the following sentence, seems to belong more to fourth-century discussions about the ordained ministry than to an earlier context. This much was admitted by Powell, but he still regarded the whole passage as part of the original text.[3] We would suggest that only the first sentence is part of the original core of the document, and that the rest grew by stages, probably in the fourth century as successive redactors sought to clarify the relationship among the three orders, a subject of intense debate at that period.

■ **1** Even the first sentence is a little clumsily expressed because the clause in the Latin, "as we have prescribed," should not relate to the bishop alone laying on his hand but the general ordination procedure.[4] It should also be noted that although the plural "hands" (*manus*) is used by the Latin, the more usual practice in ordination was for one hand alone (the right) to be laid on the candidate, as in the oriental texts here (cf. also the Latin ver-

sion of *Ap. Trad.* 7.1). Hence the plural form in the Latin text is probably the result of an error in the translation of the original Greek verb (see the commentary on chap. 11).

■ **11** The first part of the prayer is found in both the Latin and Ethiopic. In two places Botte thought that readings in the Ethiopic were to be preferred: the Latin appeared to have added "holy" to "spirit" and to have accidently translated the one word twice as "caring and diligence."[5] As the Latin breaks off part way through the prayer, the only witnesses to its latter half are the Ethiopic and *Testamentum Domini*, since both the *Canons of Hippolytus* and *Apostolic Constitutions* seem not to have employed the *Apostolic Tradition* as a source for the compilation of their prayers. This means that any attempt at reconstruction of this part of the text must be very cautious. For example, the Ethiopic asks that the deacon "may acquire . . . the great levels of ordination," but the *Testamentum Domini* has instead "be counted worthy of this high and exalted office." It seems likely that here the *Testamentum Domini* is closer to the original reading, an allusion to 1 Tim 3:13, "may attain a good standing," and that the tradition behind the Ethiopic amended this phrase when the diaconate had ceased to be normally a lifelong ministry and had become more commonly a stepping-stone to higher office.

■ **12** For the form of the doxology, see the commentary on *Ap. Trad.* 6.4 above.

Comment

■ **1** Since a deacon was to be "chosen according to those things that have been said above," what was envisaged seems to be an election to office by the people. This procedure is mentioned in *Did.* 15.1, but both Cyprian and the Syrian *Didascalia Apostolorum* state that the bishop was to appoint deacons, although the former observed that he usually consulted the clergy and people before acting,[6] and remnants of a popular approbation can be

---

1   Frere, "Early Forms," 285–86.
2   Bartlet, "Ordination Prayers," 250–54.
3   Douglas Powell, "Ordo Presbyterii," *JTS* 26 (1975) 308–11.
4   See Botte, *Tradition*, 23 n. 5.
5   Ibid., 27 n. 2.
6   Cyprian *Ep.* 32.1; 64.3; 67.4–5; *Didasc.* 3.12.1.

seen in a number of later ordination rites.[7] Although the practice of the bishop alone laying his hand on a candidate for the diaconate seemingly has to be defended here, it is the standard and unquestioned practice in virtually all later ordination rites, both Eastern and Western.[8]

■ **2** In contrast to chap. 7, where the presbyterial office is nowhere defined in sacerdotal terms, the presbyter is here said to participate in a priesthood from which deacons are excluded. The oldest explicit reference to presbyters sharing in the priesthood of the bishop occurs in Tertullian, who says that they belong to the *ordo sacerdotalis* (*De ex. cast.* 7). Cyprian similarly understood them to participate in the episcopal *sacerdotium* (see, e.g., *Ep.* 1.1.1; 61.3.1), and *Didasc.* 2.26.3 also compares presbyters to priests in the Old Testament. But the latter passage concerns the offering of tithes and extends the image to include both orphans and widows, and so the comparison may be intended more to justify their financial support than to ascribe cultic status to them.

■ **3** The "counsel of the presbyterate" was mentioned in the prayer for a presbyter in *Ap. Trad.* 7.2, but here the term "clergy" (Latin *clerus*; Greek κλῆρος) is employed instead. The use of this word to denote ordained ministers is first encountered in Clement of Alexandria (*Quis dives salvetur* 42) and became standard thereafter. The word originally meant a "lot," both in the sense of the token used in a lottery and in the sense of an allotment of land, but, because priestly duties were allocated by lot in the Old Testament (e.g., 1 Chr 24:5; 25:8), it came to be used by Christians in the sense of "ecclesiastical duties" (as in *Ap. Trad.* 3.4–5, in the Sahidic of 8.7, and in 30A.2), and then by extension to designate the ordained themselves. While here deacons are clearly understood not to be part of the clergy, other ancient writers do use the term to include deacons but exclude the bishop (e.g., Tertullian *De monog.* 12.1).

The deacon's office is here defined in terms that suggest that it was primarily an administrative role exercised under the close supervision of the bishop. The deacon is ordained, according to the Latin version, "to the service of the bishop, that he may do those things that are ordered by him . . . taking care of and indicating to the bishop what is necessary."[9] The Sahidic is more specific, indicating that the care is directed toward the sick, as is also the case in the parallel passage in the *Canons of Hippolytus, Apostolic Traditon* 34, and *Didascalia*.[10]

■ **10–12** The model for the diaconate here is not Stephen or the Seven in Acts 6 (a connection first encountered in Irenaeus[11] that recurs in the *Apostolic Constitutions* and *Canons of Hippolytus* as well as many later rites) but Christ himself, who was "sent to serve your will"[12]—a typology found as early as the writings of Ignatius of Antioch[13] and repeated in *Didasc.* 2.26.5—just as the deacon now will "serve for your church," another expression reminiscent of Ignatius.[14] To this (at least in the Ethiopic) is added an allusion to the ministry of the Levite in the Old Testament, although the word itself is not used: "to offer in your Holy of Holies that which is offered to you by your ordained high priest." The first explicit references to the deacon as Levite in early Christian writings are in *Didasc.* 2.26.3 and in Origen (*Hom. on Josh.* 2.1; *Hom. on Jer.* 12.3). This prayer in its present form therefore seems to belong to the same stratum of material as the episcopal ordination prayer in chap. 3, which also speaks of the bishop as "high priest," as does *Apostolic Tradition* 34. It is interesting to note that the ordination prayers for the bishop and the deacon in the *Sacramentary of Sarapion* may also belong together in a stratum of material separate from that for a presbyter.[15]

The principal theme of the prayer is that of service. What form this service was to take, however, is not revealed as clearly as it was in the preceding directions, which may therefore be an indication that it belongs to a different stratum of material. Here the deacon was to "serve for your church" and not serve the bishop specifically. "Caring" is mentioned, but there is no indication

7   Bradshaw, *Ordination*, 21–25.
8   Ibid., 72.
9   Cf. *Didasc.* 2.44.3–4; 3.13.1, 7.
10 Ibid.
11 Irenaeus *Haer.* 3.12.10; 4.15.1.
12 Botte (*Tradition*, 27 n. 1) sees in this phrase an allusion to the LXX of Isa 9:5, "messenger of great counsel" (μεγάλης βουλῆς ἄγγελος), also found in *Ap. Trad.* 4.4.
13 See *Magn.* 6.1; *Trall.* 3.1. For other ante-Nicene examples, see Ludwig Ott, *Le sacrement de l'Ordre* (Paris: Cerf, 1971) 31–40.
14 *Trall.* 2.3: "servants of the church of God."
15 See above, p. 59.

of the form that this was to take. There also seems to have been some reference to a liturgical ministry of assistance to the bishop in his eucharistic offering, unless this feature was added independently by the compilers of the Ethiopic and of the *Testamentum Domini*, although this seems unlikely, especially as the presenting of the oblation to the bishop is also designated as a diaconal function in chaps. 4 and 21.

Text	Comment

For the order of this chapter in relation to others, see the Introduction above (p. 15). The Sahidic seems to have preserved the better readings here, with the Arabic and Ethiopic betraying a lack of clear understanding of the text. The *Canons of Hippolytus* keeps the general sense but summarizes and paraphrases the source and adds a reference to the case of slaves. The *Apostolic Constitutions*, on the other hand, completely changes the meaning of the chapter, obviously having difficulty in accepting that a confessor could be regarded as a member of the diaconate or presbyterate without receiving the imposition of the hand. On the use of the singular/plural of "hand" here, see the commentary on chap. 11.

■ **3–5** The second half of the chapter switches subject matter abruptly, from the confessor to the bishop's freedom to extemporize eucharistic praying. The authenticity of this juxtaposition is supported not only by all the oriental translations but also by the *Canons of Hippolytus* and *Testamentum Domini*, even though the Arabic and Ethiopic change the sense entirely by omitting the negative of the Sahidic ("not at all") and the *Canons of Hippolytus* and *Testamentum Domini* appear not to understand the meaning of this section: both abbreviate it drastically, and the *Testamentum Domini* takes it as referring in some way to the bishop's ordination prayer. Obviously the Arabic and Ethiopic translators had difficulty in believing that the text could have intended to permit extemporized praying, since that custom had been abolished by their day. Yet the lack of any logical connection with what precedes or follows suggests either some accidental dislocation from an earlier point in the document (perhaps just before chap. 5, where there is a similar reference to the use of different words but the same sense in praying), or at the very least the absence of an editorial hand shaping the arrangement of the various additions to an earlier core of the document.

■ **1–2** The earliest extant instance of the term "confessor" being used to distinguish those who had suffered persecution but survived from other witnesses who had died for their faith ("martyrs") occurs in the letter of the martyrs of Lyon of 177 CE (Eusebius *Hist. eccl.* 5.2.2–3), but some later authors continue to use the words interchangeably. Although confessors were certainly held in high regard in the early church, the *Apostolic Tradition* and the church orders dependent on it appear to be the only evidence for them being admitted to the clergy without ordination. As Dix has observed,[1] Tertullian looked sourly on the privileges that were granted to confessors, but gave no hint at all that this was one of them (*De pud.* 22; *Adv. Prax.* 50), and Cyprian explicitly records his intention to ordain two confessors to the presbyterate (*Ep.* 39.5; 40.1). It seems unlikely, therefore, that the recognition granted in the *Apostolic Tradition* was a widespread custom.

It was not only ancient authors who had difficulty in accepting that a person could be regarded as a presbyter or deacon without ordination. Some modern scholars, too, have puzzled over its significance, not least because it seems to open the door to presidency at the Eucharist without ordination, although it should be noted that in the early centuries presbyters did not often preside apart from their bishop. Some have emphasized the word "honor" in the text, and attempted to draw a distinction between the possession of the honor of the presbyterate and possession of the presbyterate itself with its liturgical functions.[2] Others, however, have defended the admission of confessors to the clergy without imposition of hands on the grounds that confessors and martyrs were seen as the successors of the apostles and prophets and so as possessing the same gifts of the Spirit.[3] Bernard Cooke has suggested that the concession was granted because "the kind of elder status (presumably

---

1   Dix, "Ministry," 223–24.

2   See, e.g., Bernard Botte, "Le rituel d'ordination dans la 'Tradition apostolique' d'Hippolyte," *BCE* 36 (1962) 11; Joseph Lécuyer, *Le sacrement de l'ordination: Recherche historique et théologique* (ThH 65; Paris: Beauchesne, 1983) 41–43; Vilela, *Condition*, 357–60.

3   See, e.g., Marc Lods, *Confesseurs et martyrs, successeurs des prophètes dans l'Eglise des trois premiers siècles* (Le point théologique 19; Neuchâtel: Delachaux, 1950); Cyrille Vogel, "Le ministre charismatique de l'eucharistie: Approche rituelle," in Pierre Grelot et al., *Ministères et célébration de l'eucharistie* (Studia Anselmiana 61; Rome, 1973) 181–209, esp. 194–95;

Latin	Sahidic	Arabic	Ethiopic
	34 Concerning the confessors (ὁμολογητής)	*24 Concerning the confessors who are punished for the name of Christ: that they should have the rank of deacons and presbyters*	*24 Concerning those who confess and are condemned for the name of Christ*

1 And (δέ) the confessor (ὁμολογητής), if he was in bonds because of the name of the Lord, shall not have hand laid on him for diaconate (διακονία) or presbyterate (—πρεσβύτερος), for (γάρ) he has the honor (τιμή) of the presbyterate (—πρεσβύτερος) by his confession (ὁμολογία). But (δέ) if he is appointed (καθίστανται) bishop (ἐπίσκοπος) he will have hand laid on him.

The confessor, if he has been bound for the sake of the name of Christ, should not have hands laid on him in order to serve as a deacon or a presbyter. He has the honor of the presbyterate through his confession. And if he is made bishop, then hands should be laid on him.

If the one who confesses is in the tribunal, in chains for the name of Christ, they are not to place a hand on him for service for that is the work of a deacon, rather than of the presbyterate, and the one who confesses has the honor of the presbyterate. The bishop is to ordain [him] by placing a hand on him.

2 And (δέ) if he is a confessor (ὁμολογητής) who was not taken before an authority (ἐξουσία), or (οὐδέ) punished (κολάζειν) in bonds, or (οὐδέ) shut in prison, or (οὐδέ) condemned (κατακρίνειν) by any judgment (καταδίκη), but (ἀλλά) by (κατά) chance he was greatly scorned for the name of our Lord and punished (κολάζειν) under house arrest (κόλασις), yet (δέ) confessing (ὁμολογεῖν), hand shall be laid on him for every office (κλῆρος) of which he is worthy.

And if he has been a confessor without being brought before the authorities, or being punished with bonds or prison, or being oppressed, but only by incidental humiliation for [the sake of] his Lord, and being punished in his own home, and confessed the faith, he is worthy of all the priestly rites. Hands are laid on him

And if the confessor has not gone to the judges and has not been condemned in chains, and if he has not been shut up in prison and has not come into distress; but yet they have mocked him only because of his Lord and was given a small punishment.
And he is faithful in the entire work of the priesthood that is proper for him, they are to place a hand on him and make him.

3 And (δέ) the bishop (ἐπίσκοπος) shall give thanks (εὐχαριστεῖν) according (κατά) to what we said before.

and the bishop gives thanks as we have said before.

And the bishop is to give thanks as we have said before.

4 It is not at all (οὐ πάντως) necessary (ἀνάγκη) for him to repeat these same words that we said before, as if (ὡς) recited (μελετᾶν) by rote (ἀπόστηθος) giving thanks (εὐχαριστεῖν) to God, but (ἀλλά) according to (κατά) each one's ability he shall pray.

It is essential that we refer to what we have said before so that he should recite from memory and thank God and pray according to each one's ability.

And the reason that we mention what we said before is that he may serve openly, while guarding himself, and give thanks to God. And as each is able they are to pray.

5 If, on the one hand (μέν), he has ability to pray sufficiently (ἱκανός) with a prayer (προσευχή) that is honorable, then it is good (ἀγαθόν). But (δέ) if, on the other hand, he prays and recites a prayer (προσευχή) briefly, no one hinder (κωλύειν) him, only (μόνον) let him pray being sound in orthodoxy (ὀρθόδοξος).

If there is one who is able to pray quietly a magnificent and elevated prayer, that is good. And if one says a prayer of praise adequately, no one should prevent him if he prays rightly and in order.

And if there is one who is able to pray with devotion or a great and exalted prayer, it is a good thing. And if he prays and says glory moderately, no one is to prevent him from praying, when he is truly righteous.

Apostolic Constitutions 8.23.1–4

And I, James, [son] of Alphaeus, order concerning confessors: A confessor is not ordained, for [he is] this by intent and perseverance. And he has become worthy of great honor as one who has confessed the name of God and of his Christ before nations and kings. But if there is need for him, he may be ordained as bishop, presbyter, or deacon. But if any confessor not ordained seizes for himself some such honor on account of [his] confession, let such a one be condemned and rejected. For he is not, since he has denied the command of Christ, and is worse than a nonbeliever.

Canons of Hippolytus 6

When someone has been worthy of appearing before an assembly because of the faith, and of enduring punishment because of Christ, and then has been freed by the help of grace, that man in this way has been worthy of the order of the presbyterate from God. Thus he is not to be ordained by the bishop, because his confession is his ordination. But if he becomes bishop, he is to be ordained. When someone has confessed [the faith] but has not undergone punishment, he has become worthy of the presbyterate, but he is to be ordained by the bishop. If the slave of anyone has endured punishment because of Christ, that man thus is presbyter of the flock; even though he has not received the mark of the presbyterate, he has received the spirit of the presbyterate.

The bishop has not to pray reciting, but by the Holy Spirit.

Testamentum Domini 1.39

If [one] be borne witness to and confess that he was in bonds and in imprisonment and in afflictions for the name of God, a hand is not therefore laid on him for the diaconate. Similarly not for the presbyterate. For he has the honor of the clergy, having been protected by the hand of God, by [his] confessorship. But if he is appointed bishop, he is also counted worthy of laying on of the hand. And [even] if he is a confessor who has not been judged before the power, and has not been buffeted in bonds, but only has confessed, he is counted worthy of laying on of the hand. For he receives the prayer of the clergy.

But let him not pray over him repeating all these words; but when the shepherd advances, he will receive the effect.

with proved virtue, prudence, fidelity, etc.) recognized by the presbyteral ordination would already have been sufficiently indicated by the individual's heroic behavior in the face of persecution."[4]

■ **3–5** The liberty of bishops to extemporize prayer is well attested in the early church, and has been extensively treated elsewhere.[5] The brevity (and apparent misunderstanding) of the reference to the practice in the *Canons of Hippolytus* and *Testamentum Domini*, and its complete omission from the *Apostolic Constitutions*, suggest that it had become less usual by the mid-fourth century, as indeed other sources confirm. Alan Kreider has suggested, somewhat improbably, that the last few sentences of the chapter refer not simply to the bishop praying but to a situation where "each one" in a congregation might offer up a different sort of prayer.[6]

reprinted in idem, *Ordinations inconsistantes et caractère inamissible* (Turin: Bottega d'Erasmo, 1978) 210–11; Edward Schillebeeckx, *The Church with a Human Face,* trans. John Bowden (New York: Crossroad, 1985) 137.

4   Bernard Cooke, *Ministry to Word and Sacraments* (Philadelphia: Fortress Press, 1976) 544.

5   See Anthony T. Hanson, "The Liberty of the Bishop to Improvise Prayer in the Eucharist," *VC* 15 (1961) 173–76; Allan Bouley, *From Freedom to Formula: The Evolution of the Eucharistic Prayer from Oral Improvisation to Written Texts* (Catholic University of America Studies in Christian Antiquity 21; Washington, D.C.: Pastoral Press, 1981).

6   Alan Kreider, *Worship and Evangelism in Pre-Christendom* (JLS 32; Nottingham: Grove, 1995) 32.

Text

For the order of this chapter in relation to others, see the Introduction above (p. 15). On the use of the singular/plural of "hand," see the commentary on chap. 11. The Ethiopic is particularly confusing here, because it uses for "appoint" the same verb that it employs elsewhere for "ordain" and adopts the term "seal" to denote "ordain."

■ **4–5** Since this section begins by largely repeating what was said at the beginning and then goes on to try to justify the lack of imposition of hands, it may well be a later addition to the core of the document, in the same way that the later parts of chaps. 7 and 8 appear to be.

Comment

The earliest firm evidence for the existence of a clearly recognizable order of widows in the Christian church, as distinct from a more loosely defined group who were recipients of charity (e.g., as in Acts 6:1), occurs in 1 Tim 5:3–16, where rules are set forth concerning the "enrollment" of those who are "real" widows, that is, who have no family to provide financial support for them. They must be not less than sixty years old, have had only one husband, and be well attested for their good deeds. Reference is also made in 1 Tim 5:5 to their perseverance in prayer night and day, and second- and third-century sources bear out all these expectations of the order of widows. In return for their "pension" from the gifts of their fellow believers, they are to be examples of Christian behavior to the community, especially in displaying the virtue of continence, and they are to engage in the ministry of constant intercession and contemplation, and in some cases in visiting the sick and praying with them.[1] For this reason, they are accorded special honor within the congregation, being described as an "altar," probably because it is on them that the charitable offerings of the community are placed,[2] and also as having received a particular form of "priestly" consecration.[3] Cornelius, bishop of Rome in the mid-third century, stated that his church supported fifteen hundred widows and other poor persons.[4] The order of widows declined during the fourth century, being replaced to some extent by the order of deaconesses, who are not mentioned in the *Apostolic Tradition*.

It would appear to be the granting of this honored position within the community, akin to that given to the clergy, that is the reason why the *Apostolic Tradition* insists here that they must not be ordained but simply nominated. That question would not have arisen if they had simply been regarded as poor people deserving charitable support. The strong insistence may also be a sign that the *Apostolic Tradition* is attempting to reverse a trend that was already allowing women to function liturgically and trying to impose a new norm instead.[5]

Widows are mentioned again in chaps. 23, 24 (= 29B), and 30A.

---

1   See further Roger Gryson, *The Ministry of Women in the Early Church* (Collegeville, Minn.: Liturgical, 1976); Bonnie B. Thurston, *The Widows: A Women's Ministry in the Early Church* (Minneapolis: Fortress Press, 1989).

2   See Carolyn Osiek, "The Widow as Altar: The Rise and Fall of a Symbol," *Second Century* 3 (1983) 159–69.

3   E.g., Tertullian *Ad uxor.* 1.7.

4   Eusebius *Hist. eccl.* 6.43.

5   So argues Anne Jensen, *Gottes selbstbewusste Töchter* (Freiburg: Herder, 1992) 76–79. See also Ute E. Eisen, *Women Officeholders in Early Christianity: Epigraphical and Literary Studies,* trans. Linda M. Maloney (Collegeville, Minn.: Liturgical Press, 2000) 143–57.

10

Latin	Sahidic	Arabic	Ethiopic
	37 Concerning the widows (χήρα)	**25 Concerning the establishment of widows**	**25 Concerning the ordination of widows**
1	If a widow (χήρα) is appointed (καθίσταναι), she shall not be ordained (χειροτονεῖν), but (ἀλλά) she shall be chosen by the name.	If a widow is established, she is not ordained, but is [simply] given the name.	If a widow is ordained, she is not to be sealed but should act by nomination.
2	If, however, (δέ) her husband has been dead a long time, then let her be appointed (καθίσταναι).	If her husband has died a long time before, let her be established,	And if her husband died a long time ago, she is to be ordained.
3	But (δέ) if it has not been long since her husband died, do not trust (πιστεύ-ειν) her. But (ἀλλά) if she is an old woman, let her be tested (δοκιμάζειν) for a time (χρόνος). For often (πολλάκις γάρ) passions (πάθος) also become old with the one who will make an opportunity for them in himself [sic].	but if her husband has died recently, let confidence not be placed in her. If she is old, let her be tested for a time, for the symptoms persist in whoever allows them room.	And if her husband died recently, they should not trust her; but if she is aged, she is to be tested for a time because lust contends with those who are ordained to a position.
4	Let the widow (χήρα) be appointed (καθίσταναι) with the word only, and (δέ) let her be bound with the rest. But (δέ) hand shall not be laid on her because she does not offer up the offering (προσφορά) or (οὐδέ) the liturgy (λει-τουργία).	Let a widow be established by word only, and be bound to the rest of the widows. No hands should be laid on her because she does not make offerings and has no service.	The widow is to be ordained by word alone and she is to be joined with the rest of the widows, and they are not to place a hand on her because she does not offer the oblation and does not have a service.
5	But (δέ) the ordination (χειροτονία) is for the clergy (κλῆρος) for the sake of the liturgies (λειτουρ-γία), and (δέ) the widow (χήρα) is appointed (καθί-σταναι) only for the sake of the prayer; and (δέ) this belongs to everyone.	Ordination is in the case of the clergy for service, and in the case of the widow for prayer, which is for everyone.	For sealing is for the priests because of the service, but prayer is a widow's duty. And this is the way it is for everyone.

Apostolic Constitutions 8.25.1–3

And I, Lebbaios, called Thaddaeus, order this concerning widows: A widow is not ordained, but if a long time has passed since she lost her husband and she has lived chastely and above reproach and has taken excellent care of [her] family, as the respectable women, Judith and Anna, let her be appointed to the order of widows. But if she has lost [her] spouse only recently, let her not be believed, but let her youth be judged in time. For there is a time when also the passions grow old in people unless prevented by a better bridle.

Canons of Hippolytus 9

. . . Then, one is not to ordain the widows who are appointed there are in effect for them the precepts of the apostle. They are not to be ordained, but one is to pray over them, because ordination is for men. The function of widows is important by reason of all that is incumbent on them: frequent prayer, the ministry of the sick, and frequent fasting.

Testamentum Domini 1.40

Let a widow be appointed, being chosen, if for a long time past she has lived without a husband; if though often pressed by men to be married, because of the faith she has not been married. But if not, it is not yet right that she should be chosen; but let her be proved for a time. . . .
[41] Let her appointment be thus: as she prays at the entrance of the altar and looks down, let the bishop say quietly, so that the priests may hear, thus:
. . . .

Concerning a Reader

Latin	Sahidic	Arabic	Ethiopic
	35 Concerning the reader (ἀναγνώστης)	*26 Concerning readers and virgins and subdeacons and the grace of healing*	*26 Concerning the reader and virgins and subdeacons and concerning the grace of healing*
	When the reader (ἀναγνώστης) shall be appointed (καθίσταναι), the bishop (ἐπίσκοπος) shall give the book of the apostle (ἀπόστολος) to him and pray over him, but (δέ) shall not lay hand on him.	When a reader is established, the bishop presents him with the book and does not put a hand on him.	[As for] a reader who is to be ordained, the bishop is to hand the book to him and he is not to place a hand on him.

Text

For the order of this chapter in relation to others, see the Introduction above (p. 15). Because the *Epitome* appears to have preserved the original Greek for this short section in preference to the form in the *Apostolic Constitutions*, which in contrast prescribes an imposition of hands and a prayer, no problems of reconstruction arise. It is worth noting, however, that what is rendered in English as "a hand is imposed" is in Greek not a phrase but simply a passive verb on its own, χειροθετεῖται, which could equally well be translated as "hands are imposed." The singular has been adopted here because that was the usual practice in other ancient ordination rituals (cf., e.g., *Ap. Trad.* 7.1); but it suggests that the appearance of a plural form in the different linguistic versions of other directions about ordination elsewhere in the text (*Ap. Trad.* 8.1, 6; 9.1–2; 10.4; 13–14) is probably simply the result of the translator rendering in a different manner either this Greek verb or the parallel expression χειροτονεῖν, and not a sure indication that some definite plural expression stood in the missing Greek text.[1]

Comment

We have no clear evidence for the existence of the office of reader before the third century. Justin speaks of "the one who reads" (*1 Apol.* 67.4) as does *2 Clement* (19.1), usually dated mid-second century; but neither may have had an appointed official in mind. The function could have been exercised by different members of the congregation in turn, as was the Jewish practice, where the individual was handed the scroll from which to read— exactly the same gesture as the bishop uses here to make the appointment (cf. Luke 4:16, where Jesus reads in the synagogue). Tertullian implies that he did know a formal office of this kind. He criticizes the way in which among the Gnostics ecclesiastical offices were not permanent, but individuals moved freely from one to another: "today one is deacon, who tomorrow will be a reader" (*De praescr.* 41). Cyprian makes frequent reference to readers in his correspondence,[2] and the letter of Cornelius of Rome in 251 also mentions their existence there.[3] It is clear from this last source, however, that at Rome readers occupied a lowly place in the ecclesiastical hierarchy, being ranked after subdeacons, acolytes, and exorcists but before doorkeepers, in contrast to the *Apostolic Tradition*, where they appear to have come before subdeacons, and where exorcists and doorkeepers are not mentioned. Hanssens used this discrepancy as part of his argument for the Alexandrian rather than Roman origin of the document, since in Egyptian sources of the third century only readers and not subdeacons were mentioned.[4] Alexandre Faivre, however, supported the Roman provenance of the *Apostolic Tradition* by arguing

---

1 See Botte, *Tradition*, 31 n. 5.
2 Cyprian *Ep.* 23; 29.2; 32.2; 35.1; 38; 39.
3 In Eusebius *Hist. eccl.* 6.43.11.
4 Hanssens, *Liturgie,* 371–76.

Epitome 13	*Canons of Hippolytus* 7	*Testamentum Domini* 1.45
Concerning a reader		
A reader is appointed when the bishop gives him the book. For a hand is not imposed [on him].	When one chooses a reader, he is to have the virtues of the deacon. One is not to lay the hand on him before, but the bishop is to give him the Gospel.	A reader is instituted pure, quiet, meek, wise, with much experience, learned and of much learning, with a good memory, vigilant, so that he may deserve a higher degree. First let the book be given him in the sight of the people, on the first day of the week. But a hand is not laid on him. But he hears from the bishop [the following]: . . . .

that it represented an earlier situation at Rome, when readers enjoyed more prestige than they did by the mid-third century.[5]

The custom of appointing a reader by handing over the book from which he was to read continues to be found in later Eastern rites, but nearly always in conjunction with an imposition of hands and prayer, as it already is in the *Apostolic Constitutions*. The later Roman tradition, on the other hand, seems to be unfamiliar with the practice. *Ordo* XXXIV, the oldest extant account of Roman ordination practice, dating from the mid-eighth century, makes provision solely for the ritual appointment of acolytes and subdeacons. *Ordo* XXXV, originating in France about 1000 CE, does describe a Roman rite for appointing a reader, but this involved only a simple blessing by the pope. It appears that by this time the office was usually conferred on adolescents whose parents wished them to embark upon an ecclesiastical career rather than on those intended primarily to exercise the liturgical function. Some Gallican rites do include the handing over of the book, but their source appears to be the fifth-century *Statuta Ecclesiae Antiqua*, which in turn derived the custom from the *Apostolic Tradition* itself.[6]

All this might seem to point to the East rather than the West as the original home of this particular directive.

---

5   Alexandre Faivre, *Naissance d'une hierarchie: Les premières étapes du cursus clérical* (ThH 40; Paris: Beauchesne, 1977) 299–308.

6   See Bradshaw, *Ordination*, 96–98, 100–102.

Latin	Sahidic	Arabic	Ethiopic
	38 Concerning the virgins (παρθένος)		
	Hand shall not be laid on a virgin (παρθένος), but (δέ) her choice (προαίρεσις) alone is what makes her a virgin (παρθένος).	Hands are not laid on a virgin; it is her inner life alone that makes her a virgin.	Concerning virgins, he is not to place a hand on a virgin but [it is] in her heart alone that she has become a virgin.

Text

For the order of this chapter in relation to others, see the Introduction above (p. 15).

Comment

Virgins are first mentioned by Ignatius, who in one of his letters sends greetings to "the virgins called widows" (*Smyrn.* 13.1). These were presumably women who had pledged themselves to a life of sexual abstinence in the same way as those officially enrolled as widows (see chap. 10).[1] Thereafter, we encounter frequent references in early Christian literature to those of both sexes who practiced voluntary continence as part of their ascetic life. It is not until the late fourth century, however, that we have any account of a consecration ceremony associated with this vow.[2]

The distinction drawn between widows who are appointed by being named (*Ap. Trad.* 10.1) and virgins who simply choose the life for themselves (12) no doubt reflects a difference in status between the two groups, the former being a clearly defined order to which entry was controlled by ecclesiastical authority, and the latter a purely voluntary grouping of ascetics. Virgins are only mentioned twice again in the document, in chaps. 23 and 25.

1   See Roger Gryson, *The Ministry of Women in the Early Church* (Collegeville, Minn.: Liturgical, 1976) 13; Peter Brown, *The Body and Society: Men, Women, and Sexual Renunciation in Early Christianity* (New York: Columbia Univ. Press, 1988) 260–84; Francine Cardman, "Women, Ministry, and Church Order in Early Christianity," in Ross Shepard Kraemer and Mary Rose D'Angelo, *Women and Christian Origins* (New York: Oxford Univ. Press, 1999) 300–329; and, on Ignatius, William R. Schoedel, *Ignatius of Antioch: A Commentary on the Letters of Ignatius of Antioch* (Hermeneia: Philadelphia: Fortress Press, 1985) 252–53.

2   See, e.g., Ambrose *De virginibus* 3.1–4; Jerome *Ep.* 130.2; also René Metz, *La consécration des vierges dans l'Eglise romaine* (Paris: Presses Universitaires de France, 1954).

Apostolic Constitutions 8.24

The same concerning virgins. A virgin is not to be ordained. For we have no command from the Lord. For of the resolve is the prize of the contest, not for a slander against marriage, but for a school of piety.

Canons of Hippolytus

[See below, chap. 13]

Testamentum Domini 1.46

A male or female virgin is not instituted or appointed by man, but is voluntarily separated and named [a virgin]. But a hand is not laid on him, as for virginity. For this division is of [their] own free will. . . .

Latin	Sahidic	Arabic	Ethiopic
	36 Concerning the sub- deacon (ὑποδιάκονος)		
	Hand shall not be laid on a subdeacon (ὑποδιάκονος), but (ἀλλά) he shall be named (ὀνομάζειν) to fol- low the deacons (διάκονος).	**Hands are not laid on the subdeacon; rather they are given the name of follow- ers of the deacons.**	**Concerning a subdeacon, he is not to place a hand on a subdeacon but they are to employ the name over them so they may serve the deacons.**

Text

For the order of this chapter in relation to others, see the Introduction above (p. 15). On the use of the singu- lar/plural "hands," see the commentary to chap. 11.

Comment

Evidence for the existence of subdeacons is first found in the mid-third century. They are mentioned frequently by Cyprian in his correspondence,[1] and they are also listed first, after deacons, in the letter of Cornelius of Rome in 251.[2] In later Eastern ordination rites, where again the subdiaconate was regarded as a lower degree of the diaconate, they tend to be appointed by prayer and the imposition of the hand, as their ordination was gradually assimilated to that of a deacon. In the West it was conferred by the handing over of a symbol of office: from at least the sixth century onward subdeacons in Rome received a chalice, and in other Western traditions a chalice and paten tended to be given.[3]

1   Cyprian *Ep.* 8.1; 9.1; 29.2; 34.4; 36.1; 45.4; 47.2; 79.1.
2   In Eusebius *Hist. eccl.* 6.43.11.
3   Bradshaw, *Ordination*, 93–103.

Apostolic Constitutions 8.21	*Canons of Hippolytus*	*Testamentum Domini* 1.44
Concerning subdeacons, I, Thomas, command you bishops: When ordaining a subdeacon, O bishop, lay hands on him and say. . . .	The subdeacon [is to be appointed] according to this arrangement: he is not to be ordained still celibate and if he has not married, unless his neighbors bear witness for him and testify that he has kept himself away from women during the time of his maturity. One is not to lay the hand on someone in the state of celibacy, unless he has reached his maturity or is entering into mature age and is thought [worthy], when one bears witness for him. . . .	Similarly let a subdeacon be appointed who is chaste, the bishop praying over him. Let the bishop say over him on the first day of the week, in the hearing of all the people, thus: . . . .

Latin	Sahidic	Arabic	Ethiopic
	39 Concerning the gift of healing		
	(δέ) **If one says, "I received gifts of healing through a revelation," hand shall not be laid on him, for (γάρ) the work itself will reveal if he speaks [the] truth.**	**If anyone says, "I have received the grace of healing by a revelation," hands are not laid on him because events will show whether he is telling the truth.**	**Concerning the grace of healing, if someone says, "I have obtained the gift of healing through prophetic means," they are not to place a hand on him until his action shows whether he is trustworthy.**

Text

For the order of this chapter in relation to others, see the Introduction above (p. 15). On the use of the singular/plural "hands," see the commentary on chap. 11.

Comment

"Gifts of healing" are mentioned among the list of charisms bestowed by the Holy Spirit in 1 Cor 12:9, and there is abundant testimony in the Christian literature of the first few centuries for the expectation that any member of the church might possess these gifts.[1] In the West a specific group of exorcists (whose work was closely related to the ancient understanding of healing) first makes an appearance in the mid-third century, in the list of offices of the church at Rome in the letter of Cornelius written in 251.[2] In the East the power of healing was later associated with ordination, and features in the ordination prayer for a bishop in the *Canons of Hippolytus* and that for a presbyter in the *Apostolic Constitutions* (see above in chaps. 3 and 7). See also *Apostolic Tradition* 34 below, where visiting the sick is the responsibility of the bishop.

It would seem that this chapter is resisting the creation of a specific class or order of "healers" who are officially appointed by the church, preferring to allow the results themselves to verify any claim to possess the power of healing.

---

1   See, e.g., Justin *Dial.* 39; Irenaeus *Haer.* 2.31.2; 2.32.4–5.

2   In Eusebius *Hist. eccl.* 6.43.11.

Apostolic Constitutions 8.26.2	*Canons of Hippolytus* 8	*Testamentum Domini* 1.47
. . . For the one receiving the gift of healing is revealed through revelation from God, the grace in him being shown to all. . . .	If someone asks for his ordination, saying, "I have received the gift of healing," he is to be ordained only when the thing is manifest and if the healing done by him comes from God.	If anyone appears in the people to have a gift of healing or of knowledge or of tongues, a hand is not laid on him, for the work is manifest. But let them have honor.

15

	Latin	Sahidic	Arabic	Ethiopic
		40 Concerning newcomers, those who will give their assent to the faith (πίστις)	*27 Concerning new people who are beginning to enter the faith and the activities they must give up*	*27 Concerning new people who want to be baptized and concerning the occupation they must leave*
1		(δέ) Let those who will be brought newly to the faith (πίστις) to hear the Word be brought first to the teachers before the people (λαός) arrive.	Those who are newcomers to hearing the Word, let them be taken first to the teachers before all the people come in,	New individuals who are to be baptized so that they may hear the Word, they are to bring to the teachers before all the people come,
2		And let them be asked the reason (αἰτία) why they have given their assent to the faith (πίστις). And let those who have brought them bear witness as to whether they are able to hear the Word.	and be asked the reason why they are seeking the faith. Let those who have brought them bear witness for them, whether they are able to listen.	and they are to ask them the reason why they were seeking the faith. And those who brought them are to be witnesses for them [about] whether they are able to hear.
3		And (δέ) let them be asked about their life (βίος): What sort is it? (ἤ) Does he have a wife?	They are asked what their life is like, whether they have wives, whether they are slaves.	And they are to examine them regarding their way of life as to what [sort of people] they are: if he has a wife or if he is a slave.
4		(ἤ) Is he a servant of a believer (πιστός)? Does his master permit (ἐπιτρέπειν) him? Then, let him hear. If his master does not testify on his behalf, that he is good, let him be cast out.	If one of them is the slave of a believer who has given his permission, let him hear, but if his master does not report in his favor, let him be sent out.	And if his owner permitted him, then he is to hear. And if his owner is not a witness, he is to go out.
5		If his master is a heathen (ἐθνικός), teach him to please his master so that there shall be no scandal (βλασφημία).	And if [his master] is a heathen, let it be found out whether his master is willing lest a scandal be caused.	And if his master is an idolater, then they are to find out whether it was with the permission of his owner so that there may not be a quarrel.
6		And (δέ) if there is one who has a wife or a woman who has a husband, let them be taught to be content with his wife, and the woman with her husband.	And if one has a wife or a woman has a husband, let them be taught that the man should be content with his wife and the woman should be content with her husband.	And if he is a man who has a wife or a woman who has a husband, they are to find out whether the man lives with his wife and the woman with her husband.
7		And (δέ) if there is one who did not dwell with a wife, let him be taught not to fornicate (πορνεύειν), but (ἀλλά) either let him take a wife according to (κατά) the law (νόμος) or (ἤ) remain [as he is] according to (κατά) the law (νόμος).	If a man is single, he should not stay with a woman; let him be told not to commit fornication but to marry according to the law, or remain as he is.	And if the man is one who does not live with his wife, they are to indicate that he should not commit adultery but should marry legally or be as he is.
8		And (δέ) if there is one who has a demon (δαιμόνιον), he shall not hear the word of instruction until he is purified.	And if there is one who has a demon, let him not hear the words of the teacher.	And if he is a man who has a demon, he is not to hear the word of teaching.

Apostolic Constitutions 8.32.2–6

Canons of Hippolytus 10

Testamentum Domini 2.1

Let those first coming to the mystery of the godly life be brought by the deacons to the bishop or to the presbyters, and let them be examined as to why they came to the Word of the Lord. Let those who brought them give witness to them, after examining the things concerning them. And let them examine also their manner and life and whether they are slave or free. And if someone is a slave, let him be asked who his master is; and if he is a slave of one of the faithful, let his master be asked if he testifies to him. But if not, let him be rejected until that time he may show himself worthy to the master. But if he does testify to him, let him be accepted.

Those who come to the church in order to become Christians are to be examined with all rigor for what motive have they abandoned their religion, for fear lest they enter out of mockery. If he comes with a true faith, he is to be received with joy, questioned about his occupation, and instructed by the deacon. In this manner he is to be instructed in the Scriptures, so that he may renounce Satan and all his service. All the time he is being catechized, he is from now on reckoned with the people.
But if he is a slave and his master idolatrous, and his master forbids him, he is not to be baptized, but it suffices that he is a Christian; even if he dies without having received the gift, he is not to be excluded from the flock.

Let those who first come to hear the Word, before they enter among all the people, first come to teachers at home, and let them be examined as to all the cause [of their coming] with all accuracy, so that their teachers may know for what they have come, or with what will. And if they have come with a good will and love, let them be diligently taught. But let those who bring them be such as are well on in years, faithful who are known by the church; and let them bear witness about them, if they are able to hear [the Word]. Also let their life and conversation be asked about: if they are not contentious, if quiet, if meek, not speaking vain things or despisers or foul speakers, or buffoons or leaders astray, or ridicule mongers. Also if any of them have a wife or not. . . . And also let him who comes be asked if he is a slave or free; and if the slave of one who is faithful, and if also his master permit him, let him hear.

But if he is a household slave to a heathen, let him be taught to please his master in order that the Word not be blasphemed. If, then, he has a wife, or the woman a husband, let them be taught to be content in themselves. But if they are not married, let them be taught not to fornicate but to marry in the law. But if his master, being of faith and knowing that he fornicates, does not give him a wife, or a husband to the woman, let him be separated. And if anyone has a demon, let him be taught the godly life, but do not let him enter into the community before he has been purified. But if death is hastening, let him be accepted.

But if his master is not faithful and does not permit him, let him be persuaded to permit him. And if [his master] says truly about him that he wishes to become a Christian because he hates his masters, let him be cast out. But if no cause be shown of hatred of servitude, but [if] he [really] wishes to be a Christian, let him hear. But if his master is faithful and does not bear witness to him, let him be cast out. Similarly if [a woman] is the wife of a man, let the woman be taught to please her husband in the fear of God. But if both of them desire to serve purity in piety, they have a reward. Let him who is unmarried not commit fornication, but let him marry in the law. But if he desires to persevere thus, let him abide in the Lord. If anyone is tormented with a devil, let him not hear the Word from a teacher until he is cleansed. For the intelligence, when consumed with a material spirit, does not receive the immaterial and holy Word. But if he is cleansed, let him be instructed in the Word.

Text

The lacuna in the Latin version continues throughout these initiatory chapters until the beginning of the second baptismal interrogation in *Ap. Trad.* 21.15. The oriental versions display no textual differences of any great significance in this chapter. The Sahidic and Arabic are consistent in using the expression "let those" or "let them" in reference to the catechumens.[1]

Comment

This chapter begins an entirely new section of the document and, together with chaps. 16–21, describes the ritual process of Christian initiation from a presentation, preliminary examination of motives and life, and enrollment of "newcomers" into the catechumenate (15), to various prohibited occupations for both catechumens and fully initiated Christians (16), to the duration of the catechumenate as well as other rites during the catechumenal process (17.1–20.4), all the way to the rites of Christian initiation themselves and their culmination in the baptismal Eucharist (20.5–21).

Rites of enrollment in the catechumenate and preliminary examinations of "newcomers" to the faith have no explicit parallels within early Christian liturgical sources prior to the second half of the fourth century. The existence of similar practices, however, may be discernible from, or assumed on the basis of, other Christian literature prior to that time period. In his *First Apology,* Justin Martyr appears to make a passing reference to such a process: "as many as are persuaded and believe that these things which we teach and describe are true, and undertake to live accordingly, are taught by us to pray and ask God, while fasting, for the forgiveness of their sins; and we pray and fast accordingly."[2] But the closest explicit parallel to entrance into the catechumenate and examinations of those seeking to enter is not provided until the mid-third century, in Origen's *Contra Celsum*:

But as far as they can, Christians previously examine the souls of those who want to hear them, and test them individually beforehand; when before entering the community the hearers seem to have devoted themselves sufficiently to the desire to live a good life, then they introduce them. They privately appoint one class consisting of recent beginners who are receiving elementary introduction and have not yet received the sign that they have been purified, and another class of those who, as far as they are able, make it their set purpose to desire nothing other than those things of which Christians approve. Among the latter class some are appointed to inquire into the lives and conduct of those who want to join the community in order that they may prevent those who indulge in secret sins from coming to their common gathering; those who do not do this they whole-heartedly receive and make them better every day.[3]

■ **1** None of the oriental versions specifies who "the teachers" are. *Apostolic Constitutions*, however, refers specifically to "deacons" presenting the newcomers "to the bishop or to the presbyters"; the *Canons of Hippolytus* notes that the newcomers are to be "instructed by the deacon"; and the *Testamentum Domini* later states that the bishop is the one who will provide the instruction. This clericalization of the "teacher" reflects the fourth-century context of these documents, in which such a tendency was increasing,[4] and should not be read back into an earlier period, even though *Apostolic Tradition* 39 also refers to deacons teaching in the assembly, as that section of the church order probably belongs to a fourth-century stratum.

■ **2** All the versions and the derivative documents refer both to an examination of the newcomers' motives as well as to the necessity of sponsors testifying on their behalf. Only the *Canons of Hippolytus* provides a rationale for this, adding the phrase, "for fear lest they enter

---

1   On the variations in address throughout chaps. 15–20, see Robert Cabié, "L'ordo de l'initiation chrétienne dans la 'Tradition apostolique' d'Hippolyte de Rome," in *Mens concordet voci, pour Mgr A. G. Martimort* (Paris: Desclée, 1983) 543–58.

2   Justin *1 Apol.* 61; ET from E. C. Whitaker, *Documents of the Baptismal Liturgy* (London: SPCK, 1970) 2.

3   Origen *Contra Celsum* 3.51; ET from Henry Chadwick, *Origen: Contra Celsum* (Cambridge: Cambridge Univ. Press, 1965) 163.

4   On this see Paul F. Bradshaw, *Liturgical Presidency in the Early Church* (GLS 36; Nottingham: Grove, 1983) 15–20.

out of mockery." And only the *Canons of Hippolytus* notes that catechumens are, from the time of their acceptance, "reckoned with the people."

■ **3** All versions and derivative documents refer to an examination of the lifestyles of the newcomers (including "occupation" in the *Canons of Hippolytus*), as well as their social status (slave or free). Marital status is also included in this examination in the versions and in the *Testamentum Domini*, but not in the *Apostolic Constitutions* or *Canons of Hippolytus*.

■ **4–7** Specific concerns about whether slaves might become catechumens, questions about the permission of their masters to do so or not, and about the marital status of catechumens in general, are not clearly reflected in early Christian literature outside the extant versions and derivative documents. At the same time, nothing in these texts is inconsistent with the general Christian attitude toward slavery itself in the first three centuries of the Common Era:

> Christian writers from the second century onward . . . accepted . . . slaves as members of the Church, and they urged masters to treat slaves well. They recommended mutual respect between master and slave, and they hoped that masters would try to convert their non-Christian slaves. But repeatedly Christians told slaves to honor their masters and accept their lot. Although from the fourth century onward there was a practice called *manumissio in ecclesia,* a legal act by which a master freed a slave in church, no evidence indicates that this encouraged masters to free their slaves. In fact, its main importance lay in the recognition it gained for the Church's role in civic affairs. . . . Christians also recognized the rights of slaves in marriage. Pope Callistus I (217–222), an ex-slave, went beyond the prevailing Roman civil code and recog-

nized the validity of marriages between a male slave and a free woman.[5]

Of possible relevance in the above quotation is the well-known conflict between Callistus and Hippolytus of Rome over the question of marriages between free women and male slaves. For Hippolytus, this permission constituted one of the grounds for his charge of severe moral laxity against Callistus and within his heretical "sect" at Rome.[6] Nevertheless, nothing in the versions or derivative documents would permit us to conclude that this particular conflict played any role in the development of the *Apostolic Tradition* or is to be interpreted as reflected in the directions provided in this section. Even the *Apostolic Constitutions*, it is to be noted, is not concerned with marriage relationships between free women and male slaves but simply with the marriage relationship among slaves themselves.

■ **6–7** Directions regarding marital status appear in all the versions, the *Apostolic Constitutions*, and the *Testamentum Domini*. While the context might suggest that these directions are concerned specifically with the marital status of slaves, only the *Apostolic Constitutions* unambiguously interprets them this way, referring to a master "being of faith and knowing that he fornicates." The directions in any case parallel Paul's instructions about marriage and celibacy with regard to all believers in 1 Corinthians 7.

Nothing in this chapter would either contradict or be inconsistent with the traditional assumption of an early-third-century date for the document. Such consistency, however, proves nothing about the date, authorship, or provenance of this chapter. Rather, the only thing that can be concluded with any degree of certainty is that it *may* reflect a third-century context. Even so, however, questions about the relationship between Christianity

5   Joseph F. Kelly, *The World of the Early Christians* (Collegeville, Minn.: Liturgical, 1997) 144–45. See also Robert M. Grant, *From Augustus to Constantine: The Thrust of the Christian Movement into the Roman World* (New York: Harper & Row, 1970) 269–70; Helmut Koester, *Introduction to the New Testament,* vol. 1: *History, Culture and Religion of the Hellenistic Age* (Berlin: de Gruyter, 1982) 59–62, 331–32. Among early Christian writers who make some reference to slavery, see Ignatius *Pol.* 4.3; Athenagoras *Legatio* 35.1; *Shepherd of Hermas*; Eusebius *Hist. eccl.* 5.1.14; Tertullian *Apol.* 7.3. Although *Const.* 4.9.2

does recommend the emancipation of slaves, such a recommendation does not appear within the parallel materials here, and, for that matter, seems to be limited to the context of persecution. For a discussion of slavery in the NT world of the 1st century CE, see Dale Martin, *Slavery as Salvation: The Metaphor of Slavery in Pauline Christianity* (New Haven: Yale Univ. Press, 1990); Keith Bradley, *Slavery and Society at Rome* (Key Themes in Ancient History; Cambridge: Cambridge Univ. Press, 1994).

6   See Hippolytus *Ref.* 7. Whether Hippolytus is the author of this work is disputed.

and slavery continued well into the late fourth century and beyond,[7] and so there is also nothing here that would not be quite consistent with a fourth-century context.

■ **8** All the versions and derivative documents agree on the prohibition of one with a demon or devil from catechesis. Only the Sahidic, *Apostolic Constitutions*, and *Testamentum Domini*, however, refer specifically to some kind of "purification" or "cleansing" being needed in this context. Similarly, only the *Apostolic Constitutions* and *Canons of Hippolytus* refer to catechumens near death or dying during the catechumenal process. The *Canons of Hippolytus* directs that slaves of idolatrous masters who forbid their baptism are, nevertheless, even if they die "without having received the gift, . . . not to be excluded from the flock." It thus witnesses to what others in the patristic period would refer to as a "baptism of desire."[8]

---

7 See, e.g., Basil *The Second Canonical Letter*, canons 40 and 42; Augustine *City of God* 19.15.

8 See William R. Rusch, "Baptism of Desire in Ambrose and Augustine," *StPatr* 15 (1984) 374–78.

Text

The versions and derivative documents show considerable variation in this chapter as to the catalog of prohibited occupations, the order of their appearance in the list, and, occasionally, their interpretation. This wide variation, together with the lacuna in the Latin version, makes it impossible in many cases to determine which, if any, of the versions most closely reflects or approximates what the earliest stratum of the text would have contained. Nevertheless, the equivalent catalogs of prohibited occupations present in all of the derivative documents certainly underscore that the text of chap. 16 was in a form much like what appears in the versions by the mid-fourth century.

■ **1** In the Sahidic the Greek verb καθισταναι is the one normally used of making ecclesiastical appointments. Botte believed that the translator had confused it with κατηχεισθαι, "to be catechized," which seems to be confirmed by the other versions, and we have corrected the translation accordingly.

■ **9** Because the Sahidic version refers to the military oath here ("nor let him swear"), a direction paralleled in the *Canons of Hippolytus* ("they are not to pronounce a bad word"), some have assumed that it represents the more primitive text.[1] Certainly Tertullian's statement in *De idol.* 19 that "there is no agreement between the divine and the human sacrament" parallels this prohibition, although Tertullian also notes that even the silent acceptance of a military crown, without speaking the words of the oath, is itself an idolatrous response for Christians.[2]

Because of the more rigorist position on this issue presented in the Ethiopic version, however, Eoin de Bhaldraithe has recently argued that both the Ethiopic and *Testamentum Domini*, coming from communities on the periphery of the empire, are examples of "peripheral conservatism," retaining the more ancient practice. According to him, it is more likely that the Ethiopic prohibition against accepting "soldiers of an official" and requiring the expulsion of both catechumens and believers who wish to become soldiers is the original reading, which would have given rise to a "correction" or "concession" made later both in the Ethiopic itself ("and if he is given an order to kill . . .") and in the other versions. De Bhaldraithe dates the original prohibition reflected in the Ethiopic version to the beginning of the second century, with its correction or concession being made near the middle of that century. The Arabic version, with its correction but without any reference to the military oath, would be dated later in the second century (c. 170), and the Sahidic at the beginning of the third.[3] On the other hand, rather than being an example of "peripheral conservatism," the Ethiopic reading may just as likely be

---

1   See, e.g., Cuming, *Hippolytus,* 16.

2   See *De cor.* 12; also ibid., 1, for his praise of a Christian soldier who refused to accept the crown and so suffered its consequences in martyrdom.

3   Eoin de Bhaldraithe, "Early Christian Features Preserved in Western Monasticism," in Alan Kreider, ed., *The Origins of Christendom in the West* (Edinburgh: T. & T. Clark, 2001) 153–78. De Balthraithe's analysis is generally followed by Alan Kreider, "War and the Culture of Peace in Early Christianity," a paper presented on May 5, 1999, at Regent's Park College, Oxford, England. We are grateful to Dr. Kreider for making this unpublished paper available to us. On the question of military service and early Christianity, see John Helgeland, "Christians and the Roman Army: AD 173–337," *CH* 43 (1974) 149–63; idem, "Christians and the Roman Army from Marcus Aurelius to Constantine," *ANRW* 2.23.1 (1979) 724–834; John Helgeland, Robert Daly, and J. Patout Burns, *Christians and the Military: The Early Experience* (Philadelphia: Fortress Press, 1985); L. J. Swift, "War and the Christian Conscience 1: The Early Years," *ANRW* 2.23.1 (1979) 835–68; idem, *The Early Fathers on War and Military Service* (Message of the Fathers of the Church 19; Wilmington, Del.: Glazier, 1983); David Hunter, "A Decade of Research on Early Christians and Military Service," *RelSRev* 18/2 (1992) 87–94; idem, "The Christian Church and the Roman Army in the First Three Centuries," in Marlin Miller and Barbara Gingerich, eds., *The Church's Peace Witness* (Grand Rapids: Eerdmans, 1994) 161–81; and Jean-Michel Hornus, *It Is Not Lawful for Me to Fight: Early Christian Attitudes toward War, Violence, and the State,* trans. Alan Kreider and Oliver Coburn (Scottdale, Pa.: Herald, 1980).

Latin	Sahidic	Arabic	Ethiopic
	41 Concerning the crafts and professions (ἐπιστήμη)	*Concerning the activities and what should be the correct behavior after [certain] activities and the activities that should be followed by those who come for catechesis*	*Concerning the occupation and what is good after the occupation and the work that is for those who bring them to exhortation*
1	(δέ) They shall inquire about the crafts and work of those who will be brought in to be catechized (καθιστᾶναι) as to what they are.		
2	If one is a brothel keeper (πορνοβοσκός) who is a caretaker of prostitutes (πόρνη), either (ἤ) let him cease or (ἤ) be cast out.	If one is a whore master he should stop or be excluded.	If there is one who is a fornicator, he is to be expelled.
3	If he is a maker of idols or (ἤ) painter (ζωγράφος), let them [sic] be taught not to make idols (εἴδωλον); either (ἤ) let them cease or (ἤ) be cast out.	If one is a maker of idols or a painter, he should learn that he should not make idols; and if he is not convinced that he should stop, he should be excluded.	And if there is one who makes idols or a painter, they are to teach him not to make idols; but if he does not wish to stop, he is to be expelled.
4	If one is an actor (θεατρικός) or (ἤ) he does performances (ὑπόδειξις) in the theater (θέατρον), either (ἤ) let him cease or (ἤ) be cast out.	If one attends the circus, he should stop or be excluded.	And if there is one who goes to the circus, he is to stop or be expelled.
5	If he teaches young children, it is good indeed (μέν) for him to cease. If he has no trade (τέχνη), then let him be forgiven.	If one is a teacher of young children, it is better that he stop, but if he has no other trade, he should be forgiven.	And if there is one who teaches children an occupation of this world, it is good if he stops; and if he does not have a second occupation by which to live, they are to excuse him.
6	Likewise (ὁμοίως), a charioteer (ἡνίοχος) who contends (ἀγωνίζεσθαι) and who goes to the games (ἀγών), either (ἤ) let him cease or (ἤ) be cast out.	He who attends pagan festivals should stop or be excluded.	One who goes to sacrifices for gods is to stop or be expelled.
7	One who is a gladiator (μονομάχος) or (ἤ) who teaches gladiators (μονομάχος) to fight, or (ἤ) a hunter (κυνηγός) who performs hunts (κυνήγιον), or (ἤ) an official (δημόσιος) who regulates the gladiatorial contests (μονομάχιον), either (ἤ) let them cease or (ἤ) be cast out.	One who is a gladiator or teaches gladiators or swordsmanship or military skills or weapons training should stop or be excluded.	And if one is a hunter or teaches hunting or teaches killing or warfare or is a master of horse racing, he is to stop or be expelled.
8	One who is a priest of the idols (—εἴδωλον), or (ἤ) who is a watchman of the idols (—εἴδωλον), either (ἤ) let him cease or (ἤ) be cast out.	One who is a pagan priest or guardian of idols should stop or be excluded.	And if he is a priest of gods or one who guards gods, he is to stop or be expelled.
9	A soldier who has authority	A soldier in the sovereign's	They are not to accept

Apostolic Constitutions 8.32.7–13

If anyone is a brothel keeper, either let him stop his pimping or be rejected. Let a prostitute who comes either stop or be rejected. Let an idol maker who comes either stop or be rejected. If any of them belongs to the theater, whether man, woman, charioteer, gladiator, stadium runner, trainer of athletes, one who participates in the Olympic Games, or one who accompanies the chorus on flute, lute, or lyre, or who puts on a display of dancing or is a fraudulent trader, let them either stop or be rejected. Let a soldier who comes be taught to do no injustice or to extort money, but to be content with his given wages. Let the one who objects be rejected. A doer of unmentionable things, a lustful person, a lascivious person, a magician, a mob leader, a charmer, an astrologer, a diviner, a charmer of wild beasts, a pimp, a maker of charms, one who purifies by applying objects, a fortune-teller, an interpreter of oracles, an interpreter of bodily vibrations, one who, upon encountering them, observes defects of eyes or feet or birds, or cats, or loud noises, or significant chance remarks—let them be examined for a time, for the evil is hard to wash out. Then, let those who stop be received, but let those not persuaded be rejected.

Canons of Hippolytus 11

Every craftsman is to be told not to make any image, or any idol, whether he is a sculptor, silversmith, or painter, or of any other art. If they happen after baptism to make any such thing, except what the people need, they are to be excluded until they repent. [12] Whoever becomes director of a theater, or a wrestler, or a runner, or teaches music, or plays before the processions, or teaches the art of the gladiator, or a hunter, or a hairdresser, or a fighter with savage beasts, or a priest of idols, all these, one is not to reveal to them any of the Holy Word, until they are purified first from these impure occupations. Then, during forty days they are to hear the Word, and if they are worthy they are to be baptized. The teacher of the church is the one who judges this matter. A schoolmaster who teaches little children, if he has not a livelihood by which to live except for that, may educate, if he reveals at all times to those he teaches and confesses that what the heathen call gods are demons, and says before them every day there is no divinity except the Father, the Son, and the Holy Spirit. If he can teach his pupils the excellent word of the poet, and better still if he can teach them the faith of the word of truth, for that he shall have a reward.

Testamentum Domini 2.2

If a fornicatress, or a brothel keeper, or a drunkard, or a maker of idols, or a painter, or one engaged in shows, or a charioteer, or a wrestler, or one who goes to the contest, or a combatant [in the games], or one who teaches wrestling, or a public huntsman, or a priest of idols, or a keeper of them, be [among those that come], let him not be received. If any such desires to become faithful, let him cease from these [things]; and being in deed faithful, and being baptized, let him be received and let him partake. And if he does not cease, let him be rejected. If anyone is a teacher of boys in worldly wisdom, it is well if he ceases. But if he has no other craft by which to live, let him be excused.

Latin	Sahidic	Arabic	Ethiopic
	(ἐξουσία), let him not kill a man. If he is ordered (κελεύεσθαι), let him not go to the task nor (οὐδέ) let him swear. But (δέ) if he is not willing, let him be cast out.	army should not kill, or if he is ordered to kill, he should refuse. If he stops, so be it; otherwise he should be excluded.	soldiers of an official, and if he is given an order to kill, he is not to do it, and if he does not stop, he is to be expelled.
		28 Concerning those who wear red or believers who become soldiers or astrologers or magicians or such like: let them be excluded	*28 Concerning other people, either a believer who becomes a soldier or an astrologer or magician or the like*

	Latin	Sahidic	Arabic	Ethiopic
10		One who has authority (ἐξουσία) of the sword, or (ἤ) a ruler (ἄρχων) of a city (πόλις) who wears the purple, either (ἤ) let him cease or (ἤ) be cast out.	One who has the power of the sword or the head of a city and wears red, let him stop or be excluded.	An official who has a sword or a chief of appointed people and who wears purple is to stop or be expelled.
11		A catechumen (κατηχούμενος) or (ἤ) faithful (πιστός) [person] if he wishes to become a soldier, let them [*sic*] be cast out because they despised (καταφρονεῖν) God.	A catechumen or a believer, if they want to be soldiers, let them be excluded because they distance themselves from God.	A catechumen or believer, if they wish to become a soldier, are to be expelled because they are far from God.
12		A prostitute (πορνή), or (ἤ) profligate man, or (ἤ) one who castrated himself, or (ἤ) again, another who did other things that it is not proper to mention, let them be cast out, for (γάρ) they are defiled.	A woman who commits fornication, or a person of no integrity, or a person who has done unspeakable things, let them be excluded because they are unclean,	An adulteress or a man without mercy or a man who does what it is not proper to mention are to be expelled because they are impure.
13		Nor (οὐδέ) shall a magician (μάγος) be considered for examination (κρίσις).	because a magician cannot be admitted to the ranks of the believers.	For it is not proper that they bring a magician into the congregation of the believers.
14		The enchanter or (ἤ) the astrologer (ἀστρολόγος), or (ἤ) the wizard, or (ἤ) the one who interprets dreams or (ἤ) the one who stirs up crowds, or (ἤ) the one who ruins the hems of garments, those who are the stutterers (ψελλιστής), or (ἤ) the one who makes phylacteries (φυλακτήριον), either (ἤ) let them cease or (ἤ) be cast out.	The astrologer, the owner of an astrolabe, the fortune-teller, anyone who causes divisions in the community, anyone who buys cloth from body snatchers, and anyone who makes phylacteries, let them stop or be excluded.	An astrologer and one who divines by the sun and a soothsayer or a dream interpreter or one who misleads people or one who buys beautiful clothes for the years or one who makes medicine is to stop or be expelled.

Apostolic Constitutions	Canons of Hippolytus	Testamentum Domini
	[13] Whoever has received the authority to kill, or else a soldier, they are not to kill in any case, even if they receive the order to kill. They are not to pronounce a bad word. Those who have received an honor are not to wear wreaths on their heads. Whosoever is raised to the authority of prefect or the magistracy and does not put on the righteousness of the gospel is to be excluded from the flock and the bishop is not to pray with him.	If anyone be a soldier or in authority, let him be taught not to oppress or to kill or to rob, or to be angry or to rage and afflict anyone. But let those rations suffice him that are given to him. But if they wish to be baptized in the Lord, let them cease from military service or from the [post of] authority, and if not let them not be received.
	[14] A Christian must not become a soldier, unless he is compelled by a chief bearing the sword. He is not to burden himself with the sin of blood. But if he has shed blood, he is not to partake of the mysteries, unless he is purified by a punishment, tears, and wailing. He is not to come forward deceitfully but in the fear of God.	Let a catechumen or a believer of the people, if he desires to be a soldier, either cease from his intention, or if not let him be rejected. For he has despised God by his thought, and leaving the things of the Spirit, he has perfected himself in the flesh, and has treated the faith with contempt.
	[15] A fornicator or one who lives on the proceeds of fornication, or an effeminate, and especially one who speaks of shameful [things], or an idler, or a profligate, or a magician or an astrologer, or a diviner, or an interpreter of dreams, or a snake charmer, or an agitator who agitates the people, or one who makes phylacteries, or a usurer, or an oppressor, or one who loves the world, or one who loves swearing, that is, oaths, or one who makes reproaches against the people, or one who is a hypocrite, or a slanderer of people, or who decides if the hours and the days are favorable, all these and the like, do not catechize them and baptize them, until they have renounced all occupations of this sort, and three witnesses have testified for them that they really have renounced all these vices, because often a man remains in his passions until his old age, unless he is enabled by a great power. If they are found after baptism in vices of this sort, they are to be excluded from the church until they repent with tears, fasting, and alms.	If a fornicatress or a dissolute man or a drunkard do not do [these things], and desire, believing, to be catechumens, they may [be admitted]. And if they make progress, let them be baptized; but if not let them be rejected.

	Latin	Sahidic	Arabic	Ethiopic
15			**29 Concerning concubines; and if we have omitted anything, make a suitable judgment**	**29 Concerning concubines, and if there is something that we have omitted, decide by what is proper**
		Someone's concubine (παλλακή), if (μέν) she is his servant, if she rears her children and is intimate with him alone, then let her hear. If not, let her be cast out.	One who is a concubine, if she is a slave and brings up her children and cohabits only with her master, let her hear, but if the situation is other than this, let her be excluded.	[As for] a man's concubine, if she is his servant, if she has raised her children and if she does not approach someone other than him, they are to accept her; but if there is another, he is to be expelled.
16		A man who has a concubine (παλλακή), let him cease, and let him take a wife according to (κατά) the law (νόμος). But (δέ) if he is unwilling, then let him be cast out.	If a man has a concubine, he should stop and marry according to the law, and if he is unwilling, let him be excluded.	And a man who has a concubine is to stop and marry legally. And if he does not want to [stop], he is to be expelled.
17		Therefore, if we have left out any other thing, the things themselves will inform you, for (γάρ) we all have the Spirit (πνεῦμα) of God.	If we have omitted anything, make a suitable judgment, for the Spirit of God is in us all.	And if there is something that we have omitted, decide by what is proper because all of us have the Spirit of God.

the result of a mistranslation of the text from which it was made.

■ **14** Botte suggested that the Greek loanword in the Sahidic translated as "stutterers" (ψελλιστής) was probably intended to be ψαλιστής, "cutters."[4] Since it serves to modify "the one who ruins the hems of garments," such people would hardly be called "stutterers." Although ψελλιστής is the *lectio difficilior* and might best explain why a later editor would want to change it, ψαλιστής would also fit with the references to clothing in the Arabic ("one who buys clothes from body snatchers") and Ethiopic ("one who buys beautiful clothes for the years"). Against the view of Botte that "coin trimmers," that is, those who dealt dishonestly with imperial coinage, was the intended reference at this point, Henry Chadwick countered by noting that the overall context is that of magic and that fringes or tassels on clothing "were often regarded in antiquity as a means of protecting the wearer against evil."[5]

■ **17** John Stam has suggested that this sentence is probably an interpolation based on *Ap. Trad.* 43.4,[6] and this suggestion is supported by the grammatical change from third-person singular to first-person plural here.

Comment

Chapter 15 called for a preliminary examination of the lives and motives of those seeking entrance into the catechumenate. Chapter 16 continues this initial examination by providing a catalog of prohibited occupations

---

4   Botte, *Tradition*, 39 n. 2; idem, "ΨΕΛΛΙΣΤΗΣ-ΨΑΛΙΣΤΗΣ," *Revue des Études Byzantines* 16 (1958) 162–65.

5   In Dix, *Apostolic Tradition*, m–n.

6   John E. Stam, "Charismatic Theology in the *Apostolic Tradition* of Hippolytus," in Gerald F. Hawthorne, ed., *Current Issues in Biblical and Patris-*

tic Interpretation: Studies in Honor of Merrill C. Tenney (Grand Rapids: Eerdmans, 1975) 270.

Apostolic Constitutions	*Canons of Hippolytus*	*Testamentum Domini*
Let a concubine who is a slave of some unbeliever, who devotes herself to that one alone, be received. But if she behaves licentiously toward others, let her be rejected. If a person of faith has a concubine, if a slave, let him stop and marry in the law. But if free, let him marry her in the law. But if not, let him be rejected.	[16] A Christian who has a concubine, especially if she has had a child by him, if he marries another, it is a homicide unless he catches her in fornication.	If a concubine of a man is a servant, and desires to believe, if she educates those who are born [of her] and she separates from her master, or be joined to him alone in marriage, let her hear; and being baptized let her partake in the offering, but if not let her be rejected. He who does things that may not be spoken of, or a diviner or a magician or a necromancer, these are defiled and do not come to judgment. Let a charmer, or an astrologer, or an interpreter of dreams, or a sorcerer, or one who gathers together the people, or a stargazer, or a diviner by idols, either cease, and when he ceases let him be exorcised and baptized; or if not, let him be rejected. If a man has a concubine, let him divorce her and marry in the law and hear the word of instruction.

that would bar someone from admission into the catechumenal process. These prohibited occupations are linked together throughout the chapter by the recurring literary refrain, "let him cease or be cast out," or, simply, "let [them] be cast out."

General parallels to the prohibited occupations in this chapter have often been noted in the writings of Tertullian, especially *De idololatria* (c. 211) and *De spectaculis* (c. 197–202),[7] although they have seldom been documented in detail. While Tertullian himself never produced a "list" of prohibited occupations in relationship to those seeking to enter the catechumenate, the various occupations listed in chap. 16 certainly reflect the kinds of ethical, moral, and social concerns that Tertullian had in mind for those who were already Christians or were seeking to become Christians in the church of his day. As such, much of the chapter is consistent with an early-third-century context, at least in North Africa, but some of it may be even older still.

■ 1 Only the Sahidic specifically directs that a preliminary inquiry be made about the various crafts and professions of those being presented.

■ 2 Only the Sahidic, Arabic, *Apostolic Constitutions*, and *Testamentum Domini* include "brothel keepers." The Ethiopic and *Testamentum Domini* include "fornicators," the *Apostolic Constitutions* lists "prostitutes," and the *Testamentum Domini* includes "drunkards." No similar reference occurs at this point in the *Canons of Hippolytus* (but see *Ap. Trad.* 16.12 below). Injunctions against lust and fornication, in parallel to the prohibition against "brothels" and "brothel keepers," appear in prebaptismal catechesis as early as *Did.* 3.2. Similarly, Tertullian (*De idol.* 11) declares that Christians should not engage in or manage brothels.

---

7   See, e.g., Cuming, *Hippolytus*, 15 n. 16.

■ **3** All versions and derivative documents include "idol makers." Only the Sahidic, Arabic, and *Testamentum Domini* also refer specifically to "painters" (of idols?). Tertullian strongly attacks idol makers in *De idololatria*, especially chaps. 5, 6, and 7.

■ **4** "Actors" are included only in the Sahidic, *Canons of Hippolytus* ("director of a theater"), *Apostolic Constitutions* ("those who belong to the theater"), and *Testamentum Domini* ("one engaged in shows").[8] The Arabic and Ethiopic also include here reference to one "who attends the circus." Rejection of the acting profession as unsuitable for Christians appears in Tertullian (*De spect.* 17), and he also condemns attendance at the circus (ibid., 8), in both cases because of the "immodesty" of what went on there.

■ **5** "Teachers of children" are included at this point in all the oriental versions but appear elsewhere in the list in the *Canons of Hippolytus* and *Testamentum Domini*, and not at all in the *Apostolic Constitutions*. A prohibition against Christians being teachers of classical literature is particularly strong in Tertullian (*De idol.* 10), on the grounds that it would be necessary for them to teach about pagans gods and observe their festivals. He permitted believers to learn literature, however, because the principle was different: teachers necessarily commended what they taught, while learners did not, and would reject what was false. Tertullian was here more rigorist than are the oriental versions of *Apostolic Tradition*, which permit the person to continue teaching if he has no other means of employment. Although located at a different point in their texts, both the *Canons of Hippolytus* and *Testamentum Domini* also make this concession, with the former adding that the schoolmaster is to reveal "at all times to those he teaches and confesses that what the Gentiles call gods are demons, and says before them every day there is no divinity except the Father, the Son, and the Holy Spirit." Such leniency may suggest development on this issue after the time of Tertullian himself or, alternatively, it may merely be nothing other than a concession made for pastoral reasons.

■ **6** The prohibition against "charioteers," which is found in the Sahidic, *Apostolic Constitutions*, and *Testa-mentum Domini*, also receives special treatment in Tertullian (*De spect.* 9). He regards this activity as a form of idolatry, because the racing colors were dedicated to pagan deities. The absence of any mention of this practice in the Arabic and Ethiopic texts may be because chariot racing was not held in the communities through which the text was transmitted and so it was deleted as irrelevant, or it may be because involvement in it was no longer viewed as idolatrous.

■ **7** Gladiators and teachers of gladiators, as well as all other occupations associated with the gladiatorial games, are also condemned by Tertullian (*De idol.* 11; *De spect.* 12, 19), both on the grounds that human deaths were made the means of public entertainment and also because of a historical connection of the practice with offerings to the dead.

■ **9** Prohibitions against particular kinds of high-ranking soldiers are attested in all the versions and derivative documents. The particular prescriptions regarding these "soldiers in authority," however, varies. While the Sahidic and Arabic permit such soldiers to enter the catechumenate if they refrain from killing, the Ethiopic initially appears much more rigorist ("they are not to accept soldiers of an official") but then immediately makes the concession provided in the other versions.

On soldiers and killing, whether during warfare or in administering capital punishment, the witness of Tertullian is generally consistent with the Sahidic and Arabic texts (*De cor.* 11; *De idol.* 19), although he was also well aware that some of his contemporaries were already rationalizing the legitimacy of military service by reference to the words of John the Baptist in Luke 3:14, which are also alluded to in the *Apostolic Constitutions* here.

■ **10** The prohibition against admitting rulers into the catechumenate is paralleled in Tertullian by an attack on Christians assuming an office that required involvement in pagan sacrifices, temples, festivals, and such like, or even their wearing the dress and insignia of the office without performing any of those functions, since such things themselves carried the implication of idolatry (*De idol.* 17–18). It is difficult to be sure whether the *Apo-*

---

8   According to James Cooper and Arthur J. Maclean, *The Testament of Our Lord Translated into English from the Syriac* (Edinburgh: T. & T. Clark, 1902) 117 n. 8, this reference in the *Testamentum Domini* is equivalent to that in the *Apostolic Constitutions* here.

stolic Tradition is concerned with the cessation of wearing the purple of office or with the office itself.

■ **11** See the commentary on *Ap. Trad.* 16.9 above.

■ **12** See the commentary on *Ap. Trad.* 16.2 above.

■ **13–14** Prohibitions against diviners, astrologers, and magicians appear as early as *Did.* 3.4 as well as in Tertullian (*De idol.* 9).

■ **15–16** The prohibitions against unfaithful concubines and men with concubines are not reflected in early Christian literature outside the *Apostolic Tradition* and its derivative documents, although of course the practice of concubinage is well attested in the ancient Greco-Roman world.[9]

■ **17** The claim made by Paul to possess the Spirit of God (1 Cor 7:40) for the purpose of making moral decisions is applied here to the whole Christian community. Tertullian (*De ex. cast.* 4) similarly acknowledges that all believers have the Spirit, but distinguishes between its possession fully by apostles and partially by others.

---

9   See, e.g., Brown, *Body*, 29, 147, 151, 390, 393; idem, *Augustine of Hippo* (Berkeley: Univ. of California Press, 1967) 61–63, 88–90, 248.

Concerning the Time of Hearing the Word after the Examination of Crafts and Professions

Latin	Sahidic	Arabic	Ethiopic
	42 Concerning the time (χρόνος) of those who hear the Word after the crafts and professions (ἐπιστήμη)	**30 Concerning the time for listening to the Word after [giving up] the [above] activities**	**30 Concerning the time when they hear teaching after an occupation**
1	**Let the catechumens (κατη-χούμενος) hear the Word for three years.**	**Let the catechumens listen to the Word for three years.**	**The catechumens are to continue hearing the word of teaching for three years.**
2	**But (δέ) if one is earnest (σπουδαῖος) and perseveres (προσκαρτερεῖν) well (καλῶς) in the work, the time (χρόνος) is never judged (κρίνειν), but (ἀλλά) the character (τρό-πος) only is that which shall be judged (κρίνειν).**	**If they learn and meditate well, do not judge them for the time, but let them be judged only by their action.**	**And if one becomes knowledgeable and knows what is good, [a length of] time is not to be required for him but his conduct alone is what decides for him.**

Text

There are no significant textual variations in this chapter.

Comment

The reference to a three-year catechumenate in the *Apostolic Constitutions* as well as all the oriental versions demonstrates that this chapter was certainly part of the text of the *Apostolic Tradition* in the second half of the fourth century. But was it already there at an earlier date? Scholars have often pointed to a three-year tree-planting allegory in Clement of Alexandria as an early Alexandrian parallel in this context:

> And it [the Law] does not allow imperfect fruit to be plucked from immature trees, but *after three years*, in the fourth year; dedicating the first-fruits to God after the tree has maintained maturity. This type of husbandry may serve as a mode of instruction, teaching that we must cut the growth of sins, and the useless weeds of the mind that spring up round the vital fruit, till the shoot of faith is perfected and becomes strong. For in the fourth year, *since there is need of time to him that is being solidly catechized*, the four virtues are consecrated to God, the third alone being already joined to the fourth, the person of the Lord.[1]

It is not clear, however, if Clement is referring to the prebaptismal catechumenal period, to the length of philosophical and theological training given at his famous catechetical school in Alexandria, or to something else all together.[2] For that matter, there is an apparent reference to a *three-month* catechumenate in the mid-third-century Syrian *Pseudo-Clementine Recognitions* (3.67): "Whosoever will, then, let him come to Zacchaeus and give his name to him, and let him hear from him the mysteries of the kingdom of heaven. Let him attend to frequent fastings, and approve himself in all things, that at the end of these *three months* he may be baptized on the day of the festival."[3] A reference to a three-year probationary period appears in canon 1 of Peter of Alexandria (bishop 300–311 CE), but here related not to

---

1   Clement of Alexandria *Strom.* 2.18; ET from ANF 2:368 (emphasis added).
2   See Paul F. Bradshaw, "Baptismal Practice in the Alexandrian Tradition, Eastern or Western?" in idem, ed., *Essays in Early Eastern Initiation* (JLS 8; Nottingham: Grove, 1988) 10. Clement is summarizing and reworking Philo of Alexandria, *De virtutibus* 156–58, which is an allegorical interpretation of Lev 19:23-25. The fact that Clement is quoting Philo

makes it even less likely that this passage is a reference to a three-year catechumenate.
3   ANF 8:132 (emphasis added).

Apostolic Constitutions 8.32.16	**Canons of Hippolytus** 17	**Testamentum Domini** 2.3
Let the one coming to be catechized be instructed for three years. But if anyone is eager and has zeal for the task, let him be received, for it is not the time but the way that is judged.	. . . The catechumen who is worthy of the light, the time is not to be an obstacle for him, because his conduct is a proof: the teacher of the church is the one who judges this matter.	Let him who is instructed with all care and hears the perfectness of the gospel, be instructed not less than three years, and if he, loving, strives to be baptized, let him [then] be baptized. But if he be quiet and meek and earnest, and persevering and abiding with him who teaches him, with labor, with watching, with confession, with subjection, and with prayers, and [if] he desires to be baptized sooner, let him be baptized. For it is not the time that is judged, but the will of faith.

preparation for baptism but to the duration of penance for penitent apostates.[4] One of the mid-fourth-century *Canonical Letters* of Basil makes a similar requirement of a three-year abstinence from the Eucharist for a "soldier with unclean hands."[5]

It is possible, but certainly not conclusive or an exact parallel, that a three-year catechumenate was modelled on Qumran practice and, hence, could have been an early Christian adaptation. Josephus, for example, describes the three-year trial period required by the Essenes before they were allowed into the ritual meals (*Jewish War* 2.8.7). Hippolytus, in his very sympathetic description of the Essenes, quotes verbatim from Josephus's description:

> Now for the space of a year they set before (the candidates) the same food, while the latter continue to live in a different house outside the Essenes' own place of meeting. When, at the expiration of this period, one affords proof of self-control, he approaches nearer to the sect's method of living, and he is washed more purely than before. Not as yet, however, does he partake of food along with the Essenes. For, after having furnished evidence as to whether he is able to acquire

self-control—but for two years the habit of a person of this description is on trial—and when he has appeared deserving, he is thus reckoned amongst the members of the sect.[6]

Hippolytus also quotes Josephus's description of a subsect of Essenes who encourage marriage over celibacy, but practice a three-year-long betrothal: "However, they make a trial of their betrothed women for a period of three years. . . ."[7] There are other references to a three-year period in antiquity. In his description of the woman who gave up her seven sons to martyrdom under Antiochus IV, Cyprian of Carthage refers to three years as the length of time a mother breast-feeds her children.[8] Similarly, the *Protoevangelium of James* 7.1 suggests that at three years a child no longer desires her parents.

Outside these documents the only clear parallel statement about such a lengthy catechumenal period in the early church is canon 42 of the Council of Elvira (c. 305), which specifies a two-year general catechumenate. Michel Dujarier interprets this as a reduction or "relaxation of discipline" in relation to both Clement and the *Apostolic Tradition*. But, as Dujarier himself notes, this same council mandates that serious faults could prolong

---

4   ET in ANF 6:269.
5   *Ep.* 188.13; ET in Philip Schaff and Henry Wace, eds., *The Nicene and Post-Nicene Fathers* 8 (reprinted Grand Rapids: Eerdmans, 1983) 228.
6   *Ref.* 9.18, trans. ANF.
7   *Ref.* 9.38, trans. ANF.
8   *Ad Fortunatum* 11.

the catechumenate to three years (canon 4), five years (canon 73), or even to the end of one's life (canon 73). Similarly, as Dujarier again notes, the Council of Nicea (canon 2) also sought to ensure that a period of adequate preparation for baptism be provided in order to guarantee that the transition from pagan to Christian life not be as abrupt as apparently it had been previously.[9]

Other allusions to the length of prebaptismal catechesis tend to suggest that this period was only three weeks in duration within several places in the early church (Rome, Jerusalem, Syria). It is uncertain, however, whether this three-week period constituted the total length of prebaptismal preparation or merely the final period immediately preceding baptism.[10]

Is this chapter, therefore, a fourth-century addition to the text, when a concern for the length of baptismal preparation was clearly being expressed elsewhere in the church? Like the canons of the Council of Elvira, the reference to a three-year catechumenate here—for which no undisputed third-century corroboration is available—may perhaps best be interpreted as a parallel attempt to ensure adequate catechumenal preparation in the early fourth century. If so, the traditional assumption that the pre-Nicene church knew a general catechumenate of three years would fall to the wayside.

9   Michel Dujarier, *A History of the Catechumenate* (New York: Sadlier, 1979) 69.

10   On this see Maxwell E. Johnson, "From Three Weeks to Forty Days: Baptismal Preparation and the Origins of Lent," *StLit* 20 (1990) 185–200; reprinted in idem., ed., *Living Water, Sealing Spirit: Readings on Christian Initiation* (Collegeville, Minn.: Liturgical, 1995) 118–36; idem, "Preparation for Pascha? Lent in Christian Antiquity," in Paul Bradshaw and Lawrence Hoffman, eds., *Passover and Easter: The Symbolic Structuring of Sacred Seasons* (Notre Dame: Univ. of Notre Dame Press, 1999) 36–54.

Text

There are only slight variations among the versions in this chapter.

■ **2** The oriental versions agree that women, whether catechumens or members of the faithful, are to stand separately "in a place in the church" for prayer. The *Canons of Hippolytus*, however, although including the phrase "in a place," makes no reference to this place as being "in the church." If the phrase "in the church" in the versions refers to the building rather than the community, as seems likely,[1] then it is possible that it is a later addition to an earlier simple reference to women catechumens and faithful being separated "in a place."

Comment

■ **1–2** A parallel for liturgical assemblies being segregated according to sex and status appears in the mid-third-century Syrian *Didascalia Apostolorum*:

> For thus should it be, that in the most easterly part of the house the presbyters sit with the bishops, and next the lay men, and then the women; so that when you stand up to pray, the leaders may stand first, and after them the lay men, and then the women too.... The young girls should also sit separately, or if there is no room, they should stand up behind the women. Young women who are married and have children should stand separately, and elderly women and widows should sit separately.[2]

There is no evidence of Jewish synagogue worship being segregated according to gender in the early Christian period. In Greco-Roman antiquity, however, such practices, including even at the theater, were common. Segregation by gender in the Christian liturgical assembly, then, undoubtedly reflects this cultural context.[3]

■ **3–4** References to prayer being concluded by a kiss appear as early as Justin Martyr (*1 Apol.* 65) and also in Tertullian (*De or.* 18). The kiss of peace, which often concluded various liturgical rites in early Christianity, was regularly reserved to the baptized alone. Since the kiss was an actual exchange of *pneuma* ("breath" or "spirit"), the catechumens and the elect, who had not yet received the Spirit in baptism, were excluded from it.[4] There is no evidence elsewhere, however, for the segragation of the sexes for the kiss in early Christian communities. Indeed, Tertullian (*Ad uxor.* 2.4) notes that the practice of kissing the "brothers" could pose a problem for women married to unbelievers.

■ **5** The earliest parallel for the necessity of full head coverings for women is found in Tertullian (*De virg. vel.* 17). Veiling was a common practice in antiquity, used to enforce decorum and modesty on women. Early Christianity inherited this cultural practice; authors such as Tertullian often defended it vigorously, even for virgins who were not normally veiled in pagan society, as externalizing "the sexual shame associated with women old enough to undergo the 'common slur' of the marriage bed."[5]

---

1. Dix (*Apostolic Tradition*, lv) argued that "everywhere in the *Apostolic Tradition* 'the Church' means *the congregation, not the building*." According to Cuming (*Hippolytus*, 16), however, this interpretation is incorrect here and elsewhere in the document. See chaps. 21, 35, 39, and 41.

2. *Didasc.* 2.57; ET from Brock and Vasey, *Didascalia*, 15–16.

3. See Ross S. Kraemer, *Her Share of the Blessings: Women's Religions among Pagans, Jews, and Christians in the Greco-Roman World* (New York: Oxford Univ. Press, 1992) 106–7, 126; idem, "Jewish Women and Women's Judaism(s) at the Beginning of Christianity," in Ross Shepard Kraemer and Mary Rose

D'Angelo, eds., *Women and Christian Origins* (New York: Oxford Univ. Press, 1999) 64–65.

4. See Phillips, *Ritual Kiss*, 19–21; Michael Penn, "Performing Family: Ritual Kissing and the Construction of Early Christian Kinship," *Journal of Early Christian Studies* 10 (2002) 15–58.

5. Brown, *Body*, 80. See also Mary Rose D'Angelo, "Veils, Virgins, and the Tongues of Men and Angels: Women's Heads in Early Christianity," in Howard Eilberg-Schwartz and Wendy Doniger, eds., *Off with Her Head! The Denial of Women's Identity in Myth, Religion, and Culture* (Berkeley: Univ. of California Press, 1995) 131–64.

Latin	Sahidic	Arabic	Ethiopic
	43 Concerning the prayer of those who hear the Word	*31 Concerning the prayer of the catechumens and the kiss*	*31 Concerning the prayer of one who hears instruction and the kiss*
1	When (ὅταν) the teacher has finished instructing (κατηχεῖσθαι), let the catechumens (κατηχούμενος) pray by themselves separated from the faithful (πιστός).	When the teacher has finished his preaching, let the catechumens pray on their own separately from the believers.	When the teacher completes admonishing, the catechumens are to pray by themselves, separated from the believers.
2	And let the women stand praying in a place in the church (ἐκκλησία) all by themselves, whether (εἴτε) women faithful (πιστός) or (εἴτε) women catechumens (κατηχούμενος).	Let the women stand in a [separate] place in the church to pray on their own, whether women believers or women catechumens.	And the women are to stand in a place in the church and pray alone—the women believers and the female catechumens.
3	And (δέ) when they finish praying, they do not give [the] peace (εἰρήνη), for (γάρ) their kiss is not yet holy.	When they finish praying, the women catechumens should not give the greeting, because their kiss is not yet pure,	If the prayer is finished, the catechumens are not to kiss one another with the believers because their kiss has not yet become pure.
4	But (δέ) let the faithful (πιστός) greet (ἀσπάζεσθαι) each other only, men with men, and women with women. Men (δέ) do not greet (ἀσπάζεσθαι) women.	and let the women believers kiss each other. The men should kiss the men and the women the women, and the men should not kiss the women.	And the believers are to kiss one another—a man is to kiss a man and women are to kiss women. And men are not to kiss women.
5	But (δέ) let all women clothe the heads in a pall (πάλλιον), but (ἀλλά) [not] in a piece (εἶδος) of linen only, for this is not a head covering (κάλυμμα).	All the women should cover their heads with their robes or their cloaks and not only with a piece of linen, because this is not [enough] for a veil for them.	And all the women are to veil their head with a cover or with a mantle and not with a linen cloth alone, because this is not what has been given to them.

Apostolic Constitutions	*Canons of Hippolytus* 18	*Testamentum Domini* 2.4
	After the teacher has finished instructing each day, they are to pray separated from the Christians. . . .	Let those who are instructed, after the teacher ceases, pray apart from the faithful and go out, so that the faithful may learn, when the presbyter or deacon reads the New [Testament] or Gospels.
	The women are to be separated in a place. They are not to give the kiss to any man. The teacher is to lay the hand on the catechumens before dismissing them.	Let the faithful women stand in the church by themselves and the female catechumens by themselves apart from the faithful [women]. But all the [women] apart from the men; the girls also apart, each according to her order. The men on the right and the women on the left; the faithful virgins first, and the [women] who are being instructed to virginity behind them. After the prayer let the female catechumens give the peace to one another; also men to men; also women to women.
	The girls, when the period of their adolescence is over, are to cover the head, like the adult women, with their shawl, not with a thin cloth. . . .	Let every woman cover her head with her hair also. Let the women becomingly and decorously show their modesty in their adornment, and let them not be adorned with plaited hair or with [precious] stones, lest the young men who are in the church be caught, but with modesty and knowledge. But if not, let them be instructed by the widows who sit in front. But if they rebelliously resist, let the bishop reprove them.

Latin	Sahidic	Arabic	Ethiopic
	44 Concerning the way of laying hand on the catechumens (κατηχούμενος)	*32 Concerning laying hands on the catechumens*	*32 Concerning laying the hand on catechumens*
1		When the one who teaches, after the prayer, lays hand on the catechumens (κατηχούμενος), let him pray and dismiss them. Whether (εἴτε) a cleric (ἐκκλησιαστικός) is the one who teaches or (εἴτε) a layperson (λαϊκός), let him act the same way.	After the prayer, if the teacher lays hands on the catechumens, let him pray and dismiss them. He should do this whether it is a cleric or a layman who does the teaching.	And after the prayer, when the teacher has placed a hand on the catechumen, he is to pray and dismiss them. And if the one who teaches is a cleric or a layperson, he is to act in this way.
2		If a catechumen (κατηχούμενος) is arrested for the name of the Lord, he is not to be double-minded concerning the testimony. For (γάρ) if it happens and they act violently against him and kill him during the forgiveness of his sins, he will be justified, for (γάρ) he received baptism (βάπτισμα) in his own blood.	If they arrest a catechumen for the sake of the Lord, let him not be double-minded concerning martyrdom. If he is wronged and killed before gaining forgiveness of his sins, he will be vindicated because he will have been baptized in his own blood.	If they arrest a catechumen on account of the name of our Lord Jesus Christ, he is not to be double-hearted about the testimony. For if they overpower him and harm him and kill him before he receives baptism for the forgiveness of his sin, he is justified because he was baptized by his own blood.

Text

■ **1** All the versions agree that the "teacher" who is to lay hands on and dismiss the catechumens after prayer may be either a cleric or a layperson. But as the word in reference to an ordained person is otherwise found only from the fourth century onward, it is possible that the reading of the *Apostolic Constitutions*, "if the teacher is also a layperson," may be a more faithful rendering of the Greek text.[1]

■ **2** Where we have translated the Sahidic as "during the forgiveness of his sins," the phrase is literally, "in the forgiveness. . . ." Even though the Bohairic supports the Sahidic, most translators have preferred to follow the Arabic and Ethiopic and render it as "before."

Comment

■ **1** If the commonly accepted early-third-century date for the *Apostolic Tradition* as a whole is correct, then this passage constitutes the sole testimony in the first three centuries of the Common Era to the liturgical rite of the imposition of hands and dismissal of catechumens. All other witnesses to this practice belong to the late fourth century: for example, *Const.* 8.6.1–9.11 in the context of dismissals of various categories of people in the eucharistic liturgy, and the *Pilgrimage of Egeria* within the context not only of prebaptismal catechesis itself but within a variety of liturgical occasions.[2]

The lack of early corroborating evidence does not, of course, mean that this passage does not belong to the early third century or that what we see in fourth-century documents does not reflect a consistent evolution in relationship with what came before. But it does suggest that considerable caution needs to be exercised with regard to drawing firm conclusions from this text about early-third-century liturgical practice in general.

---

1   See Bradshaw, "Redating," 12 n. 30.
2   Egeria *Peregrinatio* 24.2–25.6.

Apostolic Constitutions 8.32.17	*Canons of Hippolytus*	*Testamentum Domini* 2.5
If the teacher is also a layperson, but experienced in the Word and the way of good character, let him teach, for all shall be taught of God.	[See above, p. 101]	After the catechumens pray, let the bishop or presbyter, laying a hand on them, say the prayer of the laying on of the hand of catechumens. . . . After this let them be dismissed.
	[19] When a catechumen is arrested because of witness and killed before having been baptized, he is to be buried with all the martyrs, because he has been baptized in his own blood.	If anyone, being a catechumen, is apprehended for my name and be judged with tortures, and hastens and presses forward to receive the laver, let the shepherd not hesitate, but let him give [it] to him. But if he suffer violence and be killed, not having received the laver, let him not be anxious. For having been baptized in his own blood, [he is] justified.

■ **2** References to baptism by martyrdom or blood do occur in some third-century documents. Tertullian (*De bapt.* 16) refers to a "baptism by blood," but it is by no means clear whether martyrdom is intended there. More obviously parallel is the description of the death of Saturus in the famous *Passion of St. Perpetua* (21.2; see also 18.3), sometimes ascribed to Tertullian himself: "And immediately at the conclusion of the exhibition he was thrown to the leopard; and with one bite of his he was bathed with such a quantity of blood, that the people shouted out to him as he was returning, the testimony of his second baptism, 'Saved and washed, saved and washed.'"[3] Other references come from the mid-third century in the context of the Decian persecution. Cyprian writes that catechumens who suffer martyrdom before they have received baptism with water "are not deprived of the sacrament of baptism. Rather, they are baptized with the most glorious and greatest *baptism of blood*, concerning which the Lord said that he had another baptism with which he himself was to be baptized."[4] In a similar way Origen writes in his *Exhortation to Martyrdom* 30: "Let us also remember the sins that we have committed, and that it is impossible to receive forgiveness of sins apart from baptism, that it is impossible according to the laws of the Gospel to be baptized again with water and the Spirit for the forgiveness of sins, and that the *baptism of martyrdom* has been given to us."[5]

3 ET from ANF 3:705.
4 *Ep.* 73.22 (emphasis added).
5 ET from Rowan A. Greer, ed., *Origen* (New York: Paulist, 1979) 61.

103

Latin	Sahidic	Arabic	Ethiopic
	45 Concerning those who will receive baptism (βάπτισμα)	*33 Concerning those who are baptized*	*33 Concerning one who is baptized*
1	And (δέ) when those appointed to receive baptism (βάπτισμα) are chosen, their life (βίος) having been examined (if they lived virtuously [−σεμνός] while they were catechumens [κατηχούμενος], and if they honored the widows [χήρα], and if they visited those who are sick, and if they fulfilled every good work),	After one or whoever is chosen to prepare for baptism, his way of life should be examined. Has he lived virtuously while they were being catechized? Have they honored the widows, visited the sick, fulfilled all good works?	When one has been chosen or who has prepared himself for baptism, they are to make an examination regarding their way of life, whether they have lived in the fear of God before they are baptized; whether they honored the widow or visited the sick or if they fulfilled all good works.
2	and when those who brought them in testify in his [*sic*] behalf that he acted thus, then let them hear the gospel (εὐαγγέλιον).	If those who have brought them bear witness that they have done so, let them hear the gospel from the day on which they are put forward	And if those who brought them become a witness for them and if they have acted in this way, they are to hear the gospel from the day they were separated.
3	And (δέ), from the time that they will be separated, let hand be laid on them daily, exorcising (ἐξορκίζειν) them. And (δέ) when the day draws near when they will be baptized (βαπτίζειν), let the bishop (ἐπίσκοπος) exorcise (ἐξορκίζειν) each one of them so that he may know that they are holy.	and let hands be laid on them every day and let them be exorcised. When the day on which they are to be baptized draws near, let the bishop gain a solemn assurance from each one to know that they are pure.	And they are to place a hand on them every day and teach them. And when the day on which they will be baptized has arrived, the bishop is to make each one of them swear so that he may know whether they are pure.
4	But (δέ) if there is one who is not good (καλός) or (ἤ) undefiled (καθαρός), let him be put aside because he did not hear the Word faithfully (−πίστις), since it is never possible to hide the stranger.	And if one is not pure, let him be set aside because he has not heard the Word faithfully, because it is never possible that an outsider should be baptized.	And if there is one who is not pure, they are to remove him thither by himself because he did not hear the word of instruction with faith, for it is not appropriate to do [this] for a stranger at all.
5	And (δέ) let those who are appointed for baptism (βαπτίζειν) be taught to wash and make themselves free, and wash themselves on the fifth day of the week (σάββατον).	They instruct those who are to be baptized that they should bathe and wash on the fifth [day] of the week.	And they are to teach those who are baptized that they should wash themselves and be exorcised on the fifth [day] of the week.
6	But (δέ) if a woman is in her time of menstruation, let her be set aside and receive baptism (−βάπτισμα) on another day.	If there is among them a woman who is menstruating, she should be set aside and be baptized on another day.	And if there is among them a woman who is menstruating, she is to be removed away so that she may be baptized on another day.

104

Apostolic Constitutions	Canons of Hippolytus	Testamentum Domini 2.6
	The catechumen, when he is baptized, and he who presents him attests that he has been zealous for the commandments during the time of his catechumenate, that he has visited the sick or given to the needy, that he has kept himself from every wicked and disgraceful word, that he has hated vainglory, despised pride, and chosen for himself humility, and he confesses to the bishop that he [takes] responsibility for himself, so that the bishop is satisfied about him and considers him [worthy] of the mysteries, and that he has become truly pure, then he reads over him the gospel at that time, and asks him several times, "Are you in two minds, or under pressure from anything, or driven by convention? For nobody mocks the kingdom of heaven, but it is given to those who love it with all their heart."	But if they are severally chosen to receive the laver, let them be proved and investigated first, how they have lived while catechumens, if they have honored widows, if they have visited the sick, if they have walked in all meekness and love, if they were earnest in good works. But let them be attested by those who bring them. And when they hear the gospel, let a hand be laid on them daily. Let them be exorcised from that day when they are chosen. And let them be baptized in the days of Pascha. And when the days approach, let the bishop exorcise each one of them separately by himself, so that he may be persuaded that he is pure. For if there be one that is not pure, or in whom is an unclean spirit, let him be reproved by that unclean spirit. If then anyone is found under any such suspicion, let him be removed from the midst [of them], and let him be reproved and reproached because he has not heard the word of the commandments and of instruction faithfully, because the evil and strange spirit remained in him.
	Those who are to be baptized are to bathe in water on the fifth day of the week and eat. They are to fast on Friday. If there is a woman and she has her menstrual period, she is not to be baptized on that occasion but she is to wait until she is purified.	Let those who are about to receive the laver be taught on the fifth day of the last week only to wash and bathe their heads. But if any woman then be in the customary flux, let her also take in addition another day, washing and bathing beforehand.

	Latin	Sahidic	Arabic	Ethiopic
7		Let those who will receive baptism (—βάπτισμα) fast (νηστεύειν) on the day of preparation (παρασκευή) of the Sabbath (σάββατον). (δέ) On the Sabbath (σάββατον), when those who will receive baptism (—βάπτισμα) gather in one place under the direction (γνώμη) of the bishop (ἐπίσκοπος), let them all be commanded to pray and to bend their knees.	Those who want to be baptized fast on the Friday. On the Saturday the bishop gathers together those who are to be baptized in one place and tells them all to pray and kneel.	And those who wish to be baptized are to fast on Friday, and on Saturday the bishop is to assemble in one place those who are to be baptized and command all of them to pray and bow down.
8		And when he has laid his hand on them, let him exorcise (ἐξορκίζειν) every foreign spirit (πνεῦμα), that they flee from them and not return to them ever again. And when he has finished exorcising (ἐξορκίζειν), let him blow into them. And when he has sealed (σφραγίζειν) their foreheads and their ears and nostrils, let him raise them up.	When he puts his hand on them, he exorcises every strange spirit [commanding them] to leave them and never return. After adjuring them, he breathes on them and signs their foreheads, their ears, and their nostrils. Then let him raise them up	And when he has placed his hands on them, he is to anathematize every unclean spirit to flee from them and not come back upon them again. And if he has completed anathematizing them, he is to breathe on them
9		And let them spend the whole night awake, being read to and instructed (κατηχεῖσθαι).	and let them keep the whole night listening to readings and preaching.	and they are to read to them and exhort them.
10		And (δέ) those who will receive baptism (—βάπτισμα) are not to have any other thing except only (εἰ μήτι) that which each one will bring in for the Eucharist (εὐχαριστία), for (γάρ) it is proper for the one who is worthy to bring his offering (προσφορά) at that time.	He who is to be baptized should not bring anything with him. Only let each one give thanks, and it is right that he who is worthy should bring his offering at [that] hour.	And those who are being baptized are not to bring with them a gold ornament, a ring, a gem or anything [of that kind], but each one is to give thanks. It is fitting for those for whom it is proper to bring their oblation at its time.

Apostolic Constitutions	Canons of Hippolytus	Testamentum Domini
	On Saturday the bishop assembles those who are to be baptized. He makes them bow the head toward the east,	Let them fast both [on] the Friday and [on] the Saturday. [7] On the Saturday let the bishop assemble those who will receive the laver, and let him bid [them] to kneel while the deacon proclaims.
	extends his hand over them, and prays and expels every evil spirit from them by his exorcism, and these never return to them from that time on through their deeds. When he has finished exorcising them, he breathes on their face and signs their breast, their forehead, their ears, and their nose.	And when there is silence, let him exorcise [them], laying a hand on them, and saying. . . . After the priest exorcises those who have drawn near, or him who is found unclean, let the priest breathe on them and seal them on their foreheads, on the nose, on the heart, on the ears; and so let him raise them up. [8] In the forty days of Pascha, let the people abide in the temple, keeping vigil and praying, hearing the Scriptures and hymns of praise and the books of doctrine.
	They are to spend all their night in the sacred Word and prayers.	But on the last Saturday let them come early in the night, and when the catechumens are being exorcised till the Saturday midnight. Let those who are about to be baptized not bring anything else with them except one loaf for the Eucharist.

Concerning Those Who Are to Receive Baptism

Text

As early as 1968, Jean-Paul Bouhot suggested that the rites of initiation in *Apostolic Tradition* 20–21 reflected two strata of development: an earlier Roman document focusing on the role of the bishop; and an "African" interpolation beginning with 21.6, which focused on the roles of presbyters and deacons and continued throughout the remainder of chap. 21.[1] While Bouhot's conclusion is stronger than the evidence permits, the numerous parallels between chaps. 20–21 (and 15–20, for that matter) and the North African initiation rites described by Tertullian and Cyprian makes North African influence on the final redaction of this section quite plausible.

Furthermore, it appears that the directions associated with the role of the bishop may themselves be additions to an even earlier text and, hence, constitute a middle stratum between a "core document" and the final addition of specific rubrical directions for presbyters and deacons. (Indeed, it has been suggested that these latter directives may have been drawn from a set of baptismal instructions intended for use when a presbyter presided over the rite in the absence of a bishop.)[2] For up to 20.3 in the initiatory section of the *Apostolic Tradition*, the process is described only in a very general manner, in impersonal and hortatory terms (e.g., "let those . . ."; "let prayer be made . . .") without clarifying the precise roles of particular ministers. Indeed, no specific ordained ministers are mentioned at all, and it is generally the catechumens or candidates themselves who function as the subjects of the various directives. From this point on, however, rubrical directions concerning the various roles of the ordained ministers in Christian initiation—bishops, presbyters, and deacons—appear with greater frequency, and the text now alternates between more general directives concerning Christian initiation and specific detailed directives regarding the ministers. This suggests that it may be made up of at least three

strata, and so the reference to the bishop's action in *Ap. Trad.* 20.3, to his "direction" in 20.7, and to episcopal exorcism in 20.8 are later interpolations in the text of this chapter.[3]

■ **4** The concluding phrase, "since it is never possible to hide the stranger" (Sahidic), "because it is never possible that an outsider should be baptized" (Arabic), or "for it is not appropriate to do [this] for a stranger at all" (Ethiopic), poses a difficulty in translation. But Botte and Cuming suggested that the original Greek word translated here as "stranger" or "outsider" was ἀλλότριος, which was used to denote the devil.[4] Support is given to this by the Sahidic word ϢⲘⲘⲞ, which occurs here and is also used to translate ἀλλότριος in, for example, the Sahidic version of John 10:5. Note also ⲠⲚⲈⲨⲘⲀ ⲚⲀⲖⲖⲞⲦⲢⲒⲞⲚ (a Sahidic transliteration of the Greek πνεῦμα ἀλλότριον, lit. "alien spirit") in the sense of "demon" in the Sahidic of *Ap. Trad.* 38.2. Thus what is envisaged here is not the seemingly impossible situation of a baptismal candidate still being at this point in the catechumenal process a stranger, but rather that the episcopal exorcism (at least in the Sahidic) is concerned with revealing or determining whether the power of the real stranger, outsider, or alien has been overcome (see also *Ap. Trad.* 21.5 below).

■ **5** The phrase "and make themselves free" appears only in the Sahidic version and, according to Botte, is an error by a scribe, misreading ⲚⲤⲈⲀⲀⲨ, "and make themselves," for ⲚⲤⲈⲈⲒⲀⲀⲨ, "and wash themselves," and then adding "free," ⲢⲘ̄ⲎⲈ, to create an allusion to either Rom 8:2, 21, or Gal 5:2. Subsequently this false reading was combined with the genuine one in the extant Sahidic text.[5] The Ethiopic adds an exorcism here.

■ **10** The phrase "only let each one give thanks" (Arabic) or "each one is to give thanks" (Ethiopic) probably reflects a textual corruption of "for the Eucharist" (Sahidic) at some point in the history of its transmission.

1 Jean-Paul Bouhot, *La confirmation, sacrement de la communion ecclésiale* (Lyon: Chalet, 1968) 38–45. See also Robert Cabié, "L'ordo de l'initiation chrétienne dans la 'Tradition apostolique' d'Hippolyte de Rome," in *Mens concordet voci, pour Mgr. A. G. Martimort* (Paris: Desclée, 1983) 543–58.

2 Bradshaw, "Redating," 14.

3 See further ibid.

4 Botte, *Tradition*, 43 n. 6; Cuming, *Hippolytus*, 17.

5 Botte, *Tradition*, 43 n. 7.

Comment

■ **1–2** This section provides for an "election" and examination of candidates for baptism and inaugurates an unspecified period of final baptismal preparation including a ritual of daily exorcism. Because of the distinction between these two periods of catechumenal instruction—a three-year general catechumenate in chap. 17 and an election for baptism here—this passage has been commonly viewed as the first historical reference to two categories of "catechumens" in early Christianity: (1) catechumens or "hearers" themselves; and (2) after election, what various traditions refer to as *electi* (Rome), *competentes* (in the non-Roman West), and *photizomenoi* or *illuminandi* (in the East). It is the conduct of the catechumens that is examined for this transition: Have they lived virtuously, honored the widows (cf. 1 Tim 5:3), visited the sick (cf. Matt 25:36), and done good works?

■ **2** Against the commonly accepted theory that in the early church catechumens were universally and regularly dismissed from the liturgy of the word *after* the reading of the gospel and homily, it has been suggested that this sentence may witness to an early tradition of withholding the reading of the gospel itself from the catechumens until a late stage in their prebaptismal preparation.[6]

■ **3–4** This section is obviously referring to what would come to be called "scrutinies," that is, solemn public examinations of the candidates at various intervals throughout the final period of baptismal preparation. These scrutinies, which were originally three in number within the Roman liturgical tradition and took place on the third, fourth, and fifth Sundays in Lent (later expanded to seven and shifted to weekdays), eventually became highly exorcistic in character.[7] Significantly,

however, *Apostolic Tradition* contains only one such solemn scrutiny and tells us nothing about when during the final preparation process it was to take place (other than near to baptism). Further, since both the Ethiopic and the *Canons of Hippolytus* refer to a scrutiny that is clearly an examination alone and not exorcistic, they may be witnessing to an earlier form of the text before references to daily exorcism or to an exorcistic scrutiny rite by the bishop were added.

Although some references to prebaptismal exorcism do appear within Gnostic literature of the first three centuries,[8] as well as in Cyprian (*Ep.* 69.15), it is only in the fourth century that *daily* exorcism in the context of final baptismal preparation is clearly attested in Eastern (West Syrian and Syro-Palestinian) liturgical sources.[9] Western sources provide no corroboration for the practice; the liturgical documents we possess (e.g., Augustine and the Roman sacramentaries and *ordines*) seem to know nothing of a daily exorcism, and instead relate the exorcisms of the *electi* to the (three or seven) solemn scrutinies of the Lenten period. While it is possible, therefore, that this passage may reflect a third-century practice, it could equally well reflect a subsequent development and hence be a later addition to the text. In this regard, its omission in the Ethiopic and *Canons of Hippolytus* may indicate that the version of the *Apostolic Tradition* at their disposal also did not yet contain it, or, alternatively, that these two documents merely reflect the single, nonexorcistic "scrutiny" assumed to have been a characteristic of the early Alexandrian liturgical tradition.[10]

■ **6** There are no parallels in other liturgical sources to this prohibition against the baptism of menstruating women. According to R. J. Zwi Werblowsky, there is also no precedent for such a prohibition in Rabbinic

6 Paul F. Bradshaw, "The Gospel and the Catechumenate in the Third Century," *JTS* 50 (1999) 143–52.

7 See further Maxwell Johnson, *The Rites of Christian Initiation: Their Evolution and Interpretation* (Collegeville, Minn.: Liturgical, 1999) 180–82; Aidan Kavanagh, *The Shape of Baptism* (New York: Pueblo, 1978) 57–60, 67.

8 See Elizabeth A. Leeper, "From Alexandria to Rome: The Valentinian Connection to the Incorporation of Exorcism as a Prebaptismal Rite," *VC* 44 (1990) 6–24, who argues that rites of prebaptismal exorcism in Rome come directly from Valentinian

Gnostic rituals of initiation.

9 Cyril of Jerusalem *Baptismal Catechesis* 1.5–6; Egeria *Peregrinatio* 46.1; John Chrysostom *Baptismal Hom.* 2.12.

10 On this see Bradshaw, "Baptismal Practice," 10–12; and Maxwell Johnson, *Liturgy in Early Christian Egypt* (JLS 33; Nottingham: Grove, 1995) 10.

Judaism, where menstruation did not appear to constitute an obstacle in the baptism of female proselytes.[11] Early Christianity, of course, did inherit from Leviticus (esp. chap. 15) the notion of ritual impurity or pollution resulting from menstruation and sexual emissions. But, according to the very limited evidence, this was related to eucharistic reception and not to baptism. Thus, for example, Dionysius of Alexandria (248–265 CE) states that "menstruous women ought not to come to the holy table, or touch the Holy of Holies, nor to churches, but pray elsewhere."[12] Such prohibitions would continue through the early Middle Ages.[13] But this was by no means a universal position. Indeed, *Didasc.* 6.21 argues strongly that neither menstruation nor any kind of sexual emission constitutes ritual impurity or serves as an impediment to eucharistic reception.

With regard to this verse, Werblowsky conjectures "that the menstruous woman is *e definitione* still in the grip of the demonic powers," but he offers no evidence in support of seeing a relationship between menstruation and the demonic.[14] The simplest explanation is that this prohibition against menstruous women is a baptismal extension of the inherited notion of ritual impurity encountered elsewhere in relationship to the Eucharist.

■ **7** The *Didache* (7.4), Justin Martyr (*1 Apol.* 61), and Tertullian (*De bapt.* 20) clearly testify that some kind of fast was part of baptism's immediate preparation. The references to Friday and Saturday here have led to the common assumption that the all-night vigil referred to in *Ap. Trad.* 20.9 took place between Saturday night and cockcrow (see *Ap. Trad.* 21.1) on Sunday morning. This is not, however, completely clear. Not only does the Ethiopic make no reference to any vigil taking place, but the references to "Sabbath" or "Saturday" in all the versions need not necessarily indicate Saturday *morning*: it is at least possible that the Friday fast was to be followed immediately by the final exorcism rites at the beginning

of the Sabbath, namely, after sundown on Friday. If so, the vigil referred to in *Ap. Trad.* 20.9 would be Friday to Saturday, not Saturday to Sunday.[15]

Because the Alexandrian liturgical tradition apparently knew a baptismal rite that was celebrated on the sixth day (Friday) of the sixth week of a forty-day prebaptismal period of fasting and preparation, which was not paschal in orientation or character,[16] Hanssens believed that this section, with its possible Friday to Saturday baptismal vigil, supported his view that the *Apostolic Tradition* was not Roman but Alexandrian in origin.[17] If Hanssen's hypothesis on the Alexandrian origins of this document has not been widely accepted by scholars, his caveat against making assumptions about the text based on later Roman practice, especially with regard to the particular days of the week in question, still merits strong consideration.

It has often been further assumed that what is described here is the equivalent of what later Roman evidence reports as the ritual pattern of bathing on Maundy Thursday, fasting on Good Friday, immediate preparation for baptism taking place on Holy Saturday morning, and the rites themselves being celebrated during the paschal vigil between Holy Saturday night and Easter Sunday morning. Gregory Dix, for example, was so convinced of this that in his edition he added the subtitle "Friday and Saturday in Holy Week" before *Ap. Trad.* 20.7 and the subtitle "The Paschal Vigil" before 20.9.[18] However, nowhere in chaps. 15–21 is it indicated that paschal baptism is the practice intended in the *Apostolic Tradition*. The reference to a Friday fast before baptism need refer to nothing other than baptismal candidates joining in the traditional weekly fast days, a tradition as old as *Did.* 8.1. While *Ap. Trad.* 21.1 will make clear that baptism itself is to take place at "cockcrow" after an all-night vigil, that the text does not indicate this clearly as Easter, or as we have seen, necessarily even Sunday, may be a sign of antiquity. Moreover, the

---

11   Werblowsky, "Baptismal Rite," 97.
12   Dionysius of Alexandria *Ad Basilidem* 2.
13   See Brown, *Body*, 433–34, 145–46.
14   Werblowsky, "Baptismal Rite," 97.
15   Hanssens, *Liturgie,* 448–51.
16   See Thomas J. Talley, *The Origins of the Liturgical Year* (2d emended ed.; Collegeville, Minn.: Liturgical, 1991) 163–224.
17   Hanssens, *Liturgie,* 450–51.
18   Dix, *Apostolic Tradition*, 32.

Commentary on Daniel by Hippolytus does make a clear association between baptism and Easter (13.15), and paschal baptism is likewise known to have been the preference in the North African tradition in the early third century, as witnessed by Tertullian (*De bapt.* 19). If, therefore, the *Apostolic Tradition* is the work of Hippolytus, the absence of any reference to Easter initiation in this text is strange. And, since Pascha is a topic treated in chap. 33, one might expect that if Easter baptism were the practice intended here, there would be some indication of it there. But there is not.[19] The most logical assumption, as Raniero Cantalamessa notes, is that chap. 20 refers to a structure and process would have been followed whenever baptisms were celebrated.[20]

■ **8** The exorcism and other rites performed by the bishop at the Saturday gathering do not find any explicit parallels in other Christian literature from the first three centuries. Episcopal ceremonies equivalent to these (i.e., a final exorcism of the *electi* and *apertio* or *ephatha* rites) on Holy Saturday morning are first known from Ambrose of Milan in the late fourth century as well as from later Roman practice.[21] And, while the rite of breathing on the faces of the candidates and the signing of their foreheads, ears, and noses has often been interpreted as an *apertio* or *ephatha*,[22] its close association with the immediately preceding exorcism suggests rather that it is to be seen here as more of a "closing" of the senses to evil than as an "opening" of them for the reception of catechesis.

The phrase "that they flee from them and not return to them ever again" may refer to an actual liturgical formula of exorcism.[23] The rubrical directions in the Ethiopic version appear less developed than in the Sahidic or Arabic, where both insufflation and signing of the foreheads, ears, and nostrils, in addition to an imposition of hands, are present. It is thus possible that the Ethiopic version reflects here an earlier form of the text.

■ **9** Evidence for vigils other than at Easter may be sparse for the first three centuries of the Christian era, but it is not completely absent (see, e.g., Tertullian *Ad uxor.* 2.4; Pontius *De vita et passione Cypriani* 15; and canon 35 of the Council of Elvira). Later evidence indicates that vigils on other feasts (e.g., Pentecost and Epiphany), Sundays, at the tombs of martyrs, and on other occasions were common and widespread.[24]

■ **10** The practice of the faithful bringing offerings or oblations to the Eucharist is well attested in early Christian literature,[25] although apart from *Apostolic Tradition* and its derivatives there are no explicit parallels to the newly baptized doing so. That the practice did exist in some places at the baptismal Eucharist, however, is certainly indicated by Ambrose's refusal to allow it at Milan. There the newly baptized were not permitted to offer oblations at the Eucharist until the following Sunday.[26] The directive that those to be baptized are to bring nothing else with them is probably best understood in relationship to *Ap. Trad.* 21.5 below.

---

19   On the development of paschal baptism in early Christianity, see Paul F. Bradshaw, "'Diem baptismo sollemniorem': Initiation and Easter in Christian Antiquity," in Johnson, *Living Water*, 137–47.

20   See Raniero Cantalamessa, *Ostern in der alten Kirche* (Bern: Lang, 1981) 79.

21   See Ambrose *De sacr.* 1.2. For an example of later Roman practice, see *Sacramentarium Gelasianum* XLII, in Leo Cunibert Mohlberg, *Liber Sacramentorum Romanae Aeclesiae ordinis anni circuli* (Rerum ecclesiasticarum documenta; Series major, Fontes 4; Rome: Herder, 1960) 68.

22   See Edward Yarnold, *The Awe-Inspiring Rites of Initiation: Baptismal Homilies of the Fourth Century* (Slough: St. Paul, 1972) 16.

23   See Cuming, *Hippolytus*, 17. Cuming refers to Mark 9:25 as a possible biblical source for the formula.

24   On vigils in Christian antiquity, see Robert F. Taft, *The Liturgy of the Hours in East and West: The Origins of the Divine Office and Its Meaning for Today* (Collegeville, Minn.: Liturgical, 1986) 165–77.

25   See Irenaeus *Haer.* 4.28.2; Tertullian *De cor.* 4; Cyprian *On Works and Alms* 15.

26   See Ambrose *Exposition of Ps. 118*, Prologue 2.

21

Latin	Sahidic	Arabic	Ethiopic
	46 Concerning the tradition (παράδοσις) of holy baptism (βάπτισμα)	**34 Concerning the order for baptizing and the recitation of the creed and the confession at baptism and the liturgy and concerning the milk and honey**	**34 Concerning the order of baptism and teaching the faith and confession of their sins at baptism and the oblation; and regarding milk and honey**
1	And (δέ) at the hour when the cock (ἀλέκτωρ) crows, let the water be prayed over first.	At the time when the cock crows, let the first prayer be said over the water.	When the cock crows, they are to pray first over the water.
2	Let the water be drawn into the pool (κολυμβήθρα) or (ἤ) flow down into it. And (δέ) let it be thus if there is no exigency (ἀνάγκη). But (δέ) if there is an exigency (ἀνάγκη) that persists and is urgent, use (χρῆσθαι) the water that you will find.	Let the water be flowing into the font, or trickling into it. Let it be so, unless there is an emergency, in which case any water that can be found should be poured.	And if it is possible, there is to be water that flows to the place of baptism or that they make flow over it. And this is the way it is to be if it is not difficult. And if it is difficult, they are to pour water into the baptistries, after drawing [it].
3	And (δέ) let them strip naked.	Let them strip naked	And they are to set their clothes [aside] and are to be baptized naked.
4	And first baptize (βαπτίζειν) the small children. And (δέ) each one who is able to speak for themselves [sic], let them speak. But (δέ) those not able to speak for themselves, let their parents or (ἤ) another one belonging to their family (γένος) speak for them.	and let them begin by baptizing the small children. And insofar as [the child] can speak and swear for himself, let him speak, and whoever cannot, let his parents or one of his family speak for him.	And first the little children are to be baptized; and if he is able to speak for himself, he is to speak; and if they are not able, their parents are to speak on their behalf or one of their relatives.
5	Afterward, baptize (βαπτίζειν) the grown men, and (δέ), finally, the women, loosing all their hair and laying aside the jewelry (κόσμησις) of gold and silver that they are wearing. Let no one take any foreign (ἀλλότριος) thing (εἶδος) down into the water with them.	And then the adult men should be baptized, and finally the women, and they should loosen their hair and take off any gold jewelry they are wearing. No one should take anything into the water with him.	After this they are to baptize the old men, and after this all the women are to loosen their hair and they are to withhold from themselves their ornaments and their gold on them. And no one at all is to go down into the water who has anything foreign with him.
6	And (δέ) at the hour that has been set to baptize (βαπτίζειν), let the bishop (ἐπίσκοπος) give thanks (εὐχαριστεῖν) over the oil, and put it in a vessel (σκεῦος) and call it the oil of thanksgiving (εὐχαριστία).	While they are being baptized, the bishop gives thanks over the oil, which he has put in a vessel and which is called the oil of thanksgiving.	And at the time they are to be baptized, the bishop is to give thanks over the oil when it is in its container, and it is called exorcised oil.
7	And let him take another oil and exorcise (ἐξορκίζειν) it, and call it the oil of exorcism (ἐξορκισμός).	And he takes another oil and says prayers of exorcism over it, and it is called the oil of exorcism.	And he is to take other oil and curse it; and it is called oil that purifies from every impure spirit.

Apostolic Constitutions	Canons of Hippolytus	Testamentum Domini
	One is to position them at cockcrow near the water, water from a river, running and pure, prepared and sanctified.	But let them be baptized thus. When they come to the water, let the water be pure and flowing.
	Those who reply for the little children are to strip them of their clothes first;	First the infants, then the men, then the women. But if anyone desires to approach as it were to virginity, let that person first be baptized by the hand of the bishop. Let the women, when they are baptized, loose their hair. Let all the children who can answer in baptism make the responses and answer after the priest. But if they cannot, let their parents make the responses for them, or someone from their houses.
	then those who are capable of answering for themselves; then the women are to be last of all to divest themselves of their clothes; they are to remove their jewels, whether they are of gold or others, and loosen the hair of their head, for fear that something of the alien spirits should go down with them into the water of the second birth.	But when those who are being baptized go down [to the water], after they make the responses and speak, let the bishop see if there be any of them — either a man having a gold ring or a woman wearing gold on herself; for no one should have with him any strange thing in the water, but let him hand it over to those who are near him.
	The bishop blesses the oil of exorcism and gives it to a presbyter; then he blesses the oil of anointing, that is the oil of thanksgiving, and gives it to another presbyter. He who holds the oil of exorcism stands on the left of the bishop, and he who holds the oil of anointing stands on the right of the bishop.	But when they are about to receive the oil for anointing, let the bishop pray over it and give thanks, and let him exorcise the other [oil] with an exorcism, the same as in the case of catechumens. And let the deacon carry that which is exorcised, and let the presbyter stand by him. Let him then who stands by that on which the thanksgiving over the oil [was said] be on the right hand; but he who stands by that which has been exorcised, on the left.

113

	Latin	Sahidic	Arabic	Ethiopic
8		And a deacon (διάκονος) shall take the oil of exorcism (ἐξορκισμός) and stand at the left hand of the presbyter (πρεσβύτερος), and another deacon (διάκονος) shall take the oil of thanksgiving (εὐχαριστία) and stand at the right hand of the presbyter (πρεσβύτερος).	The deacon, holding the oil of exorcism, stands to the left of the presbyter, and another deacon takes the oil of thanksgiving and stands to his right.	And there is to be a deacon who is to carry the oil by which they curse, and he is to stand on the left of the presbyter and another deacon is to take the exorcised oil and is to stand on his right.
9		And when the presbyter (πρεσβύτερος) grasps each one of those who will receive baptism (βάπτισμα), let him command him to renounce (ἀποτάσσεσθαι), saying, "I renounce (ἀποτάσσεσθαι) you, Satan (σατανᾶς), with all your service and all your works."	Then the presbyter takes hold of those who are being baptized one by one and orders him to make the renunciation. And he says, "I renounce you, Satan, and all your service and all your unclean works."	And when the presbyter has grasped each of those who are to be baptized, he is to command that they renounce and say: "I renounce you, Satan, and all your angels and your every impure work."
10		And when he has renounced (ἀποτάσσεσθαι) all these, let him anoint him with the oil of exorcism (ἐξορκισμός), saying, "Let every spirit (πνεῦμα) be cast far from you."	And if he declares this, he is anointed with the oil of exorcism, saying, "Let every mischievous spirit leave him."	And if he believes in this, he is to anoint him with the oil that purifies from every evil, saying: "Let every unclean spirit be far from him."
11		And in this way let him give him naked to the bishop (ἐπίσκοπος) or (ἤ) the presbyter (πρεσβύτερος) standing by the water to baptize (βαπτίζειν).	And the bishop or the presbyter who is standing by directs him naked to the baptismal water.	In this way he is to deliver him naked to the bishop or to the presbyter who stands over the water of baptism.
12		And (δέ) likewise (ὁμοίως), let the deacon (διάκονος) go with him down into the water and let him say to him, enjoining him to say, "I believe (πιστεύειν) in the only true God, the Father, the Almighty (παντοκράτωρ), and his only begotten (μονογενής) Son, Jesus Christ (χριστός) our Lord and Savior (σωτήρ) with his Holy Spirit (πνεῦμα), the giver of life to everything, three (τρίας) in one substance (ὁμοούσιος), one divinity, one Lordship, one kingdom, one faith (πίστις), one baptism (βάπτισμα), in the holy catholic (καθολική) apostolic (ἀποστολική) church (ἐκκλησία), which lives forever. Amen (ἀμήν)."	Then the deacon walks with him to the water and says to him, prompting him, "[Do] you believe in one God, the Father, the Almighty, and his only Son, Jesus Christ our Lord and Savior, and his Holy Spirit, who gives life to the whole creation, the Trinity, coequal, one divinity, one Lordship, one kingdom, one faith, one baptism, in the catholic church [and] everlasting life. Amen."	The deacon is to go down with him to the water and say to him and teach him: "Do you believe in the one God, the Father, the Lord of all, and in his only Son, Jesus Christ our Lord and our Savior, and the Holy Spirit, the one who gives life to all creation, the Trinity whose divinity is equal; and one Lord and one kingdom and one faith and one baptism in the holy catholic church and the life everlasting. Amen?"

Apostolic Constitutions	Canons of Hippolytus	Testamentum Domini

He who is to be baptized turns his face toward the west and says, "I renounce you, Satan, and all your service." When he has said that, the presbyter anoints him with the oil of exorcism that has been blessed, so that every evil spirit may depart from him. He is handed over by a deacon to the presbyter who stands near the water. A presbyter holds his right hand and makes him turn his face toward the east, near the water. Before going down into the water, his face toward the east and standing near the water, he says this after having received the oil of exorcism: "I believe, and submit myself to you and to all your service, O Father, Son, and Holy Spirit."

Thus he descends into the waters; the presbyter places his hand on his head and questions him, saying, "Do you believe in God the Father Almighty?"

And when he takes hold of each one, let him ask (the one being baptized turning to the west) and let him say, "Say, 'I renounce you, Satan, and all your service, and your theaters, and your pleasures, and all your works.'" And when he has said these things and confessed, let him be anointed with that oil that was exorcised, the one who anoints him saying thus: "I anoint [you] with this oil of exorcism for deliverance from every evil and unclean spirit, and for deliverance from every evil." And also (turning him to the east) let him say, "I submit to you, Father and Son and Holy Spirit, before whom all nature trembles and is moved. Grant me to do all your wishes without blame."

Then after these things let him hand him over to the presbyter who baptizes. And let them stand in the water naked. But let the deacon descend with him similarly. But when he who is being baptized goes down into the water, let him who baptizes him say (putting his hand on him) thus: "Do you believe in God the Father Almighty?"

	Latin	Sahidic	Arabic	Ethiopic
13	(73.1—74.35)	And (δέ) the one who receives it, let him say to (κατά) all this, "I believe (πιστεύειν) thus."	The baptized also says similarly, "I believe," and so on.	And the one who is to be baptized is again to say in this way: "Yes, I believe."
14	... having [his] hand laid on his head, let him baptize [him] once.	And the one who gives will put his hand on the head of the one who receives and dip him three times, confessing (ὁμολογεῖν) these things each time (κατά—).	The one who is baptizing keeps his hand on the one being received and immerses him three times, declaring this at each immersion,	And in this way he is to baptize him and place his hands on him and on the one who stands as a guarantor for him. And he is to baptize him three times, and the one who is baptized speaks openly in this way each time according to the number [of times] he has been baptized.
15	And afterward let him say, "Do you believe in Christ Jesus, the Son of God, who was born by the Holy Spirit from the Virgin Mary and crucified under Pontius Pilate, and died and was buried and rose on the third day alive from the dead, and ascended into heaven and sits on the right hand of the Father, and will come to judge the living and the dead?"	And afterward, let him say, "[Do] you believe (πιστεύειν) in our Lord Jesus Christ (χριστός), the only Son of God the Father, that he became man wondrously for us in an incomprehensible unity, in his Holy Spirit (πνεῦμα) from Mary, the holy virgin (παρθένος), without human seed (σπέρμα); and he was crucified (σταυροῦν) for us under Pontius Pilate; he died willingly for our salvation; he rose on the third day; he released those who were bound; he went up to heaven; he sat at the right hand of his good (ἀγαθός) Father in the heights; and he comes to judge (κρίνειν) the living and the dead by (κατά) his appearance with his kingdom;	and after that he says to him, "[Do] you believe in Jesus Christ our Lord, the only Son of God the Father, that he became man by an incomprehensible miracle from the Holy Spirit and Mary the virgin without human seed, and was crucified in the time of Pontius Pilate and died by his own will for the salvation of us all, and rose from the dead on the third day and loosed those who were bound and ascended into heaven and sat at the right hand of the Father; and he will come to judge the living and the dead in his appearing and his kingdom?	And after this he is to say to him: "Do you believe in the name of Jesus Christ our Lord, the only Son of God the Father, that he became human, through a miracle that is incomprehensible, from the Holy Spirit and from Mary the virgin without the seed of a man; and he was crucified in the time of Pontius Pilate, and he died by his will at the same time for our salvation, and he rose from the dead on the third day and released the prisoners and ascended into heaven and sat at the right hand of the Father, and he will come to judge the living and the dead at his appearing and in his kingdom?
16	And when he has said "I believe," let him be baptized again.			
17	And again let him say: "Do you believe in the Holy Spirit and the holy church and the resurrection of the flesh?"	and [do] you believe (πιστεύειν) in the Holy Spirit (πνεῦμα), the good (ἀγαθός) and the giver of life, who purifies the universe in the holy church (ἐκκλησία) ...	[Do] you believe in the Holy Spirit, the good one, the purifier, [and] in the holy church? And [do] you believe in the resurrection of the body that will be for everyone, and the kingdom of heaven and the everlasting judgment?"	Do you believe in the Holy Spirit, the good and purifying one, and in the holy church? And do you believe the resurrection of the body that will be for all people and in the kingdom of heaven and the eternal judgment?"

116

Apostolic Constitutions	Canons of Hippolytus	Testamentum Domini
	He who is baptized replies, "I believe." Then he immerses him in the water once, his hand on his head.	Let the one who is being baptized say, "I believe." Let him immediately baptize him once.
	He questions him a second time, saying, "Do you believe in Jesus Christ, Son of God, whom the virgin Mary bore by the Holy Spirit, who came for the salvation of the human race, who was crucified in the time of Pontius Pilate, who died and was raised from the dead the third day, ascended into heaven, is seated at the right hand of the Father, and will come to judge the living and the dead?"	Let the priest also say: "Do you also believe in Christ Jesus, the Son of God, who came from the Father, who is of old with the Father, who was born of Mary the virgin by the Holy Spirit, who was crucified in the days of Pontius Pilate, and died, and rose the third day, alive from the dead, and ascended into heaven, and sat down on the right hand of the Father, and comes to judge the living and the dead?"
	He replies, "I believe." Then he immerses him in the water a second time. He questions him a third time, saying, "Do you believe in the Holy Spirit, the Paraclete flowing from the Father and the Son?"	And when he says, "I believe," let him baptize him the second time. And also let him say, "Do you also believe in the Holy Spirit in the holy church?"

Latin	Bohairic	Arabic	Ethiopic
18 Then let him who is being baptized say, "I believe." And so let him be baptized a third time.	Again (πάλιν) let him say, "I believe."	And he replies to all this, saying, "I believe in this."	And he is to answer regarding all this, saying: "Yes, I believe in this."
19 And afterward, when he has come up, let him be anointed by the presbyter with that oil which was sanctified, saying: "I anoint you with holy oil in the name of Jesus Christ."	And let him ascend from the water, and let the presbyter (πρεσβύτερος) anoint him with oil of thanksgiving (εὐχαριστία), saying, "I anoint you with an anointing of holy oil in the name of Jesus Christ (χριστός)."	After that, when he has come up out of the water, the presbyter anoints him with the oil of thanksgiving, saying, "I anoint you with the holy oil."	And then when he has come up from the water, the presbyter is to anoint him with the oil of exorcism, saying: "I anoint you with holy oil."
20 And so individually wiping themselves, let them now dress and afterward enter into the church.	Likewise he anoints the rest, one by one. And, thus, when he dresses the rest, let them go into the church (ἐκκλησία).	And after that they put on their clothes. Then they go into the church	And after this they are to put on their clothes. And after this they are to enter the church,
21 And let the bishop, laying [his] hand on them, invoke, saying: "Lord God, who have made them worthy to receive the forgiveness of sins through the laver of regeneration of the Holy Spirit, send on them your grace, that they may serve you according to your will; for to you is glory, Father and Son with the Holy Spirit in the holy church, both now and to the ages of ages. Amen."	Let the bishop (ἐπίσκοπος) put his hand on them, fervently, saying, "Lord God, as (κατά) you have made these worthy to receive forgiveness of their sins for the coming age, make them worthy to be filled with your Holy Spirit (πνεῦμα); and send upon them your grace in order that (ἵνα) they may serve you according to (κατά) your will, because yours is the glory, Father, Son, and Holy Spirit (πνεῦμα) in the holy church (ἐκκλησία), now and always, and forever and ever."	and the bishop puts his hand on them and prays and says, "O Lord, O God, who have made these people worthy of the bath that is for the second birth and forgiveness of sins, make them worthy to be filled with the Holy Spirit and that there should be sent upon them grace for your service according to your will. Glory to you, O Father, Son, and Holy Spirit, in the holy church, from now and forever. Amen."	and the bishop is to place his hands on them and pray, saying: "O God, you who have made these worthy of the washing of a second birth and the forgiveness of sin, make them worthy to be filled by the Holy Spirit. May you send your grace upon them so that they may serve you by your will. Praise be to you, O Father, Son, and Holy Spirit in the holy church, from now and forever. Amen."
22 Afterward, pouring the sanctified oil from [his] hand and placing [it] on the head, let him say: "I anoint you with holy oil in God the Father Almighty and Christ Jesus and the Holy Spirit."	And he pours oil of thanksgiving (εὐχαριστία) on his hand and lays his hand on his head, saying to him, "I anoint you with anointing of holy oil in God the Father, the Almighty (παντοκράτωρ), with Jesus Christ (χριστός) and the Holy Spirit (πνεῦμα)."	After that, he pours into his hand some of the oil of thanksgiving and pours it on the head of each one of them, saying, "I anoint you with the holy oil in the name of God the Father Almighty and Jesus Christ the only Son and the Holy Spirit."	And after this when he has placed the exorcising oil in his hands, he is to put it on the head of them all, saying: "I anoint you with holy oil in the name of God the Father, the Lord of all, and in Christ Jesus, his only Son, and the Holy Spirit."
23 And signing [him] on the forehead, let him offer [him] a kiss and let him say, "The Lord [be] with you." And let him who has been signed say, "And with your spirit."	And he seals (σφραγίζειν) his forehead, giving him the kiss, and saying, "The Lord be with you." And the one who has been sealed (σφραγίζειν) says to him, "And with your spirit."[a]	And when he has anointed each one of them on his forehead, he kisses them and says, "The Lord be with you." And the one who is kissed also replies and says, "The Lord be with your spirit."	And when he has sealed them all on their forehead, he is to kiss them, saying: "God be with you." And the one who was signed is to respond again and say, "God be with your spirit."

[a] Although the greeting is in Bohairic, this response is in Greek.

118

Apostolic Constitutions	Canons of Hippolytus	Testamentum Domini
	When he replies, "I believe," he immerses him a third time in the water. And he says each time, "I baptize you in the name of the Father, of the Son, and of the Holy Spirit, equal Trinity."	And let him who is being baptized say, "I believe," and thus let him baptize him the third time.
	Then he comes up from the water. The presbyter takes the oil of thanksgiving and signs his forehead, his mouth, and his breast, and anoints all his body, his head, and his face, saying, "I anoint you in the name of the Father, of the Son, and of the Holy Spirit." And he wipes him with a cloth, which he keeps for him. He dresses him in his clothes, and takes him into the church. The bishop lays his hand on all the baptized and prays thus: "We bless you, Lord God Almighty, for the fact that you have made these worthy to be born again, that you pour your Holy Spirit on them, and to be one in the body of your church, not being excluded by alien works; but, just as you have granted them forgiveness of their sins, grant them also the pledge of your kingdom; through our Lord Jesus Christ, through whom be glory to you, with him and the Holy Spirit, to ages of ages. Amen."	Then when he comes up [from the water], let him be anointed by the presbyter with oil over which the thanksgiving was said, [the presbyter] saying over him, "I anoint you with oil in the name of Jesus Christ." . . . [9] Then let them be together in church, and let the bishop lay a hand on them after baptism, saying and invoking over them thus: "Lord God, who by your beloved Son Jesus Christ filled your holy apostles with [the] Holy Spirit, and by the Spirit permitted your blessed prophets to speak; who counted these your servants worthy to be counted worthy in your Christ of forgiveness of sins through the laver of rebirth, and have cleansed them of all the mist of error and darkness of unbelief; make them worthy to be filled with your Holy Spirit, by your love of humanity, bestowing on them your grace, that they may serve you according to your will, truly, O God, and may do your commandments in holiness, and cultivating always those things that are of your will, may enter into your eternal tabernacles; through you and through your beloved Son Jesus Christ, by whom [be] to you praise and might with the Holy Spirit forever and ever."
	Next he signs their forehead with the oil of anointing and gives them the kiss, saying, "The Lord be with you." And those who have been baptized also say, "And with your spirit."	Similarly, pouring the oil, placing a hand on his head, let him say: "Anointing, I anoint [you] in God Amighty and in Jesus Christ and in the Holy Spirit, that you may be to him a laborer, having perfect faith, and a vessel pleasing to him." And sealing him on the forehead, let him give him the peace and say, "The Lord God of the meek be with you." And let him who has been sealed answer and say, "And with your spirit."

	Latin	Bohairic	Arabic	Ethiopic
24	Let him do thus to each one.	This he does to each one of them.	And after this, when each one has finished with this,	And then, after every single part of this has come to an end,
25	And afterward let them then pray together with all the people, not praying with the faithful until they have carried out all these things.	And let all the people ($\lambda\alpha\acute{o}\varsigma$) pray together,	he prays with all the people. They should not pray with the believers until they have carried out what we have described.	they are to pray with all the people, and they are not to pray first with the full Christians but after they have done the action that we mentioned before.
26	And when they have prayed, let them offer the peace with the mouth.	and when all those who have received baptism ($\beta\acute{\alpha}\pi\tau\iota\sigma\mu\alpha$) pray, let them give peace ($\epsilon\grave{\iota}\rho\acute{\eta}\nu\eta$) with [their] mouth.	And when they have finished praying and giving the peace to each other with their mouths,	And after they have finished praying, they are to give the peace to one another with their mouth.
27	And then let the oblation be presented by the deacons to the bishop and let him give thanks [over] the bread for the representation (which the Greek calls "antitype") of the body of Christ; [and over] the cup mixed with wine for the antitype (which the Greek calls "likeness") of the blood that was shed for all who have believed in him;	Let the deacons ($\delta\iota\acute{\alpha}\kappa\sigma\nu\sigma\varsigma$) bring the offering ($\pi\rho\sigma\sigma$-$\phi\sigma\rho\acute{\alpha}$) to the bishop ($\grave{\epsilon}\pi\acute{\iota}\sigma\kappa\sigma\pi\sigma\varsigma$), and he shall give thanks over bread because it is the likeness of the flesh ($\sigma\acute{\alpha}\rho\xi$) of Christ ($\chi\rho\iota\sigma\tau\acute{o}\varsigma$), with a cup of wine, because it is the blood of Christ ($\chi\rho\iota\sigma\tau\acute{o}\varsigma$) that will be poured on all who believe in him;	let the deacon bring in the offerings to the bishop, and let the bishop give thanks over the bread and the cup that they should become the body of Christ and his blood, which he shed for all of us who have believed in him.	And the deacons are to bring the oblation to the bishop, and the bishop is to give thanks over the bread and the cup—the bread so that it may become the body of Christ, and the cup, the wine mixed, so that it may become the blood of Christ, that which was poured out for us and for all of us who believe in him.
28	[and over] milk and honey mixed together for the fulfillment of the promise that was to the fathers, which he said, "a land flowing [with] milk and honey" and which Christ gave, his flesh, through which, like little children, those who believe are nourished, making the bitterness of the heart sweet by the gentleness of the word;	and milk and honey mixed together, to fulfill the promise to the fathers, because he said, "I will give to you a land that flows with milk and honey." [Sahidic] . . .This is the flesh ($\sigma\acute{\alpha}\rho\xi$) of Christ ($\chi\rho\iota\sigma\tau\acute{o}\varsigma$), which was given to us so that the ones who believe ($\pi\iota\sigma\tau\epsilon\acute{\upsilon}\epsilon\iota\nu$) in him may be nourished by it like small children. It will cause the bitterness of the heart to melt through the sweetness of the word ($\lambda\acute{o}\gamma\sigma\varsigma$).	As for the milk and honey mixed together, they give them to them to drink to fulfill the promise he made to our fathers, saying to them, "a land flowing with milk and honey." This is the body of Christ, which he gave us and by which we are fed like little children born of him, who have believed, and which makes every bitterness of the heart perfectly sweet.	And the milk and the honey [are] mixed together, and they are to have them drink from it because of the fulfillment of the promise that he made to our ancestors, saying: "I will give you a land that is flowing with milk and honey." This is the body of Christ, which he has given to us, through which we believe in him, like young children who have been born from him, who believed in him so that he could make sweet by the sweetness of his word everyone bitter of heart."
29	and [over] water for an offering as a sign of washing, that the inner man also, which is the soul, may receive the same things as the body.			
30	And let the bishop give an explanation about all these things to those who receive.	All of these things shall the bishop ($\grave{\epsilon}\pi\acute{\iota}\sigma\kappa\sigma\pi\sigma\varsigma$) recount ($-\lambda\acute{o}\gamma\sigma\varsigma$) to those who will receive baptism ($\beta\acute{\alpha}\pi$-$\tau\iota\sigma\mu\alpha$).	Let the bishop impress all this on the one being baptized.	All this the bishop is to go through for those who are to be baptized.

Apostolic Constitutions	Canons of Hippolytus	Testamentum Domini
	He does this to each of the baptized.	And so each one severally.
	After that they pray with all the people of the faithful and they give them the kiss and rejoice with them with cries of gladness.	[10] Thenceforward let them pray together with all the people.
	Then the deacon begins the liturgy and the bishop completes the Eucharist of the body and blood of the Lord. When he has finished, he communicates the people, he himself standing near the table of the body and blood of the Lord and the presbyters holding the cups of the blood of Christ and other cups of milk and honey, so that those who partake may know that they are born again like little children, because little children partake of milk and honey.	Let the oblation be offered by the deacon. And so let the shepherd give thanks. But the bread is offered for a type of my body. Let the cup be mixed with wine—mixed with wine and water, for it is a sign of blood and of the laver; so that also the inner man (that is to say, that which is of the soul) may be counted worthy of those things that are like [them], that is to say, [those things of] the body also.

Latin	Sahidic	Arabic	Ethiopic
31 And breaking the bread [and] distributing individual pieces, let him say: "Heavenly bread in Christ Jesus."	When the bishop (ἐπίσκοπος) now, therefore, breaks the bread, let him give a piece (κλάσμα) to each one of them, saying, "This is the bread of heaven, the body (σῶμα) of Christ (Χριστός) Jesus."	When the bishop divides the bread, let him give a part of it to each one, and he says, "This heavenly bread is the body of Christ."	And when the bishop then has distributed the bread, he is to give a part of it to each one and say: "This heavenly bread is the body of Christ";
32 And let him who receives respond: "Amen."	Let the one who receives it answer, "Amen (ἀμήν)."	And the one receiving Communion replies and says, "Amen."	and the one who receives it is to answer and say: "Amen."
33 And if the presbyters are not sufficient, let the deacons also hold the cups, and let them stand with appropriateness and with restraint: first he who holds the water, second he who [holds] the milk, third he who [holds] the wine.	And (δέ) if there are not sufficient presbyters (πρεσβύτερος) there, let the deacons (διάκονος) take possession of the cup (ποτήριον) and stand in proper order (εὐταξία) and give them the blood of Christ (Χριστός) Jesus our Lord, and the one with the milk and honey.	If there are not enough presbyters, let the deacons hold the cup. And they stand in order and distribute the body of our Master Jesus Christ, and this is the milk and honey.	And if there are not enough presbyters, the deacons are to take the cups and stand in order—the first with the honey and the second with the milk.
34 And let those who receive taste of each, he who gives saying three times, "In God the Father Almighty." And let him who receives say, "Amen."	Let the one who gives the cup (ποτήριον) say, "This is the blood of Jesus Christ (Χριστός) our Lord." And let the one who receives it answer, "Amen (ἀμήν)."	And the one who gives the cup says, "This is the blood of our Master Jesus Christ." And the one who partakes says, "Amen."	And the one who hands [it] over is to say: "In God the Father, Lord of all." And the third [is the] one with the wine. And the one who hands over the cup is to say: "This is the blood of our Lord Jesus Christ." And the one who receives is to say, "Amen and amen." And when he receives the body, he is to say, "Amen." And with the blood he is to say, "Amen and amen." As therefore this Trinity takes place, each one is to be eager to do good work[s] that are pleasing to God, living in uprightness and joined to the church, doing the teaching, increasing in the service of God.
35 "And in the Lord Jesus Christ."			
36 "And in the Holy Spirit and the holy church." And let him say, "Amen."			
37 So let it be done with each one.			
38 And when these things have been done, let each one hasten to do good work. . . .	And (δέ) when these things are done, let each one hasten (σπουδάζειν) to do all that is good and to please God, and to live (πολιτεύεσθαι) uprightly, occupied with the church (ἐκκλησία), doing the things that he learned, advancing (προκόπτειν) in the service of God.	And so each one disciplines himself and does all that is good and pleasing to God and devotes himself to going to church and doing as he has learned and growing in the service of God.	
39	And (δέ) we have given these things to you in brief concerning the holy baptism (βάπτισμα) and the holy offering (προσφορά), since (ἐπειδή) you have already been instructed (κατηχεῖσθαι) concerning the resurrection of the flesh (σάρξ) and all the other things as (κατά) written.	We have openly taught you this concerning baptism and the liturgy. We have finished catechizing you about the resurrection of the body and the rest, as it is written.	This that he makes known we have taught you concerning baptism and the order of the oblation. And now we have finished the instruction that we give to you regarding the resurrection of the body and what remains, as it is written.

Apostolic Constitutions	Canons of Hippolytus	Testamentum Domini
		And let all the people, according to what has been said before, receive with an "Amen" of the Eucharist that has been offered. Let the deacons hover over [the offering], as has been said before. Let him who gives [the Eucharist] say, "The body of Jesus Christ, the Holy Spirit, for the healing of soul and body." Let the one who receives say, "Amen."
	If there are no presbyters to hold them, the deacons are to hold them. And so the bishop gives them the body of Christ, saying, "This is the body of Christ." They reply, "Amen."	
	He who gives them from the cup says, "This is the blood of Christ." They reply, "Amen." Then they partake of the milk and honey, in remembrance of the age to come, and of the sweetness of its blessings, which does not return to bitterness and does not fade away. . . .	He who spills from the cup gathers up judgment for himself. Similarly also, he who sees and is silent and does not reprove him, whoever he may be.
		Let those who receive the offering be exhorted by the priests to be careful to do good works, to love strangers, to labor in fasting, and in every good work to cultivate servitude. And let them be taught also about the resurrection of bodies; before anyone receives baptism, let no one know the word about the resurrection, for this is
	29. . . All the mysteries concerning life, resurrection, and the sacrifice, the Christians alone [are] those who hear them. This is because they have received the seal of baptism because they are the participants [in it].	

Latin	Sahidic	Arabic	Ethiopic
40	And (δέ) if there are other things that are appointed to recite, let the bishop (ἐπίσκοπος) say it quietly to those who will receive baptism (βάπτισμα). And (δέ) do not let the unbelievers (ἄπιστος) know, unless (εἰ μήτι) they first receive baptism (βάπτισμα). This is the white stone (ψῆφος) of which John said, "There is a new name written on it, which no one knows except (εἰ μήτι) the one who will receive the stone (ψῆφος)."[a]	If anything remains that should have been mentioned, let the bishop speak of it to whoever receives on his own. Do not instruct an unbeliever in this until after he has first received this holy witness[?] that John said has written on it a new name that no one knows except him who receives the witness[?]. And these chapters come after baptism.	And if there is something remaining, mention of which is proper, the bishop is to mention it to those who receive. He is to take[?] and no people other than believers are to know this, but after they first receive this holy blessing about which John said that a new name is written on it. [It is] this blessing that no one except those who receive are to know.

[a] Rev 2:17.

Text

For the suggestion that this chapter is made up of at least three strata—an original core, lacking specific ministerial directions; additional episcopal directives; and detailed instructions concerning the roles of presbyters and deacons—see the commentary on chap. 20 above. The core seems to consist of: *Ap. Trad.* 21.1–5; followed by an earlier version of 21.12–18; and then 21.20, 25, and 26. Parts of *Ap. Trad.* 21.27, 28, 31, 32, 34, 37, and the beginning of 21.38 may also belong to this stratum, although this is less clear. In the light of parallels with the *Didache* and Justin Martyr's *First Apology*, the core material may well go back to the mid-second century.

■ **2** The oriental versions agree that the water for baptism is either flowing into or collected in a "pool," "font," or "place of baptism." The derivative documents, however, contain no equivalent terms but state that the water is to be "from a river, running and pure, prepared and sanctified" *(Canons of Hippolytus),* or simply, "pure and flowing" (*Testamentum Domini*). This suggests the possibility that the terms in the oriental versions may be a later addition to the text when baptism had ceased to be normally administered in natural rivers and pools but was now usually in manufactured tanks or fonts.[1]

■ **6–11** After having provided rather complete baptismal instructions in 1–5, the text now seems to begin anew with more detailed instructions including: (1) the initiatory roles of bishops, presbyters, and deacons in the consecration of the two baptismal oils; (2) the renunciation of Satan; and (3) the prebaptismal (exorcistic) anointing. All this is quite different from what has come immediately before, and in the process even duplicates some of what has already been said (e.g., references to the time fixed for baptism, another prebaptismal exorcism, and the nakedness of the candidates). This lends support to the hypothesis that the baptismal order is made up of more than one stratum.

■ **6** The Ethiopic consistently but illogically calls the first oil over which the bishop gives thanks the "oil of thanksgiving," and not "exorcised oil" here and in *Ap. Trad.* 21.19–26.

■ **12–14** The oriental versions diverge from one another in this section, introducing either declaratory (Sahidic) or interrogative (Arabic and Ethiopic) creedal formulae. Dix viewed these formulae as an interpolation,[2] and

1   Bradshaw, "Redating," 11 n. 29. On the development of baptismal fonts, see John G. Davies, *The Architectural Setting of Baptism* (London: Barrie and Rockliff, 1962); and S. Anita Stauffer, *On Baptismal Fonts: Ancient and Modern* (JLS 29–30; Nottingham: Grove, 1994).

2   Dix, *Apostolic Tradition,* 35.
3   Botte, *Tradition,* 49.
4   On this see esp. Gabriele Winkler, *Das armenische Initiationsrituale* (OrChrA 217; Rome: Pontifical Oriental Institute Press, 1982) 383, 387–88; Yarnold, *Awe-Inspiring Rites,* 18.

Apostolic Constitutions	Canons of Hippolytus	Testamentum Domini
	[30] The catechumens are to hear the word concerning the faith and the teaching only. It is the judgment of which John speaks: "No one knows it except he who receives it."[a]	the new decree that has a new name that no one knows except the one who receives [it].

Botte saw this section as having been "profoundly altered."[3] Since reference is made in the formulae to "three in one substance, one divinity" (Sahidic), "Trinity, coequal, one divinity" (Arabic), and "the Trinity whose divinity is equal" (Ethiopic), the contents have been decidedly influenced by post-Nicene, orthodox, trinitarian theology.

It is important to note, however, that the first immersion in both the *Canons of Hippolytus* and *Testamentum Domini* is accompanied not by a similar formula but by the simple interrogation, "Do you believe in God the Father Almighty?" And, at the place corresponding to the creedal formulae in the oriental versions, those versions place a postrenunciation *syntaxis* or "Act of Adherence," a ritual change of ownership and allegiance known to be a characteristic especially of Syrian baptismal rites in the late fourth century.[4]

The presence of the introductory creedal formula in the oriental versions, therefore, appears to be the result of the later addition to the text of a form of *syntaxis*,[5] replacing what would have been the first of three interrogations, for the original form of which the *Canons of Hippolytus* and more especially the *Testamentum Domini* are probably our best witnesses.[6] Similarly, the odd rubric in *Ap. Trad.* 21.14 directing a threefold confession and immersion, which is then followed in 21.15–18 by only two creedal interrogations regarding Christ and the Holy Spirit, suggests that there has been considerable reworking at this point, and again the *Canons of Hippolytus* and *Testamentum Domini*, but this time together with the reemerging Latin text, seem to reflect the older

reading, that only one immersion takes place in relationship to this interrogation.

It is also unclear who it is that administers baptism. If, in the oriental versions and *Testamentum Domini*, it is a deacon who accompanies the candidate into the baptismal waters and asks the questions, the identity or ecclesiastical order of the actual baptizer is not indicated. Instead, they revert stylistically to the use of the third-person hortatory subjunctive that was standard in the earlier chapters (15–20) of the initiatory material, either in reference to the baptizer ("let him who baptizes"), to the candidate ("let him be baptized"), or to both. Such changes seem to suggest again that at some point prior to the insertion of rubrics about bishops, presbyters, and deacons in *Ap. Trad.* 21.6–11, the older core of the document was not specific in this regard.

■ **15–18** The creedal formulae in the oriental versions, in contrast to those in the Latin, *Canons of Hippolytus*, and *Testamentum Domini* (with the exception of the added christological clause "who came from the Father, who is of old with the Father" in the second interrogation), reflect either considerable expansion at this point or a different creedal tradition altogether. Because of close parallels between the baptismal interrogations in the Latin and what is called the Roman Creed, known to us in Greek from a letter of Marcellus of Ancyra to Julius of Rome in 340/341 CE and in Latin from a commentary by Rufinus of Aquileia in about 404 CE, scholars have often taken the Latin text here as evidence that such a creed was in existence already as a fixed formula by the end of the second century at Rome.[7] Hanssens was a

---

5   The presence of a possible *syntaxis* here was seen by Hanssens (*Liturgie,* 1:457–61) as evidence of the Alexandrian rather than Roman origins of the *Apostolic Tradition.*

6   Except for the reference to the imposition of the hand on the candidate at this point; see Bradshaw, "Redating," 12 n. 32. See also Botte, *Tradition,* 49 n. 1.

7   See Kelly, *Creeds,* 126–30. See also Bernard Botte, "Note sur le symbole baptismal de saint Hippolyte,"

in *Mélanges Joseph de Ghellinck, S.J.* (Gembloux: Duculot, 1951) 189–200; Bernard Capelle, "Les origines du Symbole romain," *RThAM* 2 (1930) 5–20; idem, "Le Symbole romain au second siécle," *RBén* 39 (1927) 33–45; David L. Holland, "The Earliest Text of the Old Roman Symbol: A Debate with Hans Lietzmann and J. N. D. Kelly," *CH* 34 (1965) 262–81.

notable exception. Because of what appeared to be the non-Western phrasing of *Christum Iesum* (rather than *Iesum Christum*) and *qui natus est de Spiritu sancto* ex *Maria virgine* ("who was born of the Virgin Mary by the Holy Spirit") and the addition of the word *vivus* ("alive") to *et resurrexit die tertia a mortuis* ("and rose on the third day from the dead"), Hanssens held, primarily on the basis of parallels in Egyptian patristic authors, that such terminology could only indicate Alexandrian origins.[8] While he was correct to underscore the Eastern origins of the Western Apostles'/Roman Creed, parallels to *Christum Iesum* and *qui natus est de Spiritu sancto ex Maria virgine* do appear in some manuscripts of early Latin creedal formulae recounted in various *Acta* of the martyrs.[9] Even *Contra Noetum*, which has often been attributed to Hippolyus, offers a parallel to *Christum Iesum*, χριστόν Ἰησοῦν (8.1).

On the other hand, by omitting the obvious post-Nicene language in the oriental creedal formulae, we are left with short statements that provide some, if not exact, parallel to early brief creedal statements known from the second-century *Epistula Apostolorum* and the later Deir Bala'izah papyrus.[10]

Epistula Apostolorum
. . . in (the Father) the ruler of the universe, and in Jesus Christ (our Redeemer) and in the Holy Spirit (the Paraclete) and in the holy Church, and in the forgiveness of sins.

Deir Balyzeh papyrus
I believe in God the Father Almighty, and in His only-begotten Son our Lord Jesus Christ, and in the Holy Spirit, and in the resurrection of the flesh in the holy catholic Church.

In his study of the development of creeds, Hans Lietzmann pointed to the Deir Bala'izah papyrus as preserving a second-century creedal tradition from Rome, from which the later texts of the specifically Roman creed would evolve.[11] But a very similar profession of faith also appears in the current Coptic Orthodox rite of baptism immediately after an exorcism and *syntaxis* and before a threefold profession:

I believe in one God, God the Father Almighty, and his Only-Begotten Son, Jesus Christ our Lord, and the holy lifegiving Spirit, and the resurrection of the flesh, and the one only catholic apostolic Church. Amen.[12]

And in the Roman rite, as late as the eighth-century manuscript of the *Sacramentarium Gelasianum*, the baptismal interrogations themselves are also formulated in a rather simple and corresponding manner:

Do you believe in God the Father Almighty?
R. I believe.
And do you believe in Jesus Christ his only Son our Lord, who was born and suffered?
R. I believe.
And do you believe in the Holy Spirit; the holy Church; the remission of sins; the resurrection of the flesh?
R. I believe.[13]

Both Wolfram Kinzig and Markus Vinzent, therefore, have argued that the baptismal creed in the Latin version of the *Apostolic Tradition* is not the authentic third-century text of the Roman/Apostles' Creed, but an updating that was done when the translation into Latin was made in order that it might correspond to the form of that creed then existing.[14] Thus, in spite of assertions that the formulae in the oriental versions are late intruders,[15] or "an interpolation,"[16] or "profoundly altered,"[17]

---

8   Hanssens, *Liturgie,* 463–70. See also idem, "Note concernant le Symbole baptismal de l'ordonnance ecclésiastique latine," *RechSR* 54 (1966) 241–64.

9   See Wolfram Kinzig, "'. . . *natum et passum* etc.' Zur Geschichte der Tauffragen in der lateinischen Kirche bis zu Luther," in Wolfram Kinzig, Christoph Markschies, and Markus Vinzent, *Tauffragen und Bekenntnis* (AKG 74; Berlin: de Gruyter, 1999) 128–32.

10 ET from Kelly, *Creeds*, 82, 89.

11 See Hans Lietzmann, "Die Urform des apostolischen Glaubensbekenntnisses," in idem, *Kleine*

Schriften 3 (TU 74; Berlin: Akademie, 1962) 163–81.

12 ET from Whitaker, *Documents,* 94.

13 Mohlberg, *Liber Sacramentorum,* 74.

14 Kinzig, "*Natum et passum,*" 93–94; Markus Vinzent, "Die Entstehung des 'Römischen Glaubensbekenntnis,'" in Kinzig, Markschies, and Vinzent, *Tauffragen und Bekenntnis,* 189.

15 Richard H. Connolly, "On the Text of the Baptismal Creed of Hippolytus," *JTS* 25 (1924) 132–39.

16 Dix, *Apostolic Tradition*, 35.

17 Botte, *Tradition*, 49 n. 1.

they may actually reflect a minor expansion and adaptation of what the baptismal interrogations in the *Apostolic Tradition* once contained, that is, three very short interrogations and responses in conjunction with the three baptismal immersions.

■ **17** Whether the phrase "in the Holy Spirit *and* the holy church" in the Latin version is to be preferred to "in the Holy Spirit *in* the holy church" as in the oriental versions has been the subject of scholarly debate. Botte, Dix, Kelly, and Pierre Nautin all preferred the reading "*in* the holy church" as being the earliest, while Connolly and Heinrich Elfers favored the reading in the Latin version.[18] D. L. Holland has surveyed this debate and conjectures on theological grounds, in the context of the rebaptism controversy between Cyprian of Carthage and Pope Stephen, that the phrase "*and* the holy church" must reflect the earliest *Roman* terminology of the creed and hence should be preferred as authentically early third century and Hippolytan for that reason.[19] The most that can be concluded, however, is that the wording of this phrase in the Latin version also belongs to that process of updating to which Kinzig and Vinzent refer above. We simply do not know the precise formulation of this phrase in the Roman creedal tradition prior to the Latin version itself.

■ **18–28** A folio has been torn out of the Sahidic manuscript here, and so we have substituted a translation of the Bohairic text for the missing portion.

■ **19–26** If the hypothesis is correct that an earlier core may lie behind the development of, first, episcopal and, second, presbyteral and diaconal assignments and rites,

then immediately following some form of the creedal interrogation and immersion, the original rite may have concluded with only *Ap. Trad.* 21.20, 25, and 26. Such a conclusion to the rite would again show a remarkable degree of consistency with Justin Martyr's description of what took place immediately after baptism in the mid-second century (*1 Apol.* 65).

■ **21** In contrast to the oriental versions and *Testamentum Domini*, the episcopal hand-laying prayer in the Latin version asks only for "grace" rather than making "them worthy to be filled with your Holy Spirit" (Sahidic) in addition to grace. There has been a long scholarly debate as to whether the Latin is corrupt here and whether the explicit language about the bestowal of the Holy Spirit in the oriental versions is preferable. Dix, for example, was so convinced of the corrupt nature of the Latin at this point that, although normally following the Latin version throughout rest of his edition, he based his English translation of this prayer on the oriental versions and entitled the entire section as "Confirmation."[20] In a similar manner, Botte suggested that a line referring to the gift of the Holy Spirit in this prayer had fallen out here from either the Latin translation or the Greek text from which it was made.[21]

The scholarly evaluation of the Latin text, however, has changed since the work of Dix and Botte. For example, Geoffrey W. H. Lampe noted that there are no grammatical problems with the Latin at this point and that the text as it stands translates quite clearly.[22] Anthony Gelston conjectured that the Greek original would have referred here to the Holy Spirit twice, first,

18 Ibid., xi–xvii; idem, "Note," 189–200; Dix, *Apostolic Tradition*, 37; Kelly, *Creeds*, 91; Pierre Nautin, *Je crois à l'Esprit dans la Sainte Église pour la résurrection de la chair* (Paris: Cerf, 1947) 13–20; Connolly, "On the Text," 131–39; Heinrich Elfers, *Die Kirchenordnung Hippolyts von Rom* (Paderborn: Bonifacius, 1938). Already in 1938 Elfers claimed (38–39) that the version of the creed in the *Apostolic Tradition* was not original to the text but, based on its contents, was most likely an interpolation from the end of the 4th century.

19 A major part of Holland's argument rests on the assumption that had "in the Holy Spirit *in* the holy church" been part of the 3d-century *Roman* baptismal profession of faith, Cyprian would have used it to his advantage in arguing that the Holy Spirit is

given only *in* the church, outside of which there is no salvation. See David L. Holland, "The Baptismal Interrogation conerning the Holy Spirit in Hippolytus' *Apostolic Tradition*," *StPatr* 10 (1970) 360–65; idem, "'Credis in spiritum sanctum et sanctam ecclesiam et resurrectionem carnis?' Ein Beitrag zur Geschichte des Apostolikums," *ZNW* 61 (1970) 126–44.

20 Dix, *Apostolic Tradition*, 38.
21 Botte, *Tradition*, 53 n. 1.
22 Geoffrey W. H. Lampe, *The Seal of the Spirit: A Study in the Doctrines of Baptism and Confirmation in the New Testament and the Fathers* (London: SPCK, 1967) 138–41.

in relation to the initial section of the postbaptismal hand-laying prayer ("through the laver of regeneration of the Holy Spirit," as in the subordinate clause in the Latin version), and, second, in connection with the petition for grace in the hand-laying prayer ("make them worthy to be filled with your Holy Spirit," as in the main clause in the oriental versions). According to Gelston, both the Latin and oriental copyists accidentally omitted one of the references but kept the other.[23]

Cuming argued in response that two different errors made by two different copyists in the same place seemed improbable and that any direct references to Titus 3:5 and to the Holy Spirit may themselves be additions to an earlier form of the text, attached to the subordinate clause in the Latin and to the main clause in the oriental versions. In support of this, Cuming preferred the Bohairic version as closest to the original at this point, where there is reference only to the eschatological "forgiveness of their sins for the coming age" but to neither the "laver of regeneration" nor the Holy Spirit in the initial subordinate clause. He noted that the *Canons of Hippolytus* likewise contains no reference to the "laver of regeneration" but does connect the "forgiveness of sins" eschatologically with "the pledge of your kingdom."[24] Nevertheless, it was the Latin that Cuming translated in his edition.[25] More recently, Aidan Kavanagh has argued strongly for the reliability of the Latin.[26]

As Cuming suggested, some corroborating evidence that the original version of the prayer did not contain a reference to an explicit bestowal of the Holy Spirit subsequent to baptism itself may be provided by the equivalent prayer in the *Canons of Hippolytus*. Although this differs from all the other versions and thus may reflect "local tradition" more than translation,[27] in a manner quite similar to the Latin it also connects being "born again" with the gift of the Holy Spirit in baptism. And while the reference to "the pledge of your kingdom" may

be an allusion to biblical language about the Holy Spirit (see Eph 1:14 in particular), it is not an explicit statement and, in any event, does not negate the close relationship between new birth and Holy Spirit already stated in the opening of the prayer.

■ **22** In one manuscript of the *Canons of Hippolytus* the bishop merely signs the forehead of the neophyte with "the sign of love" and no reference is made to either anointing or oil. Hanssens claimed that this manuscript provided the original reading at this point.[28] If correct, this would mean that at some stage the *Apostolic Tradition* may have had prayer with imposition of hands and some kind of "signing" by the bishop, but this had not yet become a second postbaptismal anointing. But Hanssens was unable to provide any concrete evidence that this was the case.

■ **25** The Bohairic seems to have accidentally omitted part of this section.

■ **27–42** In relation to what has come before, this concluding section of the initiation material represents a rather uncharacteristic mix of rubrical directions with catechetical and theological interpretations. The instruction on the meaning of the eucharistic bread and cup, as well as the theological significance of the other cups to be distributed, reads rather like a catechetical excursus in 27–30, interspersed between the directions for the oblation and eucharistic prayer and the distribution. Similarly, following the lacuna in the Latin version from the middle of 21.38 onward, all the others conclude this section of the document with references to additional episcopal catechesis (e.g., on resurrection) that is said to have been given earlier (even though nothing of the sort has appeared prior to this in the text) or that will be taught during what later liturgical sources will call the period of postbaptismal mystagogy. Here, significantly, the Arabic notes that "these chapters come after baptism." In addition, all the oriental versions end with a

23   Anthony Gelston, "A Note on the Text of the *Apostolic Tradition* of Hippolytus," *JTS* 39 (1988) 112–17.

24   Geoffrey J. Cuming, "The Post-baptismal Prayer in *Apostolic Tradition*: Further Considerations," *JTS* 39 (1988) 117–19.

25   Cuming, *Hippolytus*, 20.

26   Aidan Kavanagh, *Confirmation: Origins and Reform*

(New York: Pueblo, 1988) 47.

27   See Bradshaw, *Canons*, 24.

28   Jean Michel Hanssens, "L'édition critique des Canons d'Hippolyte," *OrChrP* 32 (1966) 542–43. See also Bradshaw, *Canons*, 24. It has been suggested that this "sign of love" was originally the baptismal kiss, but, at least here, it appears to be a separate act from the kiss that immediately follows.

warning against instructing unbelievers who have not "received"[29] and a reference to the "white stone" of Rev 2:17. Moreover, beginning in *Ap. Trad.* 21.39 the style of the text changes from third person (e.g., "let him . . .") to second-person direct address ("And we have given these things to you in brief . . ."). It may be significant that the *Canons of Hippolytus* has here merely a brief description of the subsequent exemplary life that the newly baptized are now to lead. If something similar was all that existed in the original, the differences in the versions here may merely reflect the remnant of the conclusion of a catechetical or mystagogical instruction that was interpolated into the text sometime during the period that mystagogical instruction was becoming more frequent and popular.

■ **27** While the Bohairic refers to the bread as the "likeness of the flesh of Christ" and the *Testamentum Domini* refers to it as a "type of my body," only the Latin uses the language of "representation" and "antitype," and also "antitype" and "likeness," *similitudinem* (which Botte thought possibly should have been ὁμοίωμα),[30] to refer to the "blood." There can be no question but that the technical sacramental vocabulary here in the Latin reflects either a reworking of the Greek text behind this section or an editorial interpolation. If a Greek text is merely being translated here, references to "which the Greek calls . . ." make no sense, especially when the other versions do not do the same. Furthermore, if the commonly accepted early-third-century date for the *Apostolic Tradition* is correct, the specialized Greek vocabulary of "type" and "antitype" would be problematic, as their specific eucharistic use appears to be characteristic of the mystagogues (e.g., Cyril of Jerusalem and Ambrose of Milan) and liturgical sources (e.g., the *Apostolic Constitutions*) from the fourth century.[31] Similarly, if Botte's interpretation is correct that the Greek ὁμοίωμα

(see Rom 6:5) is intended by the Latin *similitudo,* the earliest equivalent use of this word in a Greek eucharistic context appears to be the mid-fourth-century anaphora in the prayer collection of Sarapion of Thmuis[32] (although the expression is found in Syriac in the 3d-century *Didasc.* 26.22.2), and in a Latin Christian context *similitudo* appears in reference to the blood of Christ in Ambrose (*De sacr.* 4.20).[33] Prior to the fourth century, Latin authors, such as Tertullian, seem to have preferred the term *figura* to speak of the relationship between the eucharistic bread and wine and Christ's body and blood.[34]

■ **28–37** The versions disagree considerably with regard to specific details here, especially over the number of cups (including whether milk and honey are to be distributed together or separately), the formulae to be used with them, and apparently whether the distribution occurs between the distribution of the eucharistic bread and wine (Latin, Ethiopic) or afterward (Sahidic, Arabic). In particular, only the Latin speaks of giving a separate cup of water. It may have been omitted by the others because it was a practice unknown in their own traditions, or it may be an addition to the document made by the Latin.

Comment

■ **1** An initial prayer over the water is attested also in third-century North Africa by Tertullian (*De bapt.* 4) and Cyprian (*Ep.* 70.1).

■ **2–3** These two verses have a decidedly archaic ring to them—especially if the term "pool," "font," or "place of baptism" is bracketed and the simple reference to water "pure and flowing" (*Testamentum Domini*) is preferred—and the similarity to the description of baptism in *Did.* 7.1–3 is striking:

---

29   While the Sahidic refers here to the reception of *baptism*, both the Arabic and Ethiopic omit the word. Botte (*Tradition*, 59 n. 5) preferred the Arabic and Ethiopic reading. It is possible that "reception," then, is to be taken as referring to the Eucharist and not to baptism. At the same time, however, both the *Canons of Hippolytus* and *Testamentum Domini* clearly refer to baptism in this context.

30   Botte, *Tradition*, 55 n. 2.

31   See Geoffrey W. H. Lampe, *A Patristic Greek Lexicon*

(Oxford: Oxford Univ. Press, 1961) 159, 1418–20.

32   See Johnson, *Sarapion*, 226–32.

33   On this see Reginald Grégoire, "Il sangue eucaristico nei testi eucologici di Serapione di Thmuis," in F. Valtioni, ed., *Sangue e antropologia nella liturgia* (Centro Studi Sanguis Christi 4; Rome: Pia unione Preziosissimo Sangue, 1984) 1283–84.

34   See Tertullian *Adv. Marc.* 4.40.3; Victor Saxer, "Figura corporis et sanguinis Domini," *Rivista di archeologia cristiana* 47 (1971) 65–89.

As for baptism, baptize in this way: Having said all this beforehand, baptize in the name of the Father and of the Son and of the Holy Spirit, in running water. If you . . . do not have running water, however, baptize in another kind of water; if you cannot [do so] in cold [water], then [do so] in warm [water]. But if you have neither, pour water on the head thrice in the name of Father and Son and Holy Spirit.

Niederwimmer has also drawn attention to the parallels here between the two texts.[35]

■ **4–5** Although there is no exact parallel elsewhere in early Christian literature for this list of the order in which the candidates are to be baptized (children, men, women), the practice of infant initiation is attested for the third century also in Tertullian (*De bapt.* 18), Cyprian (*Ep.* 64), and Origen (*Hom. on Lev.* 8.3). It is important to note, however, that those "who cannot answer for themselves" here are not necessarily infants but could well include children from infancy all the way to the age of seven years (i.e., the ancient Roman interpretation of *infantes*).[36] Even after attaining the age of seven in Roman society, and until puberty, children were limited as to their legal rights to conduct their own affairs; and, if not under the direct authority of their fathers (the paterfamilias), they were often placed under the system of tutelage. A similar parallel with betrothal and marriage laws and customs in the ancient Roman world wherein marriages themselves were often arranged by the paterfamilias may also be operative here.[37] Margaret Miles has argued that women would have been baptized last because of an attitude that saw them as being far-

thest from the state of innocence,[38] but Mary Rose D'Angelo suggests that "the simplest explanation is that it was not expected that [women] would be aroused by seeing the men baptized,"[39] something that could not be assumed of men watching naked women baptized.

■ **5** It has been argued that in the ancient world knotted hair was frequently viewed as a dwelling place for demons and evil spirits and so its loosening is to be interpreted in an exorcistic or antidemonic manner.[40] But according to R. J. Zwi Werblowsky,

it also suggests the Rabbinic rules for the monthly lustration of women after the menses. Loosening the hair (and even washing and combing it) is enjoined by the Talmud and all later rituals as necessary before immersion. . . . The Talmud gives as one of the reasons for this ordinance (ascribed to Ezra and therefore, perhaps, a tradition of some standing) the fear that "a knot may have formed itself in the hair," thereby impeding the access of water.[41]

Hence it may simply have been an attempt "to ensure that all the hair got wet."[42]

Some kind of exorcistic or antidemonic intent, however, may lay behind the phrase "let nothing foreign down into the water with them" (Sahidic). Since the Greek ἀλλότριος, "foreign, alien," is used to denote the devil (see also *Ap. Trad.* 20.8, 38), it is possible that the jewelry to be laid aside before baptism was an object such as an amulet or charm, which was interpreted as being "in the power of the Devil."[43] This interpretation is explicit in the *Canons of Hippolytus*.

■ **9** All the versions agree on a single declaratory form

---

35 Niederwimmer, *Didache*, 128–29.

36 On early Christian sponsorship at infant baptism, see Joseph H. Lynch, *Godparents and Kinship in Early Medieval Europe* (Princeton: Princeton Univ. Press, 1986) 117–42.

37 See Suzanne Dixon, *The Roman Family* (Baltimore: Johns Hopkins Univ. Press, 1992) 64–65, 105–6, 117–18; Judith E. Grubbs, *Law and Family in Late Antiquity: The Emperor Constantine's Marriage Legislation* (Oxford: Clarendon, 1995) 140–42. Our thanks to Professor Blake Leyerle of the University of Notre Dame for directing us to these references.

38 Margaret Miles, *Carnal Knowing: Female Nakedness and Religious Meaning in the Christian West* (Boston: Beacon, 1989) 48.

39 Mary Rose D'Angelo, "Veils, Virgins, and the

Tongues of Men and Angels: Women's Heads as Sexual Members in Ancient Christianity," in Howard Eilberg-Schwartz and Wendy Doniger, eds., *Off with Her Head! The Denial of Women's Identity in Myth, Religion, and Culture* (Berkeley: Univ. of California Press, 1995) 158 n. 76.

40 See Frank Gavin, "Rabbinic Parallels in Early Church Orders," *Hebrew Union College Annual* 6 (1929) 57–67; Willem Cornelis van Unnik, "Les chevaux defaits des femmes baptisées: Un rite de baptême dans l'Ordre Ecclésiastique d'Hippolyte," *VC* 1 (1947) 77–100.

41 Werblowsky, "Baptismal Rite," 99. Henry Chadwick (in Dix, *Apostolic Tradition*, m) concurred.

42 Cuming, *Hippolytus*, 18.

43 Ibid. See also Botte, *Tradition*, 47 n. 2.

of renunciation of Satan, with some minor variation in wording. According to Hanssens, these declaratory formulae find their closest parallels in later Alexandrian, Syrian, and Armenian liturgical sources, but not in Roman, North African, and Byzantine documents, where the renunciation is generally formulated in a threefold (or even fivefold) interrogative style. Consistent with his hypothesis that the *Apostolic Tradition* is of Alexandrian origins, Hanssens concluded that the form of the renunciation must reflect an Alexandrian context.[44]

This conclusion, however, is far from certain. An Alexandrian or Egyptian context for the Sahidic or Ethiopic versions would not be surprising and, as such, tells us nothing certain about what the shape and contents of the renunciation may have been in the Greek original, especially when a lacuna exists here in the Latin. Furthermore, we do not know exactly when Western rites began to formulate the renunciation in an interrogative manner. Our earliest Western witness to the rite of renunciation is Tertullian, who does not indicate the manner in which this rite was performed, but simply describes it:

> In short, to begin with baptism, when on the point of coming to the water we then and there, as also somewhat earlier in church under the bishop's control [*sub antistitis manu*] affirm that we renounce the devil and his pomp and his angels.[45]

> . . . we bear public testimony that we have renounced the devil, his retinue, and his works.[46]

> Now the compact you have made respecting him [the devil] is to renounce him, and his pomp, and his angels.[47]

Even here, the reference to "angels" shows a parallel with the Ethiopic version, and the word "pomp" (*pompa* or πομπή) appears as well in some of the Alexandrian and Syrian sources that Hanssens quotes in support of his hypothesis.[48] It would appear, then, that no strong case for a uniquely Alexandrian or non-Western origin or character of the renunciation can be made.

■ **10** Because the exorcistic prebaptismal anointing is located immediately after the renunciation, Hanssens again concluded that it did not reflect Roman liturgical usage, where the anointing was located before the renunciation.[49] While this may be true of the Roman initiation rites within the eighth-century *Sacramentarium Gelasianum*, the lack of early Roman liturgical sources that witness to a prebaptismal anointing of any kind does not permit this conclusion. Although Tertullian in the early third century refers both to a consecration or blessing of the baptismal waters (*De bapt.* 4) and, as we saw above, to a renunciation of Satan before baptism, there is no evidence before the mid- to late fourth century (i.e., in Sarapion of Thmuis,[50] Cyril of Jerusalem *Myst. Cat.* 2.3, and John Chrysostom *Baptismal Homilies* 3.27) of the use of "exorcised oil" for a prebaptismal exorcism. Similarly, prayers, or references to prayers, for the consecration of baptismal oils are known to us only from a variety of relatively early (mid-third-century) and later Eastern liturgical sources[51] but not from any available sources in the West, except for a passing reference in Cyprian to the consecration of oils at the Eucharist (*Ep.* 70.2). For that matter, there is no early Western evidence anywhere to corroborate the presence of a prebaptismal anointing at all prior to the witness of Ambrose (*De sacr.* 1.5), where it does appear immediately before the renunciation itself.

In the Syrian East, however, such an anointing—but pneumatic and messianic rather than exorcistic in orientation—is attested much earlier.[52] Similarly, contemporary scholarship has argued, in contradistinction to Hanssens, that a prebaptismal anointing in the Egyptian liturgical tradition was originally also nonexorcistic in nature and became an exorcism only in the context of the fourth century, when a postbaptismal anointing in relationship to the gift of the Holy Spirit was imported

44 Hanssens, *Liturgie*, 1:452–56.
45 *De cor.* 3; ET from Edward C. Whitaker, *Documents of the Baptismal Liturgy* (2d ed.; Alcuin Club Collection 42; London: SPCK, 1970) 9–10.
46 *De spect.* 4; ET from Whitaker, *Documents*, 9.
47 *De anima* 35; ET from ANF 3:216.
48 See esp. Cyril of Alexandria *Explicatio in psalmos* 45.2; Cyril of Jerusalem *Myst. Cat.* 1.4–9; *Const.* 8.41.
49 Hanssens, *Liturgie*, 452.
50 Prayer 15; see Johnson, *Sarapion*, 63.
51 See the various consecration of oil prayers in Whitaker, *Documents*, 14–19; Johnson, *Sarapion*, 64–67.
52 See Gabriele Winkler, "The Original Meaning of

and introduced into Egypt from elsewhere.[53] The presence of a prebaptismal exorcistic anointing in the *Apostolic Tradition*, therefore, may well be a fourth-century addition to the text.

■ **12–18** That the profession of faith took place interrogatively in the context of the baptismal immersions themselves in at least early- to mid-third-century North African Christianity is well documented in the writings of both Tertullian and Cyprian.[54] That an interrogative profession of faith and the baptismal immersions were also joined together in the Roman rite is also clear and remained so, as the *Gelasianum* attests, well into the early medieval period.[55] Indeed, the replacement of such short interrogations with a more complete creedal text, as appears in the Latin, was not a pattern followed by any liturgical rite in subsequent history. Instead, complete creeds, most often that of Nicea-Constantinople, were delivered at the *traditio symboli* and returned by the candidates at the *redditio symboli* at some point prior to baptism itself during the final stages of the catechumenate.[56]

■ **19–24** According to the witness of Tertullian (*De bapt.* 7–8; *De res. carn.* 8) and Cyprian (*Ep.* 70.2; 73.9; 74.5), a postbaptismal anointing, an imposition of hands with prayer for the Holy Spirit, and a possible subsequent signing of the newly baptized are not inconsistent with the state of, at least, North African initiation rites in the early to mid-third century. Similarly, Hippolytus himself, in his *Commentary on Daniel* (1.16.3), testifies to what may have been a pneumatic-oriented postbaptismal anointing at Rome in the same time period. Nevertheless, as we have seen, the postbaptismal rites of the *Apostolic Tradition* have proven to be an area for considerable scholarly debate.

■ **21** No one reading the Latin version would automatically conclude that either the episcopal imposition of the hand or the accompanying prayer are related to a postbaptismal gift of the Holy Spirit. Rather, the Latin reads as a prayer for grace, and the operating assumption in the prayer appears to be that the gift of the Spirit is not subsequent to baptism but already bestowed in and connected to the water rite itself, in complete harmony with Titus 3:5 and John 3:5.[57]

The fourth century in general was an era in which various postbaptismal ceremonies throughout the Christian world were added to rites that did not have them, and the ceremonies that were added—most often, at least in the East, a single postbaptismal chrismation—were those associated with the conferral of the gift or seal of the Holy Spirit.[58] Something similar, then, may have been happening generally in the West as well, but there the pneumatic focus became attached not specifically to an anointing but to an episcopal hand-laying prayer. Since the years between the first Council of Nicea (325) and the first of Constantinople (381) were years of intense pneumatological debate and doctrinal dispute and emerging consensus regarding the Holy Spirit, such ritual development is perfectly logical.

The existence in the fourth century of a postbaptismal hand-laying with prayer closely connected to the ministry of bishops is attested by Jerome, secretary to Pope Damasus at Rome 382–385 CE, in his *Altercation of a Luciferian with an Orthodox* (6, 9), but our earliest corroborating witness to an episcopal, pneumatic, postbaptismal hand-laying prayer in a corresponding Roman liturgical text is the eighth-century manuscript of the *Sacramentarium Gelasianum*.[59] In his description of the "spiritual seal" in *De sacr.* 3.8–9, Ambrose appears to be referring to a similar postbaptismal hand-laying prayer in use at Milan, but it is by no means certain if this is the case or what ritual act or gesture accompanied this "seal."[60]

the Prebaptismal Anointing and Its Implications," *Worship* 52 (1978) 24–45.

53 See Georg Kretschmar, "Beiträge zur Geschichte der Liturgie, insbesondere der Taufliturgie, in Ägypten," *Jahrbuch für Liturgik und Hymnologie* 8 (1963) 1–54; Bradshaw, "Baptismal Practice"; Maxwell Johnson, *Liturgy in Early Christian Egypt* (JLS 33; Nottingham: Grove, 1995) 7–16.

54 See Tertullian *De spect.* 4; *Adv. Prax.* 26; *De cor.* 3; Cyprian *Ep.* 69.7; 70.2.

55 See Mohlberg, *Liber Sacramentorum*, 74.

56 See Yarnold, *Awe-Inspiring Rites*, 12–13. Our earliest *Roman* references to these practices are the early-6th-century *Letter of John the Deacon to Senarius* 4 (see Whitaker, *Documents*, 155–56); and the *Sacramentarium Gelasianum* XXXV, in Mohlberg, *Liber Sacramentorum*, 48–51.

57 Kavanagh, *Confirmation*, 47.

58 On this development see Winkler, "Original Meaning," 24–45.

59 See Mohlberg, *Liber Sacramentorum*, 74.

60 See Maxwell Johnson, "The Postchrismational

Thanks to the witness of both Tertullian and Cyprian, there is, of course, no reason why an early postbaptismal prayer for the gift of the Holy Spirit should be ruled out as a possibility also in the *Apostolic Tradition*. The fact remains, however, that the earliest version of this prayer that we possess—the Latin—is a prayer not for the Holy Spirit but for grace so that the neophytes might live out the implications of their new birth in water and the Holy Spirit. Nevertheless, it must be noted that even within the oriental versions this hand-laying prayer refers only to the neophytes being made "worthy to be filled with [the] Holy Spirit." It does not indicate precisely when in the rite or by what gesture this "filling with the Spirit" is to take place.

■ **22** A second postbaptismal episcopal anointing such as this within liturgical texts of Christian initiation rites has no parallel prior to the eighth-century *Sacramentarium Gelasianum*. And, depending on how one interprets the "spiritual seal" of Ambrose mentioned above, the earliest description of it seems to be the famous fifth-century letter of Pope Innocent I to Decentius of Gubbio (416 CE).[61]

That an episcopal hand-laying and prayer, followed however by some kind of "signing" rather than anointing, was part of the structure of the postbaptismal rites in mid-third-century North Africa may be corroborated by the witness of Cyprian: "they who are baptized in the church are brought to the prelates of the church, and by our prayers and by the imposition of the hand obtain the Holy Spirit, and are perfected with the Lord's seal (*signaculo dominico*)."[62] Although it is difficult to tell whether Cyprian intends to say that this perfecting "with the Lord's seal" is the consequence of the imposition of the hand and prayer or a subsequent ritual gesture afterward, scholars have tended here to favor the latter interpretation.[63] If this is correct, it provides a clear parallel to what may have been the case in an earlier version of

the *Apostolic Tradition*. In other words, prior to composition of the Latin version, the postbaptismal episcopal rites added to the core rite in chap. 21 may have consisted simply of a hand-laying prayer and consignation.

That this "signing" would be connected eventually to an anointing is no surprise, at least in the context of fourth-century liturgical development, where many churches throughout the world were receiving postbaptismal anointings into their initiation rites. While what evidence there is (e.g., Tertullian and Hippolytus) suggests that both North Africa and Rome had some form of postbaptismal anointing from early times corresponding to the presbyterial anointing in *Ap. Trad.* 21.19, Rome alone came to adopt a second postbaptismal anointing and, as in 21.22, reserved it exclusively to the bishop as the concluding act of what had become his pneumatic hand-laying prayer. If Hanssens was correct about the original reading of *Canons of Hippolytus* 19 ("sign of love" without an anointing), then the first witness that this signing was connected to an anointing is the Latin text of the *Apostolic Tradition* itself, a fifth-century Italian manuscript. Similarly, while Jerome in his *Altercation of a Luciferian* (6.9) does note that "neither priest nor deacon has the right of baptizing without chrism and the bishop's order," and, as we have seen, refers to bishops imposing hands and praying for the Holy Spirit, it is only Innocent I—in the same era as the Verona Latin manuscript—who can refer explicitly to this signation as connected to an anointing following the imposition of the hand and prayer. Again, as with the hand-laying prayer and its evolution in the direction of a Spirit epiclesis, it may well be in regard to the episcopal anointing as well that we are witnessing here, in the words of Aidan Kavanagh, "a development of [the *Apostolic Tradition*] on this matter which was unknown when the document was written."[64]

Structure of *Apostolic Tradition* 21, the Witness of Ambrose of Milan, and a Tentative Hypothesis Regarding the Current Reform of Confirmation in the Roman Rite," *Worship* 70 (1996) 16–34; Pamela Jackson, "The Meaning of 'Spiritale Signaculum' in the Mystagogy of Ambrose of Milan," *EO* 7 (1990) 77–94.

61   Innocent I, *Ep.* 25.3.

62   *Ep.* 73.9; ET in Whitaker, *Documents*, 11.

63   See Frank Quinn, "Confirmation Reconsidered: Rite and Meaning," in Johnson, *Living Water*, 223–25; also Maxwell Johnson, *The Rites of Christian Initiation: Their Evolution and Interpretation* (Collegeville, Minn.: Liturgical, 1999) 186–92, 204–6, 356–60.

64   Kavanagh, *Confirmation*, 47.

■ **23** The postbaptismal kiss is attested as early as Justin Martyr (*1 Apol.* 65), although in Justin it corresponds structurally to the kiss of peace in *Ap. Trad.* 21.26 below. It is possible that this kiss is to be interpreted as a postbaptismal bestowal of the Holy Spirit and that the phrase "sign of love," the manuscript reading of the *Canons of Hippolytus* preferred by Hanssens, is itself a reference to the postbaptismal kiss. The postbaptismal kiss as imparting the gift of the Spirit may also be implied by the fact that within the hand-laying prayer in *Ap. Trad.* 21.21 the oriental versions only request that the neophytes might be made "worthy to be filled with [the] Holy Spirit" without indicating precisely when, where, or how that "filling" is to take place in the rite. Similarly, the greeting and response that accompany the kiss, "The Lord be with you" . . . "and with your spirit," may be parallel to a connection between "spirit" and the "holy kiss" advocated in several Pauline letters.[65]

■ **25** The rites of Christian initiation constitute admission not only to the Eucharist but to the neophytes' first participation in the intercessory "prayers of the faithful" as early as Justin Martyr (*1 Apol.* 65). See also the commentary on *Ap. Trad.* 18.1–2 above.

■ **26** This is the "kiss of peace" shared after the prayers of the faithful, as is attested in Justin (*1 Apol.* 65), Tertullian (*De or.* 18), and Origen (*Comm. on Rom.* 10.13). Here it is distinguished from the postbaptismal kiss in *Ap. Trad.* 21.23 and may be interpreted as the common pneumatic "seal" of prayer.[66] See also the commentary on *Ap. Trad.* 18.3–4 above. The expression "peace with the mouth," however, is most unusual; see the commentary on 4.1 above.

■ **28–29, 33–37** The origins of this particular practice are obscure. Traditional scholarship conjectured that it was somehow the remnant of the early Jewish meal context

of the eucharistic liturgy itself, "a stylized form consisting of the Messianic mixture of milk and honey . . . observed at the Easter vigil to symbolize the entrance into the land of promise accomplished sacramentally."[67] But there is simply no proof for this. Nor, for that matter, as we have seen, is it by any means clear that it is the Easter vigil that is intended as the occasion for baptism in the *Apostolic Tradition*.

Moreover, what documentary evidence there is for the use of such additional cups in the baptismal Eucharist is limited to Egyptian, Ethiopic, North African, and Roman sources.[68] A metaphoric use of "milk and honey" to refer to baptism as eschatological entrance into Christ, "the promised land," appears first in *Barn.* 6.18–19; and it is possible, but by no means certain, that Clement of Alexandria knew a ritual practice that included baptismal cups of water, milk, and honey as signifying eschatologically the means by which Christ the Logos in baptism cleanses (water), purifies, and sweetens (honey and milk), and in the Eucharist nourishes the communicant with himself, who is the "milk" of God.[69] Although the practice of giving milk and honey after communion in the baptismal rite only continued until the beginning of the eighth century in the Coptic Orthodox Church, it remains part of the concluding rites of the baptismal liturgy in the Ethiopian Orthodox Church still today.[70]

In early-third-century North Africa, Tertullian notes that "made welcome then [into the assembly], we partake [or 'foretaste,' *praegustare*] of a compound of milk and honey, and from that day for a week we abstain from our daily bath" (*De cor.* 3). But whether this eschatological "foretaste" came between the rites of baptism and Eucharist is not made clear. That in the North African tradition a blessing for the offering of milk and honey

65 Phillips, *Ritual Kiss*, 7–15, 18–19.
66 Ibid., 19–21.
67 Edward Kilmartin, "The Baptismal Cups Revisited," in E. Carr et al., eds., *Eulogema: Studies in Honor of Robart Taft, S.J.* (Studia Anselmiana 110; Analecta Ligurgica 17; Rome: Pontificio Ateneo S. Anselmo, 1993) 265–66. Examples of traditional scholarship include Josef Jungmann, *The Mass of the Roman Rite, Its Origin and Development*, trans. Francis A. Brunner (2 vols.; New York: Benzinger, 1951–55) 1:15; Jean Daniélou, *The Theology of Jewish Christianity*, trans. and ed. John A. Baker (London: Darton, Longman & Todd, 1964) 333–34; and Georg Kretschmar, "Die Geschichte des Taufgottesdienstes in der alten Kirche," in *Leitourgia: Handbuch des evangelischen Gottesdienstes* 5 (Kassel: J. Stauda-Verlag, 1970) 108.
68 See Kilmartin, "Baptismal Cups"; Hanssens, *Liturgie*, 481–88; Johannes Betz, "Die Eucharistie als Milch in früchristlicher Sicht," *ZKTh* 106 (1984) 1–25, 169–85.
69 Clement *Paed.* 1.6.34.3; 1.6.36.1; 1.6.45.1; 1.6.50.3–52.2. For the Father's nourishing milk, cf. also *Odes Sol.* 19.13.
70 See Heinrich Denziger, *Ritus Orientalium Coptorum,*

must have at one time occurred within the context of the eucharistic prayer itself, as seems similarly implied in the Latin version of the *Apostolic Tradition*, appears to be clear from late-fourth-century conciliar prohibition against the practice.[71]

Apart from the possible witness of the *Apostolic Tradition* itself, the earliest Roman evidence for the use of milk and honey, but not water, in the baptismal Eucharist appears in Jerome's *Altercation of a Luciferian with an Orthodox*, where Jerome quotes Tertullian as a witness to this "universal ecclesiastical practice" but adds the theological interpretation that the practice signifies baptismal infancy or new birth. The *Letter of John the Deacon to Senarius* (12) in about 500 also witnesses to the continuation of giving a cup of milk and honey to the newly baptized at the Easter vigil Eucharist. At about the same time, the earliest clear Roman reference to a baptismal cup of water in addition to that of milk and honey appears in a blessing formula in the *Sacramentarium Veronense* within a collection of materials assigned to the baptismal Mass at Pentecost, although the origins of this prayer are obscure.[72]

Thus the Latin version of the *Apostolic Tradition* has no precise parallels anywhere: where evidence for the practice of distributing milk and honey is clearly witnessed, the normal location for its distribution is after eucharistic Communion itself and its theological significance has to do with baptism, either eschatologically as entrance into the promised land or as baptismal rebirth. And a separate cup of water is almost otherwise unknown. According to Edward Kilmartin, "the commentary and instructions concerning the baptismal cups in [the *Apostolic Tradition*] represent the work of a superior theologian":[73]

The commentary on the cups and the directives for distribution complement one another, providing a rather comprehensive view of baptism, Eucharist and their relation to one another. The water points back to the interior ablution effected by baptism; the milk and honey mixture forward to the eucharistic flesh of Christ, which has the effect of sweetening the bitterness of human existence. . . . The order of administration provides a symbolic expression of the intimate relation between baptism and eucharist. The prior reception of water signifies that baptism, as insertion into Christ, is the precondition for the sacramental participation in the promised land: the sharing in the eucharistic flesh of Christ signified by the cup of milk and honey. The insertion of the two cups between the administration of the eucharistic bread and wine conveys the idea that the eucharistic nutriment is the sacramental event of full unification with Christ. . . . A traditional eschatological interpretation of the land flowing with milk and honey (Clement, Tertullian) is omitted in favor of a christological understanding, to which is added a eucharistic specification. The milk and honey . . . point . . . to the sharing in the eucharistic flesh which has a sweet spiritual effect.[74]

The theological sophistication and unparalleled practice of the cups of water and milk and honey being distributed between baptism and Eucharist in the Latin version, therefore, may well suggest that, although the baptismal practice of milk and honey is an attested early practice in some churches, here it is the Latin version of *Apostolic Tradition* that appears to reflect the greatest degree of development. That is, whatever the original Greek may have contained at this point, it is quite possible that the Latin reflects the liturgical practice of Rome at the time the Verona translation was made. To that end, Hanssens asked whether some form of the blessing prayer in the *Sacramentarium Veronense* had influenced the *Apostolic Tradition* itself.[75]

Synorum et Armenorum in administrandis sacramentis (1863; reprinted 2 vols. in 1; Graz: Akademische Druck- und Verlagsanstalt, 1961) 1:38.

71 See Kilmartin, "Baptismal Cups," 260–61.
72 Kunibert Mohlberg, ed., *Sacramentarium Veronense* (Rome: Herder, 1956) no. 205, p. 26. See Pierre M. Gy, "Die Segnung von Milch und Honig in der Östernacht," in Balthasar Fischer and Johannes Wagner, eds., *Paschatis Sollemnia: Studien zu Österfeiern und Österfrömmigkeit. Festschrift für Josef A. Jungmann* (Basel: Herder, 1959) 206–12; Hanssens, *Liturgie,* 485–87.
73 Kilmartin, "Baptismal Cups," 267.
74 Ibid., 263–64.
75 Hanssens, *Liturgie,* 488.

Latin	Sahidic	Arabic	Ethiopic
1			And on the Sabbath and on the first [day of] the week the bishop, if it is possible, by his own hand is to deliver to all the people, as the deacons break [the bread],
2			and the presbyters are to break the baked bread. And if a deacon offers to a presbyter, he is to spread out his garment, and the presbyter himself is to take and deliver to the people with his hands.
3			And on the other days they are to receive by command of the bishop.

Text

Because this whole chapter is omitted by the Sahidic and Arabic versions, in his edition Easton treated it as a later addition to the text.[1] Dix, however, argued strongly for its authenticity on the grounds of the presence of at least somewhat similar material in the *Canons of Hippolytus* and *Testamentum Domini*,[2] a position supported by Botte.[3] The textual tradition behind the Sahidic and Arabic may well have omitted the section because its contents were not applicable to their situation or because they were unable to make sense of it,[4] since exactly what the original intended to say here is difficult to determine.

Dix, however, did regard the reference to Saturday in the Ethiopic as an interpolation because it does not appear in the *Canons of Hippolytus* and was not a day on which the Eucharist was celebrated at Rome in ancient times.[5] Botte similarly thought that this reference was added later than the third century and had been influenced by subsequent Eastern practice, which did make Saturday a eucharistic day.[6] Dix was challenged by Clifford William Dugmore, who thought that Christians were practicing public worship on the Sabbath in the third century,[7] and by Willy Rordorf, who believed that a "new regard" for the Sabbath was beginning to emerge among Gentile Christians in the third century and that "from the time of Hippolytus onwards, particularly in the fourth century, there is an increasing amount of evidence for the Christians' practice of worshiping on the sabbath."[8]

1 Easton, *Apostolic Tradition*, 31, 58.
2 Dix, *Apostolic Tradition*, 82–83.
3 Botte, *Tradition*, 61 n. 1.
4 So ibid., xxxi–xxxii.
5 Dix, *Apostolic Tradition*, 43 n. 1.
6 Botte, *Tradition*, 61 n. 2.
7 Dugmore, *The Influence of the Synagogue upon the Divine Office* (1944; 2d ed. London: Faith, 1964) 28–37.
8 Willy Rordorf, *Sunday: The History of the Day of Rest and Worship in the Earliest Centuries of the Christian Church,* trans. A. A. K. Graham (London: SCM, 1968) 145–46.

Apostolic Constitutions	*Canons of Hippolytus*	*Testamentum Domini*
	On Sunday, at the time of the liturgy, the bishop, if he is able, is to communicate all the people from his hand. If the presbyter is sick, the deacon is to take the mysteries to him, and the presbyter is to take [them] himself. [31] The deacon is to communicate the people when the bishop or the presbyter allows him.	The deacon does not give the offering to a presbyter. Let him open the disc or paten, and let the presbyter receive. Let the deacon give [the Eucharist] to the people in their hands.

Comment

Although the precise meaning of this chapter is unclear, it obviously has something to do with the distribution of Communion and seems primarily concerned about the appropriate roles for bishop, presbyter, and deacon in this ministry. Such precision of roles seems more likely to belong to the fourth century or later rather than the third (cf. the directions about the positioning of those holding oils in *Ap. Trad.* 21.6–8), as does any evidence for parallels to the practices here described, and this suggests that this chapter belongs to one of the later strata of material in the church order.

■ **1** In spite of the assertions by Dugmore and Rordorf, the only evidence for public assemblies for worship on Saturdays before the fourth century—as distinct from respect for the day—is a passage in Origen (*Hom. on Num.* 23.4), which even Dugmore admitted was not necessarily to be taken literally. And all the evidence for celebrations of the Eucharist on a Saturday belongs to the fourth century or later. Similarly, eucharistic celebrations "on other days" would have been rare prior to this period, usually being restricted to the feasts of local martyrs and then only at their place of burial.

■ **2** Dix regarded this part of the chapter as "the earliest witness to certain peculiarly Roman customs" and as referring to a practice described in the *Liber Pontificalis* and attributed there to Pope Zephyrinus (199–217) whereby at a papal liturgy the concelebrating presbyters consecrated on glass patens held before them by deacons.[9] However, even Dix admitted that the ascription to Zephyrinus was unreliable. Moreover, not only is the use of the term *sacerdos* to denote a presbyter in this section of the *Liber Pontificalis* anachronistic for the period, but the further statement that Pope Urban I (222–230) substituted twenty-five patens of silver for glass indicates that the custom was understood as referring to eucharistic celebrations on station days when the presbyters of the twenty-five parishes of Rome attended the pope's mass,[10] a practice unlikely to have been so organized as early as the first quarter of the third century.

9   Dix, *Apostolic Tradition*, 82.
10   See Geoffrey Grimshaw Willis, *Further Essays in Early Roman Liturgy* (London: SPCK, 1968) 4–15.

23

Latin	Sahidic	Arabic	Ethiopic
	47 Concerning the fast (νηστεία)	*35 Concerning the widows and virgins and at what time the bishop should fast*	*35 Concerning widows and virgins and at which time the bishop should fast*

1 | | Let the widows (χήρα) and the virgins (παρθένος) fast (νηστεύειν) often, and let them pray in the church (ἐκκλησία). The presbyters (πρεσβύτερος), likewise (ὁμοίως) with the laity (λαϊκός), let them fast (νηστεύειν) at the time they wish. | They do as we have said before many times and they pray in the church. The presbyters and deacons fast at the time they wish to, | They are to do as we have said: Widows and virgins are to fast many times; and they are to pray in the church. The presbyters and deacons may fast when they wish. And in the same way the people are to fast.

2 | | But (δέ) it is not possible for the bishop (ἐπίσκοπος) to fast (νηστεύειν) except (εἰ μήτι) on the day when all the people (λαός) will fast (νηστεύειν). | but the bishop can fast only on the day on which all the people are fasting. | And it is not for the bishop to fast except on days when all the people fast.

3 | | For (γάρ) it will happen that there is one who wishes to take something to the church (ἐκκλησία) and it is not possible for him to be denied (ἀρνεῖσθαι). But (δέ) when he divides the bread, certainly (πάντως) he will taste the bread. And (δέ) when he eats it with some others of the faithful (πιστός) with him, | It may be that someone wants to bring something to church and cannot be refused. If he divides the bread, he tastes it and eats with the other believers who are with him. | For whenever they bring along something to bring into the church, it is not possible to refuse it; and if he has broken the bread, he himself is to taste the bread, and he is to eat with the other believers who are with him

4 | | let them receive from the bishop's (ἐπίσκοπος) hand a single piece (κλάσμα) of bread before each one breaks his own bread. For (γάρ) it is a blessing and not a thanksgiving (εὐχαριστία) as in the body (σῶμα) of the Lord. | They receive the bread piece by piece from the bishop's hand before each one breaks the bread in front of him, because this is a blessing and not an offering like the Lord's body. | who receive from the hand of the bishop piece by piece of the baked bread before they participate—which is a blessing. Each one is to take the bread that they have presented, because this is the bread of blessing and not an offering like the body of our Lord.

Epitome	Canons of Hippolytus 32	Testamentum Domini 2.13
Let widows and virgins fast often and pray for the church. Let presbyters, when they wish, and likewise laypeople fast.	The virgins and the widows are to fast often and pray in the church. The clergy are to fast according to their choice and their opportunity.	
A bishop is not able to fast except when all the people [fast].	The bishop is not to be held to the fast, unless the clergy fast with him.	
For it happens when someone wishes to offer, and he is not able to refuse; but, having broken, he always tastes.	If someone wants to make an offering [continued in chap. 29B].	
		In the supper or feast, let those who have come together receive thus from the shepherd, as for a blessing.

What is apparently the Greek text of this chapter has for some inexplicable reason been preserved in just one manuscript of the *Epitome* (see the Introduction above, p. 6) and has been translated here. The most significant differences between this and the oriental texts are that the *Epitome* refers to the widows and virgins praying "for the church" rather than "in the church," and it omits the word "bread," which occurs twice in the equivalent of its last few words in the other texts. With regard to these words and the additional material at the end of the other versions, see the discussion on chaps. 24 and 25 below and the commentary on chap. 29C.

Comment

Voluntary fasting was a normal part of early Christian asceticism for everybody but was especially expected of widows and virgins, as was the ministry of intercession

for the church (see chap. 10). The absence of any explicit reference to specific, regular fast days observed by all may perhaps be a sign of the antiquity of this passage, or at least of its origin in a Christian community that did not follow what was becoming the mainstream custom. For we have abundant testimony that Wednesdays and Fridays were the normal weekly fast days in many churches. Thus *Did.* 8.1 instructs its readers to observe these days rather than the Mondays and Thursdays that were the standard Jewish days for this purpose; Clement of Alexandria and Origen attest to the existence of this custom elsewhere in the second and third centuries; the second-century Roman treatise, *The Shepherd of Hermas*, speaks of customary fasts that it calls "stations"; and Tertullian in North Africa indicates that these were kept on Wednesday and Fridays every week.[1]

---

1   Clement *Strom.* 7.12; Origen *Hom. on Lev.* 10.2; *Herm. Sim.* 5.1, on which see Carolyn Osiek, *The Shepherd of Hermas: A Commentary* (Hermeneia; Minneapolis: Fortress Press, 1999) 168–69; Tertullian *De ieiun.* 10; see also *De or.* 19.

24/25

Original Placement of 29B, C

Although the additional material at the end of chap. 23 in the oriental versions may look like nothing more than a later amplification of the chapter by a translator or copyist, there is a doublet of this passage in the Ethiopic at the end of chap. 29C, and this was one of the factors that led Botte to conclude that the material in the Ethiopic version that we have designated as chaps. 29B and 29C had actually been displaced from their original position as chaps. 24 and 25. The Sahidic and Arabic omit these two chapters entirely, passing directly from 23 to 26 (apart from the closing lines of 25 left at the end of 23) and from 29 to 30. In the Latin, which resumes after a lacuna with the last part of 26, chap. 30 similarly follows immediately after 29.

In his edition Dix accepted the Ethiopic order as authentic at this point. Botte, however, noted that traces of these two chapters in the *Canons of Hippolytus* and *Testamentum Domini* supported their original location as lying between chaps. 23 and 26.[1] Chadwick concurred with this conclusion in his revised edition of Dix, adding that no objection could be raised against their authenticity on the grounds of their absence from the Latin because there was a lacuna in the Latin text at that point.[2] Botte claimed that the chapters had not fallen out of the Sahidic and Arabic texts accidentally but, along with chap. 22, had been deliberately suppressed by a redactor because of their obscurity. He explained the Ethiopic order by claiming that the translator must have had access to two versions of the text—one like the Sahidic and Arabic and one that was more complete—and in his efforts to reconcile the two, had inserted chaps. 24 and 25 in the wrong position, along with a repetition of the end of chap. 25.

We accept Botte's conclusion with regard to the original order here, but have continued to print the two chapters where they actually occur in the Ethiopic so that readers may have a clearer impression of that manuscript tradition. We suspect, however, that these chapters fell out or were suppressed at an earlier stage than the translation into Sahidic. We believe that they were already missing in the version known to the compiler of the *Epitome* and that an earlier copyist/redactor had inserted the words, "but having broken, he always tastes," into chap. 23 in order to provide a transition to the final lines of chap. 25 still left in the text.[3]

---

1   Botte, *Tradition*, xxxi–xxxii.
2   Dix, *Apostolic Tradition*, j.
3   See Cuming, *Hippolytus*, 24.

26

Latin (75.1–4)	Sahidic	Arabic	Ethiopic
	48 Concerning the hour of eating	*36 Concerning the time for eating and that the catechumens should not eat with the believers*	*36 Concerning the time at which it is proper to eat; it is not proper that catechumens eat with believers*
1 . . . you who are present, and so feast.	And (δέ) it is proper for everyone, before they drink, to receive a cup and to give thanks (εὐχαριστεῖν) over it, and drink and eat, being purified in this way.	Each one before drinking should take a cup and give thanks over it and drink and eat, being pure.	It is proper that everyone, before they taste and drink anything, take the cup and give thanks over it and drink and eat because they are pure.
2 But to the catechumens let exorcised bread be given and let them each offer a cup.	But (δέ) let the catechumens (κατηχούμενος) be given exorcised (ἐξορκισμός) bread and a cup.	Thus the catechumens are given the bread of blessing and a cup.	They are to give the catechumens the bread of blessing and the cup.

Text

In his edition Botte treated the end of chap. 23 in the oriental versions as constituting the first half of chap. 26 (since chaps. 24 and 25 are missing from the Sahidic and Arabic and are displaced in the Ethiopic), even though there is no break in the actual texts, and he supplied it with a title, "Of the Common Meal." He went on to ignore the title that these versions then do give for the next chapter, "Concerning the Hour of Eating," because it does not correspond with the contents of what follows.[1] We, however, have followed the arrangement of the texts themselves.

■ 1 The Latin reappears part way through this, but with a different grammatical construction from the oriental witnesses (second-person plural instead of third person), which raises suspicions that there has been some emendation of the text here in one or the other tradition.

■ 2 The substitution of "of blessing" for "of exorcism" in the Ethiopic follows its standard practice throughout the church order, but here the Arabic does the same.

Comment

The chapter appears to have in view a common meal during which individuals will offer their own thanksgiving over a cup rather than participate in a communal benediction. Such a picture immediately suggests a parallel with Jewish practice, where the custom was for people to say their own blessings over wine during (but not at the end of) a meal.[2]

This chapter may well refer to the same event as in chap. 29C, which apparently originally preceded it in the text (see the discussion on chaps. 24 and 25). However, because the first half speaks of individual thanksgivings over the cup rather than the common cup of that chapter, it may be an insertion from a different (though still early) source, especially as the Latin suggests that it was written in the second-person plural rather than the third. If so, there would be a clearer contrast between the common cup and blessed bread of the faithful in chap. 29C.15–16 and the exorcised bread and individual cups of the catechumens in 26.2. A major concern here seems to be ritual purity—the segregation of the faithful from catechumens at Christian communal meals, with the latter being excluded from whatever it is that the faithful are eating and given exorcised bread instead—just as in chap. 18 there is concern that the two groups never pray together or exchange the kiss of peace. The exclusion of catechumens from Christian meals is also dealt with in *Ap. Trad.* 27.1.

---

1   Botte, *Tradition*, 67 n. 9.
2   See *m. Ber.* 6.6.

Apostolic Constitutions	Canons of Hippolytus	Testamentum Domini
	33. . . . After the offering one is to give them the bread of exorcism before they sit down.	

Latin (75.5–9)	Sahidic	Arabic	Ethiopic
[Title]	*49 Concerning that it is not proper for the catechumens (κατηχούμενος) to eat with the faithful (πιστός)*	*That the catechumens should not eat with the believers*	*Concerning that it is not proper for catechumens to eat with believers*
1 Let a catechumen not sit at the Lord's Supper.	Do not let the catechumens (κατηχούμενος) sit at the supper (δεῖπνον) of the Lord with the faithful (πιστός).	The catechumens should not sit at the Lord's banquet with the believers.	And catechumens are not to sit at the table of the Lord with believers.
2 But through the whole offering let him who offers be mindful of him who invited him, because for that reason he entreated that he should enter under his roof.	But (δέ) let the one who eats remember the one who invited him continuously (κατά—) while they are eating. For (γάρ) it was for this that he invited them that they should enter under his roof.	He who eats, every time he eats, should remember whoever invited him, for it is for this that he invited him to enter under his roof.	And it should be [the case] that the one who eats should remember the one who invited him every time he eats. And it was for this reason that he asked them to enter under his roof.

Text

■ **2** The major discrepancy between the versions in this chapter is in the references to "offering" (*oblationem*) and "him who offers" (*qui offert*) in the Latin, which are not present in any of the other witnesses. In his edition Dix followed Easton and rendered the Latin words in this way, but claimed in his notes that the Greek προσφορά, "offering," could mean a "meal" and that the word "eats" in the oriental versions was a translation of the middle voice of the Greek verb προσφέρειν rather than the active, as in the Latin, though admitting that he did not know which was correct.[1] By the time that he published *The Shape of the Liturgy*, however, he had opted for "meal" and "eats."[2] Botte and Cuming both followed suit.[3] On the other hand, the language of offering is freely used throughout the *Apostolic Tradition* (see the commentary on chap. 29C), and hence the readings "offering" and "offers" here should not be so lightly dismissed. It is possible that the scholars who have rejected these translations may have been influenced by a desire to make a clearer distinction than early Christians might have done between eucharistic and noneucharistic meals (for this see also the commentary on chap. 29C).

Comment

■ **1** The Pauline term "Lord's supper" (1 Cor 11:20) is rare in early Christian usage, but not completely unknown: Tertullian, for instance, speaks of the *dominicum convivium* (*Ad uxor.* 2.4). However, it is no more clear there than here whether the term refers to the Eucharist or to a Christian meal that was distinguished from the Eucharist.

The first sentence continues the theme of the segregation of the catechumens begun in chap. 26, and may appear to contradict what is said there, where catechumens apparently shared in the meal, albeit with different foodstuffs from the faithful. Easton dealt with the problem by suggesting that the sentence may have meant that "catechumens *stood* during the agape" or "ate at a separate table."[4] Dix adopted the same interpretation, noting the parallel with Jewish rules against table fellowship with the uncircumcised (see Acts 11:3).[5] Botte, however, explained the sentence as meaning that after the faithful had received blessed bread and the catechumens exorcised bread, the latter were then dismissed before the rest of the meal began.[6] Cuming adopted a similar reading, but treated "Lord's supper" as referring to the

---

1 Dix, *Apostolic Tradition*, 46 n. 6.
2 Dix, *Shape*, 82.
3 Botte, *Tradition*, 69 n. 3; Cuming, *Hippolytus*, 25.
4 Easton, *Apostolic Tradition*, 100 (emphasis added).
5 Dix, *Shape*, 83, though he goes on to draw the erroneous conclusion that this is the origin of the Angli-

can rule against *unconfirmed* Christians (not the unbaptized) being excluded from the Eucharist.
6 Botte, *Tradition*, 69 n. 2.

Apostolic Constitutions	*Canons of Hippolytus*	*Testamentum Domini*
	None of the catechumens is to sit down with them for the supper of the Lord.	But let not a catechumen receive. . . .

Eucharist proper, from which the catechumens would be excluded.[7]

■ **2** The reference here to a host who invited Christians to supper led Dix to conclude that the original Christian community meal had been transformed as a result of the abstraction of the Eucharist from it: "It is no longer a communal supper of the church which all Christians can attend in their own right, but a private party to which the guests can come only by the invitation of their host, whose bounty they are expected to repay by their prayers."[8] It is not impossible, however, that at least in some places if not everywhere, Christian meals had always had this character. Christians would have needed a room in which to hold their regular gatherings; what would have been more natural than to be invited to the home of one of the wealthier members of the local congregation, who would probably have provided much of the food with only relatively small contributions to the meal being made by others, and might even originally have assumed the position of presidency within the Christian community?[9]

---

7 Cuming, *Hippolytus*, 25.

8 Dix, *Shape*, 84.

9 On the role of the host in the ancient world, see further Charles A. Bobertz, "The Role of Patron in the Cena Dominica of Hippolytus' Apostolic Tradition," *JTS* 44 (1993) 170–84.

Latin (75.10—76.3)	Sahidic	Arabic	Ethiopic
[Title]	*50 Concerning that it is proper to eat judiciously (ἐπιστήμη) and moderately*	*That they should eat modestly and with restraint and not get drunk*	*Concerning that it is proper that they eat what is sufficient in fear and with moderation, and they are not to become drunk*

1 When eating and drinking, do it with appropriateness and not to the point of drunkenness, and not so that anyone may ridicule [you] or he that invites you may be grieved by your disorderly behavior, but that he may pray that he may be made worthy that the saints may enter in to him, for "you," he said, "are the salt of the earth."[a]

2 But if an offering is made in common to all, which is called in Greek *apophoreton,* take of it.

3 But if [it is] so that all may eat enough, eat so that both some may remain and he who invited you may send [it] to whomever he wishes, as though from the leftovers of the saints, and he may rejoice in confidence.

4 And let those who are invited, when eating, receive in silence, not contending with words but what the bishop has exhorted, and if he has asked anything, reply shall be given to him. And when the bishop says a word, let everyone keep silent, praising him with modesty, until he again asks.

And (δέ) when you eat and drink appropriately, do not drink to become drunk, so that people shall not laugh at you, and the one who invited you shall not grieve (λυπεῖν) at your dissoluteness, but (ἀλλά) so that, rather, he shall pray that those who are holy go in to him. For (γάρ) he said, "You are the salt of the earth."[a]

If all of you are given portions (μερίς) at once, then you shall take your share only.

But (δέ) if they summon you to eat, you are to eat only what is sufficient, so that the one who invited you will send those things that are left after you to whom he wishes, as (ὡς) they are the leavings of those who are holy. And he will rejoice at your coming in to him.

And (δέ) those who were invited to eat, (δέ) let them eat in silence, not quarreling. But (ἀλλά) when the bishop (ἐπίσκοπος) commands (προτρέπειν) one to ask for a word, let him answer him. And when the bishop (ἐπίσκοπος) speaks, let everyone remain silent in soberness until he asks them again.

You should eat and drink in order and not drink so as to get drunk, lest people ridicule you and he who invited you regret your dissoluteness. Rather let him pray that the saints should enter his house. He said, "You are the salt of the earth."[a]

If the portions of all of you are given to you together, you should take only your own share,

and if you are invited to eat, eat modestly and no more, so that what you leave can be sent by the one who invited you to whomever he wishes, as what was left by the saints, and he will rejoice when you enter.

And he who eats should remember him who invited him each time he eats. It is for this reason he asked them under his roof. And let those who are invited eat in a united spirit without quarreling, and if the bishop allows someone to ask about a saying, let him address him.

37 If the bishop speaks, let everyone be silent, and if the bishop is not present, let the blessing be taken from a presbyter or deacon If the bishop speaks, let everyone be silent until he asks them,

---

They are to eat and drink in order, and they are not to drink until they are drunk so that people may not make fun of them and so that the one who invited them should not be sad because of their foolishness. But they are rather to pray that holy ones may enter the house. And he said: "You are the salt of the earth."[a]

And now he has given to you so that you could take your portion after all those [who are] with him.
Eat with moderation and drink with moderation so that there should be something left and so that what is left from you the one who invited you may send to whom he will. For this food and this drink are the leftover[s] of the holy ones, and they are to rejoice when you come to them and are to eat your leftovers as food from the holy ones. . . . those who have been invited. They are to rejoice in your coming as they eat. And furthermore those who have been invited are to eat without contention. But when the bishop permits, they may speak and ask whatever there is [to ask] and he is to respond. And then, when he has finished saying to them everything that he wanted to ask them, they are again to be silent with moderation until the bishop once more asks them.

---

[a] Matt 5:13

Apostolic Constitutions	*Canons of Hippolytus*	*Testamentum Domini*
	They are to eat and drink sufficiently, not to the point of drunkenness, but peacefully, to the glory of God. [34] No one is to talk too much and shout, lest anyone laugh at you, and you are a scandal for the people, and he who invited you is insulted, because you are disorderly. But he himself, let him be allowed to participate and all his household, and see the decency of each one of us, and receive a great blessing such as he sees in us, and he will pray that the saints come under his roof, because our Savior said, "You are the salt of the earth."[a]	Let those who are called with the bishop to the house of one who is faithful eat with gravity and knowledge, not with drunkenness or to debauchery, and not so that he who is present may laugh, or so as to annoy the household of him that called him; but so let them enter that he who called [them] may pray that the saints may enter into his house. For "you are the salt of the earth,"[a] [as] you have heard.
		Because when they eat, let them eat abundantly, [but] so that there may be left over both for you [and] also for those to whom he that called you wishes [to] send, so that he may have them as foods left over by the saints, and that he may rejoice at that which remains over. Let those who come to a feast, being called, not stretch out a hand before them that are older. But let them eat last when the first shall have done. Let not those who eat strive in speech, but let them eat in silence; but if anyone desires, or the bishop or presbyter ask [a question], let him return answer.
	When the bishop says a word, being seated, they are to gain benefit from it and [he also] is to gain profit [from it].	But when the bishop says a word, let everyone quietly, giving praise, choose silence for himself, until he also be asked [a question].

	Latin	Sahidic	Arabic	Ethiopic
	Latin	**Sahidic**	**Arabic**	**Ethiopic**
5	Even if without the bishop the faithful are at the supper, with a presbyter or deacon present, let them similarly eat appropriately. And let everyone hasten to receive the blessing from the hand, whether from a presbyter or from a deacon. Similarly a catechumen also shall receive it exorcised.	And (δέ) if there is no bishop (ἐπίσκοπος) there, but (ἀλλά) some faithful (πιστός) only, let those who are at the dinner (δεῖπνον) receive a blessing (εὐλογία) from the presbyter (πρεσβύτερος), if he is there. But (δέ) if there is none, let them receive it from a deacon (διάκονος). Likewise (ὁμοίως), let the catechumen (κατηχού-μενος) receive exorcised (ἐξορκισμός) bread.	and if there is no bishop present but only believers at the meal, let them take a blessing from the hand of a presbyter if one is present, and if one is not present, from the hand of a deacon. Let the catechumens also take the bread of exorcism.	And if the believers should be without a bishop at the supper, they are to take the blessing by hand from a presbyter or from a deacon. Similarly catechumens are to take an exorcised portion from the bread.
6	If the laity are together, let them act with moderation, for a layman cannot make the blessing.	But (δέ) when the laity (λαϊκός) are together without clergy (κληρικός), let them eat prudently (ἐπιστήμη). But (δέ) the layman (λαϊκός) is not able to give a blessing (εὐλογία).	And if they are all lay people together, let them eat quietly; a layman should not do the blessing.	And if there are laity among them, they are to eat in silence. And it is not proper for a layman to do the blessing.

Apostolic Constitutions	*Canons of Hippolytus*	*Testamenatum Domini*
	If the bishop is not present and the presbyter is present, they are all to pay attention to him, because he is higher than them in God. They are to honor him with the honor with which the bishop is honored, and are not to dare to oppose him. He is to give them the bread of exorcism before they sit down, so that God may free their meal from the disturbance of the enemy and they may rise well in peace.	
	[35] A deacon at a meal in the absence of a presbyter is to replace the presbyter for the prayer over the bread; he is to break it and give it to the guests. With regard to the layman, it is not given to him to sign the bread but to break it only, if there is no cleric there.	

Text

Unlike chap. 27, but in line with the Latin fragment of chap. 26, this chapter addresses its readers directly in the second-person plural throughout its first half (though the Sahidic oscillates between singular and plural). It reverts to the more usual third person for the rest, thus suggesting the possibility that the first part, the exhortation to moderation in food and drink at Christian community meals (1–3), may be an insertion from a different source, before the instructions in how to order the meal resume (4–6).

The several versions exhibit a number of textual divergences here, especially in the latter part of the chapter. Although the general sense may be clear, it is often difficult to determine which of them comes closest to the original reading. We should also note that a doublet of the last part of the chapter occurs in the Ethiopic, beginning from the middle of *Ap. Trad.* 28.4 at exactly the point where the Arabic introduces a new heading. The doublet is located just before chap. 30 (= chap. 29D below), and more closely reproduces the Arabic (including its title) than does the Ethiopic version here. This suggests that the Ethiopic translator had access to more than one text of the *Apostolic Tradition*, in which some material was not in exactly the same order.

■ **2** Dix, followed by Botte, treated the phrase "which is called in Greek" as an insertion by the Latin translator.[1] Hanssens, on the other hand, claimed that the other versions implied that the original word in the Greek text was simply μερίς, "share," and that the translator had instead introduced *apophoreton*, "that which is carried away," because it was the more usual term for such distributions in the region of Italy from which he came, as other sources confirmed.[2]

■ **3** Dix proposed that the Latin "in confidence" (*in fiducia*) was translating the Greek ἐν παρρησίᾳ, and "at your coming/when you enter/when you come to them" in the oriental versions were rendering ἐν παρουσίᾳ but that

the more likely original text was ἐν ὑπερουσίᾳ, "at what is left over," preserved by the *Testamentum Domini*.[3]

■ **4** Botte thought that "what the bishop has exhorted" (*quae hortatus fuerit episcopus*) in the Latin was probably the result of a mistranslation of the Greek verb ἐπιτρέπειν, "to allow," which he said was correctly preserved in the Sahidic.[4] However, the Greek loanword in the Sahidic is clearly προτρέπειν, "to command," not ἐπιτρέπειν. Cuming suggested that the Latin "praising him" may have been a copyist's error in reading *laudans* for *audiens*, "hearing,"[5] but it should be noted that "praising" is also found in the *Testamentum Domini* and there is no sign of either participle in the oriental texts.

Comment

■ **1** Behavior at Christian suppers was apparently not always of the most seemly kind. Not only does Paul inveigh against selfish abuses in the Corinthian church (1 Cor 11:17-22), but Clement of Alexandria also criticizes the conduct of some at such gatherings (*Paed.* 2.1-2). Furthermore, we can see in the claims of sobriety and moderation at these meals that Tertullian advanced (in the passage quoted in the commentary on chap. 29C) that there was a concern to defend Christians against pagan charges of drunkenness and excess.

■ **2-3** Like chap. 27, these directions seem to presuppose a supper to which Christians have been invited as guests. However, two different possible situations seem to be envisaged, the first a simple distribution of edibles for people to take away without sharing a meal together, and the other a common meal with any leftovers being sent by the host to others. A similar distinction also appears in chap. 30A.

■ **4** The existence of some sort of informal ministry of the Word in connection with Christian community meals seems to be indicated in 1 Cor 14:26 ("When you come together, each one has a hymn, a lesson, a revelation, a tongue, or an interpretation . . ."), if we may pre-

---

1   Dix, *Apostolic Tradition*, 47; Botte, *Tradition*, 71.
2   Hanssens, *Liturgie,* 489–91. On the meaning of *apophoreton,* see also Charles A. Bobertz, "The Role of Patron in the Cena Dominica of Hippolytus' Apostolic Tradition," *JTS* 44 (1993) 174–76.
3   Dix, *Apostolic Tradition,* 47.
4   Botte, *Tradition,* 71 n. 5.
5   Cuming, *Hippolytus,* 25.

sume that this passage is referring to the same occasion as 1 Cor 11:17–34.[6] The passage from Tertullian already cited refers to the participants singing psalms or hymns after the meal. But here in the *Apostolic Tradition* the bishop seems to be firmly in control of everything that is said, and the participants are allowed only to speak in response to questions that he may put to them. Stewart-Sykes has claimed that this usurping by the bishop of what would have been the patron's role in normal Roman society is a sign of a challenge to an older ecclesiology in which the patrons would have assumed the leadership positions in the Christian community.[7]

■ **5–6** In the absence of the bishop, a presbyter or even a deacon may replace him in giving thanks over the common cup and blessing the bread that is shared. When the gathering is without either a presbyter or a deacon, however, the bread cannot be blessed. In Ignatius of Antioch we encounter the directive: "Let that be considered a valid *eucharistia* which is done by the bishop or one to whom he entrusts it. . . . It is not permitted either to baptize or hold an *agape* without the bishop" (*Smyrn.* 8). Although scholars have often taken *eucharistia* ("thanksgiving") and *agape* ("love feast") as describing different events, there is no clear evidence that either the terms or the events themselves were so distinguished at this early period. In any case, it seems unlikely that Ignatius would be prescribing more stringent rules for the presidency of an *agape* than for the Eucharist, and so it seems better to treat them as referring to the same celebration.

---

6   See C. K. Barrett, *A Commentary on the First Epistle to the Corinthians* (Harper's New Testament Commentaries; New York: Harper & Row, 1968) 325.

7   Stewart-Sykes, "Integrity," 114–15.

29A

Latin (76.4–6)	Sahidic	Arabic	Ethiopic
[Title]	**51 Concerning that it is proper to eat with thanksgiving**		
Let everyone eat in the name of the Lord. For this is pleasing to God, that we should be competitors also among the nations, all alike and sober.	And (δέ) let each one eat with thanksgiving in the name of God. For (γάρ) this is proper (πρέπειν) for the service of God so that we all shall be sober (νήφειν), and the heathen (ἔθνος) shall be envious of us.		And when they give thanks, each one is to eat in the name of God and drink with moderation as they call on his name, because this is the way it is suitable to God, that we should be zealots among the peoples, all of us being equal and serene and pure and without spot. For God rejoices in us, in his workmanship, because we are his workmanship if we have become pure.

Text	Comment

Text

This very brief chapter (which is missing from the Arabic) raised several textual questions for Botte. He questioned the references to thanksgiving both in the title and in the text of the Sahidic and Ethiopic, regarding them as an addition by a translator.[1] But since they also occur in the *Canons of Hippolytus*, the interpolation, if that is what it is, must have been made very early in the process of transmission. The divergence in what follows ("pleasing to God/proper for the service of God/ suitable to God") he thought might be attributed to different renderings of the Greek adjective θεόπρεπες. The reading "competitors" in the Latin he thought was assured by the agreement of the Ethiopic, and he believed that the Sahidic and *Canons of Hippolytus* had read the word ζηλωταί, "admirers, emulators," as ζηλωτοί, "objects of envy." He also suspected that the word rendered as "alike" by the Latin and as "equal" by the Ethiopic (but omitted by the Sahidic) was ὁμόνοοι, "of one mind, united," which had become corrupted into ὅμοιοι, "similar."[2]

Comment

This short chapter adds nothing to what was said in the first part of chap. 28, but if that section was indeed a later addition, as we have suggested, then these may have been at one time the only directives in the document concerning behavior at meals.

1   Botte, *Tradition apostolique*, 73 nn. 2, 3.
2   Ibid., 73 nn. 4–6.

Apostolic Constitutions	Canons of Hippolytus	Testamentum Domini
	Each one is to eat what he brings with thanksgiving in the name of the Lord, so that the Gentiles may see your purpose and envy you.	

Latin	Sahidic	Arabic	Ethiopic
			Concerning the gift for the sick
1			A deacon in a [time of] difficulty is with eagerness to give the sign/sealing to the sick if there is no presbyter.
2			When he has given as often as is appropriate that he should take what has been distributed, he is to give thanks and there they should consume [it]. And because they took so as to serve eagerly, he is to give the blessing.
3			If there is one who takes in order to bring [it] to a widow and to someone who is sick and to one who is involved with the church, he is to bring [it] on its day.
4			And if he does not bring it on the second [day], after he has added something from his own, he is to bring [it] because the bread of the poor remained with him.

Text

For the order of this chapter in relation to others, see the discussion on chaps. 24 and 25 above. It was regarded as an interpolation by Easton, chiefly because it is found only in the Ethiopic,[1] but defended by Dix because of the support given by the *Canons of Hippolytus* and *Testamentum Domini*.[2] Botte believed that it had not fallen out accidentally but had been deliberately omitted by the Sahidic and Arabic because of the obscurity of its contents.[3] The text in the Ethiopic is certainly very confused at the beginning of the chapter, and requires much conjecture in translation.

■ **2** Botte thought that the phrase rendered here, "because they took so as to serve eagerly," was meant to be the title of the section that followed ("That those [who] receive should serve diligently"), and that the words after that, "he is to give the blessing," were a gloss inserted by a later hand in an attempt to make some sense of the passage.[4]

Comment

■ **1** The meaning of the word "sign" or "sealing" is far from clear, and the alternative reading in one manuscript, "attention," looks like an attempt to make sense

1   Easton, *Apostolic Tradition*, 31, 58.
2   Dix, *Apostolic Tradition*, 83.
3   Botte, *Tradition*, xxxi–xxxii, where "23" is a misprint for "24."
4   Botte, *Tradition*, 63 nn. 3 and 4.

Apostolic Constitutions	Canons of Hippolytus 32	Testamentum Domini 2.10
	[continued from chap. 23] if there is not a presbyter present in the church, the deacon is to replace him in everything, except for the offering of the great sacrifice alone and the prayer.	[continued from chap. 22] When the presbyter is not present, let the deacon of necessity baptize.
	If one gives an offering to be given as alms to the poor, it is to be distributed before sunset to the poor of the people. But if there is more that is needed, one is to give [it] the next day, and if anything remains, the third day. Nothing is to be credited to the donor alone. He is not to receive [anything], because the bread of the poor remained in his house by his negligence.	[11] If anyone receives any service to carry to a widow or poor woman or anyone constantly engaged in a church work, let him give it the same day; and if not, on the morrow, let him add something to it from his own [property] and so give it. For the bread of the poor has been kept back in his possession. . . .

of the obscurity rather than an indication of the original text. The *Testamentum Domini* appears to have understood it as referring to baptism, but that appears unlikely to be its true import as that act is never otherwise described in this way in the *Apostolic Tradition*, unless this passage comes from an entirely different source from all the rest. Dix thought that the Ethiopic "perhaps has in mind unction,"[5] but Botte was unwilling to offer any conjecture.[6] We may note that there is an apparent contradiction here with *Apostolic Tradition* 34, where it is the deacon rather than the presbyter who principally ministers to the sick. On the other hand, a mid-third-century letter of Dionysius of Alexandria records that it is the responsibility of presbyters to take the reserved sacrament to the sick.[7]

■ **2** This part of the chapter is so unintelligible in the Ethiopic that it is impossible to know precisely what is meant, beyond that it has something to do with the distribution of food and its blessing.

■ **3–4** This part of the chapter seems to be concerned with the prompt distribution of charity to widows, those who are sick, and church workers, with a penalty of an additional donation being required from those who delay for more than a day.

5   Dix, *Apostolic Tradition*, 49 n. 14.
6   Botte, *Tradition*, 63 n. 3.
7   Dionysius of Alexandria *Ad Fabium Antiochenum* 4; Eusebius *Hist. eccl.* 6.44.

29C

Concerning the Bringing in of the Lamps at the Supper of the Congregation

Latin	Sahidic	Arabic	Ethiopic
			Concerning bringing in lamps at the supper of the congregation
			With the bishop present, when evening has come, a deacon is to bring in a lamp,
			and, standing among all the faithful who are there, he is to give thanks. He is first to offer a greeting in this way, saying: "The Lord be with you."
			And the people are to say: "With your spirit."
			"Let us give thanks to God."
			And they are to say: "It is right, and just; greatness and exaltedness with glory are fitting for him."
			But they are not to say the lifting up the hearts because it is said at the oblation.
			And he will pray in this way, saying: "We give you thanks, O God, through your Son Jesus Christ our Lord, through whom you have enlightened us, revealing to us the light that does not perish.
			After we have, therefore, finished the length of the day and have arrived at the beginning of the night, having been filled with the light of the day that you created for our satisfaction, now, since we do not lack the light of the evening by your own grace, we praise you and glorify you
			through your Son Jesus Christ our Lord, through whom you have glory, might, and honor with the Holy Spirit, now and always and forever and ever. Amen."
			And everyone is to say "Amen."
			And when they have then risen after the supper and have prayed, the children and the virgins are to say the psalms.
			After this a deacon, holding the mixed cup of the oblation, is to say a psalm from the ones over which "Hallelujah" is written.
			And after this a presbyter, if he has commanded, [is also to read] in this way from those psalms.
			And after this, the bishop, when he has offered the cup, is to say the psalm that is appropriate for the cup, with all of them saying every Hallelujah. When they read the psalms they are all to say Hallelujah, that is to say, we praise the one who is God glorified and praised, who established the entire world with one word.
			And in this way, when the psalm has been completed, he is to give thanks [for] the cup and he is to give some of the crumbs to all the faithful.
	[See chap. 23]	[See chap. 23]	And as those believers who are there are eating the supper, they are to take a little bread from the bishop's hand before they break their own bread, because it is a blessing and not the Eucharist like the body of our Lord.

156

Apostolic Constitutions 8.37.3	*Canons of Hippolytus*	*Testamentum Domini*
	If there is a meal or supper made by someone for the poor—it is [a supper] of the Lord—the bishop is to be present at the time when one lights a lamp. The deacon is to light it, and the bishop is to pray over them and over him who has invited them.	Let the lamp be offered in the temple by the deacon, saying: "The grace of our Lord [be] with you all." And let all the people say: "And with your spirit."
"You lead us the length of day and bring on the beginning of night . . ."		
	It is necessary [to do] for the poor the thanksgiving at the beginning of the liturgy. They are to be dismissed so that they depart before dark, and they are to recite psalms before their departure.	And let the little boys say spiritual psalms and hymns of praise by the light of the lamp. Let all the people respond "Hallelujah" to the psalm and to the chant sung together, with one accord, with voices in harmony; and let no one kneel until he who speaks ceases. Similarly also when a lection is read or the word of doctrine is spoken. If then the name of the Lord is spoken, and the rest, as has sufficiently been made known, let no one bow, having come creeping in.

Text

For the order of this chapter in relation to others, see the discussion on chaps. 24 and 25 above. As indicated there, the final part of the chapter in the Ethiopic also occurs again at the end of chap. 23, and has parallels there in the Sahidic and Arabic. Just as in the case of chap. 29B, Easton regarded the whole chapter as an interpolation because it occurs only in the Ethiopic,[1] but Dix defended its place in the text because of the support given by the *Apostolic Constitutions*, *Canons of Hippolytus*, and *Testamentum Domini*.[2] Dix, however, subsequently regarded it as an interpolation "from some oriental source" but "not necessarily much, if at all, later in date than Hippolytus' genuine work."[3] Botte, on the other hand, treated the chapter as authentic, alleging that it had been deliberately omitted by the Sahidic and Arabic because of the obscurity of its contents.[4]

The Ethiopic certainly gives the impression of having undergone major modification and expansion in the course of its history, and is in places very obscure, but in the absence of other versions of the full text of the chapter, it is difficult to be sure what the earliest form might have been.

■ **9** For the form of the doxology, see the commentary on *Ap. Trad.* 6.4.

■ **11** Dix conjectured that this sentence might have been either added or placed out of order, because he believed that in the Jewish tradition the meal would have followed the offering of the cup and the breaking of bread.[5] Botte agreed that the sentence was "manifestly" out of place.[6]

■ **13** Dix was inclined to strike out the first sentence "as an intrusion."[7]

Comment

Dix attempted to demonstrate the Jewish roots of the practices described in this chapter,[8] but he may have overstated the case. Scholars would generally today not be as confident as he was that we can know exactly what Jewish practices were in the first century CE, and in particular would dispute the idea of the *haburah* meal that Dix saw as the antecedent of the Christian community supper.[9] That is not to deny the possibility that at least some of the customs here described may have arisen from first-century Jewish-Christian circles but only to acknowledge that we do not have enough evidence to say so with certainty. Thus, although the daily Christian ritual lighting of the lamp has often been seen as derived from the Jewish Sabbath eve light, it is perhaps more likely to have arisen from the widespread pagan custom of a daily ritual greeting of the evening lamp.[10]

The bringing in of the lamps at a Christian community supper is first attested by Tertullian, although it would appear that the order known to him was different from that in the *Apostolic Tradition*, where the lighting of the lamp precedes rather than follows the meal itself:

They do not recline before prayer to God is first tasted. Only as much is eaten as satisfies the hungry; only as much is drunk as is fitting for the chaste. They are satisfied as those who remember that even during the night they have to worship God; they talk as those who know that the Lord hears. After washing the hands and the lighting of lamps, each is invited to stand in the middle and sing a hymn to God, from the holy scriptures or of his own composition, as he is able. This proves how little is drunk. Similarly, prayer ends the feast. (*Apol.* 39.15)

■ **2** While commentators have assumed that the subject of the verb "give thanks" is meant to be the bishop, which is certainly how the *Apostolic Constitutions* and *Canons of Hippolytus* understood it, as it stands it could conceivably be the deacon, as in the *Testamentum Domini*.

---

1   Easton, *Apostolic Tradition*, 31, 58.
2   Dix, *Apostolic Tradition*, 83.
3   Dix, *Shape*, 85, 86.
4   Botte, *Tradition*, xxxi–xxxii.
5   Dix, *Shape*, 89.
6   Botte, *Tradition*, 65 n. 1.
7   Dix, *Shape*, 88.

8   Ibid., 87–90.
9   See Joachim Jeremias, *The Eucharistic Words of Jesus*, trans. Norman Perrin from 3rd German ed. (New York: Scribner, 1966) 29–31.
10   See further Taft, *Liturgy*, 36–37.

■ **7–9** The only other liturgical text used at lamplighting to have been preserved from early times is the hymn *Phos hilaron*, cited as being ancient by Basil the Great in the second half of the fourth century:

> it seemed good to our fathers not to receive in silence the gift of the evening light but as soon as it appeared to give thanks. Who was the author of those words of thanksgiving at lamp lighting we cannot say, but the people pronounce the ancient formula and nobody ever thought them impious to say, "We praise the Father, the Son, and the Holy Spirit of God."[11]

The full text of this hymn, still used in the evening office of the Byzantine tradition, displays a similarity of theme to that in the *Apostolic Tradition*:

> O joyous light of the holy glory of the immortal Father,
> heavenly, holy, blessed Jesus Christ!
> As we come to the setting of the sun and behold the evening light,
> We praise you Father, Son, and Holy Spirit of God!
> It is fitting at all times that you be praised with auspicious voices,
> O Son of God, giver of life.
> That is why the whole world glorifies you![12]

■ **11–14** The instructions about the psalmody seem a little too precise and detailed for a second- or third-century text, and have probably been subsequently expanded.[13] However, the use of the communal Hallelujah refrain to psalms that contain it in the biblical text is also attested by Tertullian, who says that "those who are more diligent in praying are accustomed to include in their prayers Alleluia and this type of psalms, with the endings of which those who are present may respond" (*De or.* 27).

■ **12** The expression "the mixed cup of offering," if indeed these words were part of the earlier Greek text, sounds as though it might have eucharistic connotations. Justin Martyr apparently speaks of wine mixed with water being offered in the Eucharist;[14] the custom was strongly defended by Cyprian (*Ep.* 62); and it became standard eucharistic practice in later centuries.

■ **13** The use of the term "offer" here in connection with the cup does not help to settle the question of whether this rite was seen as a Eucharist, because the language of offering is widely used throughout the church order, especially in the Latin: not only are bread and wine described as the "offering" and said in the eucharistic prayer to be offered to God (*Apostolic Tradition* 4), but so are oil (5), cheese and olives (6), water (21), firstfruits (31), and flowers (32). Catechumens each "offer a cup" (26), and the *apophoreton* is described as an "offering" (28; see also 27).

■ **15** Dix viewed the ritual surrounding the cup as the equivalent of the Jewish *kiddush*, a special blessing over a cup of wine pronounced at the beginning of each Sabbath or festival.[15] But we should note that there is other evidence for the existence of early Christian community meals in which the cup ritual preceded that of the bread[16] (which would result if the sentence after the thanksgiving for light were eliminated as Dix and Botte suggested), including *Didache* 9, which an increasing number of scholars would now regard as being a form of eucharistic rite.[17] Moreover, as Cuming notes,[18] the word

11 Basil *De Spiritu Sancto* 29.73.
12 On this hymn see further Antonia Tripolitis, "*ΦΩΣ ΙΛΑΡΟΝ*: Ancient Hymn and Modern Enigma," *VC* 24 (1970) 189–96.
13 Cuming (*Hippolytus*, 24) described this section as "confused."
14 *1 Apol.* 65.3; 67.5. For the possibility that this may be an interpolation into Justin's text, see Adolf von Harnack, "Brod und Wasser: Die eucharistischen Elemente bei Justin," in *Über das gnostische Buch Pistis-Sophia; Brod und Wasser: die eucharistischen Elemente bei Justin. Zwei Untersuchungen* (TU 7; Leipzig: Hinrichs, 1891) 115–44.
15 Dix, *Shape*, 88.
16 For a summary of the evidence, see Andrew McGowan, "'First regarding the cup . . .': Papias and the Diversity of Early Eucharistic Practice," *JTS* 46 (1995) 551–55.
17 See, e.g., Louis Ligier, "The Origins of the Eucharistic Prayer: From the Last Supper to the Eucharist," *StLit* 9 (1973) 177–78; Mazza, *Origins*, 12–97; Thomas J. Talley, "The Eucharistic Prayer of the Ancient Church according to Recent Research: Results and Reflections," *StLit* 11 (1976) 146–50.
18 Cuming, *Hippolytus*, 24.

translated as "crumbs" here represents the Greek κλάσ-ματα, which occurs in *Did.* 9.3–4.[19]

■ **16** Although the final clause clearly characterizes this meal as not being the Eucharist proper, these words may well be a later addition to the text, and so eucharistic and noneucharistic meals should perhaps not be so sharply and simply differentiated from one another in the very early period of the church's history as other commentators have tended to do.[20] More recent research would recognize the existence of quite a wide range of forms of Christian sacred meals in the first two or three centuries before the classic eucharistic shape emerged as preeminent.[21]

19   Cf. also Matt 14:20 par. Mark 6:43 par. Luke 9:17; Matt 15:27 par. Mark 8:8; 1 Cor 10:16.
20   For example, Botte, *Tradition*, 61 n. 6; Cuming, *Hippolytus*, 22.
21   See McGowan, *Ascetic Eucharists*, esp. 10–14.

29D

	Latin	Sahidic	Arabic	Ethiopic
				37 And when the bishop speaks, let everyone be silent; and if there is no bishop, they are to take the bread of blessing from a presbyter or from a deacon
1	[See 28.4]	[See 28.4]	[See 28.4]	And when the bishop speaks, all of them are to be silent and are not to answer one another until the bishop asks them.
2	[See 28.5]	[See 28.5]	[See 28.5]	And if there is no bishop but only believers at the meal, they are to take the blessing from the hand of a presbyter. And if there is no presbyter, they are to take [it] from the hand of a deacon. But the catechumens are to take the bread of the exorcised portion.
3	[See 28.6]	[See 28.6]	[See 28.6]	If there are laymen among them, they are to eat quietly. And it is not proper for a layman to do the blessing.

Text

This is a doublet of *Ap. Trad.* 28.4b–6 found in the Ethiopic alone, another sign of the dislocation that had occurred to the text of the church order in that linguistic tradition. Interestingly, it conforms more closely than the earlier version did to the Arabic version of chap. 28, and both of them introduce a new title at this point.

Although this passage was included in early reconstructions that were made of the work, its existence was merely noted by Easton,[1] and it has been entirely omitted from all later editions, except that of Hanssens, who rather unhelpfully prints it alongside the other versions of chap. 28 and leaves the first occurrence of it without parallels.[2] It adds nothing to our understanding of chap. 28.

---

1   Easton, *Apostolic Tradition*, 30.
2   Jean Michel Hanssens, *La liturgie d'Hippolyte: Documents et études* (Rome: Liberia Editrice dell'Universita Gregoriana, 1970) 127, 131.

30A

Latin (76.7–13)	Sahidic	Arabic	Ethiopic
[Title]	*52 Concerning the supper (δεῖπνον) of the widows (χήρα)*	*38 Concerning the widows' meal*	*Concerning the meal of widows*
1 Widows, if anyone wishes that they should be fed, [being] already mature in age, let him send them away before evening.	If someone wishes on occasion to invite the widows (χήρα), everyone who is old, let him feed them and send them away before nightfall.	If someone would like from time to time to invite the widows, all those who are elderly, let him feed them and send them away before nightfall.	And if one desires at any time to invite widows and all who are old, he is to satisfy them and send them away before it is evening.
2 But if he cannot on account of the lot that he has been assigned, giving them food and wine, let him send them away and let them partake of it at their own homes, however it pleases them.	And if it is not possible for them, because of the lot (κλῆρος) that he has drawn (κληροῦν), let him give them wine with something to eat, and they shall eat in their house as they wish.	And if they are not able [to come] because of the rank they have attained, let him send them wine and food and let them eat in their own houses as they wish.	And if it is not possible, because of the ordained individuals who have been invited, he is to give them food, and after giving [them] wine, he is to send them away. And each one of them is to do as they wish in their houses.

Text

■ **2** The discrepancy over "lot/rank/ordained individuals" among the versions appears to be the result of a misunderstanding of the Greek κλῆρος. As indicated in the commentary on *Ap. Trad.* 3.4–5 and 8.3, this word (which originally meant "lot") began to be used for an ecclesiastical duty, because in the Old Testament these were assigned by lot; then later it came to mean "clergy." The Latin and Sahidic have probably preserved the correct sense here, that it is the host who may be prevented by an ecclesiastical duty from exercising hospitality.

Comment

As noted in the commentary on chap. 10 above, widows were the regular recipients of the charity of the Christian community, but a constant need was felt to keep them under control lest their behavior should appear scandalous—hence the references here to their age and to the need to send them away before evening. The practice of either providing a common meal for them to share or instead giving them edibles to take away parallels what is said in chap. 28 of the activity of a host toward his guests. Widows are also mentioned in chaps. 23 and 24 (=29B).

Apostolic Constitutions	*Canons of Hippolytus*	*Testamentum Domini*
	When someone wishes to feed widows, he is to feed them and send them away before sunset. If they are numerous, lest they should be excited and not manage to depart before evening, he is to give each of them enough to eat and drink, and they are to depart before night comes.	

30B

Latin	Sahidic	Arabic	Ethiopic
[See chap. 1]			*39 Concerning the statute of the gift of apostles*

1 [As for] that which concerns the Word, we have written rightly regarding the gifts—how much God in his plan has given to humankind from the beginning, as he brings humankind, the image that had gone astray, close to him.

2 But now as we come to the one beloved among all the saints, we have arrived at the summit of the tradition that is proper in the churches,

3 so that those who have been well taught, keeping the tradition that has existed until now, as they know our statute, may become strong concerning what has been found,

4 although they at present have stumbled in their ignorance and those who do not know,

5 as the Holy Spirit gives the perfect grace to those who truly believe so that they may know how those who stand in the church must pass along and keep.

This is the version of the prologue in the Ethiopic text, displaced to this point for reasons that are not immediately obvious (see above, pp. 15 and 22). It is followed in the Ethiopic alone by a lengthy baptismal rite, which is an obvious interpolation and has therefore not been reproduced here. The text is in Duensing, *Aethiopische Text*, 81–127; ET in Horner, *Statutes*, 162–78.

Text

The titles of this and the following chapter appear to have been reversed, since that of chap. 32, "The Blessing of Fruits," would be more appropriate here and this title more suitable to the contents of that chapter.[1]

There is an additional source, in Greek, for the text of part of this chapter. The prayer, together with the list of fruits that may be offered from chap. 32, is found in Byzantine *euchologia*, beginning with the oldest extant manuscript, Barberini *gr.* 336 (8th century).[2] It is, however, of limited value, as the text is in a defective state. Because of this, and because its restriction of the offering to fruit alone does not correspond with Eastern canonical legislation, one may suspect that it was not a prayer in current use but simply a piece of venerated antiquity copied out from generation to generation. That the *euchologia* contain other texts for use at the presentation of firstfruits increases this suspicion.

Contrary to its usual practice, the Sahidic does not omit the full text of the prayer here, though why this should be an exception to the rule is not obvious. Could it be that the prayer was in current use in the translator's tradition?

■ **1** As Botte suggests, "as soon as they shall begin them" in the Latin is probably the result of a misreading of the Greek word for firstfruits, ἀπαρχή, as ἀπ᾽ ἀρχῆς, "from the beginning."[3]

■ **5** For the form of the concluding doxology, see the commentary on *Ap. Trad.* 6.4 above.

Comment

The earliest reference to the Christian adoption of the Old Testament and Jewish offering of firstfruits occurs in *Didache* 13. The directions there include firstborn oxen and sheep, as well as firstfruits of the winepress and of the threshing floor. The obligation to offer firstfruits is extended from the primary producers to consumers who make bread or open a jar of wine or oil, and even to all possessions, thus effectively turning it from a harvest offering into a tax on total income. The wide-ranging nature of those ordinances and the repeated direction that the firstfruits were to be given to the prophet suggest that the primary concern was not theological but economic. Prophets needed to receive material support if they were to be free to exercise their ministry, and hence the Old Testament commandments were invoked to justify the provision of that support by the Christian community. What was really in view there, therefore, was a tithe for the financing of the prophetic ministry rather than an offering of firstfruits as an expression God's lordship over creation.

A more direct citation of Numbers 18 concerning the rights of the priests and Levites to the offerings reappears in the *Didascalia Apostolorum*, where it is used as the authority for the community's obligation to provide financial support for its clergy and the relief of the poor. Here firstfruits and tithes are mentioned together, with no distinction being drawn between them: "set apart special offerings and tithes and first fruits for Christ the true high-priest, and for his ministers, as tithes of salvation."[4] Other patristic writings show the same tendency to regard firstfruits and tithes as synonymous and to stress the quantity that ought to be given to provide for the adequate support of the clergy and the poor. In general, the fathers criticize Christians for being less generous in their giving than the Old Testament law had required.[5]

Only in Irenaeus do we find a different, more traditional understanding of the purpose of the presentation of firstfruits, although he relates this to Christ's institution of the Eucharist: "the Lord instructed his disciples to offer firstfruits to God from his own creatures, not because God needed them, but so that they themselves might not be unfruitful or ungrateful."[6]

This chapter, however, provides the earliest known Christian rite for the offering of firstfruits, and it contains no suggestion that what was offered was intended for the support of the clergy or of the needy, and indeed

1   Botte, *Tradition*, 79 n. 1.
2   For further details of this, see above, p. 6.
3   Botte, *Tradition*, 75 n. 2.
4   *Didasc.* 9; ET from Brock and Vasey, *Didascalia*, 11.
5   See Lukas Vischer, *Tithing in the Early Church,* trans.

Robert C. Schultz (Philadelphia: Fortress Press, 1966) 15–30.
6   Irenaeus *Haer.* 4.17.5; see also 4.18.1.

Concerning the Fruit That It Is Proper to Bring to the Bishop

Latin (76.14–28)	Sahidic	Arabic	Ethiopic
[Title]	*53 Concerning the fruit (καρπός) that it is proper to bring (προσενέγκαι) to the bishop*	*39 Concerning the first-fruits that are brought to the bishop and the naming of them*	*39 Concerning the fruit that it is fitting for them to bring*
1 Let all hasten to offer to the bishop the new fruits as soon as they shall begin them;	Let each one hasten (σπου-δάζειν) to take in to the bishop (ἐπίσκοπος) on every occasion the first-fruits (ἀπαρχή καρπός) of first growth (γέννημα).	Let everyone make haste to come to the bishop with the firstfruits of his harvest,	Each one is to give the firstfruits of the grain and be eager to bring it to the bishop;
2 and let him who offers bless and name him who brought [them], saying:	And (δέ) let the bishop (ἐπίσκοπος) also receive them with thanksgiving, and bless them, and name (ὀνομάζειν) the name of the one who brought them in, saying:	and the bishop will take them and bless them and remember the name of the one who brought them to him, and he will say,	and he is to bring [it] as he blesses and names the one who brought [it], saying:
3 "We give thanks to you, God, and we offer to you the first of the fruits that you have given to us to eat, [you] nourishing them by your Word, ordering the earth to bear all fruits for the joy and nourishment of human beings and for all animals.	"We give thanks (εὐχαρισ-τεῖν) to you, Lord God, and we bring you the firstfruits (ἀπαρχή καρπός) of which you gave us to eat, having perfected them by your Word; and you commanded the earth to send forth every fruit (καρπός), for profiting, gladdening, and the nourishment (τροφή) of the human race (—γένος) and all creation.	"We thank you, O God, and bring to you the firstfruits that you have given us to eat. You have perfected them according to your Word, and you have commanded the earth to send forth all the fruits for joy and food for the human race and all the animals.	"We thank you, O God, and we offer to you the first-fruits that you have given to us for enjoyment, as you have made [the earth] fruit-ful by your Word. You commanded the earth to be fruitful with every kind[?] for satisfaction—food for people and for all animals,
4 For all these we praise you, God, and in all things with which you have helped us, adorning for us the whole creation with varied fruits,	We bless you, God, for these things, and all others with which you show kind-ness (εὐεργετεῖν) to us, having adorned (κοσμεῖν) all creation with the vari-ous fruits (καρπός),	We thank you, O God, for this and all the other things you have made for our well-being. You have arranged your creation with various fruits	for which we glorify you, O God, in all that [by] which you have profited us, all creation [with] its own fruit,
5 through your Child Jesus Christ our Lord, through whom to you [be] glory to the ages of ages. Amen."	through your holy Son Jesus Christ (Χριστός) our Lord: through him glory [be] to you with him and the Holy Spirit (πνεῦμα) forever and ever. Amen (ἀμήν)."	through your Son Jesus Christ our Lord, through whom be glory to you with him and the Holy Spirit unto ages of ages. Amen."	by your Son Jesus Christ our Lord, through whom you have glory with the Holy Spirit forever and ever. Amen."

Barberini gr. 336:

"We give thanks to you, Lord God, and we offer the first portion of the fruits that you gave us for sharing, having brought [them] to perfection through your Word and having commanded all kinds of fruits for enjoyment and nourishment for people and every living creature. In all we hymn you, O God, for all in which you have done good things for us, [having crowned] all creation with great fruits; through your Child Jesus Christ our Lord, through whom also [be] to you glory to the ages of ages. Amen."

Apostolic Constitutions 8.40.2–4	*Canons of Hippolytus* 36	*Testamentum Domini* 2.14
	Whoever has the firstfruits of the earth is to bring them to the church, the first of their floors and the first of their presses, oil, honey, milk, wool, and the first of the produce of the work of their hands, all this they are to bring to the bishop, and the first of their trees. The priest who takes them is to give thanks to God for them, first outside the veil, he who has brought them remaining standing. The priest says: "We give thanks to you, Lord, almighty God, because you have made us worthy to see these fruits that the earth has produced this year.	If any one presents fruits or the first produce of crops, let him offer [them] as firstfruits to the bishop. . . .
"We give thanks to you, almighty Lord . . . through your beloved Child, Jesus Christ our Lord, for these firstfruits offered to you . . . who brought to perfection all things through your Word and commanded the earth to produce all kinds of fruits for our enjoyment and food . . .		[16] The fruits that are offered to the bishop, let him bless thus: "O God, we give thanks to you always, and also in this day when we offer to you the firstfruits of the fruits that you have given us for food, having ripened them by your power and by your Word, having commanded from the beginning of the creation of the worlds that the earth should bring forth different fruits for the joy and delight of the sons of men and of all creatures.
	Bless, Lord, the crown of the year that is of your bounty, and may they satisfy the poor of your people. Your servant N., who has brought these things that are yours, because he fears you, bless him from you holy heaven, and all his house, and pour upon him your holy mercy, that he may know your will in everything, and cause him to inherit heavenly things, through our Lord Jesus Christ, your dear Son, and the Holy Spirit, to the ages of ages. Amen."	We praise you, O Lord, for all these things with which you have benefited us, adorning for us all the earth with various fruits. Bless also this your servant N., and receive his earnestness and his love,
through whom [be] to you glory, honor, and worship in Holy Spirit to the ages. Amen."		through your only begotten Son Jesus Christ, through whom [be] praise and honor and might to you with the Holy Spirit forever and ever. Amen."

the restriction of the offering to new *fruits* as such and not vegetables would rather imply that this was not the case. The prayer concentrates entirely on the theme of thanksgiving for what God has given, and does not contain any element of petition at all, or even provision for the naming of the offerer that is mentioned in the opening direction.[7] By contrast, brief prayers elsewhere in the document (chaps. 5 and 6) that are to be used whenever people offer oil, cheese, or olives are almost entirely petitionary in character, although as they are apparently intended for use at the conclusion of the eucharistic prayer itself, the element of thanksgiving would be supplied by that oration.

7   For later developments see Paul F. Bradshaw, "The Offering of the Firstfruits of Creation: An Historical Study," in Ralph McMichael Jr., ed., *Creation and Liturgy: Studies in honor of H. Boone Porter* (Washington, D.C.: Pastoral, 1993) 29–41.

Text

With regard to the title, see chap. 31 above. There is some variation between the versions in the items listed, but Hanssens is surely correct in concluding that the specific fruits and vegetables mentioned do not offer any clues to the place of origin of the document itself.[1]

■ **2** The statement in the Latin and Sahidic that sometimes flowers are also offered, followed immediately by the restriction of that offering to the rose and lily alone, suggests that the latter may be a later addition to the text, correcting what was seen as an excessively liberal policy. Since the Latin manuscript begins a new page between the two statements, there is sufficient space for there to have been the title of a new chapter here,[2] but there is no evidence in any of the other versions that one existed.

■ **3** There is a change here from the passive voice of the rest of the chapter to the third-person plural in the active voice for the main verb. This is another indication that this material may be an addition by a different hand, besides its lack of connection with what immediately precedes it. "The holy" God here is an unusual expression, not followed by any of the other witnesses, and may be a copyist's error, especially as the Latin words are written in a very contracted form.

Comment

■ **1** The listing of the particular fruits suitable for blessing and the exclusion of vegetables from that act has been thought to have some connection with Old Testa-ment texts referring to those foods associated with the Egyptian captivity and those with the land of promise.[3] Num 11:5 refers to "the cucumbers, the melons, the leeks, the onions, and the garlic" that had been eaten during the time in Egypt; Num 13:23 speaks of grapes, pomegranates, and figs found in the promised land; and Deut 8:8 describes that land as one of "of wheat and barley, of vines and fig trees and pomegranates, a land of olive trees and honey." There are also discussions in the Mishnah (*Ber.* 6.4; *Bik.* 1.3; 3.9) of appropriate forms of food blessings that emphasize the importance of the "seven kinds of foods of the land of Israel," referring to this list in Deuteronomy.[4]

However, these parallels more satisfactorily explain the exclusion of vegetables than the particular contents of the list of fruits. Andrew McGowan has suggested that some aesthetic category of "sweetness" (or cost or general desirability for diet) may have been responsible for shaping the list,[5] but the absence of the most substantial of the "seven kinds" of Deut 8:8, the wheat and barley, is rather surprising, as is the omission of honey, especially as it is mentioned in the baptismal Eucharist of chap. 21. Is this another indication of the composite character of the document?

■ **2** The singling out of the rose and the lily from other flowers could derive from Cant 2:1 and other biblical passages where these flowers are used as symbols of beauty and splendor.[6] Among early Christians, they also became messianic symbols: Cyprian speaks of the church being bedecked with the lily and the rose because it was white with good works and purple with the blood of martyrs.[7]

1 Hanssens, *Liturgie*, 491–92.
2 And not before all reference to flowers, as Botte erroneously states (*Tradition*, 79 n. 3).
3 See, e.g., Chadwick in Dix, *Apostolic Tradition*, m.
4 See Johannes Baptist Bauer, "Die Fruchtesegnung in Hippolyts Kirchenordnung," *ZKTh* 74 (1952) 71–75.
5 McGowan, *Ascetic Eucharists*, 125–27.
6 Easton, *Apostolic Tradition*, 102.
7 Cyprian *Ep.* 10.5; cited by Andrew F. Walls, "A Primitive Christian Harvest Thanksgiving," *Theology* 58 (1958) 336–39.

Latin (76.29—77.4)	Sahidic	Arabic	Ethiopic
[Title]	*54 The blessing (εὐλογία) of fruits (καρπός)*	*The blessing of the fruits*	*Concerning the fruits*

1

Latin: Fruits indeed are blessed, that is, grape, fig, pomegranate, olive, pear, apple, mulberry, peach, cherry, almond, plum, [but] not pumpkin, not melon, not cucumber, not onion, not garlic, or any of the other vegetables.

Sahidic: These are the fruits (καρπός) that shall be blessed: the grape, the fig, the pomegranate, the olive, the pear (ἀπίδιον), the apple, the peach (περσικόν), the cherry (καράσιον), the almond (ἀμύγδαλον). But (δέ) neither the sycamore fig, nor (οὐδέ) the onion, nor (οὐδέ) the garlic, nor (οὐδέ) the melon (gourd?) (πέπων), nor (οὐδέ) the pumpkin (μηλοπέπων), nor (οὐδέ) the cucumber, nor (οὐδέ) any other vegetable (λάχανον) shall be blessed. But (δέ) if it will happen that they offer (προσφέρειν) flowers (ἄνθος),

Arabic: These are the fruits over which a blessing is said: grapes, figs, pomegranates, olives, peaches, apples, plums. The fruits that are not blessed are sycamore figs, onions, garlic, cucumbers, and all pulses.

Ethiopic: These fruits are then to be blessed: grapes, figs, pomegranates, the fruit of olive trees, apples, prunes, quinces, cherries, almonds. And they are not to bless the Egyptian fig, not garlic, not onions, and no kind of gourd, and none of the vegetables, and no other fruits are they to offer

2

Latin: But sometimes flowers are also offered.

[?Title]
Therefore let the rose and the lily be offered, but not others.

Sahidic: let them bring the roses and the lily (κρίνον). But (δέ) do not let others be brought.

Arabic: They may bring roses also, but no other [flowers].

Ethiopic: except the flower of the rose.

3

Latin: And in all things that are eaten, let them give thanks to the holy God, eating for his glory.

Sahidic: But (δέ) everything else that shall be eaten, they shall give thanks to God for it, and taste them [*sic*] to his glory.

Arabic: For everything that is eaten let them thank God and savor it to his glory.

Ethiopic: And all that they eat they are to eat with thanks to God, to whom be glory. Give thanks to him when you take [something].

Apostolic Constitutions	Canons of Hippolytus	Testamentum Domini
	Every vegetable, all the fruits of the trees, and all the fruits of the cucumber fields are to be blessed, and [also] him who brings them, with a blessing.	Vegetables are not blessed, but fruits of trees, flowers, and the rose and the lily. [17] Let them give and return thanks and not eat with offense or scandal. Let no one taste that which is strangled or sacrificed to idols.

Barberini gr. 336:
These fruits are blessed: grape, fig, pomegranate, olive, apple, nectarine, peach, plum.

	Latin (77.5–16)	Sahidic	Arabic	Ethiopic
	[Title]	*55 Concerning that it is not proper for anyone to taste anything in the Pascha (πάσχα) before the hour when it is proper to eat*	*40 That no one should taste anything at Easter before the time when eating should take place*	*40 Concerning that it is not proper that a person eat anything during the fasts of the Pascha except at the time at which it is proper for them to eat*
1	At the Pascha let no one eat before the oblation has been made. For whoever does so, for him the fast does not count.	The fast (νηστεία) shall not count for any such one when he is greedy before the hour when the fast (νηστεία) is finished.	This fast does not count as a fast if one becomes greedy before the time when the fast comes to an end,	To ones like this his fast is not reckoned to him. . . .
2	But if anyone is pregnant and is sick and is not able to fast for two days, let them fast on the Sabbath because of [their] necessity, confining [themselves] to bread and water.	But (ἀλλά) if there is one who is sick and unable to fast (νηστεύειν) for two days, then let him fast (νηστεύειν) on the day of the Sabbath (σάββατον) because of necessity (ἀνάγκη) and (δέ) be content with bread, salt, and water.	unless it be someone who is ill and cannot fast the two days. Let him fast on the Saturday, because this is essential, and then stop but eat only bread and water.	And if there is someone who is pregnant and someone who is sick and not able to fast the two days, he is to fast on the Sabbath because it is necessary that he continue with bread and water.
3	If anyone finding himself at sea or in some necessity did not know the day, when he learned of this, let him observe the fast after Pentecost.	And if there is one at sea, or (ἤ) who was ignorant of the day of the Pascha (πάσχα), when this one knows this, let him make his fast (νηστεία) after Pentecost (πεντηκοστή).	If someone is away at sea and does not know when Easter day falls, in this case if he does not know, let him fast after Pentecost.	And if one who is on a ship or in any kind of distress errs regarding the knowledge of its day, he is to make compensation after Pentecost by fasting.
4	For the type has passed, because it ceased in the second month, and he ought to fast when he has learned the truth.	For (γάρ) it is not a Pascha (πάσχα) that we observe, for (γάρ) that which is the type (τύπος) has passed. Because of this, we did not say, "in the second month," but (ἀλλά), "When he knows the truth, he shall give his assent to the fast (νηστεία)."	He will not be keeping Easter, but it will be similar and he should keep a fast of the same length[?].	It is not the Pascha that he keeps, for its likeness has passed by. For that reason you are not to allow [it] in the second month; and when he comes, he is to perform [it], when he knows [it] with certainty.

Apostolic Constitutions	*Canons of Hippolytus* 22	*Testamentum Domini* 2.18
	During the week of the Passover of the Jews all the people are to take care with great vigilance to fast then from every evil desire. One is not to say even a word with joy but with sadness, knowing that the Lord of all, the Impassible, suffered for us at this time, so that by [his] undergoing suffering we should escape the suffering that we deserve because of our sins. Let us also take a share in the suffering that he accepted for us, so as to have a share with him in his kingdom. Food during the Pascha is bread and salt only and water. If someone is ill or in a region where there are no Christians and the time of the Pascha ends without him having known its date, or because of a sickness, these people are to fast after Pentecost and observe the Pascha with discipline.	On the days of Pascha, especially in the last days, on Friday and on Saturday, by night and by day, let the prayers be according to the number of the hymns of praise. . . . [20] Let the bishop command that they proclaim that no one taste anything until the offering is completed. . . . But if anyone before he approaches and receives of the Eucharist eats something else, he sins and his fast is not reckoned to him. . . . Similarly if a woman is pregnant [and] sick, and cannot fast these two days, let her fast that one day, taking on the first [day] bread and water. And if she cannot come, let a deaconess carry [the Eucharist] to her.
	Let their intention be clear: they are not late through lack of reverence; they do not fast in order to observe their own Pascha, to establish another foundation than that which has been laid.	

33 That It Is Not Proper for Anyone to Taste Anything in the Pascha before the Hour When It Is
Proper to Eat

Text

■ **2** "Bread and water" occur in the Latin, Arabic, Ethiopic, and *Testamentum Domini*. The use of "bread, salt, and water," found in the Sahidic and *Canons of Hippolytus*, is attested for the mid-third century also in *Didasc.* 21.18, and so it is difficult to be sure which of the two readings may have been the original.

■ **3** The Sahidic and Arabic omit "if anyone is pregnant."

■ **4** Both the Latin and *Testamentum Domini* omit the statement, "for it is not a Pascha that we observe" (Sahidic), a phrase attested also in the Ethiopic, and echoed in the Arabic. Botte argued that together with the next phrase, "for the type has passed," such a statement is unclear if it is the Christian Pascha that is intended here. To make sense out of these confusing phrases, Botte proposed that the word τύπος ("type") would have appeared twice in the Greek original: ὃ γὰρ τηροῦμεν πάσχα οὐκ ἐστι τύπος ("for the Pascha that we observe is not a type"), τύπος γὰρ παρῆλθεν ("for the type has passed"). Hence, for Botte, the reference is an intended contrast between the Christian and Jewish Pascha. The Jewish Pascha, the "type" of the Christian Pascha, has passed, and it is not the "type" but the "reality" that Christians celebrate.[1]

The phrase "because it ceased in the second month" (Latin and Ethiopic) appears in the Sahidic as "we did not say, 'in the second month.'" According to Botte, the Sahidic translator made an error in substituting the verb ϫⲱ ("to speak") for ϭⲱ ("to cease") at this point.[2] Closely related to his interpretation above, Botte saw the contrast between the Jewish and Christian Pascha continued here, with the Jewish Pascha having ended in the second month as the ending of the type itself. "It is not the same with the Christian Pascha that is no longer a figure but reality."[3]

Botte's explanations are not plausible. The alleged translator's error in the Sahidic is not as simple as it appears to be, because the intransitive verb ϭⲱ cannot take a pronominal object suffix as ϫⲱ does and so the change would have involved more than just misreading

one letter. A more likely suggestion is that the confusion is between ϫⲱ and ϫⲱⲕ ("to complete"), which does take a pronominal suffix, and with the mistake occurring between ϫⲟⲟⲥ ("say it") and ϫⲟⲕⲥ ("complete it"), a change of merely one letter. Nevertheless, the context of this section does not readily appear to be about the contrast between the Jewish and Christian Pascha, but about those who, for whatever reason, did not know the date of Pascha and so missed both the two-day paschal fast and the celebration of Pascha. As a consequence, "after Pentecost" they are expected to keep the fast. Hence, whether something has been omitted here from the Latin or not, and to whatever the word τύπος might refer, the sense seems to be simply that, although the annual date of Pascha itself had passed, those who missed it could now make up the fast itself. At this point, the Arabic ("he will not be keeping Easter, but it will be similar and he should keep a fast of the same length") and *Canons of Hippolytus* ("they do no fast in order to observe their own Pascha, to establish another foundation than that which has been laid") may well be closer, at least in interpretation, to what the original would have contained. If so, Botte's hypotheses should be dismissed as pure conjecture.

A more recent evaluation of Botte's interpretation has been offered by Raniero Cantalamessa, who writes in support of the authenticity of the phrase "for it is not a Pascha that we observe" in the Sahidic:

Contrary to Botte, . . . I understand it to mean the Pascha of the second month, which is the model (*typos*) of the Christian Pascha. . . . Christians who are prevented from keeping the Pascha at the regular time, therefore, are not asked to observe it a month later, as the Jews were, but only to fulfill the obligation of fasting, after the festive season of Pentecost. In the *Canons of Hippolytus* . . . this was not understood, and the sentence was reworded to read: "After the Pentecost, let them fast *and keep the Pascha* with discipline."[4]

The context here is obviously the prescription in Num 9:9–12 about the necessity of those who are ritually unclean or on a journey during Passover itself to

---

1   Botte, *Tradition*, 81 n. 2.
2   Ibid., 80, note to line 7.
3   Ibid., 81 n. 3.

4   Raniero Cantalamessa, *Easter in the Early Church*, trans. James M. Quigly, S.J., and Joseph T. Lienhard, S.J. (Collegeville, Minn.: Liturgical, 1993) 156.

keep the Passover on the fourteenth day of the *second* month. This prescription is repeated and discussed in rabbinic literature as well.[5] The closest parallel to this in early Christian literature is in Origen's *Hom. on Exod.* 7.4, where he interprets this "second Passover" as the type prefiguring the church's Pascha and the Eucharist, since, according to Origen, the manna from heaven was not given at the first but only at the second Passover. Although the versions display confusion on this issue, in light of Origen's comment, Cantalamessa is probably correct in concluding that the "type [that] has passed" is this "second Passover" prescribed in Num 9:9–12.

Comment

■ **1** The two-day paschal fast has an archaic ring to it. In the development of the prepaschal fast it is clear that the two days of the Friday and Saturday before Pascha constituted a primitive practice (Tertullian *De ieiun.* 13–14),

at least outside a Quartodeciman context, although already in the late second century Irenaeus of Lyons witnesses to a variety of existing practices (one day, two days, even more days, or forty hours) throughout the church of his day.[6] This practice itself probably first consisted of adding an annual Saturday fast to the Friday fast, which together with Wednesdays would already have been established as a regular fasting day each week. By the third century, at least in Syria and Egypt, this prepaschal fast was extended backward to include a total of six days, a kind of nascent "Holy" or "Great" Week.[7]

■ **3** "Pentecost" is best understood not as particular feast on the fiftieth day of Easter (which did not develop until the 4th century) but to the Easter season itself, that is, the *Pentecoste* or fifty days of Pascha.

5   See *m. Pesaḥ.* 9.3; and Avraham Davis, ed., *The Metsudah: Chumash/Rashi* 4 (3d ed.; Hoboken: Ktav, 1997) 116–18. Our thanks to Professor Hindy Najman of the University of Notre Dame for directing us to these references.

6   Cited by Eusebius *Hist. eccl.* 5.24.12.

7   On the early development of the prepaschal fast, see Thomas Talley, *The Origins of the Liturgical Year* (2d emended ed.; Collegeville, Minn.: Liturgical, 1991) 87–112; Paul Bradshaw, "The Origins of Easter," in Paul Bradshaw and Lawrence Hoffman, eds., *Passover and Easter: Origin and History to Modern Times* (Two Liturgical Traditions 5; Notre Dame: Univ. of Notre Dame Press, 1999) 81–97; Maxwell Johnson, "Preparation for Pascha? Lent in Christian Antiquity," in Paul Bradshaw and Lawrence Hoffman, eds., *Passover and Easter: The Symbolic Structuring of Sacred Seasons* (Two Liturgical Traditions 6; Notre Dame: Univ. of Notre Dame Press, 1999) 36–54; idem, "From Three Weeks to Forty Days: Baptismal Preparation and the Origins of Lent," *StLit* 20 (1990) 185–200; reprinted in Johnson, *Living Water*, 118–36.

Latin (77.17–23)	Sahidic	Arabic	Ethiopic
[Title]	*56 Concerning that it is proper for the deacons (διάκονος) to assist (προσκαρτερεῖν) the bishop (ἐπίσκοπος)*	*41 That the deacons should follow the orders of the bishop*	*41 Concerning that it is proper for deacons to serve the bishop*
Let each deacon with the subdeacons attend on the bishop. Let it also be told to him who are sick, so that, if it is pleasing to the bishop, he may visit them. For a sick person is greatly consoled when the high priest remembers him.	And (δέ) let each one of the deacons (διάκονος) and subdeacons (ὑποδιάκονος) assist (προσκαρτερεῖν) the bishop (ἐπίσκοπος), and let them inform him about everyone who is sick, so that if it seems good (δοκεῖν) to the bishop (ἐπίσκοπος), he may visit them. For (γάρ) those who are sick are consoled when they see their high priest (ἀρχιερεύς) visiting them and that they are remembered.	Every deacon and subdeacon should direct himself to the bishop and tell him who is ill so that he should visit them, because if the head of the priests visits them [. . . ?], they remember them.	Every one of the deacons with the subdeacons are to turn to the bishop and tell him about the sick so that he may visit them. For if the chief priest visits the sick, they will be greatly consoled because he remembered them.

Text

This chapter is also the basis for chaps. 39 and 40. For a discussion of the relationship between them, see p. 16. The phrase, "if it is pleasing to the bishop," occurs in the Latin and its equivalent in the Sahidic, but appears to have dropped out of the other versions. In his Latin translation of the Sahidic phrase that is rendered here, "he may visit *them*," Botte used the word *infirmos* rather than the pronoun *eos*, as in the Latin version.[1] There is, however, nothing in the Sahidic text of the phrase to correspond to *infirmos*. Botte may have misread the Sahidic word ϣⲓⲛⲉ, "visit," as ϣⲱⲛⲉ, "sick." In the final sentence of the oriental versions and *Canons of Hippolytus*, the "high priest" (bishop) "visits" the sick and "remembers" them, while the Latin version and *Testamentum Domini* omit the word "visits." The slight corruption in the Arabic text of this sentence is negligible.

Comment

The title in the oriental versions suggests the general ministry of deacons as assistants to the bishop, although the actual content of the chapter concerns the specific work of attending to the sick. According to the Latin version of chap. 8, deacons are ordained to serve the bishop, "indicating to the bishop what is necessary," but the Sahidic version of the chapter specifically mentions that the deacon is appointed to "take care of the sick and inform the bishop of them," as does the parallel of chap. 8 in the *Canons of Hippolytus*. On the other hand, chap. 29B, found only in the Ethiopic, suggests that ordinarily it would be the presbyter who would give the "sign" or "seal" to the sick, with the deacon fulfilling that role only in a "time of difficulty."[2] Chapter 34 appears to be closer to the conception of deacons in chap. 8 than in the Ethiopic text of chap. 29B.

---

1   Botte, *Tradition*, 80.
2   Note also that a mid-third-century letter of Diony-

sius of Alexandria *Ad Fabium Antiochenum* 4, preserved by Eusebius (*Hist. eccl.* 6.44), records that it is

Apostolic Constitutions	Canons of Hippolytus 24	Testamentum Domini 2.21
	A deacon is to accompany the bishop at all times to inform him of everyone's condition. He is to inform him about each sick person, because it is important for the sick person that the high priest visits him. He is relieved of his sickness when the bishop goes to him, especially when he prays over him, because the shadow of Peter healed the sick, unless his life span is over. [Continued in *Ap. Trad.* 40; see also *Ap. Trad.* 39.]	Let them take [it] up to the hearing of the bishop, so that if it seems good to the bishop, he may visit them; for the sick [person] is much comforted when the high priest remembers him, and especially when he is faithful. [See also *Ap. Trad.* 39.]

In the *Pseudo-Clementine Epistula* 12, it is the duty of the deacon to find out who is sick and report to the entire congregation, so "that they may visit them, and supply their wants according to the judgment of the [bishop]."[3] Similarly, the *Apostolic Constitutions* notes that deacons visit the sick and report to the bishop those who are afflicted.[4]

The bishop is referred to here as the "high priest," just as in the episcopal ordination prayer of chap. 3 and in the Ethiopic text of *Ap. Trad.* 8.11. On parallels to this usage in the early church, see p. 33.

It may be noted that no mention is made of "healers" (see *Apostolic Tradition* 14), nor of any pastoral ministry of healing other than the deacons informing the bishop of needs in the church.

the responsibility of presbyters to take the reserved sacrament to the sick.

3 This literature has been notoriously difficult to date, though the basic document may be a work of the 3d century and the final forms of the *Homilies* and the *Recognitions* probably date to the 4th century. For a survey of the issues, see Georg Strecker, "The Pseudo-Clementines: Introduction," in Wilhelm Schneemelcher, ed., *New Testament Apocrypha*, vol. 2: *Writings Relating to the Apostles, Apocalypses and Related Subjects,* trans. ed. R. McL. Wilson (rev. ed.; Louisville: Westminster/John Knox, 1992) 483–93.

4 *Const.* 3.19.

35

Latin (77.24–31)	Sahidic	Arabic	Ethiopic
[Title]	*57 Concerning the hour when it is proper to pray*	*42 Concerning times when one should pray*	*42 Concerning the time at which it is proper to pray*
1 Let the faithful, as soon as they have woken and risen, before they touch their work, pray to God and so hasten to their work.	And (δέ) every faithful [person] (πιστός), at the hour they shall awake, before they do any work, let them pray to the Lord, and in this way let them proceed to their work.	The believers, at the time when they awake and get up, before they work at anything, should pray to the Lord, and after that turn to their labors.	When believers awake, after they have risen, before they do anything, they are to wash their hands and pray to God. And afterward they are to go to their work.
2 And if there is any instruction by word, let him give preference to this so that he hurries and hears the Word of God for the comfort of his soul. Let him hasten to the church, where the spirit flourishes.	But (δέ) if there is the word of catechesis (κατήχησις), let them choose even better to go and listen to the Word of God, strengthening their soul (ψυχή). And (δέ) let them hasten (σπουδάζειν) to go to the church (ἐκκλησία), the place where the spirit (πνεῦμα) sprouts forth.	If there is then a sermon, they should choose it and go and hear the word of preaching, which is the Word of God that confirms the soul. Let them go quickly to the church, the place in which the spirit is and bears fruit.	And if there is a word of teaching that is to be carried out, they are to hurry to go there where the word of teaching is—which is the Word of God that strengthens souls. They are to hurry to go to the church, the place where the Spirit is, and they are to bear fruit there.

Text

Chapter 35 is a doublet of 41.1–4. On the problem of the order of the concluding chapters, see the Introduction, p. 16. Dix suggested that chap. 35 represented a condensation of the first part of chap. 41, which was the original text.[1] Botte accepted that chap. 35 was earlier, and offered the more likely explanation that chap. 41 was an expansion of chap. 35, though with the highly questionable suggestion that the expansion was made by the original author of chap. 35.[2] The presence of this shorter chapter in *Apostolic Constitutions* 8, but not in either the *Canons of Hippolytus* or *Testamentum Domini*, is further indication of its original independence from the expanded horarium of chap. 41. On the relationship of chap. 35 to chap. 41, see p. 202 below.

The title is supplied by the oriental versions. The Arabic title has the plural, "times when one should pray," possibly to conform to the use of the plural in the title of the parallel chap. 41.

Comment

This chapter directs the faithful to pray upon rising before going to the day's activities, unless there is a time of "instruction" in the church, in which case one should go first to the church before going to work. Thus preference is to be given to the communal meetings rather than to the private prayer at home. These catechetical meetings would presumably have included prayer along with the catechesis. They would have been occasional in nature, and should not be construed as an early example of a daily public office of morning prayer.[3] See the

---

1   Dix, *Apostolic Tradition*, 57 nn. 84–85.
2   Botte, *Tradition*, xxxiii. He does also offer the possibility that chap. 41 had an independent existence.
3   So Bradshaw, *Daily Prayer*, 71, disputing the earlier

assessment of Dugmore, *Influence*, 47–49. See also Taft, *Liturgy*, 25–26, who notes that this assembly was not a "matins."

Apostolic Constitutions 8.32.18	*Canons of Hippolytus*	*Testamentum Domini*
Let every faithful man and woman rising early in the morning, before they undertake their work, wash themselves and pray. But if there is a word of catechesis, let them honor the word of godly living over work.		

description of the catechetical gatherings in chap. 18 (p. 100 above).

Morning prayer is mentioned in several second- and third-century sources, but without the explicit connection to rising from sleep that we find in this chapter. The connection may be inferred, for example, in Clement of Alexandria, who describes the prayer of the true, Gnostic Christian: "He, all day and night, speaking and doing the Lord's commands, rejoices exceedingly, not only on rising in the morning and at noon, but also when walking about, when asleep. . . ."[4] Yet this is, for Clement, merely part of "prayer without ceasing," since the Gnostic prays "throughout his whole life."[5]

4   *Strom.* 7.12.
5   Ibid., 7.7.

Latin (77.32—78.2)	Sahidic	Arabic	Ethiopic
[Title]	*58 Concerning that it is proper to receive the Eucharist (εὐχαριστία) early at the time it will be offered up, before they taste anything*	*43 That they should receive the Eucharist first, at the time when it takes place, before tasting anything*	*43 Concerning that it is proper for them to receive from the Eucharist first when they go up, before they taste anything*
Let every faithful [person] take care to receive the Eucharist before he tastes anything else. For if he receives in faith, even if something deadly shall be given to him after this, it cannot harm him.	And (δέ) let every faithful [person] (πιστός) hasten (σπουδάζειν) to receive the Eucharist (εὐχαριστία) before he tastes anything. For (γάρ) if there are some faithful (πιστός) who receive it, if someone gives him [*sic*] a drug, it will not affect him.	Every believer should make it his practice that he should receive the mysteries before tasting anything. If there is faith in him and he receives it, if someone gives him deadly poison, it will not hurt him.	Every believer is to carry out the admonition that he receive from the mystery before he tastes anything. If he has faith and receives it, if there is someone who gives deadly poison to him, it will not harm him.

Greek fragment:
Let every faithful [person] try to receive the Eucharist before he tastes anything. For if he receives in faith, even if someone may give him something deadly after this, it will not overpower him.

Text

Early editors (Schwartz, Jungklaus, and Easton) regarded chaps. 36–38 as spurious, and even Dix thought that they were "very awkwardly placed . . . between two regulations about deacons' duties." Nevertheless, he still believed that they were authentic and had merely become displaced from their true location after chap. 41, where a parallel to chap. 36 is found in the *Testamentum Domini*.[1] They are, however, retained by Botte without comment in the place where the manuscripts locate them. There is some thematic connection between receiving the Eucharist in the morning referred to in this chapter and the morning prayer and assembly for instruction referred to in chap. 35. On the other hand, these chapters may owe their position in the church order not to any similarity of theme to what precedes but rather to a resemblance in the opening words to the beginning of chap. 35: "Let the faithful . . ." (plural)/ "Let every faithful person. . . ." It is even possible that these chapters were once part of an independent list of such instructions, from which they were extracted to form an addition to an older version of the *Apostolic Tradition* with 35 as its final chapter, since it appears

that chaps. 39–41 were also not included in the church order at one time.[2] This notion receives some further support from the fact that, as indicated in the Introduction (see above, p. 7), this particular chapter is preserved independently in Greek in an eighth-century collection of patristic quotations, which exists in two manuscripts, Ochrid *Mus. nat.* 86 (13th century), f. 192, and Paris BN *gr.* 900 (15th century), f. 112. Apart from the form of the verb "receives" in the second sentence (μεταλάβοι versus μεταλάβη), the two fragments are identical, and so seem to provide a fairly reliable guide to the original text.

It has been alleged that Jerome was familiar with this chapter under the authorship of Hippolytus, because he apparently refers to it in *Ep.* 71.6: "What you ask about Saturday, whether one ought to fast on that day, and about the Eucharist, whether one ought to receive it daily, observances which the Roman church and Spain recommend, has been treated of by Hippolytus, a man of great learning." Saturday fasting is discussed in Hippolytus's *Comm. on Dan.* 4.20. While chap. 36 does not specifically mention *daily* reception, it seems to be the only place in works attributed to Hippolytus that hints at it. This does not, of course, prove that Jerome knew the

1   Dix, *Apostolic Tradition*, 84.
2   See the Introduction above, p. 16.

3   See, e.g., Connolly, *Egyptian Church Order*, 79; Dix, *Apostolic Tradition*, 84–85; Cuming, *Hippolytus*, 27;

Apostolic Constitutions	Canons of Hippolytus 28	Testamentum Domini 2.25
	None of the faithful is to taste anything until after having partaken of the mysteries, especially on the days of fasting.	. . . But always let the faithful take care that, before he eats, he partakes of the Eucharist, that he may be incapable of receiving injury. . . .

whole *Apostolic Tradition*—he may simply have encountered this chapter, or chaps. 36–38 independently—or that even if the work were associated with the name of Hippolytus in his day, such an attribution was genuine.

Comment

Although Augustine believed that fasting before the reception of Communion was a universal practice that had existed since apostolic times (*Ep.* 54.8), the earliest evidence that we have for it is in Tertullian (*Ad uxor.* 2.5), who refers to the situation of a woman married to an unbeliever: "Will your husband not know what you taste in secret before any food, and if he knows it is bread, will he not believe it to be what it is called?"

While the titles given to the chapter in the oriental versions clearly interpret the injunction as referring to fasting before an actual celebration of the Eucharist, the general scholarly consensus is that the chapter was originally intended to refer to the reception of Communion at home on weekdays, as also seems to be the case in chap. 37.[3] Indeed, Dix regarded the phrase beginning in the Sahidic, "at the time . . . ," as a later interpolation since there would have been no room for such a long title in the space left in the Latin.[4] There is evidence from other sources that consecrated bread might be taken home from the Sunday celebration of the Eucharist for consumption there on weekdays. Not only does Tertullian have concerns about a believer doing this in front of an unbelieving spouse (as we saw above), but he also recommends those who have scruples about receiving the Eucharist at church on a day when they are

fasting to take the sacrament home and consume it later when the period of fasting is over (*De or.* 19). Cyprian mentions a woman who "with impure hands" tried to open the container in which she was keeping the body of Christ, but fire flared up from it—obviously intended as a cautionary tale against unworthy reception (*De laps.* 26). The custom is also clearly attested in various places in the fourth century, and although it then began to decline, it persisted in some contexts until the seventh or eighth century.[5] It should be noted that the term "Eucharist" is used here to denote the consecrated elements themselves rather than as the name for the whole rite. This is standard practice in early Christianity.

The belief expressed here that the sacrament has apotropaic power to ward off evil is a clear allusion to Mark 16:18, which says of believers that "if they drink any deadly thing, it will not hurt them"; but quasi-magical properties were often alleged for the consecrated elements by early Christian writers. For example, Ignatius describes the bread of the Eucharist as "the medicine of immortality, the antidote preventing death" (*Eph.* 20.2), a phrase that may echo the magical papyri;[6] Cyprian speaks of the Eucharist as a kind of talisman that protects the worthy but exposes the guilty (*De laps.* 26); Cyril of Jerusalem in the fourth century advises communicants to "sanctify" their eyes by touching them with the body of Christ that they have just received (*Myst. Cat.* 5.21); and Ambrose tells the story of his brother, Satyrus, who when a catechumen found himself in danger of shipwreck asked Christian fellow passengers to give him the sacrament, which he wrapped in his scarf, and then plunged into the sea (*De excessu fratris* 1.43).

Nathan Mitchell, *Cult and Controversy: The Worship of the Eucharist Outside Mass* (New York: Pueblo, 1982) 11–12.

4 Dix, *Apostolic Tradition*, 58.

5 See William H. Freestone, *The Sacrament Reserved* (Alcuin Club Collections 21; London: Mowbrays, 1917) 40–50; Otto Nussbaum, *Die Aufbewahrung der*

Eucharistie (Theophaneia 29; Bonn: Hanstein, 1979) 266–69.

6 But cf. William R. Schoedel, *Ignatius of Antioch: A Commentary on the Letters of Ignatius of Antioch* (Hermeneia; Philadelphia: Fortress Press, 1985) 97–98.

Latin (78.3–7)	Sahidic	Arabic	Ethiopic
[Title]	*59 Concerning that it is proper to watch over the Eucharist (εὐχαριστία) diligently*	*44 That care should be taken to adhere to the mysteries and that nothing should be spilled from the chalice*	*44 Concerning that it is proper that the mystery be kept with care*
Let everyone take care that an unbeliever does not taste of the Eucharist, nor a mouse or any other animal, nor that any of it falls and is lost. For the body of Christ is to be eaten by believers and not to be despised.	Let everyone take care diligently that an unbeliever (ἄπιστος) not eat of the Eucharist (εὐχαριστία), or (ἤ) a mouse, or (ἤ) another creature, or (ἤ) that any of it at all (ὅλως) fall from it and get lost. It is the body (σῶμα) of Christ (χριστός) from which all the faithful (πιστός) receive, and it is not proper to despise (καταφρονεῖν) it.	Everyone should be concerned to be sure that no unbeliever should receive the mysteries, nor any rat or other animal, and that nothing should fall from it and be lost, for it is the body of Christ and every believer eats of it and should not be careless about it.	And it is not proper that anything should be poured from the cup. Everyone is to think strictly that no one except a believer is to receive from the mystery and that none of it should fall or be thrown away. For it is the body of Christ, and all believers are to eat from it. And it is not proper that they neglect it.

Comment

As intimated in the commentary on chap. 36 above, this short instruction may originally have been part of a separate collection of such directives before being incorporated into this document. It appears to owe its place in this particular position to a connection in subject matter with that chapter: the reception of Communion at home. The faithful are exhorted to take care not to let a nonbeliever or some small creature partake of the sacrament, or to allow any of it to fall on the ground, the latter being a common admonition in early Christian writings.[1] In the first case what is at stake is the preservation of the boundaries and ritual purity of the Christian community rather than hygiene as such, just as in *Ap. Trad.* 26.2 and 27.1 there was a concern to segregate catechumens and the faithful at the community supper for the same reason. In the second case, as the text goes on to indicate, the motive is reverence for the consecrated bread as "the body of Christ," an expression also found in *Ap. Trad.* 23.4 and its parallel in 29C.16, which we suggested may have been a later addition to that passage. At a communal celebration of the Eucharist, such preventive measures are more likely to have been the responsibility of the deacons than of the whole community, and in any case the risk of nibbling by mice seems more likely to have occurred when the consecrated bread was being stored than during the eucharistic celebration itself. It is for these reasons that the injunction has been thought to be concerned rather with a domestic situation, where the sacrament would have been kept from the Sunday celebration of the community for reception on weekdays (see the commentary on chap. 36 above). Usually bread alone was reserved in this way, because of the difficulty of preserving wine for long, and that is what seems to be envisaged here, since the reference is to the body of Christ rather than the blood. The Arabic and Ethiopic translators, however, who were doubtless not personally familiar with this by now obsolete custom, take it to be referring to spillage from the cup. That, however, forms the theme of the next chapter.

---

1   See, e.g., Tertullian *De cor.* 3.4; Origen *Hom. on Exod.* 13.3; Cyril of Jerusalem *Myst. Cat.* 5.21.

Apostolic Constitutions	Canons of Hippolytus	Testamentum Domini
	The clergy are to see that they do not let anyone partake of the mysteries, except the faithful alone.	

38A — That It Is Not Proper to Spill Anything from the Cup

Latin (78.8–14)	Sahidic	Arabic	Ethiopic
[Title]	*60 Concerning that it is not proper to spill anything from the cup* ($\pi o \tau \acute{\eta} \rho \iota o \nu$)	*That nothing should be spilled from the chalice*	
1 For blessing [the cup] in the name of God, you received [it] as the antitype of the blood of Christ.	For ($\gamma \acute{\alpha} \rho$) when you bless the cup ($\pi o \tau \acute{\eta} \rho \iota o \nu$) in the name of God and receive of it as ($\dot{\omega} \varsigma$) it is the blood of Christ ($X \rho \iota \sigma \tau \acute{o} \varsigma$), watch yourself very much.	If the chalice is blessed in the name of the Lord and Communion is given from it, it is the blood of Christ.	For it is not proper that anything should be poured out from the cup, because the cup was blessed in the name of our Lord Jesus Christ so that you should receive from it, for it is the blood of Christ.
2 Therefore refrain from pouring out [any], as if you despised [it], so that an alien spirit may not lick it up. You will be guilty of blood, as one who scorned the price with which he has been bought.	Do not spill it, so that an alien ($\dot{\alpha} \lambda \lambda \acute{o} \tau \rho \iota o \nu$) spirit ($\pi \nu \epsilon \hat{v} \mu \alpha$) shall not lick it, so that God shall not be angry at you, since ($\dot{\omega} \varsigma$) you have thought scornfully ($\kappa \alpha \tau \alpha \varphi \rho o \nu \epsilon \hat{\imath} \nu$) and are guilty ($\alpha \breve{\iota} \tau \iota o \varsigma$) of the blood of Christ ($X \rho \iota \sigma \tau \acute{o} \varsigma$), while despising the price with which you were bought.	Take great care that nothing is spilled from it, lest strange spirits should lick it up and it should be you who have behaved contemptuously and been the cause of [spilling] the blood of Christ, which you have belittled, though you have been bought with it.	Be very careful and diligent that none of it be poured out or drop so that no foreign spirit licks any of it, so that it may not be [the case] that you yourself are the one who denied and rejected the glorious blood of Christ through which he redeemed you, and it becomes for you the cause, as if you denied and rejected Christ. And if a little of his body falls and if a little from the cup drops out, you will receive judgment on account of that through which he redeemed you.

Text

Although this chapter is obviously linked in subject matter to the preceding one, the shift from the third-person singular of the previous chapters to the second-person singular here, in all the linguistic versions, suggests that it may not be part of the same stratum of material. On the whole, the brevity of the Latin seems to be a better guide to the original text than the more prolix oriental versions, especially the Ethiopic, which seem to have expanded the directive considerably.

■ **1** The absence of the word "cup" from the Latin appears to be accidental rather than an older version of the text that the oriental versions have expanded, since without it the sense of the sentence is unclear. Dix suggested that, as the first word in the text, it might accidentally have been written in red like the preceding title and effaced along with it.[1]

Comment

Even if it comes from a different source, this chapter follows naturally from the desire for care in the handling of the consecrated bread in chap. 37. Christians are instructed not to allow any wine to be spilled from the chalice so that no evil spirit may lick it up.

■ **1** The warning about reverent treatment occurs in the context of an individual saying a blessing over the cup; there is no suggestion that it is necessarily addressed to an ordained minister rather than to one of the faithful,

---

1   Dix, *Apostolic Tradition*, 59.

Apostolic Constitutions	*Canons of Hippolytus* 29	*Testamentum Domini*
	The clergy are to stand with all their attention on the altar when it has been prepared. They are to stand watching over it, so that no insect climbs on to it and nothing falls from the cup: that would be a mortal sin for the presbyters. That is why everyone is to stand watching over the holy place: he who gives the mysteries and those who partake are to watch with great care that nothing falls on the ground, for fear that an evil spirit should have power over it. . . .	

and so it may well refer to Communion at home, like the preceding chapter, as only consecrated bread and not wine was usually brought home, because of the difficulty of preserving the latter. On the other hand, *Ap. Trad.* 26.1 does speak of individuals giving thanks over their own cup apparently at a common meal, and so such a context cannot be entirely excluded here. Dix suggested that the blessing may have been done by dropping a small portion of consecrated bread into the cup, as was the practice in the later Roman liturgy of the presanctified,[2] but nothing in the text lends support to that particular theory.

For the use of the word "antitype," see the commentary on *Ap. Trad.* 21.27 above.

■ **2** The term "alien/foreign (spirit)" also occurs in *Ap. Trad.* 20.4, 8, and 21.5.

---

2   Ibid., 84–85.

38B

Latin (78.15–35)	Sahidic	Arabic	Ethiopic

[Title]

1 Always try to sign your forehead respectfully. For this sign of the Passion is displayed against the devil, if anyone does [it] with faith, not to please human beings but through knowledge presenting [it] as a breastplate.

2 When the adversary sees the power of the spirit from the heart clearly displayed in the likeness of baptism, he will flee trembling, with you not striking him but breathing [on him].

3 This was what Moses [did] typologically with the sheep that was sacrificed at the Passover: he sprinkled the blood on the threshold and anointing the two posts signifies that faith that is now in us, in the perfect sheep.

4 Signing the forehead and eyes with the hand, let us escape from him who is trying to destroy us.

5 And so, when these things are heard with thankfulness and true orthodox faith, they provide edification for the church and eternal life for believers.

6 I instruct that these things be kept by those who are wise. For to all who hear the apos. . . .

Text

As explained in the Introduction (p. 16 above), this chapter is a doublet of chaps. 42 and 43 resulting from an attempt in the Latin text to conflate a longer and a shorter version of the church order. In his edition Botte labels this material as L^1, divides it, and places it with chaps. 42 and 43. Dix follows the same pattern, according to his chapter numeration of chaps. 37 and 38. Cuming numbers the material as chaps. 42A and 43A, but places it immediately after chap. 38. The chapter breaks off with a lacuna at the end of the page in the Latin manuscript. See the commentary on chaps. 42 and 43 for further details.

Latin	Sahidic	Arabic	Ethiopic
		45 The deacons and presbyters should meet every day at the place of the bishop	*45 The deacons and presbyters are to gather every day where the bishop is*

1

| | And (δέ) let the deacons (διάκονος) and the presbyters (πρεσβύτερος) gather daily in the place where the bishop (ἐπίσκοπος) will command them. And the deacons (διάκονος) are not (μέν) to neglect (ἀμελεῖν) to gather always, unless (εἰ μήτι) an illness prevents (κωλύειν) them. | The deacons and presbyters should meet every day at the place to which the bishop directs them to go. The deacons and presbyters should not be lax in meeting every day, unless they are prevented by illness. | The deacons, then, and the presbyters are to gather every day at the place of the bishop, and he will order them to go to him. And the deacons and the presbyters are not to neglect to gather every day if illness does not prevent them. |

2

| | And (δέ) when they all gather, let them inform those in the church (ἐκκλησία), and in this way, when they pray, let each one proceed to the works that are appointed to him. | When they meet, they should teach those who are in the churches and then, when they [have] pray[ed], each one should turn to his work. | And when they gather they are to teach those who are in the churches. And in this way, when they pray, each one is to return to work. |

Text

In the Introduction (p. 16) we described chaps. 39 and 40 as a later expansion of chap. 34. We reached this conclusion not only because in the text of the *Apostolic Tradititon* known to both the *Canons of Hippolytus* and the *Testamentum Domini* a version of those chapters appears to have occupied the place originally filled by chap. 34, but also because there remain some similarities of content, even though the meaning has been much changed. For instance, the reference to illness is still there in chap. 39, but now related to the deacons themselves rather than to those to whom they minister. Similarly, the unusual word in the Sahidic of chap. 39.2, ⲧⲁⲙⲉ, translated as "inform," which becomes "teach" in the Arabic and Ethiopic, is the same word used in the Sahidic of chap. 34 in the phrase "let them inform him." It is true that *Canons of Hippolytus* 24 and *Testamentum Domini*

2.21 are in many ways closer to *Apostolic Tradition* 34 than to *Apostolic Tradition* 39, which suggests that they were not familiar with the extant text of chap. 39 as such but rather with an earlier stage in the transition, in which the reference to the high priest visiting the sick still remained but some other elements of chaps. 39 and 40 had already been added. Thus the *Canons of Hippolytus* contains the phrase "at all times," which is not found in *Apostolic Tradition* 34 but does correspond to "daily" or "every day" in *Apostolic Tradition* 39. It also states that the bishop "prays" over the sick rather than "remembers" them. Again, praying is not mentioned explicitly in chap. 34, but it is in chap. 39.

The chapter also has some affinity with *Canons of Hippolytus* 21, which speaks of an assembly of the clergy. The location of this chapter in the *Canons of Hippolytus*, however, deviates from the *Apostolic Tradition* significantly, making direct dependence less likely, although

Apostolic Constitutions	Canons of Hippolytus 24	Testamentum Domini 2.21
	A deacon is to accompany the bishop at all times to inform him of everyone's condition. He is to inform him about each sick person, because it is important for the sick person that the high priest visit him. He is relieved of his sickness when the bishop goes to him, especially when he prays over him, because the shadow of Peter healed the sick, unless his life span is over. [Continued in *Ap. Trad.* 40; see also *Ap. Trad.* 34.] [21] The presbyters are to assemble each day at the church, and the deacons, the subdeacons, the readers, and all the people at the time when the cock crows. They are to perform the prayer, the psalms and reading of Scripture and the prayers, according to the precept of the apostle who said: "Apply yourself to the reading until I come." He who stays behind the clergy, except for illness, and does not hurry is to be excluded. . . .	Let them take [it] up to the hearing of the bishop, so that if it seems good to the bishop, he may visit them; for the sick [person] is much comforted when the high priest remembers him, and especially when he is faithful. [See also *Ap. Trad.* 34.]

that is not to deny that there may be some influence from one to the other.

The Sahidic continues *Apostolic Tradition* 38 here with no break, and with no evidence of a title, while the title in the Arabic and Ethiopic is little more than a repetition of the first sentence of the chapter. Since the contents do not have much in common thematically with the previous chapter, however, it seems appropriate to place a break here.

■ 1 According to the Sahidic, the deacons (the Arabic and Ethiopic texts have "deacons and priests") are "not to neglect to gather always." Botte found this expression awkward, since the reference should be to the morning gatherings, rather than gathering "always," and proposed that the Sahidic text is slightly corrupt here.[1] The

Arabic (and Ethiopic) would seem to have captured the sense of the phrase: "The deacons and priests should not be *lax in meeting every day*."

Comment

The presbyters and deacons gather daily in the morning before work at the place appointed by the bishop, which suggests that these gatherings are the same as the catechetical gatherings in chaps. 18 and 19. Chapter 19 indicates that the "teacher" at the catechetical meetings may be either a cleric or a layperson, which is likewise implied in *Ap. Trad.* 41.2. This present chapter in the Sahidic suggests that teaching is the responsibility of the deacons, although this has been "corrected" by the

---

1   Botte, *Tradition*, 87 n. 2.

Arabic and Ethiopic to read "deacons and priests."[2] If the absence of reference to lay teachers insinuates a clericalization of the teaching office in the oriental versions, however, we might expect the same clericalization in chap. 19, where, on the contrary, lay teachers are explicitly affirmed. Thus it is reasonable to assume that there was no mention of lay teachers in the Greek text underlying the oriental versions. The teaching office is not typically associated with deacons, though the third-century *Apostolic Church Order* does allude to this as a function of deacons.[3]

The order of the meeting is identical to that in chap. 18: gathering, teaching, praying, going off to work. Furthermore, the phrase "proceed to his work" appears not only here but also in chaps. 35 and 41a (albeit in the plural there), which further hints at a thematic connection between these chapters as morning gatherings. Nevertheless, the absence of lay teachers is curious, and suggests that this chapter has been added to the *Apostolic Tradition* at a later date than chap. 19.[4]

Canons of Hippolytus 21 places this morning gathering earlier still, at cockcrow, and changes the public catechetical nature of the meeting into a public prayer service, similar in order to the morning office of the Egyptian monks described by John Cassian.[5] The catechetical origin of the chapter is retained, however, in the inclusion of the reading of Scripture lessons in the order of service, usually absent from fourth-century prayer offices outside Egypt.[6]

---

2 On the disappearance of lay teachers in the 3d century, see Roger Gryson, "The Authority of the Teacher in the Ancient and Medieval Church," *Journal of Ecumenical Studies* 19 (1982) 176–87; John Kevin Loyle, "The Exercise of Teaching in the Postapostolic Church," *Église et Théologie* 15 (1984) 23–35.

3 *Apostolic Church Order* 20, a chapter dealing with the duties of deacons, includes: "some [deacons]

admonishing, some exhorting, some rebuking. . . ."

4 See the commentary on chap. 41 below for a discussion of the redactional layers of chaps. 35 and 41.

5 Cassian *De institutis coenobiorum* 3.5. See Bradshaw, *Canons*, 26.

6 Bradshaw, *Daily Prayer*, chap. 4; Taft, *Liturgy*, 57–74.

Text

For the origin and development of this chapter, see the commentary on chap. 39. The parallel in the *Canons of Hippolytus* continues to adapt the material to the care of the sick rather than the departed.

■ **1** The Greek loanword κοιμητήριον in the Sahidic (lit. "sleeping place") is a distinctive Christian usage in reference to a cemetery.[1] The word is plural in the Sahidic and Arabic, and there is little justification for Dix's preference for the singular "cemetery."[2] The Greek loanword κέραμος in the Sahidic means "tiles," though the *Canons of Hippolytus* has translated it as "earthen vessels," a common alternative meaning of the word. While the Arabic and Ethiopic omit the reference to "tiles" altogether, the evidence of the *Canons of Hippolytus* suggests that it was present in the underlying Greek text.

Comment

At the core of this chapter is concern for the proper burial of the poor within the church community. While cremation was a common Roman practice to dispose of the dead, Christians followed the Jewish practice of burial, either in a surface grave or in an underground tomb or catacomb.[3] This was a relatively expensive practice requiring the ownership of land,[4] and it was necessary for the wealthier members of the synagogue or church to provide the burial space for the poor and slaves. In the Roman church the poorer members were buried in the underground tunnels, typically in holes dug into the walls, which allowed for accommodation of a large number of graves within a limited space. These narrow, horizontal graves were sealed with stucco and tiles.[5] Christian graves used either tiles laid side by side or marble to cover the *loculi*, though marble may have been the preferred seal for wealthier Christians.[6] The Arabic and Ethiopic omission of the "tiles" could be no more than an accommodation to the Egyptian practice.[7] Likewise, the *Canons of Hippolytus* (mis)reads the Greek here as "earthen vessel."

The concern for the poor and the use of tiles indicated in chap. 40 fits well with a third-century Roman context for this material as it is preserved in the Sahidic version. Dix notes that the *Refutatio* attributed to Hippolytus records that Callistus was put in charge of the Christian cemetery by the Roman bishop Zephyrinus.[8] This cemetery may originally have been the family burial ground of Zephyrinus, who, according to the *Liber Pontificalis* (1.16.14), was buried there, probably above ground. Those who "take care of it" are apparently distinct from the grave diggers in all three versions. The direction for the bishop to support them also fits with

---

1   (Hippolytus) *Ref.* 9.12.14: "[Zephyrinus] brought him [Callistus] from Antheium and appointed him over the cemetery (τὸ κοιμητήριον)." Eusebius (*Hist. eccl.* 7.11.10) preserves a dialogue of Dionysius of Alexandria, which also refers to τὰ κοιμητήρια.

2   Dix, *Apostolic Tradition*, 60.

3   See Margaret H. Williams, "The Organisation of Jewish Burials in Ancient Rome in the Light of Evidence from Palestine and the Diaspora," *ZPE* 101 (1994) 165–82.

4   Umberto M. Fazola, "Introduction," in Fabrizio Mancinelli, *The Catacombs of Rome and the Origins of Christianity* (Florence: Scala, 1981) 6–7.

5   Thomas J. Harrington, "The Local Church at Rome in the Second Century: A Common Cemetery Emerges amid Developments in this 'Laboratory of Christian Policy,'" *Studia canonica* 23 (1989) 178; Williams, "Organisation," 176. See also Connolly, *Egyptian Church Order*, 117–18.

6   James Stevenson, *The Catacombs: Life and Death in Early Christianity* (Nashville: Nelson, 1978) 18. The preference for marble is evidenced in that even carved pieces taken from pagan sources were occasionally used, with the inscription turned inward toward the tomb so as not to be visible.

7   Dix (*Apostolic Tradition*, 60 n. 2) suggests that the Arabic and Ethiopic misunderstand the allusion. On the other hand, Hanssens (*Liturgie*, 492–93) has suggested that there was a great deal of similarity between Alexandrian and Roman practice of the 2d and 3d centuries, particularly regarding burial of the poor.

8   *Ref.* 9.12.14. See Dix, *Apostolic Tradition*, xv n. This is undoubtedly the Catacomb of St. Callixtus on the Via Appia Antica. Its prominence in the early Roman church is evident in that it contains the tombs of nine 3d-century popes.

Latin	Sahidic	Arabic	Ethiopic
	61 Concerning the places of burial	*46 Concerning cemeteries*	*46 Concerning the tomb*

1 — Sahidic: **Do not let them overcharge ($\beta\alpha\rho\epsilon\hat{\iota}\nu$) people to bury a man in the cemeteries ($\kappa o\iota\mu\eta\tau\acute{\eta}\rho\iota o\nu$). For ($\gamma\acute{\alpha}\rho$) it is the property of every poor person. Only ($\pi\lambda\acute{\eta}\nu$) let the one who digs be given the wage of the worker ($\grave{\epsilon}\rho\gamma\acute{\alpha}\tau\eta\varsigma$) with the price of the tiles ($\kappa\acute{\epsilon}\rho\alpha\mu o\varsigma$).**

Arabic: **Let no one make excessive demands of people for burial in the cemeteries. It is the work of the poor. Rather, let a wage be paid to the grave digger**

Ethiopic: **One is not to compel anyone by an order regarding burial of people in a tomb that is made for all the poor, but they are to give his wage to a wage earner who digs**

2 — Sahidic: **And ($\delta\acute{\epsilon}$) those who are in that place, who take care [of it], let the bishop ($\grave{\epsilon}\pi\acute{\iota}$-$\sigma\kappa o\pi o\varsigma$) support them, so that it [the burial place] shall not become burdensome to any who come to those places ($\tau\acute{o}\pi o\varsigma$).**

Arabic: **and to the guard who is in the place and looks after it, and let the bishop support them from what is paid to the temple.**

Ethiopic: **and to the one who guards that place, who takes thought for them; and the bishop will provide for him from what they bring to the churches.**

the brief description in the *Refutatio* of Callistus's administration of the cemetery under Zephyrinus.

The use of the plural "cemeteries" in the Sahidic (in the title and in the chapter itself) is not an argument against a Roman location for the material; there were several Christian cemeteries in Rome dating from the early third century.[9] Finally, the reference to the "tiles" that would be used to seal the tombs also fits well the Christian Roman burial of the poor in subterranean graves.[10]

Nevertheless, despite its Roman flavor, chap. 40 along with chap. 39 does not appear to belong to the earliest layer of the *Apostolic Tradition*, which is represented by the shorter ending in the Latin version.

---

9   Brent, *Hippolytus*, 439. Brent bases his argument on the reading of the same evidence by Peter Lampe, *Die stadtrömishen Christen in den ersten beiden Jahrhunderten* (Wissenschaftliche Untersuchungen zum Neuen Testament 2/18; Tübingen: Mohr-

Siebeck, 1989); ET *Christians of Rome in the First Two Centuries* (Turnbridge Wells: Burn and Oates, 1999).

10   Connolly (*Egyptian Church Order*, 117–18) understood the reference to $\kappa\acute{\epsilon}\rho\alpha\mu o\iota$, "tiles," as a strong indication of a Roman origin for the text.

Apostolic Constitutions	*Canons of Hippolytus*	*Testamentum Domini* 2.23
	[24 continued] The sick are not to sleep in the dormitory, but rather the poor. That is why he who has a home, if he is sick, is not to be moved to the house of God. Rather he is only to pray and then return home. [25] The steward is the one who has care of the sick. The bishop is to support them; even the vessel of clay necessary for the sick, the bishop is to give it to the steward.	If a poor man dies, let those who provide for each one provide for his clothing. If anyone who is a stranger dies and has no place to be buried, let those who have a place give [it]. But if the church has [a place], let it give [it]. And if he has no covering, let the church similarly give it. But if he does not have grave clothes, let him be shrouded. But if a man is found to have possessions, and does not leave them to the church, let them be kept for a time; and after a year do not let the church appropriate them, but let them be given to the poor for his soul. But if he desires to be embalmed, let the deacons provide for this, a presbyter standing by. If the church has a graveyard, and there is someone who lives there and keeps it, let the bishop provide for him from the church, so that he is no burden to those who come there.

Latin	Sahidic	Arabic	Ethiopic
	62 Concerning the hour when it is proper to pray	*47 Concerning the times when one should pray and listen to sermons and [concerning] signing the forehead with the cross*	*47 Concerning the times in which it is proper to pray, and hearing teaching and signing the forehead with the cross*

1

Latin	Sahidic	Arabic	Ethiopic
	And (δέ) every faithful man (πιστός) and woman (πιστή), when they arise early from sleeping, before they touch any work, let them wash their hands and pray to God, and in this way let them proceed to their work.	Every believer, male and female, when they get up in the morning, before they do anything, should wash their hands and pray to God and then turn to their work.	All believing men and women, when they rise early in the morning, before they do anything, it is necessary that they wash their hands and pray to God. Then they are to turn to their work.

2

Latin	Sahidic	Arabic	Ethiopic
	But (δέ) if it happens that there is catechesis (κατήχησις) of the Word of God, let each one choose to go to that place, considering this in his heart that God is the one whom he hears speaking in the one who instructs (κατηχεῖσθαι); for (γάρ) having prayed in the church (ἐκκλησία), he will be able to escape (παρελθεῖν) the evil (κακία) of the day. Let the pious one consider it a great loss when he does not go to the place where one is instructed (κατηχεῖσθαι), especially (μάλιστα δέ) if he can read or (ἤ) if the teacher comes.	If there is a sermon, everyone should choose to go to the place where the teaching takes place and take into his heart that the one he hears, it is God who is speaking through the mouth of the teacher, for he lives in the church and dispels the evil of every day. Let the God-fearing man consider it a great loss if he does not go to the place where teaching is given, especially if he can read.	And if they tell them where the word of teaching is, every one is to hurry to go there, to the place of instruction. And he is to know this in his heart and examine closely that what he heard is God who speaks from the mouth of the one who teaches, and the evil of every day passes away from the one who dwells in the church. And it will be reckoned a great loss to the one who fears God if he does not go to the place where there is teaching, especially for one who is able to read.

3

Latin	Sahidic	Arabic	Ethiopic
	Let none of you be late for the church (ἐκκλησία), the place in which they teach. Then (τότε) the one who speaks will be enjoined to proclaim those things that are profitable to everyone, and you will listen to things you do not think about, and you will benefit (ὠφελεῖν) from things that the Holy Spirit (πνεῦμα) will give to you from the one who teaches (κατηχεῖσθαι). By this your faith (πίστις) will be strengthened by the things you have heard. And (δέ) you will be told also in that place the things that it is proper for you to do in your house. Because of this, let each one hasten	If the teacher is present, let him not be late for church, the place in which the teaching is given. Then the speaker will be given to say what is profitable to everyone. You will hear what you do not expect and profit from what the Holy Spirit gives you through the one who is teaching. So your faith will be established on what you hear. You will also be told in that place what you should do at home. For this reason, let everyone hasten to the church, the place in which the Spirit shines.	If there is one who teaches, he is not to hold back from the church, the place where the teaching is. It should immediately be permitted to the one who speaks that he should speak what is profitable for everyone. And you will hear what you had not thought, and you will profit through what the Holy Spirit will give you from the one who teaches. And in this way your faith will become strong because of what you will hear. And further, they will say to you in that place what is proper for you to do in your house. And for this reason each person is to hurry to go to the

Apostolic Constitutions 8.32.18	*Canons of Hippolytus*	*Testamentum Domini* 2.24
Let every faithful man and woman rising early in the morning, before they undertake their work, wash themselves and pray. But if there is a word of catechesis, let them honor the word of godly living over work.	Each person in the order of Christians is to pray when he rises from sleep, in the morning they are to wash their hands when they wish to pray before doing anything.[a]	Let the people always take care about the early dawn, that arising and washing their hands they immediately pray. And so let each one go to the work that he wishes.

[26] When there is in a church an assembly for the Word of God, every one is to hurry and assemble there. They are to know that to hear the Word of God is better than all the glory of this world. They are to reckon it a great loss to them when a necessity prevents them from hearing the Word of God. On the contrary, they are to devote their time to the church frequently and [so] be able to expel hatred of their enemy, especially if someone can read, because it is more profitable to hear what one does not know.

For the Lord, in the place where [his] majesty is remembered, makes the Spirit dwell in those who are assembled and gives his grace to all. Those who are in two minds among them, be reassured concerning them because you have heard some of them in the Spirit. Those whose mind is preoccupied at home are not to forget what they have heard in church. That is why each one is to make it his concern to go to church every day when there are prayers.

---

[a] The material from *Apostolic Tradition* 41 has been rearranged at this point in the *Canons of Hippolytus*, probably as a result of an accidental displacement in the ms. used by the compiler: canon 25 continues below on p. 197.

Latin	Sahidic	Arabic	Ethiopic
	(σπουδάζειν) to go to the church (ἐκκλησία), the place in which the Holy Spirit (πνεῦμα) springs forth.		church, to the place where the Spirit shines.

4

Latin	Sahidic	Arabic	Ethiopic
	If there is a day when there is no catechesis (κατή-χησις), when each one is at his house, let him take a holy book and read in it sufficiently as it seems (δοκεῖν) to him that it is profitable.	If it is a day on which there is no teaching, let everyone be in his house and take a holy book and read enough for what he knows is good.	And if it is a day on which there is no teaching, everyone is to be in his house and is to take the holy book and read as long as he can, because it is a good thing.

5

Latin	Sahidic	Arabic	Ethiopic
	And if (μέν) you are in your house, pray at about the third hour and bless God. If on the other hand (μέν) you are in another place and you happen upon that time (καιρός), pray in your heart to God.	If you are in your house, pray the third hour and praise God, and if you are in some other place when that time arrives, pray in your heart to God,	And if you are in your house, pray three [sic] hour[s] and glorify God. And if you are in another place and that hour arrives, pray in your heart to God

6

Latin	Sahidic	Arabic	Ethiopic
	For (γάρ) in that hour Christ (Χριστός) was seen nailed to the wood. Because of this also, in the old (παλαιά) [testament] the law (νόμος) commanded that they offer shewbread (−πρόθεσις) at every hour as type (τύπος) of the body (σῶμα) and the blood of Christ (Χριστός) with the slaughter of the senseless (ἄλογος) sheep, this being a type (τύπος) of the perfect (τέλειος) sheep. For (γάρ) the shepherd is Christ (Χριστός). He also is the bread that came down from heaven.	for at that hour Christ was seen being nailed to the tree. For this [reason] in the old [testament?] the law orders that the bread of offering should be offered at the third hour as a figure of the holy body and blood of Christ and the slaughter of the lamb, which is a figure of the perfect lamb, for the shepherd is Christ, and he is the bread that came down from heaven.	because in that hour they stripped Christ and nailed his cross. And for this reason he commands beforehand in the law that they should give the bread that they offer in the third hour, a likeness of Christ's holy body and blood. And they sacrifice a lamb that is a likeness of the perfect Lamb. For the shepherd is Christ, and he is the bread that came down from heaven.

7

Latin	Sahidic	Arabic	Ethiopic
	Pray likewise (ὁμοίως) at about the sixth hour, for (γάρ) after Christ (Χριστός) was hung on the wood of the cross (σταυρός), that day divided and a great darkness happened. Therefore (ὥστε), at that hour, let a prayer that is powerful be prayed, being compared to the voice of the one who prayed [and] caused all creation (κτίσις) to become dark for the unbelieving Jews (Ἰουδαῖος).	Pray the sixth hour, because that is when Christ was hung on the tree and that day was divided and it became dark. So at that hour let a powerful prayer be prayed, so that you will resemble the voice of the one who prayed and made the whole creation dark for the unbelievers.	Pray in the sixth hour because the crucifixion of Christ on the tree [occurred then]. And the day was divided, and it became darkness. And they are to pray a strong prayer in that hour, and they are to imitate the word that he prayed and made all the world darkness. And cate-chumens are to make a great prayer.

Apostolic Constitutions	Canons of Hippolytus	Testamentum Domini
	[27] Each day when there is no prayer in church, take a Bible and read from it. Let the sun see the Bible on your knees at each dawn.[b]	
[8.34.3] And the third because at that time the Lord received condemnation from Pilate.	[25 continued] They are to pray again at the third hour, for it is the time when the Savior Jesus was crucified voluntarily for our salvation, so as to set us free.	Let all take care to pray at the third hour with mourning and labor, either in the church, or in the house because they cannot go [to the church]. For this is the hour of the fixing of the only begotten on the cross.
[8.34.4] And the sixth because at that time he was crucified.	And again at the sixth hour they are to pray, because it is the time when the whole creation shook because of the evil deed that the Jews did to him.	But at the sixth hour similarly let there be prayer with sorrow. For then the daylight was divided by the darkness. Let there be then that voice which is like to the prophets, and to creation mourning.

[b] Because of the dislocation of the material in the *Canons of Hippolytus* referred to above (p. 195 note a), canon 27 resumes below on p. 199.

Latin (79.1—80.14)	Sahidic	Arabic	Ethiopic
8 . . . God who does not lie, who was mindful of his saints and sent his Word to illuminate them.	And (δέ) let a great prayer and a great blessing be prayed at about the ninth hour, so that you shall know the way in which the soul (ψυχή) of the righteous (δίκαιος) blesses the Lord, the true God. This one, who remembered those who are holy, sent his Son to them, who is his Word (λόγος), to shine on them.	Let them also say a great prayer at the ninth hour and praises such that you will know how the souls of the just bless the God of truth who remembered his saints and sent them his Son, who is his Word, to enlighten them;	And in the ninth hour they are to be long in praying with praise so that they may be joined in praising with the soul[s] of the righteous ones, glorifying the living God who does not lie, who has remembered his holy ones and sent to them his Son who is his Word so that he may enlighten them.
9 Therefore at that hour Christ, pierced in his side, poured forth water and blood, and illuminating the rest of the time of the day, he brought [it] to evening. Then, beginning to sleep [and] making the beginning of another day, he completed an image of the resurrection.	For (γάρ) at that hour, they pierced Christ (Χριστός) in his rib by a spear (λόγχη). Blood and water came out, and afterward he brought light to the rest of the day, until evening. Because of this, you also, when you go to sleep, shall begin (ἄρχεσθαι) another day and make the type (τύπος) of the resurrection (ἀνάστασις).	for at that hour Christ was pierced in his side and blood and water came out, and after that he enlightened others for the remainder of that day until nightfall. For this reason you, when the daylight ends and you begin another day, in likeness of the resurrection,	For in that hour the side of Christ was pierced and blood and water flowed out. And then the rest of the day, being bright, he brought to the evening. And for this reason you, as you begin another day, make the likeness of the resurrection;
10 Pray also before your body rests on the bed.	Pray also before you lie (ἀναπαύειν) on the bed in your bedroom.	pray before you rest your body on your bed.	pray before you give rest to your body in your bed.
11 And rising about midnight, wash your hands with water and pray. And if your wife is also present, pray both together;	And when you arise in the middle of the night, wash yourself and pray. And (δέ) you shall wash yourself in water that is pure. And (δέ) if you have a wife, then pray with each other at one time.	If you get up at midnight, wash your hands with water and pray, and if you have a wife, pray together.	And at midnight pray, when you have risen and washed your hands in water. And if you have a wife, the two of you pray.
12 but if she is not yet a believer, withdrawing into another room, pray and return again to your bed.	But (δέ) if she is not yet a believer (πιστή), then withdraw (ἀναχωρεῖν) yourself to a place and pray alone, and return to your place again.	And if she is not yet a believer, go apart and pray alone and then return to your place once again.	And if she is not yet a believer, separate and pray by yourself and return again to your bed.
13 And do not be lazy about praying. He who is bound in marriage is not defiled. For those who have washed do not have necessity to wash again, because they are clean.	And (δέ) you who are bound by marriage (γάμος), do not delay in praying. For (γάρ) you are not defiled. For (γάρ) those who washed have no need (χρεία) of washing again, because they are pure and they are clean (καθαρός).	You who are bound by marriage, do not be hindered from prayer, for you are not unclean. Those who have been baptized do not need to bathe again, for they are pure.	You who are bound by marriage are not to cease praying because you are pure and have not become unclean. Those who have been baptized do not want to be washed again because they are pure.
14 Through consignation with moist breath and catching your spittle in your hand, your body is sanctified down to your feet. For when it is offered with a believing heart, just as from the font, the gift of	But (δέ) when you breathe on your hand and seal (σφραγίζειν) yourself with the spittle that you will bring up from your mouth, you are purified down to your feet. For (γάρ) this is the gift (δῶρον) of the Holy	If you breathe into your hands and sign yourself with the saliva that comes out of your mouth, the whole of you is pure [down] to your feet. This is the Holy Spirit, and drops of the baptismal water rise	And if you breathe on your hands and sign yourself with the saliva that comes from your mouth, you will become pure as far as your feet which is a gift from the Holy Spirit. And the drop of water of baptism ascends

Apostolic Constitutions	Canons of Hippolytus	Testamentum Domini
[34.5] And the ninth because all things were shaken by the crucifixion of the Lord, trembling at the daring of the impious Jews, not bearing the violation of the Lord.	At the ninth hour again they are to pray, because Christ prayed and surrendered his spirit into the hands of his Father at that time.	At the ninth hour also let prayer be protracted, as with a hymn of praise that is like to the souls of those who give praise to God who does not lie, as one who has remembered his saints, and has sent his Word and Wisdom to enlighten them. For in that hour life was opened to the faithful, and blood and water were shed from the side of our Lord.
	Again at the time when the sun sets they are to pray, because it is the end of the day. Again when one lights the lamps in the evening they are to pray, because David said, "In the night I meditate."	But at evening, when it is the beginning of another day, showing an image of the resurrection, he has caused us to give praise.
	Again in the middle of the night they are to pray, because David also did that, and Paul and Silas, the servants of Christ, prayed in the middle of the night and praised God.	But at midnight let them arise, praising and lauding because of the resurrection.
	[27 continued] The Christian is to wash his hands each time he prays. He who is bound by marriage, even he rises from beside his wife, he is to pray, because marriage is not impure and there is no need of a bath after the second birth, except for the washing of the hands only, because the Holy Spirit marks the body of the believer and purifies him completely.	But at dawn [let them arise], praising with psalms, because after he rose he glorified the Father while they were singing psalms. But if any have a consort or wife [not] faithful, let the husband who is faithful go and pray at these times without fail.

	Latin	Sahidic	Arabic	Ethiopic

the Spirit and the sprinkling of washing sanctifies him who believes.

Spirit ($\pi\nu\epsilon\hat{\upsilon}\mu\alpha$). And the drops of water are those of baptism ($\beta\acute{\alpha}\pi\tau\iota\sigma\mu\alpha$) coming up from a fountain ($\pi\eta\gamma\acute{\eta}$) that is in the heart of the faithful ($\pi\iota\sigma\tau\acute{o}\varsigma$) that purifies him who believes ($\pi\iota\sigma\tau\epsilon\acute{\upsilon}\epsilon\iota\nu$).

up from the spring, which is the heart of the believers, and purify those who believe.

from the fountain that is the heart of believers; it purifies the heart of believers.

15 Therefore it is necessary to pray at this hour. For the elders who handed [it] on to us taught us thus, because at this hour all creation is still for a moment, so that they may praise the Lord: stars and trees and waters stop for an instant, and all the host of angels [that] ministers to him praises God at this hour together with the souls of the righteous.

And ($\delta\acute{\epsilon}$) it is necessary ($\grave{\alpha}\nu\alpha\gamma\kappa\alpha\hat{\iota}o\nu$) that we pray at that hour. For moreover ($\kappa\alpha\grave{\iota}\,\gamma\acute{\alpha}\rho$) the presbyters ($\pi\rho\epsilon\sigma\beta\acute{\upsilon}\tau\epsilon\rho\varsigma$) themselves are the ones who gave this work to us, and they instructed us in this way, since from that hour all creation pauses, quietly blessing God. The stars and the trees and the waters act in the manner of those who attend. And all the host ($\sigma\tau\rho\alpha\tau\acute{\iota}\alpha$) of angels ($\check{\alpha}\gamma\gamma\epsilon\lambda o\varsigma$) worship ($\lambda\epsilon\iota\tau o\upsilon\rho\gamma\epsilon\hat{\iota}\nu$) with the souls ($\psi\upsilon\chi\acute{\eta}$) of the righteous ($\delta\acute{\iota}\kappa\alpha\iota o\varsigma$). They sing ($\acute{\upsilon}\mu\nu\epsilon\acute{\upsilon}\epsilon\iota\nu$) to God the Almighty ($\pi\alpha\nu\tau o\kappa\rho\acute{\alpha}\tau\omega\rho$) at that hour.

Prayer must be made at that hour because the elders delivered this to us. All the choirs of angels are worshiping and the souls of the just are praising God at that hour,

Then in this hour pray eagerly, because the elders, too, who transmitted [this] to us taught us in this way that in this hour all creation toils to praise God. The stars, the plants, and the waters stand for an hour, and all the armies of angels, as they serve in this hour with the souls of the just, praise God.

16 Therefore those who believe ought to take care to pray at this hour. Also bearing witness to this thing, the Lord says thus, "Behold, a shout was made about midnight of those saying, 'Behold, the bridegroom comes; rise to meet him.'" And he goes on, saying, "Therefore watch; for you do not know at what hour he comes."[c]

Because of this, it is proper for those who believe ($\pi\iota\sigma\tau\epsilon\acute{\upsilon}\epsilon\iota\nu$) to pray at that hour. And ($\delta\acute{\epsilon}$) the Lord also spoke of this, when he testified to this, saying, "At midnight, behold, there was a voice, 'Behold, the bridegroom has come. Come out to meet him.'" And he interpreted the word further, saying, "Because of this, stay awake, because you do not know the day or ($o\grave{\upsilon}\delta\acute{\epsilon}$) the hour when the Son of Man comes."[c]

and for this reason the believers should pray at that hour. The Lord also said that at midnight the cry went up, "The bridegroom has come. Go out and meet him." And again he said, "Watch, for you do not know the day or the hour in which he is coming."[c]

For this reason it is proper for those who believe to be eager to pray this hour. The Lord, being then a witness to this, said this: "Then there was a cry at midnight, saying: 'The bridegroom has now come; rise to meet [him].'" And he says [it] again, saying: "Watch, because you do not know at what hour he will come."[c]

17 And rising about cockcrow, likewise. For at that hour, when the cock crew, the sons of Israel denied Christ, whom we know by faith, looking toward this day in the hope of eternal light at the resurrection of the dead.

Likewise ($\acute{o}\mu o\acute{\iota}\omega\varsigma$), when you arise at the hour when the cock ($\grave{\alpha}\lambda\acute{\epsilon}\kappa\tau\omega\rho$) will crow, pray, because it was at that hour the children of Israel denied ($\grave{\alpha}\rho\nu\epsilon\hat{\iota}\sigma\vartheta\alpha\iota$) Christ ($X\rho\iota\sigma\tau\acute{o}\varsigma$), this one whom we have known, we who believe ($\pi\iota\sigma\tau\epsilon\acute{\upsilon}\epsilon\iota\nu$) in him, through faith ($\pi\acute{\iota}\sigma\tau\iota\varsigma$)

When you get up when the cock crows, pray, for the children of Israel denied Christ at cockcrow. We have known him by faith, watching in hope for that day of everlasting light that will enlighten us at the resurrection of the dead.

And when the cock crows, when you have risen, pray in this way because in that hour—cockcrow—the children of Israel denied our Lord Christ whom we have known by faith, to trust the eternal light, as we hope for the day of the resurrection of the dead.

[c] Matt 25:6, 13.

200

Apostolic Constitutions	*Canons of Hippolytus*	*Testamentum Domini*
	Every one is to be concerned to pray with great vigilance in the middle of the night, because our fathers have said that at that hour all creation gives itself over to glorify God, all the ranks of angels and the souls of the righteous blessing God.	Let those who are chaste not lessen [them]. For the adornments of heaven give praise, the lights, the sun, the moon, the stars, the lightnings, the thunders, the clouds, the angels, the archangels, the glories, the dominions, the whole [heavenly] army, the depths, the sea, the rivers, the wells, fire, dew, and all nature that produces rain. All the saints also give praise and all the souls of the righteous. These, then, who pray are numbered together in the remembrance of God.
	The Lord bears witness to this, saying, "In the middle of the night there will be a cry: Lo, the bridegroom has come; come out to meet him."	
	At the time when the cock crows, again it is a time when there are prayers in the churches, for the Lord says, "Watch, for you do not know at what time the master comes, in the evening, or in the middle of the night, or at cockcrow, or in the morning," that is to say that we must remember God at each hour. And when one is lying on his bed, he must pray to God in his heart.	[2.25] When you, the faithful, accomplish these things, teach and instruct one another, causing the catechumens to make progress, as loving every man; you do not perish, but will be in me and I will be among you. [This chapter continues in *Ap. Trad.* 36 above.]

Latin	Sahidic	Arabic	Ethiopic
	looking forward in hope (ἐλπίς) for the day of light eternal, which will shed light on us forever in the resurrection (ἀνάστασις) of the dead.		
18 And acting thus, all faithful ones, and making a remembrance of them and in turn teaching [them] and encouraging the catechumens, you will not be able to be tempted or to perish, when you always have Christ in remembrance.	And (δέ) these things, all of you faithful (πιστός), when you fulfill them and remember them, instructing each other and teaching the catechumens (κατηχούμενος) to do them, nothing will tempt (πειράζειν) you, nor (οὐδέ) will you ever fall, while remembering Christ (Χριστός) always.	If you fulfill this, believers, and remember and teach each other to do it, no one will tempt you and you will never fall and you will remember Christ constantly.	As then all you believers do this and remember one another, teach; and as you first build up the catechumens, do not be enticed and do not become lost as you always remember Christ.

Text

Chapter 41.1–8a is missing from the Latin version because of the lacuna, and 41.1–4 duplicates and expands chap. 35. Since it is virtually certain that this duplication did not appear in the earliest stratum of the text, scholars have proposed various solutions for the evolution and arrangement of the final chapters. We have set out our own resolution above in the Introduction (above, p. 16).[1]

The text of the chapter exhibits shifts in grammatical person and number that suggest multiple sources.[2] Furthermore, the horarium as described would appear to be idiosyncratic, including, for example, prayer at cockcrow, which is otherwise unattested in the third century, but omitting prayer at sunset, which is found in other second- and third-century horaria. We believe, therefore, that the original text of chap. 35 has undergone three stages of expansion to form chap. 41.

1. An horarium was attached, consisting of prayer at the third, sixth, and ninth hours, and at midnight. This horarium has the triple attestation of the oriental versions, *Canons of Hippolytus*, and *Testamentum Domini*. For parallels to it, see the excursus, pp. 213–15.

2. Prayers at bedtime and at cockcrow were added to the horarium. It is not clear whether one or both of these additions were made to the horarium before its inclusion in the *Apostolic Tradition* or were inserted by a later hand. Neither the *Canons of Hippolytus* nor the *Testamentum Domini* includes prayer at bedtime, but the *Canons of Hippolytus* does include prayer at cockcrow.

3. The morning prayer/catechetical instruction of chap. 35 was expanded with material from two other distinct sources to form 41.1–4.[3] While stage 2 necessarily came after stage 1, it is possible that stage 3, in whole or part, preceded stage 2 or even stage 1.

■ **1–4** The three sources here are:

(a) *Apostolic Tradition* 35 itself, which with minor discrepancies is reproduced as 41.1; the opening of 41.2; and the last sentence of 41.3. A notable change in the first paragraph of chap. 41 in a manuscript that had lost its concluding pages.

---

1   See also L. Edward Phillips, "Daily Prayer in the *Apostolic Tradition* of Hippolytus," *JTS* 40 (1989) 389–92.

2   See Metzger, "Enquêtes," 11.

3   This revises the proposal in Phillips, "Daily Prayer," 391, which suggested that chap. 35 represents the

Apostolic Constitutions	*Canons of Hippolytus*	*Testamentum Domini*
	Let us do that and instruct one another with the catechumens, in the service of God, and the demons will not be able to sadden us, if we remember Christ at each hour.	

Sahidic of 41.2 is the phrase "catechesis of the Word of God," which does not appear in the Arabic or Ethiopic, nor in the *Apostolic Constitutions*, which has "word of catechesis," and may retain the original reading.[4] The hand washing at rising in the morning is almost certainly an addition to the earliest version of this paragraph, since it is not found in chap. 35.

(b) The remainder of *Ap. Trad.* 41.2 and 41.4, which is characterized by verbs and pronouns in third-person singular, whereas source (a) prefers third-person plural (demonstrated most clearly in the Sahidic version of chap. 35). It should be noted here that the reference to "having prayed in the church" is an addition peculiar to the Sahidic version.

(c) *Ap. Trad.* 41.3 (with the exception of the last sentence), which is characterized by verbs and pronouns in the second-person singular.[5] In the Sahidic it also prefers the Coptic ⲤⲂⲰ, "to teach," over the Greek loan-word κατήχησις, "catechesis," used by source (b). It is

possible that the author/redactor is addressing Christians of lower social status in these passages and accordingly adopts a more condescending tone: "Let none of you be late . . ."; "You will be told what to do at home."[6]

■ **5–6** This section begins the horarium that is appended to *Apostolic Tradition* 35 to form chap. 41. The third and sixth hours do not appear in the Latin version because of the lacuna; but, since the Latin resumes in the middle of the ninth hour of prayer, it is reasonable to assume that the third and sixth hours were originally part of that text.[7] One should note that the oriental versions employ the grammatical second person, while the *Canons of Hippolytus* and *Testamentum Domini* maintain third-person pronouns. While the *Apostolic Constitutions* also includes a section concerning the hours of prayer that has some superficial similarities to the horarium in the *Apostolic*

---

4   Botte, *Tradition*, 89 n. 2. Cuming (*Hippolytus*, 29 n. 2) adopts the same reading.

5   The parallel material in the *Canons of Hippolytus* maintains the 3d person in several sentences where the oriental versions use 2d person. Since the *Canons of Hippolytus* does eventually shift to the second person, however, there is little reason to doubt

that the underlying text of the *Apostolic Tradition* is best represented by the oriental versions.

6   There is a similar shift in person in chaps. 28 and 38.

7   There would have been room in the missing pages of the Latin for this material.

Tradition, it employs quite different descriptions of the individual hours, which suggests that it is from a different source.[8]

■ **5** The reading of the Ethiopic, "pray three hour[s]," is clearly an error in translation. The phrase in the Sahidic, "bless God," which is reminiscent of the Jewish *birkat*, becomes in the Arabic "praise God" and in the Ethiopic "glorify God,"[9] probably in order to make it conform to a Christian pattern of prayer, as the blessing form is characteristic of Jewish prayer but not typical of Christian prayer.[10] This Jewish prayer form appears again in the Sahidic and Arabic versions at the ninth hour.

■ **6** The Sahidic notes that the shewbread was offered "at every hour"; the Arabic and Ethiopic state "at the third hour." There are no clear grounds to prefer one reading to the other.[11] According to Lev 24:5–9 and early Jewish evidence,[12] the shewbread was changed every Sabbath to maintain a "perpetual" offering, and there is no Jewish or Christian tradition that connects the shewbread to the third hour, or to the daily offering of the lamb. Therefore, either the Sahidic is "correcting" the text of *Apostolic Tradition* at this point to be more "biblical," or the Arabic and Ethiopic are correcting the text to be more relevant to the third hour. The Sahidic phrase containing the Greek loanword ἄλογος, here translated "senseless," is also obscure. Cuming translated it, "without reason,"[13] as did Botte, "sans raison."[14] Dix translated it as "dumb."[15]

■ **7** The reference in the Sahidic to the "unbelieving Jews" becomes "unbelievers" in the Arabic, while the Ethiopic appears to misconstrue the sentence as a reference to catechumens ("unbelievers" = not-yet believers, i.e., catechumens).[16] There is no other precedent linking the prayer of catechumens to the noon hour of prayer, and since the *Canons of Hippolytus* also keeps the reference to "the Jews," it is likely that the Sahidic preserves the best reading.

■ **8** The Sahidic, as at the third hour, uses the word ⲤⲘⲞⲨ, "blessing," though here in nominative form with the verb ⲈⲒⲢⲈ, "to make," in the phrase, "make a great prayer and a great blessing." In the Sahidic and Arabic, the great prayer and blessing are offered in order that the believer shall "*know* the way in which the soul of the righteous blesses God." The Ethiopic has "may join in glorifying with the soul of the righteous," and the *Testamentum Domini* reads "*like* the souls of those who praise God." Botte suggested that the reading of the *Testamentum Domini* may represent the original text.[17]

■ **11–16** This passage concerning prayer at midnight is the longest and most complex section of the horarium. There are some variations in the versions, with the Arabic exhibiting a tendency toward reduction, and the Sahidic appearing to include some additions to the original Greek text of the *Apostolic Tradition*. The *Testamentum Domini* moves some of the material concerning prayer at midnight to prayer at dawn. Generally, the Ethiopic is closer to the Sahidic than to the Arabic throughout.

■ **14** This section dealing with the consignation presents numerous difficulties. There is some confusion between the Latin and the oriental versions. Dix's translation

---

8   See Phillips, "Daily Prayer," 391–92; J. Michael Joncas, "Daily Prayer in the Apostolic Constitutions," *EphLit* 107 (1993) 113–35; Marcel Metzger, *Les Constitutions apostoliques* 2 (SC 329; Paris: Cerf, 1986) 85–86.

9   Note the use of Coptic ⲤⲘⲞⲨ, rather than the Greek loanword phrase ⲈⲦⲒ ⲈⲨⲖⲞⲄⲒⲀ, "to give a blessing," as in the Sahidic version at *Apostolic Tradition* 28.

10 See Bradshaw, *Daily Prayer*, 30–31.

11 Dix (*Apostolic Tradition*, 63 n. 3) and Botte (*Tradition*, 91 n. 2) preferred the reading of the Arabic and Ethiopic versions. Cuming (*Hippolytus*, 29 n. 3) preferred the reading of the Sahidic and suggested that the Arabic and Ethiopic translators "may have been misled by the context."

12 *M. Menaḥ.* 11.7–9; Josephus *Ant.* 3.10.7 §255.

13 Cuming, *Hippolytus*, 29.

14 Botte, *Tradition*, 91.

15 Dix, *Apostolic Tradition*, 63. He translated the phrase as an allusion to Isa 53:7, "like a sheep that before its shearers is silent."

16 So suggested Dix, *Apostolic Tradition*, 63 n. 4.

17 Botte commented, "The reading of S[ahidic] . . . makes no sense" (*Tradition*, 91 n. 5). He proposed that the Sahidic was corrupt here, and that the verb ⲈⲒⲘⲈ, "to know," should be ⲈⲒⲚⲈ, "to resemble." This would be the standard Coptic translation for the Greek ὅμοιος. However, ⲈⲒⲚⲈ takes a different object marker (Ⲛ), while the Sahidic uses the correct object marker (ⲉ) for ⲈⲒⲘⲈ here.

reverses the order of phrases in the Latin to conform somewhat to the reading in the oriental versions.[18] The translation of the Latin here supplies the pronoun "it" as the subject for the passive verb *offertur*. Cuming suggests that "it" is the "prayer" of the believer,[19] but this does not fit the passage well, since what is offered is explicitly connected to the "gift of the Spirit and the sprinkling of baptism." A better subject would be "consignation." The oriental versions have no parallel for *offertur*, but refer instead to the "gift of the Holy Spirit."[20] In the Latin version the offering is made "just as from the font" (*ex fonte*). For *fonte* Dix suggested the translation "fountain"[21] and Botte, "source."[22] "Fountain" is the word of choice for the Sahidic version as well.[23] According to the Latin version, the believer makes the sign with "moist breath" (*cum udo flatu*), after catching "spittle" in "your hand." The Latin word *spitum* is here abbreviated *spm*, which usually stands for *spiritum*. However, Botte notes that this confusion is not possible in Greek; thus the Sahidic must provide the correct translation, "spittle."[24] Dix's assertion that this paragraph in the oriental versions "is obviously badly translated" from the Greek text of the *Apostolic Tradition* may be overly harsh.[25] The oriental versions, most clearly the Sahidic, allude to John 4:14,[26] where Jesus is the living water that becomes in the believer "a spring gushing up to eternal life." In the Sahidic New Testament, John 4:14 reads: "[it] will be up from in him a spring of water."[27] In these passages from John, the Holy Spirit is within the believer and comes up from within the believer's heart (or belly).

In a similar way, the Sahidic version of *Ap. Trad.* 41.14 connects the water of saliva in moist breath with the Holy Spirit in the believer. Combined with the sign of the cross on the forehead, this moist breath sanctifies[28] the outside of the body. Given this allusion to John 4:14, the Sahidic version makes more sense than the muddled syntax of the Latin, which awkwardly links the consignation before prayer to the consignation at baptism.

■ **16** The biblical quotation of Matt 25:6 and 13 that concludes the section exhibits some interesting differences among the versions. Dix noted that the first "Behold," which is omitted in the Arabic, Ethiopic, and *Canons of Hippolytus*, does not appear in the Greek text of Matthew.[29] Generally, the Sahidic, the Ethiopic, and to a lesser extent the Arabic seem to be corrected to conform more closely to the biblical text. Thus the Latin version, corroborated in several places by the Arabic, would appear to represent the oldest form of the *Apostolic Tradition*. On the other hand, none of the versions matches the standard text of Matt 25:13: "Keep awake, therefore, for you know neither the day nor the hour." Variant readings of the Greek text of Matthew add the phrase, "in which the Son of Man is coming." This is the reading of the Sahidic version. The Arabic is close to the Sahidic, but omits the phrase "Son of Man." The Latin and the Ethiopic shorten the phrase even further and omit the word "day." The Latin and the Ethiopic are actually closer to Matt 24:42 (par. Mark 13:35), which reads "Keep awake, therefore, for you do not know on what day[30] your Lord is coming." Curiously, at this place

---

18 Dix translated: "For the gift of the Spirit and the sprinkling of the font, drawn from the heart . . . as from a fountain, purifies him who has believed" (*Apostolic Tradition*, 66).

19 Cuming, *Hippolytus*, 30. The Latin reads "believing heart" (*corde credente*), while the oriental versions read "heart of the faithful." Dix (*Apostolic Tradition*, 66 n. 11) suggested that the Latin here should read *credentis* rather than *credente*.

20 Does *offertur* equal the Greek loanword δῶρον, "gift," in the Sahidic? The next closest parallel would be the "coming up," ⲉⲩⲛⲏⲩ ⲉϩⲣⲁⲓ, of the "drops of baptismal water" from the "fountain."

21 Dix, *Apostolic Tradition*, 66.

22 Botte, *Tradition*, 95.

23 A Greek loanword, ⲡⲩⲅⲏ, more properly spelled ⲡⲏⲅⲏ, its phonological equivalent.

24 Botte, *Tradition*, 95 n. 1. So also Cuming, *Hippolytus*, 30. Dix disagreed and translated the abbreviation "spirit" (*Apostolic Tradition*, 66 n. 11).

25 Dix translated the Latin *lauacri* as "font," rather than "washing," as in the present translation. He proposed (*Apostolic Tradition*, 66 n. 11) that the Sahidic translator had substituted βάπτισμα for Greek λουτροῦ.

26 Cf. John 7:38.

27 ⲛⲁϣⲱⲡⲉ ϩⲣⲁⲓ ⲛ̄ϩⲏⲧϥ̄ ⲛ̄ⲟⲩⲡⲏⲅⲏ ⲙ̄ⲙⲟⲟⲩ.

28 Botte (*Tradition*, 95 n. 2) noted that Sahidic ⲧⲃ̄ⲃⲟ can translate Greek ἁγιάζω.

29 Dix, *Apostolic Tradition*, 67 n. 13. It does, however, appear in the Sahidic version of the Gospel of Matthew.

30 Some ancient texts of Matthew read "at what hour."

the Latin and Ethiopic are also similar to *Did.* 16.1: "Keep vigil over your life. Let your lamps not go out and let your loins not be weak but be ready, for you do not know the hour at which our Lord is coming." The *Canons of Hippolytus*, it would seem, understands this passage to be a reference to Mark 13:35, and cites the Mark passage as a warrant for prayer at cockcrow, rather than midnight. Therefore, the readings of the Latin, Ethiopic, and *Canons of Hippolytus* provide triple independent testimony to the Greek text of *Ap. Trad.* 41.16. Since the saying of Jesus quoted here does not conform to any standard text of Matt 25:13, but is similar to *Did.* 16.1, the reference itself may be quite early. The Sahidic and Arabic appear to expand and conform the text to Matt. 25:13.

■ **17** The text for the prayer at cockcrow exhibits various problems. Dix has observed that the Latin version "as it stands is meaningless"; the oriental versions "are defective and confused"; and *Canons of Hippolytus* 27 "is so much altered as to be useless."[31] The Latin omits the main verb ("pray"?) in the opening clause. The Sahidic exhibits some doubling and expansion of the paragraph.[32] Moreover, the reference to "this day" (Latin) or "the day" (Sahidic and Arabic) seems abrupt and out of context. The Ethiopic omits the reference altogether.[33]

■ **18** This conclusion to the chapter appears in all the versions as well as in the *Canons of Hippolytus* and *Testamentum Domini* with little variation. The first phrase of the Latin, *in hac itaque*, is difficult to translate, and continues from the previous paragraph without a period, though the witness of the oriental versions indicates that there should be one. Botte, following Hauler's Latin edition, proposed that the Latin should read *in ha(a)c*, and he placed a period before *itaque*.[34] Dix proposed that the *in* should be dropped from the Latin text as an error

from the previous sentence and wanted to correct the text to *Ha(e)c itaque*.[35] His translation of the Latin then conforms to the oriental versions, reading "these things."

Comment

■ **1** The phrase "wash their hands" is found in the oriental versions of *Ap. Trad.* 41.1 and in the parallel in the *Canons of Hippolytus*. It appears in *Apostolic Tradition* 35 only in the Ethiopic, where it would seem to be an attempt to harmonize with 41.1. The injunction to wash one's hands before praying after rising from sleep will appear again in the directions concerning prayer at midnight (see 41.11 below).

■ **2** The faithful offer their prayer at home, unless there is "catechesis," in which case they are to go to "that place," that is, the catechetical meetings described in *Apostolic Tradition* 18. The Sahidic version of source (b) contains directions for both catechesis and prayer, though the catechetical purpose is stressed, since, if there is no catechesis in the church, the believer is to take up a book and read at home. Apparently, this source addresses an audience of persons who will be able to read, although the text exhibits some discrepancy here, since the first reference to reading ("if he can read") implies there would be those who cannot. Furthermore, those who can read are under even more obligation ("especially") to attend the instructional meetings, since they would presumably be able to contribute to them (perhaps read for them?).[36]

Source (b) demonstrates similarity to *Apostolic Tradition* 39 in theme and language. In chap. 39 deacons and presbyters are to gather daily at the bishop's command to "inform" the laity, and to pray, which is comparable to

31 Dix, *Apostolic Tradition*, 67–68 n. 14. He proposed a reconstruction based on parallels that he found in Hippolytus's *Comm. on Dan.* 4.16, and emended the Latin to read: "daily awaiting in hope the appearing of the eternal light at the resurrection of the dead." See Dix, *Apostolic Tradition*, 85.

32 Botte, *Tradition*, 97 n. 3.

33 Dix (*Apostolic Tradition*, 67–68 n. 14; 85) proposed that the phrase should be adverbial, "daily."

34 Botte, *Tradition*, 96, n.

35 Dix, *Apostolic Tradition*, 68 n. 15.

36 While there is no way to establish with certainty the literacy rate in the early church, the number of readers would be low. Those who could read were expected to do so for those who could not. "In a community in which texts had a constitutive importance and only a few persons were literate, it was inevitable that those who were able to explicate texts would acquire authority for that reason alone" (Harry Y. Gamble, *Books and Readers in the Early Church* [New Haven: Yale Univ. Press, 1995] 9).

the direction here to gather to hear the instruction and to pray.[37] In both chapters, those with specific ministerial responsibilities (readers and teachers, deacons and presbyters) are to meet with the laity.

Here, and throughout the entire chapter, references to "the church" refer to a place where the community is to gather. *Apostolic Tradition* 39 suggests that this is not a fixed place but rather where the bishop commands them to go. *Ap. Trad.* 41.1–4 displays an increasing tendency to identify "church" with the place where the church meets, while the *Canons of Hippolytus* specifically connects the presence of the Spirit with the assembly, rather than the meeting place as such.

All the versions testify that this morning catechetical gathering enables the believer to withstand the "evil of the day." The Sahidic locates the protection from evil in the prayer of the believer; the Arabic locates it in the presence of God in the church, mediated through the "mouth of the teacher"; and the Ethiopic in the act of dwelling in the church (assembly?) itself.

■ **3** The "church" is identified as the place "in which they teach." While *Ap. Trad.* 41.2 states that God speaks through the teacher, here source (c) refers to the "Holy Spirit" as the source of teaching given through the teacher. The content of the instruction is ethical rather than doctrinal: the believers are told what is "proper" for them to do at "your house," that is, when not in the gathered community. This source (c) material fits well with the description of the catechetical meetings of *Apostolic Tradition* 18–20.

■ **4** This paragraph, from source (b), again refers to those who can read. The concluding sentence expects "each one" to be able to "take a holy book and read in it," therefore assuming that the audience will have "holy books" to use at home. This may indicate an extraordinarily high social status for the intended audience, who are literate and wealthy enough to own books. The Ethiopic modifies the last sentence to indicate that everyone is to "read as well as he can," possibly recogniz-

ing the problem with the presumption of literacy.

■ **5–6** With the beginning of the horarium, the emphasis turns to private prayer. At the third hour, the Christian is to pray and bless (Sahidic) God either at home (aloud?) or if at any other place, presumably at work, then silently. For each separate hour of prayer in the horarium, *Apostolic Tradition* provides warrants, drawn from Scripture through quotation or allusion.[38] The first warrant for the third hour is the nailing of Christ to the cross, but this is expanded with references to the shewbread and the daily morning sacrifice of the Jerusalem temple, the shewbread being described as a "type of the body and the blood of Christ." The precise meaning of this, presumably biblical, allusion is difficult to determine. Then this double analogy is further extended with a confusing twist of the metaphor drawn from the Gospel of John, which describes Christ as the "shepherd" (John 10:11) and the "bread that came down from heaven" (John 6:41, 58). As neither of these Johannine passages alludes to the shewbread or the temple sacrifice, it is unclear what the *Apostolic Tradition* means to convey by placing them together.

Otherwise in the New Testament, Hebrews 9 employs a similar double analogy in a typological depiction of the temple, whereby Christ is both priest and sacrifice; but in Hebrews 9 the sacrifice mentioned is specifically the Yom Kippur sacrifice of a calf and goats. Hebrews 10:11–12 expands the typology to include the daily sacrifices, though again the christological referent is to Christ's single offering of himself. In this description of the temple, Heb 9:2 refers to the shewbread that was offered in the Holy Place, but without any specific christological significance, since the typology focuses on the Yom Kippur sacrifice and ritual, which took place only once a year.[39]

---

37 Origen (*Second Hom. on Num.* 3.1) instructs the laity of his community to spend at least one or two hours in prayer and Bible instruction at the church daily, though it appears that many of his congregation were negligent in this regard.

38 This provides another piece of evidence to distinguish the horarium from the morning prayer/gath-

erings of *Ap. Trad.* 35/41.1–4.

39 In a lecture given at the Catholic Theological Union, Chicago (Dec. 8, 1997), Lawrence Hoffman demonstrated that Jews, at least after the destruction of the temple, and perhaps even before the destruction, used matzo as a symbol for the Passover lamb in Passover celebrations when

Patristic references to the shewbread are few. Origen interprets the story of David eating the shewbread (1 Sam 21:1–6, which Jesus refers to in Mark 2:23–28 and par.) as a type of the Eucharist,[40] as does Eusebius of Caesarea.[41] In his commentary on the Hebrews passage above John Chrysostom makes no eucharistic connection, since, as he explains, the articles found in the Holy Place are symbols of the world, rather than symbols of divine realities.[42] Basil of Caesarea, on the other hand, contrasts the shewbread (which represents the doctrine of Apollinarius) with "the Bread which came down from heaven" (which represents orthodox Christology).[43] Basil connects the John 6 image, Christ as Bread of Heaven/ Manna, with the shewbread, as does the *Apostolic Tradition*, but in a less-than-favorable light.

In his treatise on the Lord's Prayer, Origen cites John 6:58 in his commentary on the clause, "Give us this day our daily bread." For Origen, this bread is the flesh and blood of the Word or Wisdom of God that nourishes the soul of the believer.[44] While Origen must surely have understood this in some way as a eucharistic reference, he does not bring out this aspect of the Johannine passage or the reference to daily bread in the Lord's Prayer. Perhaps the shewbread/body and blood imagery in *Apostolic Tradition*, together with the quotation of John 6:41 and 58, is an allusion to the Lord's Prayer, which may have been prayed at this (or every?) hour of prayer. In short, there is no Jewish or Christian tradition, apart from this reference in *Ap. Trad.* 41.6, that explicitly connects the shewbread to the third hour or to the daily offering of the lamb.

■ **7** Prayer at the sixth hour is warranted by the darkness that the Synoptic Gospels describe "coming over the whole land" during the crucifixion at the noon hour. The paragraph states further that this prayer is meant to imitate the "voice of the one who prayed and caused all creation to become dark." But who is the "one who prayed?" According to the Synoptic Gospels, Jesus cries out with a loud voice at the moment of his death, at the ninth hour, but they do not mention any specific words at noon. Therefore, even though the Ethiopic understands the reference to be to "Christ," that is not necessarily what was originally meant. The interpretation of the *Testamentum Domini*, "like to the prophets," may be correct, since even the Gospel writer Mark almost certainly had in mind any number of Old Testament prophetic passages in describing the darkness at noon.[45] The *Longer Rule* of Basil, in the description of the daily *cursus* of monastic prayer, also contains a curious parallel to this reference to prayer at the sixth hour: "And we judge prayer to be necessary at the sixth hour *in imitation of the saints* who say: 'Evening and morning and at noon I will speak and declare, and he shall hear my voice.'"[46]

The anti-Jewish polemic of the passage may seem thoroughly Christian, but is not necessarily. If "the one who prayed" were one of the prophets, then behind this reference could be an "intra-Jewish" polemic—the "believing Jews" against the "unbelieving Jews."[47] At any

ritually sacrificed lamb was not available. Thus Passover bread represented the Passover lamb. Does the author of the horarium have a similar symbolic substitution in mind (shewbread = Lamb)? For the treatment of the cult in Hebrews, see Harold W. Attridge, *Hebrews: A Commentary on the Epistle to the Hebrews* (Hermeneia; Minneapolis: Fortress Press, 1989) 230–43.

40 Origen *Comm. on 1 Cor.* 12 (Fragments published in *Journal of Biblical Literature* 9 [1908] 232–47). See also Origen (dub.) *Selecta in psalmos* (PG 12.1069.3).

41 Eusebius *Comm. on the Psalms* (PG 23.289.31).

42 John Chrysostom *In Epistolam ad Hebraeos* 15.

43 Basil *Ep.* 265.

44 Origen *De or.* 27.

45 Deut 28:29; Amos 8:9–10; Joel 2:1–2. See Raymond

E. Brown, *The Death of the Messiah* (2 vols.; New York: Doubleday, 1994) 2:1034ff. Tertullian (*Ad Judaeos* 13) cites Amos 8:9–10 and Cyprian (*Ad Quirinum* [*Test. lib.* III] 2.23) cites Amos and Jer 15:9 as OT testimonies to the darkness at the crucifixion.

46 ET from Taft, *Liturgy*, 85.

47 The Palestinian Talmud tractate *Sheqalim* (2:3 [III.B, C]) contains the following comment on the half-shekel temple tax: "R. Judah and R. Nehemiah: One said, 'Since they sinned [in the matter of the golden calf] at midday, [when the day was half over,] they give a half-sheqel.' The other said, 'Since they sinned at the sixth hour, let them give a half-sheqel, which is a sixth of a *garmasin* [coin].'" *Pesiqta de Rab Kahana* II.X.3.C–D (ET Jacob Neusner, *Pesiqta de Rab Kahana: An Analytical Translation* [2 vols.;

rate, whether or not there is a Jewish source for this material, this particular image of Christ's prayer on the cross bringing down the darkness on the unbelieving Jews has no exact parallel in other early Christian literature.

■ **8** The warrant for the ninth hour is the harrowing of hell—Christ going to the "soul[s] of the righteous" (the "spirits in prison" mentioned in 1 Pet 3:19) at the time of his death.[48] Christ "shines" on the "souls of the righteous" and likewise brings "light to the rest of the day."

■ **9** With regard to the phrase "water and blood," Botte proposed that the Latin version was not referring to John 19:34, which reads "blood and water," but to a variant reading of Matt 27:49, which reads "water and blood."[49] Note, however, that the oriental versions read "blood and water," as does the *Testamentum Domini.*

According to the Latin, Christ's "beginning to sleep" begins a new day, which is an image of the resurrection. Connolly pointed out that the concept that the day of crucifixion was divided into two days by the three hours of darkness "goes back to at least the third-century *Didascalia Apostolorum.*"[50] This division of the day of crucifixion may be the concept behind the beginning of the new day at the conclusion of darkness by Christ's death, in which the return of the light would be a type for the resurrection.[51] On the other hand, the connection may be to the Jewish reckoning of the day as beginning in the evening, signified by Christ's "beginning to sleep." This typology would connect the beginning of the Jewish day with Jesus' resurrection.

The Latin version, which often represents the best

reading, is very obscure here: Christ's going to sleep begins a new day as a type of resurrection. The Latin translator may have in mind the Matthean connection of the death of Jesus with the opening of the tombs and resurrection of the saints (Matt 27:52–53). The oriental versions have a different reading of the typology. The Sahidic ("when *you* go to sleep, [*you*] begin another day and make the type of the resurrection") shifts the reference from Christ's death/going to sleep to the believer's going to sleep as a type of resurrection, which is no less confusing than the Latin. This is further developed in the Arabic and Ethiopic by connecting the going to sleep with bedtime rather than the ninth hour. The *Testamentum Domini* is ambiguous, but would seem to suggest that God (or Christ) causes "us to give praise" [by] "showing [us] an image of the resurrection," rather than the believer's praise itself being an image of the resurrection. This is weak, but significant, support of the reading of the Latin, which also refers to Christ's resurrection.

■ **10** All the versions conclude this hour with a direction to pray before going to bed. The oriental versions are more explicit in connecting the prayer at bedtime to Christ's death and resurrection than is the Latin. The variations suggest that the source horarium used by the redactor of chap. 41 did not originally have a separate reference to prayer at bedtime. There is no evidence in second- or third-century sources for a separate hour of prayer at bedtime. Moreover, the reference is by far the shortest in the Latin and Sahidic, and there are no warrants given for it, unlike the other "hours" of prayer.

Brown Judaic Studies 122–23; Atlanta: Scholars Press, 1987] 1:29), a rabbinic discourse on the liturgical calendar, also includes this comment, as does *Pesiqta Rabbati* 10.12 (ET William G. Braude, *Pesikta Rabbati: Discourses for Feasts, Fasts, and Special Sabbaths* [2 vols.; Yale Judaica Series 18; New Haven: Yale Univ. Press, 1968] 1:189–90). For these and later attestations of the tradition, see Louis Ginzberg, *The Legends of the Jews* (7 vols.; Philadelphia: Jewish Publication Society of America, 1909–46) 6:62 n. 315.

48 In some Jewish literature of the Second Temple period, the phrase "souls of the righteous" refers to righteous persons who have died: see Wis 3:1; also Irenaeus *Haer.* 4.22. On 1 Pet 3:19 see Paul J. Achtemeier, *1 Peter: A Commentary on First Peter*

(Hermeneia: Minneapolis: Fortress Press, 1996) 254–58.

49 Botte, *Tradition*, 93 n. 1.

50 Connolly, *Egyptian Church Order*, 103–4. He refers to *Didasc.* 5.14: "He suffered, then, at the sixth hour on the Friday. And these hours during which our Lord was crucified were reckoned a day. And afterwards, again, there was darkness for three hours; and it was reckoned a night. And again, the three hours from the ninth hour until the evening were reckoned a day" (ET from Brock and Vasey, *Didascalia*, 26).

51 See *1 Clem.* 24.1–3: "Day and night reveal to us a resurrection. Night goes to sleep, the day rises."

Indeed, the Arabic and Ethiopic rectify this deficiency of warrant by moving the resurrection imagery of the ninth hour to bedtime prayer in order to make it a separate hour.[52]

The addition of bedtime prayer to the horarium is quite understandable, given the connection of Christ's death to sleep. Even though it must be in the Greek text underlying all the versions, it is significant that no trace of bedtime prayer appears in either the *Canons of Hippolytus* or *Testamentum Domini*, which substitute prayer at lamplight or evening. This suggests that bedtime prayer may not have been in the Greek text used by these church orders. It is also significant that there is no mention of a separate evening prayer in the Latin or oriental versions. Evening prayer is found in other second- and third-century witnesses to Christian daily prayer, and it was part of the Jewish pattern. Even the *Testamentum Domini*, which expands the horarium to include the evening hour, does not have an explicit direction to offer an evening prayer. Rather, at evening the *Testamentum Domini* states, "he *caused* us to give praise," a curious shift to the past tense from the injunctive. The *Canons of Hippolytus* shifts the warrant for the ninth hour to include prayer at sunset, and then further adds prayer at lamplighting, with reference to Ps 63:6.[53] But whereas the *Testamentum Domini* uses the imagery of evening as the beginning of the day as a sign of the resurrection in order to justify prayer at the evening hour, the *Canons of Hippolytus* merely says that one should pray because it is evening, with no further justification. Thus the similarity between these two church orders on evening prayer is rather superficial. Consequently, one must conclude that the Greek text of the horarium of *Apostolic Tradition* 41 did not have any reference to evening prayer as a separate hour.[54]

■ **11** The section begins with an admonition to "wash your hands and pray," which is similar to *Ap. Trad.* 41.1. There is ambiguity here, for *Ap. Trad.* 41.13 contradicts this direction: "For those who have washed do not have necessity to wash again, because they are clean."[55] Washing one's hands upon rising and before praying is a well-attested Jewish practice.[56] Clement of Alexandria notes, "It was a custom of the Jews to wash frequently after being in bed." Yet he appears to cite this practice as a contrast to Christian practice: "It was then well said, 'Be pure, not by washing of water, but in the mind.'"[57] Tertullian gives an even stronger argument against what he calls the "superstitious" practice of washing hands before prayer.[58] He is opposed to the practice of washing the hands as a matter of ritual cleanliness, since baptism has already cleansed the body of ritual defilement. Yet hand washing before prayer must be rather widespread among Christians since he has found it necessary to investigate the practice. It is curious that Tertullian does not indicate that this is a Jewish ritual, but rather a commemoration of Pilate's washing his hands at the trial of Jesus. If Tertullian had found a Jewish precedent, this would have been reason enough to discourage the practice, and verification of Jewish practices would surely have been simple enough to obtain. Perhaps the Jews in North Africa did not wash their hands before prayer.

■ **12** On the subject of husband and wife praying together, Tertullian observes that when both are believers, this can be a tremendous source of support for prayer. In Christian marriages there is "no stealthy signing, no trembling greeting, no mute benediction."[59] Origen dissents from this opinion: "For it must be considered whether it is a holy and pure thing to intercede with God in the place of intercourse. . . . For if it is not

---

52   This is a misunderstanding of the ninth hour as bedtime, as Connolly points out in *Egyptian Church Order*, 103.

53   The *Canons of Hippolytus* apparently construes evening and lamplighting as two separate times of prayer.

54   Taft's proposal (*Liturgy*, 24–25) that prayer at lamplighting in the description of the meal in *Apostolic Tradition* 25 functions as the daily evening prayer hour is problematic, as even he acknowledges.

55   Cf. John 13:10.

56   See *Letter of Aristeas* 304–6; Kaufmann Kohler,

"Ablutions," *Jewish Encyclopedia*, ed. Isidore Singer (12 vols.; New York: Funk and Wagnalls, 1901–6) 1:70.

57   Clement *Strom.* 4.22. ET from ANF 2:871.

58   Tertullian *De or.* 13.

59   Tertullian *Ad uxor.* 2.6; *De or.* 31.4.

possible to find time for prayer as one ought, 'except it be with consent for time' (1 Cor 7:5) that a man applies himself thereto, perhaps we ought to consider also whether (such a) place is suitable."[60] Tertullian was also aware of the problems that could arise in the course of devotional practices when both husband and wife were not believers.[61]

■ **13** This paragraph refers to John 13:10. The allusion to baptism in the Latin and Sahidic is made explicit in the Arabic and Ethiopic versions. The statement that those who are baptized do not need to perform an additional washing ritual is similar to Tertullian, but contradicts the earlier instruction in *Ap. Trad.* 41.11. The *Canons of Hippolytus* clarifies the text by adding, "there is no need of a bath after the second birth, *except for the washing of the hands only.*" The *Testamentum Domini* omits the reference to washing altogether at this place, though it does mention washing the hands when rising.

■ **14** Instead of washing, believers are instructed to sign themselves with moist breath, which is baptismal water. This passage is even more problematic when compared with the other description of the sign of the cross in *Apostolic Tradition*, contained in 42.2. Here the Latin text states that the use of spittle is *not* helpful: "For when the adversary sees the power which is from the heart . . . he will be routed by the [not spitting but breathing] mouth."[62]

Both Origen and Tertullian are familiar with the practice of making the sign of the cross.[63] Origen indicates that "this sign all the faithful make before beginning tasks, especially prayers or holy readings."[64] Tertullian

indicates that the sign of the cross is to be made frequently: "At every forward step and movement, at every going in and out, when we put on our clothes and shoes, when we bathe, when we sit at table, when we light the lamps, on couch, on seat, in all the ordinary actions of daily life, we trace upon the forehead the sign."[65] He also mentions making of the sign of the cross during prayers at night. Commenting on the problems a Christian woman might have with an unbelieving husband, he states: "Shall you escape notice when you sign your bed, (or) your body; when you blow away some impurity; when even by night you rise to pray? will you not be thought to be engaged in some work of magic?"[66] Note here that Tertullian refers not only to making of the sign of the cross, but also to "blowing away some impurity," which would seem to be quite close to the practice here in *Ap. Trad.* 41.14 of signing oneself with moist breath.

The action described by *Ap. Trad.* 41.14, therefore, would not appear to be idiosyncratic. Yet the signing with moist breath is proposed as an *alternative* to washing the hands, and it is given as an example of why the believer does not need to wash again. It does not seem likely in this context that *both* the instruction to wash one's hands *and* the instruction to avoid this practice (but instead sign oneself with moist breath) could stand together in the underlying source for the horarium. But it is also unlikely that the disclaimer—"he who has washed has no need to wash again"—would have appeared in the text without the direction to "wash your hands and pray." The clarification inserted by the *Canons of Hippolytus* to the effect that this does not refer

60 Origen *De or.* 31.4, ET from Eric George Jay, *Origen's Treatise on Prayer* (London: SPCK, 1954) 212–13.
61 Tertullian *Ad uxor.* 2.4.
62 This latter reference, however, is almost certainly an addition to the text, since it is not found in the oriental versions, and it is very confused in the Latin. The regulations in the *Rule of Pachomius* attributed to Horsiesios (mid-4th century) have this curious prohibition regarding the sign of the cross: "At the beginning of our prayers let us sign ourselves with the seal of baptism. Let us make the sign of the Cross on our foreheads, as on the day of our baptism, as it is written in Ezekiel (9:4). *Let us not first lower our hand to our mouth or to our beard*, but let us raise it to our forehead, saying in our heart, 'we
have signed ourselves with the seal'" (ET from Armand Veilleux, *Pachomian Chronicle and Rules* [Pachomian Koinonia 2; Kalamazoo: Cistercian Publications, 1981] 199, emphasis added). On the other hand, it is possible that the *Canons of Hippolytus*, which does not include the signing with moist breath, better represents the Greek text of prayer at midnight.
63 See Gerardus Q. Reijners, *The Terminology of the Holy Cross in Early Christian Literature* (Graecitas christianorum primaeva 2; Nijmegen: Dekker & Van de Vegt, 1965) 148–87.
64 Origen *Selecta in Ezechielem* (*PG* 13.801).
65 Tertullian *De cor.* 3.
66 Tertullian *Ad uxor.* 2.5.

to the washing of hands before prayer underscores the problem.

■ **15** This paragraph endorses prayer at midnight by referring to a "tradition of the elders" that at midnight all creatures, including the angels, pause to give praise to God. Henry Chadwick has proposed a Jewish background for this "tradition of the elders," noting similarities between *Apostolic Tradition* and the *Testament of Adam*, a pseudepigraphal work that describes an horarium in which the orders of creation give praise to God at the various hours of the day and night.[67] The thematic similarity between the two horaria is slight. Chadwick noted that in the *Testament of Adam* at the "twelfth hour" the "hosts of heaven and the fiery orders are at rest."[68] The "twelfth hour," however, is not midnight, but six o'clock in the morning. At the sixth hour of the night, the text states that "it is necessary to be quiet and rest, because it [midnight] holds fear,"[69] which is quite different from the theme of praise in *Ap. Trad.* 41.15. The two texts share a similar angelology, but this angelology is common in Jewish and Christian writing of the period.[70] *Pereq Shirah*, a Jewish mystical text with strong parallels to the *Testament of Adam*, also describes the nightly praise of all creation along with the angels. Among the orders of creation that praise God, it includes seas, celestial bodies, and trees, and this praise is connected with the theme of the coming of the Lord. The most significant parallel, however, is the statement that "God at midnight goes to the *pious in paradise*."[71] Likewise, *Apostolic Tradition* notes that at midnight "stars and trees and waters" pause to acknowledge the praise of the heavenly hosts, "together with the *souls of the righteous*." *Pereq Shirah* is a medieval text, and, though its origins may go back to the fourth century, there cannot be any dependence of *Apostolic Tradition* on this particular treatise.

Nevertheless, we again find Jewish parallels in the horarium, which suggests that Chadwick is correct in positing a Jewish mystical source for prayer at midnight. It is likely that behind the "tradition of the elders" in *Apostolic Tradition* lie Jewish legends about the praise of God by the angels and all the orders of creation.[72]

■ **16** The concluding paragraph contains a biblical warrant for prayer at midnight, the parable of the wise and foolish virgins in Matt 25:1–13. We may note that the parable in Matthew calls for continuous prayer, rather than at midnight specifically. As a warrant for rising frequently to pray during the night, Clement cites Luke 12:35–37, which has the theme of watchfulness and is somewhat parallel to the Matthean parable of the virgins: "Be dressed for action and have your lamps lit."[73] Origen cites Ps 119:62: "But not even the time of night shall we rightly pass without such prayer, for David says, 'At midnight I rose to give thanks unto thee because of thy righteous judgements.'"[74] Cyprian cites the story of Anna (Luke 2:37), who prayed day and night in the temple.[75] The theme for the last two examples is continuous prayer, of which prayer at night is a chief instance. While the parable of the wise and foolish virgins is not used explicitly by other sources of the period as justification for prayer at midnight, *Ap. Trad.* 41.16 is thematically similar.

■ **17** The warrant for prayer at cockcrow is that at this hour "the sons of Israel denied Christ." The eschatological theme is utterly missing here, and so it would not appear to give support to looking "in hope" to the "resurrection of the dead," which is the theme of the second half of the sentence. It is obvious that the "day" here refers to the day of the Lord's coming. Moreover, the illustration is not an obvious reference to the Passion accounts in the canonical Gospels. There, of course, it is

67 Henry Chadwick, "Prayer at Midnight," in Jacques Fontaine and Charles Kannengiesser, eds., *Epektasis: Mélanges patristiques offerts au cardinal Jean Daniélou* (Paris: Beauchesne, 1972) 47–49.

68 See the critical edition of Stephen E. Robinson, *The Testament of Adam* (Society of Biblical Literature Dissertation Series 52; Chico, Calif.: Scholars Press, 1982) 57, 73, 95, 127.

69 Ibid., 121.

70 See, e.g., *Apocalypse of Paul* 11.

71 ET from Ginzberg, *Legends*, 1:44. For the critical edition, see Malachi Beit-Arié, "Pereq Shirah" (diss.,

Hebrew University, 1966).

72 For a possible Essene background for prayer during the night, see Bradshaw, "Prayer Morning, Noon, Evening, and Midnight—an Apostolic Custom?" *StLit* 13 (1979) 59–60.

73 Clement *Strom.* 2.9.

74 Origen *De or.* 12.2; ET from Jay, *Origen's Treatise on Prayer*, 115.

75 Cyprian *De dom. or.* 36.

Peter, rather than the "children of Israel" as such, who denies Christ at cockcrow. In addition to these problems, there is no mention of washing with water, even though the Christian would be rising from bed. This is odd, given the insistence in the rest of the chapter on washing the hands when rising from sleep at midnight and in the morning before going to the catechetical lectures.

These difficulties together confirm that prayer at cockcrow was not part of the earliest stratum of the horarium, and no second- or third-century source seems to know of prayer at this hour. It may be an invention of the Egyptian monastic tradition of the early fourth century, where it forms one of the two times of communal prayer.[76] This tradition could have influenced the *Canons of Hippolytus,* where cockcrow is not an hour of private prayer but a gathering in the church.

■ **18** This paragraph is a generic summary admonition to obey the preceding instructions and to teach them to the catechumens. The grammatical person and number in the horarium have typically been second-person singular, but here the number shifts to the second-person plural. There is a similar shift at the conclusion of the baptismal material in *Apostolic Tradition* 21, and also in the chapter which concludes the whole document, *Apostolic Tradition* 43. Coming as it does before the duplicate concluding chaps. 42 and 43, one may consider whether the "things" that the faithful are admonished to do and teach refer only to the daily prayer instructions or instead are meant to include all the various instructions contained in chaps. 22–41.

The reference to the catechumens is somewhat surprising since they are not explicitly mentioned elsewhere in the horarium, except for the sixth hour in the Ethiopic version. The duplicate material of chap. 35 and 41.1–4 does contain the mandate to attend the daily *catechetical* lectures where catechumens would necessarily be present. Yet the instructions concerning prayer at midnight are explicitly baptismal and could not apply to

catechumens,[77] and even the eucharistic imagery of the third hour might seem somewhat inappropriate for the catechumens. Perhaps both the change in grammatical number and the reference to the catechumens indicate that this concluding paragraph is an editorial addition to the horarium made at the time when it was attached to the text of *Ap. Trad.* 41.1–4.

Excursus: Parallels to the Hours of Daily Prayer in the Second and Third Centuries

Behind *Apostolic Tradition* 41 is an horarium that had prayer for the third, sixth, and ninth hours and at midnight, but that contained no explicit reference to prayer on rising or prayer at sunset. Was this primitive horarium a complete *cursus* of daily prayer, or was it somehow truncated or otherwise defective?

The conventional theory, most thoroughly set out by Clifford W. Dugmore,[78] is that the earliest Christian horarium consisted of morning and evening prayer taken from the synagogue, to which the church in the late second century added prayer at the third, sixth, and ninth hours. This view was challenged by Joan Hezelden Walker, who argued, with reference to the injunction to say the Lord's Prayer three times a day in *Did.* 8.3, that prayer at the third, sixth, and ninth hours formed the earliest Christian horarium.[79] She cited *Apostolic Tradition* 41 to suggest that the origin of these hours was the Markan chronology of the crucifixion. Paul Bradshaw offered a third reading of the early evidence, especially that from Alexandria, to suggest that the earliest daily prayer pattern was morning, noon, evening, and during the night, but allowing that Walker was correct in identifying the Markan crucifixion narrative as a source for the "secondary" hours.[80] He subsequently modified his position in the light of Edward Phillips's examination of the development of *Apostolic Tradition* 41.[81] He proposed that while for some early Christian communities the three times of daily prayer may have been morning, noon, and evening, for others they may well have been the third, sixth, and ninth hours instead, and that these two parallel traditions eventually coalesced to form the fivefold pattern of prayer in the morning, at the third, sixth (= noon), and ninth

---

76 Taft (*Liturgy,* 201–2) proposes that prayer at cockcrow functioned as a parallel to morning prayer in the 4th-century cathedral office. Both were the offices of prayer after rising; monks simply got up earlier than the laity.

77 Even if the reference to making the sign of the cross is a later addition to the text, as suggested above,

the references to washing are clearly baptismal in character.

78 Dugmore, *Influence,* 10, 47, 70, 112.

79 Joan Hezelden Walker, "Terce, Sext, and None, an Apostolic Custom?" *StPatr* 5 (1962) 206–12.

80 Bradshaw, *Daily Prayer,* 47–49, 61–62.

81 Phillips, "Daily Prayer."

hours, and in the evening (together with prayer in the night) found in some third-century sources.[82]

The evidence for daily prayer in the pre-Constantinian church is quite clear, but open to various interpretations. Clement of Alexandria, around 200 CE, notes the same three day hours as *Apostolic Tradition* 41, but connects them with the Trinity.[83] He also mentions prayer at various other times of the day for the especially pious, including on rising in the morning, at noon, at mealtimes, before bed, and during the night;[84] but it is significant that the only specific hours given by Clement as those practiced by the typical Christian are the third, sixth, and ninth.

Origen likewise states that prayer must be made at least three times each day, citing the practice of Daniel (Dan 6:10). He gives no scriptural warrant for the first time of daily prayer but connects the middle of the three times to Peter's prayer on the roof at noon in Acts 10:9, and the last of the day hours to the "evening sacrifice" of Ps 141:2.[85] Dugmore[86] and Walker[87] proposed that since Origen explicitly connected the middle time of prayer to the sixth hour, he must have intended the other two times of prayer to be the third and ninth hours. Bradshaw thought that because Origen connected the last of the hours to the evening sacrifice, he must have intended this to be evening prayer, and therefore the other times would have been morning and noon. As Origen went on to counsel prayer even in the middle of the night, Bradshaw concluded that the complete pattern of prayer in Origen was morning, noon, evening, and midnight.[88]

On the other hand, Tertullian states that the "regular" prayers "are due, without any admonition, on the entrance of light and of night," that is, morning and evening.[89] He exerts considerably more effort defending the observance of prayer at the third, sixth, and ninth hours, which he notes "mark the intervals of the day"[90] and have scriptural precedents in Daniel and in Acts (2:1–4; 10:9; 3:1), even if they are not mandated. In *De ieiun*. 10 Tertullian again cites the scriptural precedents, but observes that the

Montanists honor the ninth hour as the hour of Christ's death. He also adds prayer in the night to these five times of prayer during the day.

In the mid-third century, Cyprian similarly connected the prayers of Daniel to the third, sixth, and ninth hours, cited the passages from Acts as warrants for the third and sixth hours, and linked the ninth hour to the crucifixion.[91] For Cyprian, these hours constituted the "old sacraments" (i.e., OT or Jewish practice), but they were also the times observed by the apostolic church. The new, and specifically Christian, times of prayer he thought were morning, as a commemoration of the resurrection, and sunset, to honor Christ as the "true sun and true day." To this he added a reference to prayer during the night.[92]

To summarize: Origen, Tertullian, and Cyprian all employ Dan 6:10 as a biblical precedent for prayer during the day. Tertullian and Cyprian specifically link Daniel's prayers with the third, sixth, and ninth hours. Clement does not cite Daniel, but he does indicate that the third, sixth, and ninth hours were the standard hours of prayer for the day. Origen connects the middle of Daniel's prayers with the sixth hour. As noted above, Bradshaw originally argued that the last time of day prayer for Origen must be the evening because Origen cites Ps 141:2, "Let my prayers rise like incense, my hands like the evening sacrifice." Yet Josephus records that in the first century the evening sacrifice was held at the *ninth hour* of the day, rather than later in the evening.[93] Origen was acquainted with the works of Josephus and so may well have known that the hour of the evening sacrifice was three o'clock in the afternoon. Hence Walker may have been correct in her suggestion that *Did.* 8.3 (the instruction to pray the Lord's Prayer three times each day) was evidence for an apostolic pattern of prayer at the third, sixth, and ninth hours of the day.

If, however, the core pattern for the horarium in *Apostolic Tradition* 41 is similarly prayer at the third, sixth, and ninth hours, and at midnight, what is striking about it is the particular use of biblical warrants for the times of prayer. We find no hint of Dan 6:10,

---

82 See Bradshaw, *Search*, 190–91.
83 Clement *Strom*. 7.7.
84 Clement *Strom*. 2.23; 7.7; 7.12; *Paed*. 2.4; 2.9.
85 Origen *De or*. 12.2.
86 Dugmore, *Influence*, 67–68.
87 Walker, "Terce," 209.
88 Bradshaw, *Daily Prayer*, 48–49, 62–64.
89 *De or*. 25.
90 Dugmore saw here a Roman civil custom in the public proclamation of these important hours of the day. Walker, however, convincingly demonstrated that this was not a widespread Roman custom and

so could not have served as a grounds for the Christian practice of the third, sixth, and ninth hours.
91 *De dom. or*. 34–35.
92 Ibid., 36.
93 Josephus *Ant*. 14.4.3 §65.

nor are there any references to the obvious hours of prayer mentioned in Acts. The controlling symbol for the day hours is the Markan chronology of the crucifixion, although none of the other early Christian authors uses this typology.[94] Yet even more idiosyncratic are the additional warrants for the day hours of prayer: the shewbread, the "voice of the one who prayed," and the sleep/death of Christ as beginning a new day as a type of the resurrection. Prayer at midnight, too, is given strong Jewish associations, and the references to a prayer of "blessing" rather than "thanksgiving" at the third and ninth hours points in the same direction. With so many more obvious biblical examples available and in actual use in third-century Christian texts, the community from which this particular horarium originates appears either to represent a very early stage in the history of the church, when the influence of its Jewish roots was still felt, or else is a later one that was outside the mainstream of Christian practice.

94 Tertullian suggests that the ninth hour among the Montanists was warranted in the death of Christ, but he does not follow the entire typology for prayer at the third and sixth hours.

42

	Latin (80.14–29)	Sahidic	Arabic	Ethiopic
1	And always imitate to sign your forehead with reverence. For this sign of the Passion is clear and approved against the devil, if you do so with faith, not so that you may be seen by human beings but through knowledge presenting [it] like a shield.	And (δέ) make proof (πεῖρα) every hour of sealing (σφραγίζειν) your forehead respectfully. For (γάρ) this is the sign that is known and manifest; by this the devil (διάβολος) is destroyed; if you make it faithfully (–πίστις), it is not before men you reveal yourself only, but (ἀλλά) in the knowledge that you have accepted as a shield (θύρεον).	Sign your forehead at all times in fear. This is the pure and known symbol through which the devil is destroyed. If we do this in faith, not only do we declare it publicly, but knowing that it gives you strength like armor;	And always be eager to sign your forehead, because this sign of the Passion is then against the familiar Satan; and let it show whether you have acted in faith, not that which is evident to people alone, but you know that you put on the breastplate.
2	For when the adversary sees the power that is from the heart, so that a human may reveal the likeness of the Word clearly displayed, he will be routed by the not spitting but breathing mouth.	Since (ἐπειδή) the adversary (ἀντικείμενος), the devil (διάβολος), sees (θεω-ρεῖν) the power of the heart exceedingly. If he sees the man that is within, that he is sensible (λογι-κός), sealed (σφραγίζειν) within and without in the seal (σφραγίς) of the Word (λόγος) of God, he flees at that hour, being pursued by the Holy Spirit (πνεῦμα), which is in the man who gives opportunity for him in him.	for the deceiver looks only at the strength of the heart, and if he sees that the inner man is rational and that he is signed both inwardly and outwardly by the sign of the word, he flees and hastens to retreat from the Holy Spirit who is in the man who makes a place for him within himself.	And the one who opposes, when he sees the strength of a rational, inner man that is in the heart—that he has signed himself inwardly and outwardly by the sign of the Word—then he trembles and flees quickly behind the Holy Spirit. This is the one who is in a person, who has made a dwelling place with him.
3	Moses, displaying this with the sheep of the Passover that was sacrificed, sprinkled the blood on the threshold and anointed the posts [and] denoted that faith which is now in us, which is in the perfect Sheep.	This also is what Moses the prophet (προφήτης) already taught us in the Pascha (πάσχα) with the sheep that was pierced. He commanded all of them to smear the blood on the lintel with the two doorposts, telling us about the faith (πίστις) that is in us now, which was given to us by the perfect (τέλειον) Sheep.	This is what Moses first taught us through the paschal lamb that he sacrificed and ordered its blood to be smeared on the doorposts and the lintels to teach us the faith that resides in us now, which was given us by the perfect Lamb.	This is what Moses earlier taught us through the lamb in the Pascha that was slaughtered, and he commanded that its blood be smeared on the lintel of the door and the doorposts. The smearing, then, made known what we now have, the faith that has dwelt upon us, that he has given to us in the perfect Lamb.
4	And signing the forehead and eyes with the hand, let us escape him who is trying to destroy us.	By this, when we seal (σφραγίζειν) our foreheads with our hand, we will shake off those who want to kill us.	When we sign our foreheads with this [?sign] with our hands, we are saved from the one who would kill us.	If in this we sign the forehead with the hand, then we will be saved from those who want to kill us.

Apostolic Constitutions	Canons of Hippolytus 29	Testamentum Domini
	. . . Be pure at all times and mark your forehead with the sign of the cross, being victorious over Satan and glorifying in your faith. Moses did that with the blood of the lamb with which he smeared the lintels and the two door-posts, and it healed whoever lived there. How should the blood of Christ not purify more and protect more those who believe in him and manifest the sign of the salvation that is for all the world, which has been healed by the blood of the perfect Lamb, Christ?	

42

[Concerning the Sign of the Cross]

Text

The Latin has a duplicate of this material following chap. 38, numbered as 38B in our edition. As explained in the Introduction (above, p. 16), this appears to be the result of an attempt to conflate a longer and a shorter version of the text of the *Apostolic Tradition*. The two Latin texts exhibit some variation from each other, and both of them differ significantly from the oriental versions, with the result that it is not easy to reconstruct the underlying text of this chapter.[1]

Connolly thought that the duplicate already appeared in the Greek text used by the Latin translator,[2] but Hanssens suggested that the duplication of the chapters resulted from an error by the copyist who produced a manuscript that later became the Verona palimpsest.[3] Botte argued that the similarities between the two Latin chapters (excluding pronouns and particles, they have numerous words in common) indicated that they were "simply two different states of the same text."[4] Based on a comparison of the Latin texts with the oriental versions, he proposed that the Latin of chap. 42 represented the earliest form.[5] On the contrary, however, the similarity of the Latin of chap. 42 to the Sahidic is to be explained on the basis that both of them belong to the same later stage of the evolution of the text, and hence it is the Latin of 38B that reflects an older version.

■ **1** The opening phrase of this chapter is confused in all the versions. The Latin of chap. 38B, "Always try (*semper tempta*) to sign your forehead," seems excessively banal. The Latin of chap. 42, "And always imitate (*semper autem imitare*)," makes even less sense.[6] Botte noted that the word *imitare* is only partly visible in the palimpsest, and suggested that it was a corruption of *temptare*,[7] which would make it closer to chap. 38B. This reading is also closer to the Sahidic, which has the Greek loanword in nominal form, πεῖρα, "proof,"[8] related to the verb πειράζειν, "to tempt" or "to try." Botte further suggested that the awkward word *semper*, "always," is a result of a corruption in the Greek text, reading ἀεί, "always," for εἰ, "if." The underlying Greek text could then be reconstructed: εἰ δὲ πειράζῃ, σὺν εὐλάβεια σφράγιζε, "If you are tempted, then reverently sign. . . ."[9]

The "sign of the passion" becomes in the Sahidic "the sign that is known and manifest," similar to the Arabic here. The Ethiopic and *Canons of Hippolytus* agree with the Latin. The sign is made "not so that you may be seen (*appareas*) by human beings" (Latin chap. 42) or "not to please (*placens*) human beings" (Latin chap. 38B). The oriental versions have a different sense: the sign is not made *only* to be seen by human beings. The Greek word in the Sahidic, ⲑⲎⲢⲰⲚ, an unusual spelling for θυρεός, "shield,"[10] becomes "breastplate [of righteousness?[11]]," in the Ethiopic and in the Latin of chap. 38B.

1   See Dix, *Apostolic Tradition*, 68 note; Hanssens, *Liturgie,* 163–64.

2   Connolly, *Egyptian Church Order*, 100, 145. He suggested that the differences in the two Latin translations of the chapter indicated differences in the Greek text.

3   Hanssens, *Liturgie,* 10, 68–69, and 165. He proposed that a translator for some reason made two copies of the ending, which a later copyist found and included in a manuscript of the *Apostolic Tradition*.

4   Bernard Botte, "Un passage difficile de la 'Tradition apostolique' sur le signe de croix," *RThAM* 27 (1960) 7.

5   Botte, *Tradition*, 99 n. 1. Hanssens (*Liturgie* 164–65) makes the same assertion. Dix (*Apostolic Tradition*, 86) notes several places where he thinks the Latin of *Ap. Trad.* 38B preserves the best reading. Elsewhere he confesses: "There is much confusion in the text of this chapter and I do not feel much confidence in any restoration as to the details" (ibid., 68 note).

6   Cuming (*Hippolytus*, 31) translates, "Always . . . observe," which is no better.

7   Botte, "Passage," 6 n. 1.

8   Hanssens noted that this is the only place where the Latin of chap. 38B is closer to the Sahidic than the Latin of chap. 42.

9   Botte ("Passage," 9) acknowledged that this was Dix's reconstruction of the text. See Dix, *Apostolic Tradition*, 68.

10   Dix, *Apostolic Tradition*, 69 n. 1.

11   Isa 59:17; Wis 5:18; Eph 6:14.

■ **2** Botte suggested that there was a small lacuna in the Latin of chap. 42 between the words *homo* ("human") and *similitudinem* ("likeness"); based on comparison with the Sahidic, he would insert the words *interior, qui est rationalis, interiorem*.[12] Botte further proposed that the word *deformatam,* found in both the Latin texts, corresponded to Greek ἐκτυποῦν, rather than to σφραγίζειν, which appears as a loanword in the Sahidic text at this point.[13]

The phrase "likeness of baptism" (*lauacri,* lit. "washing") becomes "likeness of the Word (of God)" in the Latin of *Apostolic Tradition* 42. Dix plausibly suggested this was a confusion of λουτροῦ for λόγου in the underlying Greek.[14]

The final phrase in the Latin versions is exceedingly odd. Hauler reconstructed the Latin as *infugiatur non sputante sed flante sp[irit]u i[n] te*. Tidner, on the other hand, reconstructed the final letters as: *[h]ore*.[15] Our translation follows Tidner's reconstruction. Botte, however, proposed an explanation of the text based on Hauler's reading, suggesting that the phrase *non sputante sed flante*, which does not have a parallel in the oriental versions, is an editorial gloss by the Latin redactor intending to explain the Latin abbreviation, *spu*. The redactor wanted to ensure that the reader knew that *spu* refers to *spiritu* ("breathing") rather than *sputante* ("spitting").[16] Thus Botte's reading would harmonize with the oriental versions: "he will be routed by the [not spitting but breathing] Spirit in you."[17] The parallel in the Latin of chap. 38B contains the word *cedente* (alternative spelling of *caedente*), "strike," rather than *sputante*: "not striking but breathing." Dix and Hanssens made the ingenious proposal that the confusion here results from the similarity of the Greek words πτύοντος, "spitting," and τύπτοντος, "striking."[18] This proposal, however, requires that the phrase in the Latin versions goes back to the Greek text, whereas Botte's hypothesis requires that the phrase originates as a gloss in the Latin translation.[19]

■ **3** Moses "sprinkled" (Latin versions) or "smeared" (oriental versions and *Canons of Hippolytus*) blood on the lintel and doorposts.[20] The Latin phrase translated as "that faith which is now in us, which is in the perfect Sheep" (*in perfecta oue*, singular!) is awkward. The Sahidic and Arabic clarify that the faith is given *by* (Sahidic, ϨΙΤΝ̅) "the perfect Sheep."

■ **4** The Latin versions have signing of the "forehead and eyes," while the oriental versions have only "forehead." Botte proposed that "eyes" was another gloss in the Latin.[21]

---

12 Botte, *Tradition*, 101 n. 1; idem, "Passage," 9–10. Cuming (*Hippolytus*, 31) translates: "as the inner man, who is rational, displays the inner likeness of the word outwardly formed." Botte's reconstruction of the Latin phrase would equal exactly one line in the manuscript, and could be explained as a copyist's error.

13 Botte pointed out that Coptic translators may substitute Greek loanwords for less familiar Greek expressions. See "Passage," 10–11; *Tradition*, 101 n. 2.

14 Dix, *Apostolic Tradition*, 69 n. 2.

15 Erik Tidner, *Didascaliae apostolorum Canonum ecclesiasticorum Traditionis apostolicae versiones Latinae* (TU 75; Berlin: Akademie, 1963) 149 nn. 23–24.

16 Botte, "Passage," 13–14; idem, *Tradition*, 101 n. 3. Misreading of such abbreviations was a common occurrence. Botte reconstructed the Greek text as: τροποῦται τῷ ἐν σοι πνεύματι.

17 Note that Botte claims this reading was inspired by the parallel in the Latin of *Ap. Trad.* 38B, which has the word *inspirante* rather than *flante*. Yet the connection of the making of the sign of the cross with spittle also appears in chap. 41 at prayer at midnight. See above, p. 211. Could this gloss be an attempt to clarify with respect to the earlier reference in *Ap. Trad.* 41.14?

18 Dix, *Apostolic Tradition*, 69 n. 2; Hanssens, *Liturgie*, 165.

19 Of course, Botte assumes that the Latin of *Ap. Trad.* 42 represents the earlier reading. On the other hand, perhaps the Latin editor "corrected" the translation here on the presumption that the underlying word πτύοντος had been misread as τύπτοντος.

20 Exod 12:7.

21 Botte, *Tradition*, 101 n. 4. See also Dix, *Apostolic Tradition*, 70 n. 4; Hanssens, *Liturgie*, 165.

Comment

■ 1 The reference to the Passion in the Latin and Ethiopic versions indicates that the "sign" is the sign of the cross.[22] The sign, made "against the devil" (Latin), is not to be (or not *merely*, in the oriental versions) a public display, but is to be made "with faith," "like a shield" according to the Latin and Sahidic of *Apostolic Tradition* 42. This phrase is an obvious allusion to Eph 6:16: "take the *shield of faith*, with which you will be able to quench all the flaming arrows of the evil one."

■ 2 As noted above, this paragraph is difficult to reconstruct. Botte's proposed emendation of the second phrase would give the sense that the sign of the cross makes visible before Satan the interior shield of faith, which Satan otherwise could not see. In the Latin of chap. 38B this sign is the likeness[23] of baptism, presumably the seal given by the bishop to the newly baptized in *Ap. Trad.* 21.23. Through this sign the devil is "routed" not by striking (or spitting),[24] but by breathing. The Sahidic (and parallels in the oriental versions) adds: "which is in the man who gives opportunity for him [the Spirit] in him."[25] This entire paragraph is similar to *Ap. Trad.* 41.14, where the seal (sign) is connected to breath, baptism (and spittle!), and to the Holy Spirit, which dwells in the heart of the believer.[26]

■ 3 The visible sign of the cross is analogous to the blood of the Passover lamb,[27] which Moses smeared (or sprinkled) on the threshold and doorposts of the homes of the Hebrews. Dix found a parallel to the reference to Moses' anointing the doorposts in a sermon attributed to John Chrysostom,[28] where this "anointing" was described as the "type of the unction of Confirmation." Dix also referred to a text by Origen, *Selecta in Exodum*, which interprets Moses' smearing of the blood as an anointing, and he suggested that Origen got the idea from Hippolytus, who invented the analogy.[29] The analogy appears much earlier, however, in Justin Martyr's *Dialogue with Trypho*: "The mystery, then, of the lamb which God enjoined to be sacrificed as the Passover, was a type of Christ; with whose blood, in proportion to their faith in Him, they anoint their houses, i.e., themselves, who believe on Him."[30] Consequently, there is no need to posit a connection of this passage to Hippolytus. Yet the baptismal typology here strengthens the case for the priority of the Latin of *Apostolic Tradition* 38B over 42, which has "likeness of the word" rather than "baptism," in 42.2.

■ 4 In the Latin and Arabic versions the sign of the cross enables the believer to escape from "him [the one] who is trying to destroy [kill] us." Presumably this refers to the devil of *Ap. Trad.* 42.1–2. The shift in the Sahidic and Ethiopic to the plural, "from *those* who want to kill us," harks back to *Ap. Trad.* 42.1, where the oriental versions differ from the Latin in recognizing the public nature of the sign of the cross.[31]

---

22 This is made explicit in the *Canons of Hippolytus*.

23 Does the Latin *similitudine* equal σφραγίς in the Sahidic? See J. Blanc, "Lexique comparé des versions de la *Tradition apostolique* de S. Hippolyte," *RThAM* 22 (1954) 184.

24 Accepting Dix's proposal about the confusion of πτύοντος for τύπτοντος.

25 Cf. 2 Cor 1:22. Botte ("Passage," 15–16) thought that the original Greek text (as the Latin version) did not refer to the indwelling Holy Spirit as such, but rather to the "power" that the Holy Spirit gives to the heart of the believer.

26 Cf. John 7:38–39. The Latin of *Ap. Trad.* 38B belongs to an earlier stage in the development of the text than the horarium of chap. 41. On the connection of spitting with the sign of the cross, see above, p. 211 n. 62.

27 Cf. "perfect Sheep" in *Ap. Trad.* 41.6.

28 The sermon, *In sanctum pascha*, is no longer attributed to John Chrysostom. See Pierre Nautin, ed., *Homélies pascales* 2 (SC 27 [1950]; SC 36 [1953]; SC 48 [1957]; Paris: Cerf) 26–30. See also Enrico Cattaneo, *Trois homélies pseudo-chrysostomiennes sur la Pâque comme oeuvre d'Apollinaire de Laodicée: attribution et étude theologique* (Theologie historique 58; Paris: Beauchesne, 1981).

29 Dix, *Apostolic Tradition*, 85–86. Dix believed that Origen was quoting an authentic sermon by Hippolytus, *On the Pascha*, though this sermon is now thought to be spurious.

30 Justin *Dial.* 40.1.1. ET from ANF 1:409.

31 It is not to be made before men "only." The Sahidic word ⲚⲞⲨϨⲈ, "shake off," is used in the Sahidic versions of Luke 9:5, "shake off the dust of your feet."

[Conclusion]

Text

The Latin version has a duplicate of this material in *Apostolic Tradition* 38B. Chapter 43 follows 42 without a title or break in all the versions. While the *Testamentum Domini* does not contain a parallel to chap. 42, it does contain a parallel to this material, which is a possible indication of a chapter break. Otherwise, the break is quite artificial.

■ **1** The Latin versions employ the grammatical third person, while the oriental versions and *Testamentum Domini* use the second person. The Latin in chap. 38B, *fide recta gloriosae* (translated above as "true orthodox faith"), is a mistranslation of the Greek.[1] The oriental versions more closely parallel the Latin of chap. 43.

■ **2** The Latin versions here employ the first-person singular. This is the only place in all the versions of the entire church order to use the first-person singular.[2] The oriental versions employ the first-person plural; however, since the singular has the double attestation of Latin 38B and Latin 43, it likely represents the earliest reading.[3] The Latin breaks at nearly the same point in both chap. 38B (*apos . . .*) and chap. 42 (*apostolicam tra . . .*). Both these breaks occur at the ends of lines at the bottom of pages in the Verona palimpsest. The Sahidic version suggests that the underlying Greek phrase was ἀποστολικὴ παράδοσις. The Sahidic reads "traditions" (plural); the other versions have the singular, "tradition" or "teaching." The Sahidic adds at the end, "or any man at all."

■ **3** The Ethiopic inserts a phrase clarifying "heretics," as those who "corrupted the teaching of the apostles."

■ **4** The Sahidic "beloved" becomes "brothers" in the Ethiopic. The oriental versions differ in the concluding phrase: Sahidic, "the church that is worthy . . ."; Arabic, "him who is worthy . . ."; Ethiopic, "holy church. . . ."[4] Dix suggests that the Sahidic has mistaken ἄξιαν, "worthy," for ἁγίαν, "holy," in which case the Ethiopic preserves the correct reading.[5] The Sahidic, ⲘⲞⲞⲚⲈ, "to moor," Botte takes to be authentic.[6]

Comment

■ **1–2** The concluding chapter has been used as an important piece of evidence in the identification of the work as the *Apostolic Tradition* of Hippolytus, as the concluding words in the Latin can be reconstructed as *apostolicam traditionem* through comparison with the Sahidic. Connolly noted that chap. 1 also contained references to "the gifts" and to "tradition." Thus he proposed that the phrase *apostolicam traditionem* at the conclusion of the church order was the title of the work of Hippolytus as listed on the base of the famous statue.[7] Even regardless of the problems surrounding the statue (see Introduction, p. 4), however, the notion that the phrase could be considered a title has come under attack. Metzger, for example, has remarked that the use of "tradition" as a title of liturgical canons would be unique.[8] Furthermore, Markschies has performed a careful analysis of the phrase in its literary context, which demonstrates the unlikelihood of it being the title of the work.[9] He notes that the Latin of chap. 43 begins with the words, *Haec itaque*, "And so, these things . . . ," which must refer to the preceding collection of canons. The parallel in the oriental versions confirms this. If this is the case, then *apostolicam traditionem* must be roughly synonymous with *haec*, but as a corroborating point that situates "these things" in the larger "tradition of the apostles," meaning "the sum of church tradition altogether." He observes that this is the usual meaning of

---

1   Horner, *Egyptian Church Order*, 145 n. 2.; Dix, *Apostolic Tradition*, 71 n. 1.; Botte, *Tradition*, 102 n.; Cuming, *Hippolytus*, 28 n. 3. This is evidence that the Latin of chap. 38B was (badly) translated from a Greek text.

2   See Metzger, "Enquêtes," 12.

3   So Connolly, *Egyptian Church Order*, 147.

4   The Arabic has the variant reading, "holy church" (MS. Bodleian 40, Huntington 458). See the collation of the Arabic text in Horner, *Statutes*, 426.

5   Dix, *Apostolic Tradition*, 72.

6   Botte, *Tradition*, 103 n. 3, though he would amend ⲘⲘⲞⲞⲚⲈ to ⲈⲘⲞⲞⲚⲈ. Note that the Sahidic version of Ps 106(107):30 has the phrase ϩⲚ̄ Ⲛ̄ⲘⲀ ⲘⲘⲞⲞⲚⲈ ⲈⲦⲈϩⲚⲀⲨ ("in the mooring places that they desired"), and it might be that the redundancy, ⲘⲘⲞⲞⲚⲈ, "mooring," and ⲖⲓⲘⲏⲛ, "harbor," is an added allusion in the Sahidic to that psalm verse.

7   Connolly, *Egyptian Church Order*, 145–46.

8   The typical titles are: "canon," "order," "constitutions," "teaching" (Metzger, "Nouvelles perspectives," 247).

9   Markschies, "Wer schrieb," 30–34.

43

Latin (80.30–35)	Sahidic	Arabic	Ethiopic
1 And so, if these things are received with thankfulness and true faith, they provide edification in the church and eternal life for believers.	And (δέ) when you receive these things thankfully with faith (πίστις) that is right, you will be edified, and you will be given (χαρίζεσθαι) eternal life.	If you do this with thanks and upright faith, you will be built up and eternal life will be given to you.	If you learn this with thanks and with the right faith, then you will be strong and he will give you eternal life.
2 I give instruction that these things be kept by all the wise. For to all who hear the apostolic tra . . .	These are the things that we counsel (συμβουλεύειν) you to keep, those who have a mind for them. For (γάρ) if everyone follows the traditions (παράδοσις) of the apostles (ἀπόστολος), these things that they heard and kept, no heretic (αἱρετικός) will be able to lead them astray (πλανᾶν), or (οὐδέ) any man at all. For (γάρ) in this way many heresies (αἵρεσις) in-	We admonish you who have hearts to keep these things. If all those who hear the teaching of the apostles keep it, none of them could be led astray by any heresy.	This is the decree for you that you may be preserved through it, you who have a heart, if you keep everything. The one who keeps the teaching of the apostles no heretics will hinder.
3	creased (αὐξάνειν) because those who are leaders (προϊστάναι) did not desire to learn the purpose (προαίρεσις) of the apostles (ἀπόστολος), but (ἀλλά) according to (κατά) their own lust (ἡδονή), they do things that they desire, not those things that are proper (πρέπειν).	The heresies increased greatly because those who received them were unwilling to learn the mind of the apostles, but followed only their own desires, doing what pleased them and not what was right.	They are the rebellious ones who have gone astray and have corrupted the teaching of the apostles, if people come from them. Thus the heretics become numerous because those who have heard them do not want to learn the command of the apostles but do only their will—whatever they have chosen, and [not] that which is proper.
4	If we omitted anything, our beloved, these things God will reveal to those who are worthy, steering (κυβερνᾶν) the church (ἐκκλησία) that is worthy of mooring in the tranquil harbor (λιμήν).	If we have omitted anything, God will reveal it to those who are worthy and guide the church for him who is worthy to a tranquil harbor. These are the canons of the church.	And if there is something that we have shortened, our brothers, may God reveal [it] to those who are worthy, as he pilots the holy church into the tranquillity of the harbor.

the term "apostolic tradition" in the second and third centuries, and further that, while one example of "the tradition of the apostles" does appear in a work sometimes attributed to Hippolytus, *Contra Noetum* 17.2, there it functions as a general description of church teaching as in other third-century authors, and certainly not as a title. Finally, while it is not uncommon for titles to appear at the ends of work in patristic manuscripts, these titles come at the very end, and not, as in chap. 43, in the middle of a concluding paragraph.

Connolly thought that the shift to first-person singu-

lar was evidence that "there is no sign of any apostolic pretence" on the part of the author, since he explicitly distinguishes his own direction from the "apostolic tradition." He also took this as evidence that the church order had a single author.[10] This stretches the evidence considerably.

■ **2–3** The concern is with heretics who may lead the faithful astray. It is impossible to discern specific "heresies" that the author may have in mind, though the problem seems to involve the practices of the heretics rather than belief as such: "they *do* things that they desire, not

---

10   Connolly, *Egyptian Church Order*, 145.

Apostolic Constitutions	*Canons of Hippolytus*	*Testamentum Domini* 2.25
		[Continued from *Ap. Trad.* 36 above] When you teach these things and keep [them], you will be saved, and evil heresy shall not prevail against you. Lo, then, I have taught you now all [things] that you desire; and those things [of] which I have spoken with you from the beginning, and have taught and commanded you before I should suffer, you know.

those things that are proper." This fits well with the overall tenor of the church order since it consistently stresses correct practice (baptism, daily prayer, signing, etc.) as an antidote to heresy.

■ **4** This summary statement echoes the disclaimer at the end of chap. 21, where the bishop will tell the newly baptized "anything else," that is, anything that has been omitted. God will reveal these things "to those who are worthy." Despite the plural "those," could this refer specifically to the bishop?[11] It certainly seems possible, since the theme here is the guiding of the church into a place of safety. This seems to be the meaning of the Arabic, which indicates that "God will . . . guide the church for him who is worthy. . . ." The Ethiopic probably has the correct reading here to the effect that God guides the "holy church," rather than the "church that is worthy" as in the Sahidic and Arabic. The concluding image of the church "mooring in the tranquil harbor" is rather common in the fourth century as an illustration for heaven.[12] Hilary of Poitiers, on the other hand, employs

---

11   The bishop is called "worthy" at his ordination in the Latin version of *Ap. Trad.* 4.1.

12   E.g., Athanasius *Historia Arianorum* 79.4.5; John Chrysostom *Ad viduam iuniorem* 3.1; Chrysostom

the image of the "peaceful harbor" to describe a faith that is firm and safe from heresy.[13] The phrase "tranquil harbor" (Greek εὐδίος λιμήν) appears only once in the third century, curiously, in Hippolytus *Ref.* 7.13.3. In a similar manner to Hilary of Poitiers, Hippolytus compares heresy to a storm at sea that one should avoid "in quest of the tranquil harbor." The sense of this concluding phrase in chap. 43 would appear to be quite akin to this use by Hilary and Hippolytus. While it is more at home in the fourth century, the parallel in the *Refutatio* suggests that it is not strange to the early third century.

could also use the phrase to illustrate the peace that Christ affords the believer: *Paraeneses ad Theodorum lapsum* 2.2.

13 *De trinitate* 12.1.

Bibliography

We have attempted to present as complete a listing as possible, in chronological order, of the editions, translations, and reconstructions that have been made of the full text of the *Apostolic Tradition*, but have limited the list of secondary literature almost entirely to those studies that are primarily concerned with the *Apostolic Tradition* itself and not with other aspects of Hippolytus's life and works or with early liturgical practice in general.

1. Editions, Translations, and Reconstructions

Leutholf, Job (Ludolfus)
Ad suam historiam Aethiopicam antehac editam commentarius (Frankfurt: J. D. Zunneri, 1691) 323–29; reproduced in *Bullarium Patronatus Portugalliae Regum in Ecclesiis Africae, Asiae atque Oceaniae* III: *Documenta Historiam Ecclesiae Habesinorum illustrantia inedita vel antea iam edita* (Olisipone: Ex Typographia Nationali, 1868) 2:145–98 [incomplete Ethiopic text with Latin translation].

Tattam, Henry
The Apostolical Constitutions or the Canons of the Apostles in Coptic with an English Translation (Oriental Translation Fund of Great Britain and Ireland Publications 63; London: Oriental Translation Fund of Great Britain and Ireland, 1848) 31–92 [Bohairic text with English translation].

Lagarde, Paul de
Aegyptiaca (Göttingen: Hoyer, 1883; reprinted Osnabrück: Zeller, 1972) 248–66 [Sahidic text].

Achelis, Hans
Die ältesten Quellen des orientalischen Kirchenrechtes I: *Die Canones Hippolyti* (TU 6/4; Leipzig: Hinrichs, 1891) 38–137 [German translation of Sahidic text and incomplete Ethiopic text].

Hauler, Edmund
Didascaliae apostolorum fragmenta Veronensia latina: Accedunt canonum qui dicuntur apostolorum et aegyptiorum reliquies (Leipzig: Teubner, 1900) 101–21 [Latin text].

Horner, George W.
The Statutes of the Apostles or Canones Ecclesiastici (London: Williams & Norgate, 1904) 10–52, 95–108, 138–62, 244–66, 306–32 [Arabic and Ethiopic texts with English translations; from 1915 onward it was reissued by Oxford Univ. Press without the oriental texts].

Funk, Franz Xaver
Didascalia et Constitutiones Apostolorum (2 vols.; Paderborn: Schöningh, 1905; reprinted Turin: Bottega d'Erasmo, 1962) 2:97–119 [reconstruction in Latin].

Périer, Jean and Augustin
Les "127 Canons des Apôtres" (PO 8/4; Paris: Firmin-Didot, 1912; reprinted Turnhout: Brepols, 1971) 590–622 [Arabic text with French translation].

Schermann, Theodor
Die allgemeine Kirchenordnung, frühchristliche Liturgien und kirchliche Überlieferung I: *Die allgemeine Kirchenordnung des zweiten Jahrhunderts* (Studien zur Geschichte und Kultur des Altertums 3; Paderborn: Schöningh, 1914; reprinted New York: Johnson, 1968) 35–100 [reconstruction in Latin with Greek fragments].

Hennecke, Edgar
Neutestamentliche Apokryphen (2d ed.; Tübingen: Mohr, 1924) 569–83 [reconstruction in German].

Jungklaus, Ernst
Die Gemeinde Hippolyts dargestellt nach seiner Kirchenordnung (TU 46/2; Leipzig: Hinrichs, 1928) 121–50 [reconstruction in German].

[Edmayr, H.]
Die apostolische Überlieferung des Hl. Hippolytus (Klosterneuburg: Volksliturgisches Apostolat, 1932) [reconstruction in German].

Easton, Burton Scott
The Apostolic Tradition of Hippolytus (New York: Macmillan, 1934; reprinted Hamden, Conn.: Archon, 1962) [reconstruction in English].

Dix, Gregory
Apostolike Paradosis: The Treatise on the Apostolic Tradition of St. Hippolytus of Rome (New York: Macmillan, 1937; 2d ed. with preface and corrections by Henry Chadwick, London: SPCK, 1968; reprinted Ridgefield, Conn.: Morehouse, 1992) [reconstruction in English].

Duensing, Hugo
Der aethiopische Text der Kirchenordnung des Hippolyt (Göttingen: Vandenhoeck & Ruprecht, 1946) [Ethiopic text with German translation].

Schneider, Alfons Maria
Stimmen aus der Frühzeit der Kirche (Cologne: Pick, 1948) 103–26 [reconstruction in German].

Botte, Bernard
Hippolyte de Rome: La Tradition apostolique (SC 11; Paris: Cerf, 1946; 2d ed. SC 11bis, 1968) [reconstruction in French, with Latin text and Greek fragments].

Till, Walter, and Johannes Leipoldt
Der koptische Text der Kirchenordnung Hippolyts (TU 58; Berlin: Akademie, 1954) [Coptic text with German translation].

Botte, Bernard
La Tradition apostolique de saint Hippolyte: Essai de reconstitution (Liturgiewissenschaftliche Quellen und Forschungen 39; Münster: Aschendorff, 1963; 5th ed. 1989, with addenda by Albert Gerhards) [Latin text; Greek fragments; composite oriental text in Latin; reconstruction in French].

Tidner, Erik

Didascaliae apostolorum Canonum ecclesiasticorum
Traditionis apostolicae versiones Latinae (TU 75;
Berlin: Akademie, 1963) 117–50 [Latin text with
Greek fragments].

Deiss, Lucien

Aux sources de la liturgie (Paris: Fleurus, 1963)
39–86 [reconstruction in French; ET: Early Sources
of the Liturgy, trans. Benet Weatherhead (Staten
Island: Alba, 1967) 27–74].

Cotone, Michel

"The Apostolic Tradition of Hippolytus of Rome,"
American Benedictine Review 19 (1968) 492–514
[reconstruction in English].

Hanssens, Jean Michel

La liturgie d'Hippolyte: Documents et études (Rome:
Liberia Editrice dell'Universita Gregoriana, 1970)
[synoptic Latin translations of all relevant texts].

Novak, Maria da Glória

Tradição Apostólica de Hipólito de Roma (Fontes da
catequese 4; Petrópolis, Brazil: Vozes, 1971)
[reconstruction in Portuguese].

Tateo, R.

Ippolito di Roma: La Tradizione apostolica (Rome:
Paoline, 1972; 2d ed. 1979) [reconstruction in Ital-
ian].

Cuming, Geoffrey J.

Hippolytus: A Text for Students (GLS 8; Nottingham:
Grove, 1976) [reconstruction in English].

Anonymous

La tradición apostólica (Salamanca: Sígueme, 1986)
[reconstruction in Spanish].

Geerlings, Wilhelm

Traditio Apostolica = Apostolische Überlieferung
(Fontes Christiani 1; Freiburg: Herder, 1991)
[Botte's texts with German translation of his recon-
struction].

Ekenberg, Anders

Den apostoliska traditionen (Kristna klassiker; Upp-
sala: Katolska, 1994) [reconstruction in Swedish].

Peretto, Elio

Pseudo-Ippolito: Tradizione apostolica (Collana di testi
patristici 133; Rome: Città Nuova, 1996) [recon-
struction in Italian].

Urdeix, Josep

La Didajé: La Tradición apostólica (Barcelona: Centre de Pastoral Litúrgica, 1996) [reconstruction in
Spanish].

2. Secondary Literature

Bartlet, J. Vernon

"The Ordination Prayers in the Ancient Church
Order," JTS 17 (1916) 248–56.

Batiffol, Pierre

"Une prétendue anaphore apostolique," Revue
biblique 13 (1916) 23–32.

Bauer, Johannes Baptist

"Die Fruchtesegnung in Hippolyts Kirchenordnung," ZKTh 74 (1952) 71–75.

Béraudy, Roger

"Le sacrement de l'Ordre d'après la Tradition apostolique d'Hippolyte," BCE 38–39 (1962) 338–56.

Blanc, J.

"Lexique comparé des versions de la Tradition
apostolique de S. Hippolyte," RThAM 21 (1954)
173–92.

Bobertz, Charles A.

"The Role of Patron in the Cena Dominica of Hippolytus' Apostolic Tradition," JTS 44 (1993)
170–84.

Botte, Bernard

"Adstare coram te et tibi ministrare," QL 63 (1982)
223–26.

Idem

"L'authenticité de la Tradition apostolique de saint
Hippolyte," RThAM 16 (1949) 177–85.

Idem

"Christian People and Hierarchy in the Apostolic
Tradition of St. Hippolytus," in Roles in the Liturgical Assembly (New York: Pueblo, 1981) 61–72; ET of
L'assemblée liturgique et les différents rôles dans
l'assemblée (Rome: Edizioni Liturgiche, 1977)
79–91.

Idem

"L'épiclèse de l'anaphore d'Hippolyte," RThAM 14
(1947) 241–51.

Idem

"L'Esprit-Saint et l'Église dans la 'Tradition apostolique' de Saint Hippolyte," Disaskalia 2 (1972)
221–33.

Idem

"Extendit manus suas cum pateretur," QLP 49
(1968) 307–8.

Idem

"Les Heures de prière dans la 'Tradition Apostolique' et les documents dérivés," in Mon-
seigneur Cassien and Bernard Botte, eds., La prière
des heures (Lex Orandi 35; Paris: Cerf, 1963)
101–15.

Idem

"Note sur le symbole baptismal de saint Hippolyte," in Mélanges Joseph de Ghellinck, S. J. (Gembloux: Duculot, 1951) 189–200.

Idem

"Un passage difficile de la 'Tradition apostolique'
sur le signe de croix," RThAM 27 (1960) 5–19.

Idem

"À propos de la 'Tradition apostolique,'" RThAM
33 (1966) 177–86.

Idem

"ΨΕΛΛΙΣΤΗΣ-ΨΑΛΙΣΤΗΣ," Revue des Études
Byzantines 16 (1958) 162–65.

Idem

"Le rituel d'ordination dans la 'Tradition apostolique' d'Hippolyte," BCE 36 (1962) 5–12.

Idem

"La sputation, antique rite baptismal?" in Mélanges
offerts à Mademoiselle Christine Mohrmann (Utrecht:
Spectrum, 1963) 196–201.

Idem

"Le texte de la *Tradition apostolique*," *RThAM* 22 (1955) 161–72.

Idem

"Tradition apostolique et Canon romain," *La Maison-Dieu* 87 (1966) 52–61.

Bradshaw, Paul F.

"Ordination," in Geoffrey J. Cuming, ed., *Essays on Hippolytus* (GLS 15; Nottingham: Grove, 1978) 33–38.

Idem

"The Participation of Other Bishops in the Ordination of a Bishop in the *Apostolic Tradition* of Hippolytus," *StPatr* 18/2 (1989) 335–38.

Idem

"A Paschal Root to the Anaphora of the *Apostolic Tradition*? A Response to Enrico Mazza," *StPatr* 35 (2001) 257–65.

Idem

"The Problems of a New Edition of the *Apostolic Tradition*," in Robert F. Taft and Gabriele Winkler, eds., *Comparative Liturgy Fifty Years after Anton Baumstark (1872–1948)* (OrChrA 265; Rome: Edizioni Orientalia Christiana, 2001) 613–22.

Idem

"Redating the *Apostolic Tradition*: Some Preliminary Steps," in John Baldovin and Nathan Mitchell, eds., *Rule of Prayer, Rule of Faith: Essays in Honor of Aidan Kavanagh, OSB* (Collegeville, Minn.: Liturgical, 1996) 3–17.

Brent, Allen

Hippolytus and the Roman Church in the Third Century: Communities in Tension before the Emergence of a Monarch-Bishop (VCSup 31; Leiden: Brill, 1995).

Cabié, Robert

"L'ordo de l'initiation chrétienne dans la 'Tradition apostolique' d'Hippolyte de Rome," in *Mens concordet voci, pour Mgr A. G. Martimort* (Paris: Desclée, 1983) 543–58.

Cagin, Paul

L'anaphore apostolique et ses témoins (Paris: Lethielleux, 1919).

Idem

L'Eucharistie, canon primitif de la messe ou formulaire essentiel et premier de toutes les liturgies (Paris: Lethielleux, 1912).

Capelle, Bernard

"Hippolyte de Rome," *RThAM* 17 (1950) 145–74; reprinted in idem, *Travaux liturgiques de doctrine et d'histoire* (3 vols.; Louvain: Centre liturgique, Abbaye du Mont César, 1955–67) 2:31–60.

Idem

"L'introduction du catéchuménat à Rome," *RThAM* 5 (1933) 129–54.

Idem

"Les origines du Symbole romain," *RThAM* 2 (1930) 5–20.

Idem

"A propos d'Hippolyte de Rome," *RThAM* 19 (1952) 193–202; reprinted in idem, *Travaux liturgiques de doctrine et d'histoire* (3 vols.; Louvain: Centre liturgique, Abbaye du Mont César, 1955–67) 2:61–70.

Idem

"Le Symbole romain au second siècle," *RBén* 39 (1927) 33–45.

Casel, Odo

"Die Kirchenordnung Hippolyts von Rom," *ALW* 2 (1952) 115–30.

Chadwick, Henry

"Prayer at Midnight," in Jacques Fontaine and Charles Kannengiesser, eds., *Epektasis: Mélanges patristiques offerts au Cardinal Jean Daniélou* (Paris: Beauchesne, 1972) 47–49.

Connolly, Richard H.

"An Ancient Prayer in the Mediaeval Euchologia," *JTS* 19 (1918) 132–44.

Idem

"The Eucharistic Prayer of Hippolytus," *JTS* 39 (1938) 350–69.

Idem

"On the Text of the Baptismal Creed of Hippolytus," *JTS* 25 (1924) 131–39.

Idem

"The Ordination Prayers of Hippolytus," *JTS* 18 (1917) 55–60.

Idem

"The Prologue to the *Apostolic Tradition* of Hippolytus," *JTS* 22 (1921) 356–61.

Idem

The So-called Egyptian Church Order and Derived Documents (TextS 8/4; Cambridge: Cambridge Univ. Press, 1916; reprinted Nendeln, Liechtenstein: Kraus, 1967).

Cuming, Geoffrey J.

"The Post-baptismal Prayer in *Apostolic Tradition*: Further Considerations," *JTS* 39 (1988) 117–19.

Cuming, Geoffrey, J., ed.

Essays on Hippolytus (GLS 15; Nottingham: Grove, 1978).

Devreesse, Robert

"La prière eucharistique de saint Hippolyte," *VAL* 8 (1921–22) 393–97, 448–53.

Idem

"La 'Tradition apostolique' de S. Hippolyte," *VAL* 8 (1921–22) 11–18.

Edsman, C. M.

"A Typology of Baptism in Hippolytus," *StPatr* 2 (1957) 35–40.

Elfers, Heinrich

Die Kirchenordnung Hippolyts von Rom (Paderborn: Bonifacius, 1938).

Idem

"Neue Untersuchungen über die Kirchenordnung Hippolyts von Rom," in Marcel Reding, ed., *Abhandlungen über Theologie und Kirche: Festschrift für Karl Adam* (Düsseldorf: Patmos, 1952) 169–211.

Engberding, Hieronymus

"Das angebliche Dokument römischer Liturgie aus dem Beginn des dritten Jahrhunderts," in

Miscellanea liturgica in honorem L. Cuniberti Mohlberg (2 vols.; Rome: Edizioni Liturgiche, 1948–49) 1:47–71.

Eynde, Damien van den
"Nouvelle trace de la 'Traditio apostolica' d'Hippolyte dans la liturgie romaine," in *Miscellanea liturgica in honorem L. Cuniberti Mohlberg* (2 vols.; Rome: Edizioni Liturgiche, 1948–49) 1:407–11.

Faivre, Alexandre
"La documentation canonico-liturgique de l'Eglise ancienne," *RevScRel* 54 (1980) 204–19, 237–97.

Finn, Thomas M.
"Ritual Process and the Survival of Early Christianity: A Study of the Apostolic Tradition of Hippolytus," *Journal of Ritual Studies* 3 (1989) 69–89.

Frere, Walter Howard
"Early Forms of Ordination," in Henry B. Swete, ed., *Essays on the Early History of the Church and the Ministry* (London: Macmillan, 1918) 263–312.

Idem
"Early Ordination Services," *JTS* 16 (1915) 323–71.

Funk, Franz Xaver
"Die liturgie der Aethiopischen Kirchenordnung," *ThQ* 80 (1898) 513–47.

Galtier, Paul
"La consignation à Carthage et à Rome," *RechSR* 2 (1911) 350–83.

Idem
"La 'Tradition Apostolique' d'Hippolyte," *RechSR* 13 (1923) 511–27.

Gavin, Frank
"Rabbinic Parallels in Early Church Orders," *Hebrew Union College Annual* 6 (1929) 57–67.

Gelston, Anthony
"A Note on the Text of the *Apostolic Tradition* of Hippolytus," *JTS* 39 (1988) 112–17.

Goltz, Eduard von der
"Die Taufgebete Hippolyts und andere Taufgebete der alten Kirchen," *ZKG* 27 (1906) 1–51.

Idem
"Unbekannte Fragmente altchristlicher Gemeindeordnungen," *Sitzungsberichte der Preussischen Akademie der Wissenschaft* (1906) 141–57.

Grove, Ron
"Terminum figat: Clarifying the Meaning of a Phrase in the Apostolic Tradition," *OrChrP* 48 (1982) 431–34.

Hamel, A.
"Über das kirchenrechtliche Schriftum Hippolyts," *ZNW* 36 (1937) 238–50.

Hammerschmidt, Ernst
"Bermerkungen zum koptischen Text der Kirchenordnung Hippolyts," *Ostkirchliche Studien* 5 (1956) 67.

Hanssens, Jean Michel
La liturgie d'Hippolyte: Ses documents, son titulaire, ses origines et son charactère (1959; 2d ed.; OrChrA 155; Rome: Pontificium Institutum Orientalium Studiorum, 1965).

Idem
"La liturgie d'Hippolyte. Assentiments et dissentiments," *Greg* 42 (1961) 290–302.

Idem
"Note concernant le Symbole baptismal de l'ordonnance ecclésiastique latine," *RechSR* 54 (1966) 241–64.

Hennecke, Edgar
"Hippolyts Schrift 'Apostolische Überlieferung der Gnadengaben,'" in *Harnack-Ehrung: Beiträge zur Kirchengeschichte* (Leipzig: Hinrichs, 1921) 159–82.

Idem
"Der Prolog zur 'Apostolischen Überlieferung' Hippolyts," *ZNW* 22 (1923) 144–46.

Holland, David L.
"The Baptismal Interrogation concerning the Holy Spirit in Hippolytus' *Apostolic Tradition*," *StPatr* 10 (1970) 360–65.

Idem
"'Credis in spiritum sanctum et sanctam ecclesiam et resurrectionem carnis?': Ein Beitrag zur Geschichte des Apostolikums," *ZNW* 61 (1970) 126–44.

Jilek, August
"Bischof und Presbyterium: Zur Beziehung zwischen Episkopat und Presbyterat im Lichte der Traditio Apostolica Hippolyts," *ZKTh* 106 (1984) 376–401.

Idem
Initiationsfeier und Amt: Ein Beitrag zur Struktur und Theologie der Ämter und des Taufgottesdienstes in der frühen Kirche (Traditio Apostolica, Tertullian, Cyprian) (Frankfurt: Lang, 1979).

Johnson, Maxwell E.
"The Postchrismational Structure of *Apostolic Tradition* 21, the Witness of Ambrose of Milan, and a Tentative Hypothesis Regarding the Current Reform of Confirmation in the Roman Rite," *Worship* 70 (1996) 16–34.

Jungmann, Josef A.
"Beobachtungen zum Fortleben von Hippolyts 'Apostolische Überlieferung,'" *ZKTh* 53 (1929) 579–85.

Idem
"Die Doxologien in der Kirchenordnung Hippolyts," *ZKTh* 86 (1964) 321–26.

Küppers, Kurt
"Die literarisch-theologische Einheit von Eucharistiegebet und Bischofsweihegebet bei Hippolyt," *ALW* 29 (1987) 19–30.

Lanne, Emmanuel
"Les ordinations dans le rite copte, leurs relations avec les Constitutions Apostoliques et la Tradition de saint Hippolyte," *L'orient syrien* 5 (1960) 89–106.

Lécuyer, Joseph
"Episcopat et presbytérat dans les écrits d'Hippolyte de Rome," *RechSR* 41 (1953) 30–50.

Idem

"La prière d'ordination de l'évêque: Le Pontifical romain et la 'Tradition apostolique' d'Hippolyte," *Nouvelle revue théologique* 89 (1967) 601–6.

Lengeling, Emil J.

"Hippolyt von Rom und die Wendung 'extendit manus suas cum pateretur,'" *QLP* (1969) 141–44.

Ligier, Louis

"L'Anaphore de la 'Tradition Apostolique' dans le 'Testamentum Domini,'" in Bryan D. Spinks, ed., *The Sacrifice of Praise* (Rome: C.L.V.-Edizioni Liturgiche, 1981) 91–106.

Lods, Marc

"Le sacrifice de louange: Lecture de la liturgie eucharistique d'Hippolyte de Rome," *Foi et Vie* 70 (1971) 180–95.

Lorentz, Rudolf

De egyptische Kerkordening en Hippolytus van Rome (Haarlem: Enschede, 1929).

Magne, Jean

"Un extrait de la 'Tradition apostolique sur les charismes' d'Hippolyte sous les gloses du Constituteur, et les 'Diataxeis des saints Apôtres,'" in Franz Paschke, ed., *Überlieferungsgeschichtliche Untersuchungen* (TU 125; Berlin: Akademie, 1981) 399–402.

Idem

"En finir avec la 'Tradition' d'Hippolyte!" *BLE* 89 (1988) 5–22.

Idem

"La prétendue Tradition Apostolique d'Hippolyte de Rome s'appelait-elle *AI ΔIATAΞEIΣ TΩN AΓIΩN AΠOΣTOΛΩN, Les statuts des saints apôtres*? *Ostkirchliche Studien* 14 (1965) 35–67.

Idem

Tradition apostolique sur les charismes et Diataxeis des saints Apôtres (Origines chrétiennes 1; Paris: Magne, 1975).

Markschies, Christoph

"Neue Forschungen zur sogenannten *Traditio Apostolica*," in Robert F. Taft and Gabriele Winkler, eds, *Comparative Liturgy Fifty Years after Anton Baumstark (1872–1948)* (OrChrA 265; Rome: Edizioni Orientalia Christiana, 2001) 583–98.

Idem

"Wer schrieb die sogenannte *Traditio Apostolica*? Neue Beobachtungen und Hypothesen zu einer kaum lösbaren Frage aus der altkirchen Literaturgeschichte," in Wolfram Kinzig, Christof Markschies, and Markus Vinzent, *Tauffragen und Bekenntnis* (AKG 74; Berlin: de Gruyter, 1999) 1–74.

Martimort, Aimé-Georges

"Encore Hippolyte et la 'Tradition apostolique,'" *BLE* 92 (1991) 133–37; 97 (1996) 275–79.

Idem

"Nouvel examen de la 'Tradition apostolique' d'Hippolyte," *BLE* 88 (1987) 5–25.

Idem

"Tradition apostolique," *Dictionnaire de Spiritualité* 15 (Paris, 1991) 1133–46.

Idem

"La Tradition apostolique d'Hippolyte," *L'année canonique* 23 (1979) 159–73.

Idem

"La 'Tradition Apostolique' d'Hippolyte et le rituel baptismal antique," *BLE* 60 (1959) 57–62.

Mazza, Enrico

"Omelie pasquali e Birkat ha-mazon: fonti dell'anafora di Ippolito?" *EphLit* 97 (1983) 409–81.

Metzger, Marcel

"Enquêtes autour de la prétendue *Tradition apostolique*," *EO* 9 (1992) 7–36.

Idem

"Nouvelles perspectives pour le prétendue *Tradition apostolique*," *EO* 5 (1988) 241–59.

Idem

"A propos des règlements écclesiastiques et de la prétendue *Tradition apostolique*," *RevScRel* 66 (1992) 249–61.

Idem

"A propos d'une réédition de la prétendue *Tradition apostolique* avec traduction allemand," *ALW* 33 (1991) 290–94.

Müller, Karl

"Kleine Beiträge zur alten Kirchengeschichte 6: Hippolyts Ἀποστολικὴ Παράδοσις und die Canones Hippolyti," *ZNW* 23 (1924) 226–31.

Idem

"Kleine Beiträge zur alten Kirchengeschichte 15: Noch einmal Hippolyts Ἀποστολικὴ Παράδοσις," *ZNW* 28 (1929) 273–74.

Nairne, Alexander

"The Prayer for the Consecration of a Bishop in the Church Order of Hippolytus," *JTS* 17 (1916) 398–99.

Norwood, Percy V.

"The *Apostolic Tradition* of Hippolytus," *ATR* 17 (1935) 15–18.

O'Regan, James

"A Note on Keeping a Difficult Text in the Apostolic Tradition," *EphLit* 108 (1994) 73–76.

Orbe, Antonio

"El enigma de Hipólito y su Liturgia," *Greg* 41 (1960) 284–92.

Oliveira, Carlos-Josaphat Pinto de

"Signification sacerdotale du ministère de l'évêque dans la Tradition Apostolique d'Hippolyte de Rome," *FZPhTh* 25 (1978) 398–427.

Phillips, L. Edward

"Daily Prayer in the *Apostolic Tradition* of Hippolytus," *JTS* 40 (1989) 389–400.

Ratcliff, Edward C.

"Apostolic Tradition: Questions concerning the Appointment of the Bishop," *StPatr* 8 (1966) 266–70; reprinted in Arthur H. Couratin and David Tripp, eds., *E. C. Ratcliff: Liturgical Studies* (London: SPCK, 1976) 156–60.

Idem

"The Sanctus and the Pattern of the Early Anaphora," *JEH* 1 (1950) 29–36, 125–34; reprinted in
Arthur H. Couratin and David Tripp, eds., *E. C.
Ratcliff: Liturgical Studies* (London: SPCK, 1976)
18–40.

Richard, Marcel

"Le florilège eucharistique du Codex Ochrid.
Musée national 86," in *Charistêrion eis Anastasion
K. Orlandon* III (Athens: Publications de la Société
archéologique d'Athènes, 1966) 47–55; reprinted
in idem, *Opera Minora* 1 (Turnhout: Brepols, 1976)
no. 6.

Idem

"Quelques fragments des Pères anténicéens et
nicéens," *Symbolae Osloenses* 38 (1963) 76–83;
reprinted in idem, *Opera Minora* 1 (Turnhout:
Brepols, 1976) no. 5.

Richardson, Cyril C.

"The Date and Setting of the Apostolic Tradition
of Hippolytus," *ATR* 30 (1948) 38–44.

Idem

"A Note on the Epicleses in Hippolytus and the
Testamentum Domini," *RThAM* 15 (1948) 357–59.

Idem

"The So-Called Epiclesis in Hippolytus," *HTR* 40
(1947) 101–8.

Richter, Klemens

"Zum Ritus der Bischofsordination in der 'Apostolischen Überlieferung' Hippolyts von Rom und
davon abhängigen Schriften," *ALW* 17 (1975) 7–51.

Robinson, J. Armitage

"The 'Apostolic Anaphora' and the Prayer of St
Polycarp," *JTS* 21 (1920) 97–105.

Rordorf, Willy

"L'ordination de l'évêque selon la Tradition apostolique d'Hippolyte de Rome," *QL* 55 (1974)
137–50; reprinted in idem, *Liturgie, foi et vie des premiers chrétiens* (ThH 75; Paris: Beauchesne, 1986)
123–36.

Salaville, Severien

"Un texte romain du Canon de la Messe au debut
du IIIe siècle," *Echos d'Orient* 21 (1921) 79–85.

Salles, A.

"La 'Tradition apostolique' est-elle un témoin de la
liturgie romaine?" *RHR* 148 (1955) 181–213.

Saxer, Victor

"Figura Corporis et Sanguinis Domini: Une for-
mule eucharistique des premiers siècles chez Ter-
tullien, Hippolyte et Ambroise," *Rivista de
Archeologia Cristiana* 47 (1971) 65–89.

Idem

"La tradizione nei testi canonico-liturgici: Didachè,
Traditio apostolica, Didascalia, Constitutiones
apostolorum," in *La tradizione: Forme e modi*
(StEphA 31; Rome: Institutum Patristicum Augustinianum, 1990) 251–63.

Schermann, Theodor

*Ein Weiheritual der römischen Kirche am Schlusse des
ersten Jahrhunderts* (Munich: Walhalla, 1913).

Schwartz, Eduard

Über die pseudoapostolischen Kirchenordnungen (Strasbourg: Trubner, 1910); reprinted in idem, *Gesammelte Schriften* (5 vols.; Berlin: de Gruyter, 1938–63)
5:192–273.

Segelberg, Eric

"The Benedictio Olei in the Apostolic Tradition of
Hippolytus," *OrChr* 48 (1964) 268–81.

Idem

"The Ordination Prayers in Hippolytus," *StPatr* 13
(1975) 397–408.

Simonin, H. D.

"La prière de la consecration episcopale dans la
Tradition apostolique d'Hippolyte de Rome," *La
vie spirituelle* 60 (1939) 65–86.

Smith, Michael A.

"The Anaphora of *Apostolic Tradition* Re-consid-
ered," *StPatr* 10 (1970) 426–30.

Stam, John E.

"Charismatic Theology in the *Apostolic Tradition* of
Hippolytus," in Gerald F. Hawthorne, ed., *Current
Issues in Biblical and Patristic Interpretation: Studies
in Honor of Merrill C. Tenney* (Grand Rapids: Eerdmans, 1975) 267–76.

Idem

Episcopacy in the Apostolic Tradition of Hippolytus
(ThD 3; Basel: Reinhardt, 1969).

Stewart-Sykes, Alistair

"The Integrity of the Hippolytean Ordination
Rites," *Aug* 39 (1999) 97–127.

Turner, Cuthbert Hamilton

"The Ordination of a Presbyter in the Church
Order of Hippolytus," *JTS* 16 (1915) 542–47.

Unnik, Willem Cornelis van

*"Les chevaux defaits des femmes baptisées: Un rite
de baptême dans l'Ordre Ecclésiastique d'Hippolyte," *VC* 1 (1947) 77–100.

Vigourel, L'Abbé

"Autour de la 'Tradition apostolique,'" *La vie et les
arts liturgiques* 8 (1922) 150–56.

Walls, Andrew F.

"The Latin Version of Hippolytus' Apostolic Tradition," *StPatr* 3 (1961) 155–62.

Idem

"A Primitive Christian Harvest Thanksgiving,"
Theology 58 (1958) 336–39.

Werblowsky, Reuben J. Zwi

"On the Baptismal Rite According to St. Hippolytus," *StPatr* 2 (1957) 93–105.

Wilmart, André

"Le texte latin de la *Paradosis* de saint Hippolyte,"
RechSR 9 (1919) 62–79.

Idem

"Un réglement ecclésiastique du début du
troisième siècle. La 'Tradition apostolique' de saint
Hippolyte," *Revue du Clergé Français* 96 (1918)
81–116.

Index

f / Early Christian Literature and the Ancient Church

Paraeneses ad Theodorum lapsum
2.2 — 224

Clement of Alexandria — 42, 96[2]
Paedagogus
1.6.34.3 — 134[69]
1.6.36.1 — 134[69]
1.6.45.1 — 134[69]
1.6.50.3–52.2 — 134[69]
2.1-2 — 150
2.4 — 214[84]
2.9 — 214[84]
Quis dives salvetur
42 — 65
Stromateis
2.9 — 212[73]
2.18 — 96[1]
2.23 — 214[84]
4.22 — 210[57]
6.6 — 47
7.7 — 179[5], 214[83], 214[84]
7.12 — 140[1], 179[4], 214[84]

Clement of Rome
1 Clement — 33, 37[1]
24.1-3 — 209[51]
44.3 — 28[17]
44.4 — 36
2 Clement [spurious]
19.1 — 74

Clementine Octateuch — 22, 58[10]

Cornelius of Rome
Letter (251) — 74, 78, 80

Council of Elvira
Canon 4 — 98
Canon 35 — 111
Canon 42 — 97
Canon 73 — 98

Council of Nicea
Canon 2 — 98

Cyprian — 54, 108, 127, 127[19], 214
Ad Fortunatum
11 — 97[8]
Ad Quirinum — 208[45]
De dominica oratione
31 — 43
34–35 — 214[91]
36 — 212[75], 214[92]
De lapsis
26 — 181
Epistulae
1.1.1 — 65
8.1 — 78[1]
9.1 — 78[1]
10.5 — 169[7]
23 — 74[2]
29.2 — 74[2], 78[1]
32.1 — 64[6]
34.4 — 78[1]
35.1 — 74[2]
36.1 — 78[1]
38 — 74[2]
39 — 74[2]
39.5 — 67
40.1 — 67
45.4 — 78[1]
47.2 — 78[1]
55.8 — 27[14]
61.3.1 — 65
62 — 159
63.14 — 33[18]
64 — 130
64.3 — 64[6]
67.4-5 — 64[6]
67.5 — 27[14]
69.15 — 109
69.7 — 132[54]
70.1 — 129
70.2 — 131, 132, 132[54]
73.9 — 132, 133[62]
73.22 — 103[4]
74.5 — 132
79.1 — 78[1]
On Works and Alms
15 — 111[25]

Cyril of Alexandria
Explicatio in psalmos
45.2 — 131[48]

Cyril of Jerusalem — 46, 46[43], 129
Baptismal Catechesis
1.5-6 — 109[9]
Mystagogical Catecheses
1.4-9 — 131[48]
2.3 — 131
5.21 — 181, 182[1]

Deir Balyzeh papyrus — 126

Didache — 9, 37[1], 120
3.2 — 93
3.4 — 95
7.1-3 — 129
7.4 — 110
8.1 — 110, 140
8.3 — 213, 214
9 — 44, 159
9.3-4 — 160
10 — 44, 45
13 — 165
13.3 — 33
28, 28[17], 64
16.1 — 206

Didascalia Apostolorum — 1[6], 3, 7[56-58], 9, 99
2.26.3 — 65
2.26.4 — 33
2.26.5 — 65
2.44.3-4 — 65[9]
2.57 — 43[20], 99[2]
3.12.1 — 64[6]
3.13.1 — 65[9]

2. Authors (modern/contemporary)

Achelis, Hans
1, 1[5], 6, 10

Achtemeier, Paul J.
209[48]

Andrieu, Michel
26[4]

Attridge, Harold W.
208[39]

Baldovin, John
14[107]

Barlea, Octavian
29, 29[29]

Barrett, C. K.
151[6]

Bartlet, J. Vernon
34[23], 55, 55[7], 64, 64[2]

Bauer, Johannes Baptist
169[4]

Bebawi, Carol
17, 17[113]

Beit-Arié, Malachi
212[71]

Béraudy, Roger
35[27], 58[11]

Betz, Johannes
134[68]

Beylot, Robert
11, 11[81]

Bhaldraithe, Eoin de
87, 87[3]

Black, Matthew
28, 28[27]

Blanc, J.
220[23]

Bobertz, Charles A.
145[9], 150[2]

Botte, Bernard
2[17], 3, 3[27], 4, 4[30, 34], 5, 5[37, 45], 7[55], 8, 8[61], 10, 10[75], 12, 12[91, 92], 13, 13[99],16, 17, 18, 22, 22[2, 4], 23[10], 26, 26[1, 2], 26[5], 29, 29[31], 32, 32[5], 32[9], 33, 33[13, 14], 35, 35[27], 37, 37[6, 7], 42, 42[8, 13], 43[21], 47, 47[46], 47[51], 48, 48[54, 55, 56, 58], 49, 49[2, 5, 6], 53, 53[5], 55, 55[3, 4], 58, 58[14], 59[22], 64, 64[4, 5], 65[12], 67[2], 74[1], 92, 92[4], 108, 108[4, 5], 125, 125[3, 6, 7], 126[17], 127, 127[18, 21], 129, 129[29], 129[30], 130[43], 136, 136[3, 4, 6], 141, 141[1], 142, 142[1], 144, 144[3], 144[6], 150, 150[1, 4], 152, 152[1, 2], 154, 154[3], 155, 155[4, 6], 158, 158[4, 6], 159, 160[20], 165, 165[1, 3], 174, 174[1, 2, 3], 176, 176[1], 178, 178[2], 180, 187, 189, 189[1], 203[4], 204, 204[11, 14, 17], 205, 205[22, 24, 28], 206, 206[32, 34], 209, 209[49], 218, 218[4, 5, 7, 9], 219, 219[12, 13, 16, 17, 19, 21], 220, 220[25], 221, 221[1], 221[6]

Bouhot, Jean-Paul
108, 108[1]

Bouley, Allan
70[5]

Bouriant, Urbain
8[59]

Bouyer, Louis
5, 6[47], 37, 37[3], 42, 42[12], 47, 48, 48[52, 59]

Bradley, Keith
85[5]

Bradshaw, Paul F.
1[1], 7[55], 10[75], 11[77], 13[102], 14[107, 109], 27[9], 27[13], 28[20, 21, 22], 34[22], 34[24, 25], 42[18], 43[19, 24], 44[27, 29], 45[34], 58[15], 59[21], 65[7, 8, 10], 74[6], 78[3], 84[4], 96[2], 98[10], 102[1], 108[2, 3], 109[6, 10], 111[19], 124[1], 125[6], 128[27, 28], 132[53], 168[7], 175[7], 178[3], 190[5, 6], 204[10], 212[72], 213, 213[80], 214, 214[82, 88]

Brakmann, Heinzgard
11, 11[78]

Brennecke, Hanns Christof
54[12]

Brent, Allen
3, 3[20, 23], 4, 4[28, 29, 32], 4[33], 5[39], 13, 13[105], 27, 27[9], 33, 33[17], 35, 35[30], 59, 59[24], 192[9]

Brock, Sebastian
42, 42[15], 43[20], 165[4]

Brown, Peter
76[1], 95[9], 99[5], 110[13]

Brown, Raymond E.
208[45]

Burkitt, Francis C.
7[58]

Burns, J. Patout
87[3]

Cabié, Robert
84[1], 108[1]

Cantalamessa, Raniero
44, 44[32], 111, 111[20], 174, 174[4], 175

Capelle, Bernard
4[30], 10[68], 125[7]

Cardman, Francine
76[1]

Carr, E.
134[67]

Casel, Odo
2[16]

Cattaneo, Enrico
220[28]

Chadwick, Henry
2[15], 3, 8[58], 12, 84[3], 92, 130[41], 141, 169[3], 212, 212[67]

Charles, Robert Henry
54[10]

Chavasse, Antoine
49, 49[1]

Coburn, Oliver
87[3]

Connolly, Richard H.
2, 2[14], 4[34], 6[48], 5[44], 7[53], 10, 11, 11[84], 22[1], 22[4, 5], 32, 33, 33[10], 44[30], 47, 47[48], 48, 48[56], 55[8], 126[15], 127, 127[18], 180[3], 191[5], 192[10], 209, 209[50], 210[52], 218, 218[2], 221, 221[3, 7], 222, 222[10]

Cooke, Bernard
67, 70[4]

Cooper, James
xvii, 11[79], 17, 93[8]

Coppens, Joseph
28[25]

Coquin, René-Georges
10, 10[75], 11

Couratin, Arthur
37, 37[5]

Crehan, Joseph H.
7[58]

Cuming, Geoffrey J.
12[93], 22, 22[3], 28[22], 48[55], 53, 53[8], 87[1], 93[7], 99[1], 108, 108[4], 111[23], 128, 128[24, 25], 130[42, 43], 141[3], 144, 144[3], 145[7], 150[5], 159, 159[13, 18], 160[20], 180[3], 187, 203[4], 204, 204[11], 204[13], 205, 205[19, 24], 218[6], 219[12], 221[1]

Cutrone, E. J.
46[43]

Designer's Notes

In the design of the visual aspects of *Hermeneia*, consideration has been given to relating the form to the content by symbolic means.

The letters of the logotype *Hermeneia* are a fusion of forms alluding simultaneously to Hebrew (dotted vowel markings) and Greek (geometric round shapes) letter forms. In their modern treatment they remind us of the electronic age as well, the vantage point from which this investigation of the past begins.

The Lion of Judah used as visual identification for the series is based on the Seal of Shema. The version for *Hermeneia* is again a fusion of Hebrew calligraphic forms, especially the legs of the lion, and Greek elements characterized by the geometric. In the sequence of arcs, which can be understood as scroll-like images, the first is the lion's mouth. It is reasserted and accelerated in the whorl and returns in the aggressively arched tail: tradition is passed from one age to the next, rediscovered and re-formed.

"Who is worthy to open the scroll and break its seals. . . ."
Then one of the elders said to me
"weep not; lo, the Lion of the tribe of David,
the Root of David, has conquered,
so that he can open the scroll and
its seven seals."
Rev. 5:2, 5

To celebrate the signal achievement in biblical scholarship which *Hermeneia* represents, the entire series will by its color constitute a signal on the theologian's bookshelf: the Old Testament will be bound in yellow and the New Testament in red, traceable to a commonly used color coding for synagogue and church in medieval painting; in pure color terms, varying degrees of intensity of the warm segment of the color spectrum. The colors interpenetrate when the binding color for the Old Testament is used to imprint volumes from the New and vice versa.

Wherever possible, a photograph of the oldest extant manuscript, or a historically significant document pertaining to the biblical sources, will be displayed on the end papers of each volume to give a feel for the tangible reality and beauty of the source material.

The title-page motifs are expressive derivations from the Hermeneia logotype, repeated seven times to form a matrix and debossed on the cover of each volume. These sifted-out elements will be seen to be in their exact positions within the parent matrix.

Horizontal markings at gradated levels on the spine will assist in grouping the volumes according to these conventional categories.

The type has been set with unjustified right margins so as to preserve the internal consistency of word spacing. This is a major factor in both legibility and aesthetic quality; the resultant uneven line endings are only slight impairments to legibility by comparison. In this respect the type resembles the handwritten manuscripts where the quality of the calligraphic writing is dependent on establishing and holding to integral spacing patterns.

All of the type faces in common use today have been designed between AD 1500 and the present. For the biblical text a face was chosen which does not arbitrarily date the text, but rather one which is uncompromisingly modern and unembellished so that its feel is of the universal. The type style is Univers 65 by Adrian Frutiger.

The expository texts and footnotes are set in Baskerville, chosen for its compatibility with the many brief Greek and Hebrew insertions. The double-column format and the shorter line length facilitate speed reading and the wide margins to the left of footnotes provide for the scholar's own notations.

Kenneth Hiebert

Category of biblical writing,
key symbolic characteristic,
and volumes so identified.

1
Law
(boundaries described)
  Genesis
  Exodus
  Leviticus
  Numbers
  Deuteronomy

2
History
(trek through time and space)
  Joshua
  Judges
  Ruth
  1 Samuel
  2 Samuel
  1 Kings
  2 Kings
  1 Chronicles
  2 Chronicles
  Ezra
  Nehemiah
  Esther

3
Poetry
(lyric emotional expression)
  Job
  Psalms
  Proverbs
  Ecclesiastes
  Song of Songs

4
Prophets
(inspired seers)
  Isaiah
  Jeremiah
  Lamentations
  Ezekiel
  Daniel
  Hosea
  Joel
  Amos
  Obadiah
  Jonah
  Micah
  Nahum
  Habakkuk
  Zephaniah
  Haggai
  Zechariah
  Malachi

5
New Testament Narrative
(focus on One)
  Matthew
  Mark
  Luke
  John
  Acts

6
Epistles
(directed instruction)
  Romans
  1 Corinthians
  2 Corinthians
  Galatians
  Ephesians
  Philippians
  Colossians
  1 Thessalonians
  2 Thessalonians
  1 Timothy
  2 Timothy
  Titus
  Philemon
  Hebrews
  James
  1 Peter
  2 Peter
  1 John
  2 John
  3 John
  Jude

7
Apocalypse
(vision of the future)
  Revelation

8
Extracanonical Writings
(peripheral records)

ⲧⲉⲭⲉⲉⲣⲟⲩ · ⲛⲥⲉⲕⲁ
ⲇⲓⲕⲁⲓⲱⲟⲩ · ⲁⲡⲡⲉ
ⲡⲛⲁⲛⲟⲩⲱ ⲡⲡⲉⲧ
ⲛⲏⲩⲉⲣ ⲙⲉ ⲭⲱⲟⲩ ·
ⲡⲡⲉⲡⲣⲉⲥⲃⲩⲧⲉⲣⲟⲥ ⲅⲁⲣ
ⲱⲁ ⲩⲭⲓ ⲙⲁⲩⲗⲁⲩ ·
ⲙ ⲛⲧⲁⲩ ⲉ ⲍ ⲟⲩ ⲥ ⲓ ⲁ ⲙ ·
ⲙⲁⲩⲧⲕⲗⲏⲣⲟⲥ ·
ⲉⲧⲃⲉⲡⲁ ⲓ ⲛⲩⲛ ⲁ ⲱ
ⲕⲁⲏ ⲥ ⲧⲁⲁ ⲛ ⲕⲗⲏ
ⲣⲓⲕⲟⲥ · ⲉⲱⲁ ⲩ
ⲥ ⲫ ⲣ ⲁ ⲅⲓ ⲍⲉ ⲙ ⲡⲉ ⲡ
ⲣⲉⲥⲃⲩⲧⲉⲣⲟⲥ ⲓ ⲙⲁ
ⲧⲉ ⲉ ⲧ ⲉ ⲣⲉ ⲡⲉⲡⲓⲥⲕⲟ
ⲡⲟⲥ ⲛⲁⲭⲓⲣⲟⲇ ⲟⲛ ⲉ ⲓ ⲙ
ⲙ ⲟ ⲩ

ⲉⲧⲃⲉ ⲛ ⲍⲟ ⲙ ⲟ ⲗ ⲟ ⲅ ⲓ ⲧ ⲏ ⲥ

ⲍ ⲟ ⲙ ⲟ ⲗ ⲟ ⲅ ⲓ ⲧ ⲏ ⲥ ⲇⲉ
ⲉ ⲱ ⲁ ⲭ ⲓ ⲛ ⲧ ⲁ ⲩ ⲱ ⲡ ⲙⲡⲉ
ⲍ ⲛ ⲍⲉ ⲛ ⲙ ⲡⲣ ⲣ ⲉ ⲉ ⲧ ⲃ ⲉ
ⲡ ⲣ ⲁ ⲛ ⲙ ⲡ ⲭⲟⲉⲓⲥ · ⲛ̄
ⲛ ⲉ ⲩ ⲕ ⲁ ⲁ ⲭ ⲓ ⲭ ⲱ ⲟ ⲩ
ⲉ ⲧ ⲃ ⲉ ⲟ ⲩ ⲇ ⲓ ⲁ ⲕ ⲟ ⲛ ⲓ ⲁ
ⲏ ⲟ ⲩ ⲙ ⲛ ⲧ ⲡⲣⲉⲥ ⲃ ⲩ
ⲧⲉⲣⲟⲥ · ⲟ ⲩ ⲉ ⲛ ⲧ ⲁ ϥ
ⲅ ⲁ ⲣ ⲓ ⲙ ⲙ ⲁ ⲩ ⲛ ⲧ ⲙ ⲏ
ⲛ ⲧ ⲙ ⲛ ⲧ ⲡ ⲣⲉ ⲥ ⲃ ⲩ
ⲧ ⲉ ⲣ ⲟ ⲥ · ⲍ ⲓ ⲧ ⲛ ⲧ ⲉ ⲩ ⲍ ⲟ
ⲙ ⲟ ⲗ ⲟ ⲅ ⲓ ⲁ ⲉ ⲱ ⲁ ⲩ
ⲉ ⲇ ⲉ ⲉ ⲩ ⲛ ⲕ ⲁ ⲏ ⲥ ⲧ ⲁ
ⲓ ⲙ ⲙ ⲟ ⲩ ⲥ ⲛ ⲉ ⲡⲓⲥ ⲕ ⲟ ⲡ ⲟ ⲥ ·

ⲉ ⲓ ⲉ ⲉ ⲩ ⲛ ⲕ ⲁ ⲁ ⲓ ⲭ ⲓ
ⲭ ⲱ ⲟ ⲩ ·· ⲉ ⲩ ⲭⲉⲟ ⲩ
ⲍ ⲟ ⲙ ⲟ ⲗ ⲟ ⲅ ⲓ ⲧ ⲏ ⲥ ⲇ ⲉ
ⲡ ⲓ · ⲓ ⲟ ⲩ ⲭ ⲓ ⲟ ⲩ ⲡ
ⲣ ⲧ ⲭⲟⲟⲩ ⲟ ⲧ ⲡ
ⲉ ⲍⲟⲩ ⲛ ⲛ ⲛ ⲁ ⲍ ⲣ ⲛ
ⲉ ⲍ ⲟ ⲩ ⲥ ⲓ ⲁ · ⲟ ⲩ ⲇ ⲉ ⲓ ⲙ
ⲡ ⲟ ⲩ ⲕ ⲟ ⲗ ⲁ ⲍ ⲉ ⲓ ⲙ ⲙ ⲟ ⲩ
ⲍ ⲛ ⲍ ⲉ ⲛ ⲙ ⲡ ⲣ ⲣ ⲉ · ⲟ ⲩ
ⲇ ⲉ ⲓ ⲡ ⲟ ⲩ ⲧ ⲡ ⲉ
ⲍ ⲟ ⲩ ⲛ ⲉ ⲡ ⲓ ⲱ ⲧ ⲉ ⲕ ⲁ
ⲟ ⲩ ⲇ ⲉ ⲓ ⲡ ⲟ ⲩ ⲕ ⲁ ⲧ ⲁ
ⲕ ⲣ ⲓ ⲛ ⲉ ⲓ ⲙ ⲙ ⲟ ⲩ ⲍ ⲛ ⲁ
ⲩ ⲛ ⲕ ⲁ ⲧ ⲁ ⲇ ⲓ ⲕ ⲏ ·
ⲁ ⲗ ⲗ ⲁ ⲕ ⲁ ⲧ ⲁ ⲟ ⲩ ⲭ ⲱ
ⲛ ⲛ ⲧ ⲁ ⲩ ⲥ ⲟ ⲩ ⲱ ⲛ ϥ
ⲙ ⲁ ⲧ ⲉ ⲁ ⲭ ⲓ ⲙ ⲡ ⲣ ⲁ ⲛ ⲙ
ⲡ ⲛ ⲁ ⲇ ⲉ ⲓ ⲥ · ⲁ ⲩ ⲱ ⲁ ⲩ
ⲕ ⲟ ⲗ ⲁ ⲍ ⲉ ⲓ ⲙ ⲙ ⲟ ⲩ ⲍ ⲛ
ⲟ ⲩ ⲕ ⲟ ⲗ ⲁ ⲥ ⲓ ⲥ ⲛ ⲏ ⲓ · ⲉ
ⲁ ⲓ ⲍ ⲟ ⲙ ⲟ ⲗ ⲟ ⲅ ⲉ ⲓ ⲇ ⲉ
ⲕ ⲗ ⲏ ⲣ ⲟ ⲥ ⲛ ⲓ ⲙ ⲉ ⲩ ⲉ ⲓ ⲙ
ⲡ ⲓ ⲱ ⲁ ⲓ ⲙ ⲙ ⲟ ⲟ ⲩ ⲉ ⲩ ⲛ ⲁ
ⲕ ⲁ ⲁ ⲓ ⲭ ⲓ ⲭ ⲱ ⲟ ⲩ ·
ⲡ ⲣ ⲉ ⲡ ⲉ ⲡ ⲓ ⲥ ⲕ ⲟ ⲡ ⲟ ⲥ ⲇ ⲉ
ⲛ ⲁ ⲉ ⲩ ⲭ ⲁ ⲣ ⲓ ⲥ ⲧ ⲟ ⲩ
ⲕ ⲁ ⲧ ⲁ ⲛ ⲉ ⲛ ⲧ ⲁ ⲛ ⲩ ⲱ
ⲣ ⲓ ⲭ ⲟ ⲟ ⲩ · ⲟ ⲩ
ⲡ ⲁ ⲛ ⲧ ⲱ ⲥ ⲧ ⲁ ⲛ ⲩ ⲱ
ⲕ ⲏ ⲣ ⲟ ⲩ ⲧ ⲉ ⲉ ⲧ ⲣ ⲉ ϥ
ⲧ ⲍ ⲟ ⲩ ⲟ ⲛ ⲛ ⲉ ⲓ ⲱ ⲁ ⲭ ⲓ
ⲛ ⲟ ⲩ ⲱ ⲧ · ⲛ ⲧ ⲁ ⲛ
ⲱ ⲣ ⲓ ⲭ ⲟ ⲟ ⲩ · ⲍ ⲱ ⲥ
ⲉ ⲓ ⲙ ⲙ ⲛ ⲧ ⲁ ⲛ ⲍ ⲛ